"The most complete home-buying book you will find ... doesn't leave out any of the essentials. On my scale of one to 10, this superb new book rates an off-the-chart 12."
—Robert Bruss, syndicated real estate columnist

"Coming from a gal that knows tools, this book is a must-have tool for any home buyer. It offers so much essential information, purchasing a home without it would be like trying to drive a nail without a hammer!"
—Norma Vally, host of *Toolbelt Diva* (Discovery Home) and author of *Chix Can Fix: 100 Home Improvement Projects* and *True Tales From the Diva of Do-It-Yourself*

"Any first-time homebuyer owes it to him or herself to get this book. It's packed with information you won't find anywhere else, yet is remarkably accessible, even when covering complex financial issues."
—Elisabeth DeMarse, CEO, Creditcards.com, former CEO, Bankrate.com

"Enthusiasm, hints and tips all rolled into a great read for first-timers."
—Pat Lashinsky, President of ZipRealty

"...Provides in-depth insight and helpful advice that is easy to understand and use."
—Rob Paterkiewicz, CAE, IOM, Executive Director, American Society of Home Inspectors

"Like having over a dozen real estate experts over for dinner."
—Steve Kropper, President, Bank on Real Estate, founder of Domania.com

"Nolo's excellent guide for novice home buyers provides fresh, updated information about the whole process that even those in the know will find useful."
—Library Journal

Download Forms on Nolo.com

You can download the forms in this book at:

 www.nolo.com/back-of-book/HTBH.html

We'll also post updates whenever there's an important change to the law affecting this book—as well as articles and other related materials.

More Resources from Nolo.com

 Legal Forms, Books, & Software
Hundreds of do-it-yourself products—all written in plain English, approved, and updated by our in-house legal editors.

 Legal Articles
Get informed with thousands of free articles on everyday legal topics. Our articles are accurate, up to date, and reader friendly.

 Find a Lawyer
Want to talk to a lawyer? Use Nolo to find a lawyer who can help you with your case.

7th Edition

Nolo's Essential Guide to
Buying Your
First Home

Ilona Bray, J.D.
Attorney Ann O'Connell
& Marcia Stewart

SEVENTH EDITION	JANUARY 2020
Editor	ILONA BRAY
Cover Design	SUSAN WIGHT
Book Design	SUSAN PUTNEY
Proofreading	SUSAN CARLSON GREENE
Indexing	UNGER INDEXING
Printing	BANG PRINTING

Names: Bray, Ilona M., 1962- author. | O'Connell, Ann (Ann Kristin), 1979-
   author. | Stewart, Marcia, author.
Title: Nolo's essential guide to buying your first home / Ilona Bray, J.D.,
   Attorney Ann O'Connell, & Marcia Stewart.
Description: 7th edition. | [Berkeley, California] : Nolo, [2019] |
   Includes index.
Identifiers: LCCN 2019025747 (print) | LCCN 2019025748 (ebook) | ISBN
   9781413327007 (paperback) | ISBN 9781413327014 (ebook)
Subjects: LCSH: House buying.
Classification: LCC HD1390.5 .B734 2019 (print) | LCC HD1390.5 (ebook) |
   DDC 643/.12--dc23
LC record available at https://lccn.loc.gov/2019025747
LC ebook record available at https://lccn.loc.gov/2019025748

This book covers only United States law, unless it specifically states otherwise.

Please note

We believe accurate, plain-English legal information should help you solve many of
your own legal problems. But this text is not a substitute for personalized advice
from a knowledgeable lawyer. If you want the help of a trained professional—and
we'll always point out situations in which we think that's a good idea—consult an
attorney licensed to practice in your state.

Acknowledgments

This book was a 100% team effort and couldn't have been written without the advice, stories, and ideas of real estate experts and homebuyers from around the United States. First and foremost, we thank the members of our advisory board, who spent countless hours reviewing chapters, explaining local practices, and sharing the best and worst memories from their professional experiences.

Special thanks to **Attorney Alayna Schroeder,** one of the book's original co-authors, for playing an instrumental role in making this a book that would see many future editions. Also thanks to the late **Broderick Perkins,** a real estate journalist based in San Jose, California, who reviewed and contributed to every chapter of this book's first draft.

Our other invaluable sages included:

- **Sydney W. Andrews,** owner of the mortgage company Loanenvy.com, and licensed real estate broker
- **Amy Bach, J.D.,** consumer advocate and executive director and cofounder of United Policyholders, a national nonprofit (www.uphelp.org), based in San Francisco, California
- **Timothy Burke,** founder and CEO of National Family Mortgage (www.nationalfamilymortgage.com), based in Waltham, Massachusetts
- **Mark Daya,** owner of Sac Platinum Realty, in the Sacramento, California metro area
- **Sandy Gadow,** expert on real estate closing and escrow, and best-selling author of *The Complete Guide to Your Real Estate Closing* (www.sandygadow.com)
- **Sylvia M. Gutierrez,** loan officer in the South Florida market (sylviagutierrez.com), and author of *Mortgage Matters: Demystifying the Loan Approval Maze*
- **Colette Herwitt,** associate broker and Realtor at Berkshire Hathaway HomeServices Rocky Mountain, REALTORS® in Boulder, Colorado
- **Rob Jensen,** broker/president of Rob Jensen Company, a Las Vegas brokerage (www.robjensen.com)

- **Paul Grucza,** director of education and Client Engagement for The CWD Group, Inc. AAMC® in Seattle, Washington (www.cwdgroup.com)
- **Frank Lesh,** founder of Home Sweet Home Inspection Company and spokesman/ambassador for the American Association of Home Inspectors (ASHI)
- **Richard Leshnower,** New York-based real estate attorney
- **Greg Nino,** associate Realtor at RE/MAX Compass in Houston, Texas (www.everydaysold.com)
- **Lisa Shaffer,** loan adviser at RPM Mortgage in Alamo, California (www.rpm-mtg.com)
- **Daniel Stea,** broker/owner/attorney at Stea Realty Group in Oakland, California (www.stearealtygroup.com), and
- **Tara Waggoner, MBA,** real estate broker at eXp Realty and coach with the Tara Waggoner Group (www.linkedin.com/in/whynotwaggoner).

A number of other experts provided additional advice—you'll see many of them quoted in this book. They include now-retired real estate broker Nancy Atwood in Framingham, Massachusetts; Neil Binder, New York real estate investment expert; Alicia Champagne, real estate attorney and Realtor education teacher in Wilmington, Massachusetts; Kartar Diamond, a Southern-California feng shui analyst; Marjo Diehl, Mortgage Adviser at RPM Mortgage in Alamo, California; Debbie Ostrow Essex, child and family therapist based in Berkeley, California; Stephen Fishman, attorney and Nolo author; Kenneth Goldstein, Boston-area attorney with the law firm of Goldstein & Herndon, LLP; Joanna Hirsch, real estate agent with The Grubb Co. in Montclair, California; Joel Kinney, attorney with Sheehan Phinney in Boston, Massachusetts; Annemarie Devine Kurpinsky, professor at City College of San Francisco; Pat Lashinsky, former president, ZipRealty; Jeff Lipes, mortgage banking consultant in Hartford, Connecticut; the late Maxine Mackle, Connecticut Realtor; Paul MacLean, retired home inspector in Austin, Texas; Ken McCoy, mortgage banker with Petaluma Home Loans; Mark Nash, an Illinois Realtor; Carol Neil, retired Realtor in California; Fiore Pignataro, Realtor with Windermere Realty in Seattle, Washington; Lorri Lee Ragan, formerly of the American Land Title Association; Mary Randolph, attorney and author; Frank Rathbun, formerly of the Community Associations Institute; Paul A. Rude, retired home inspector;

Ira Serkes, Berkeley Realtor with Pacific Union (www.berkeleyhomes.com); Viviane M. Shammas, attorney and real estate broker in Ann Arbor, Michigan; Bert Sperling, founder of BestPlaces.net; the late Fred Steingold, attorney and author in Ann Arbor, Michigan; Debbie Stevens, Oregon real estate agent; Rich Stim, attorney and Nolo author; Russell Straub, founder of LoanBright in Evergreen, Colorado.

No amount of advice can substitute for a personal story, so we'd also like to thank the many homebuyers who shared the good, the bad, and the ugly of their own experiences or told us what they'd like from this book, including Amy Blumenberg, Laurie Briggs, Dave and Danielle Burge, Karen Cabot, Linda Chou, Jennifer Cleary, Jaleh Doane, Phil Esra, Lisa Guerin, Gabrielle Hecht, Pat Jenkins, Ellie Kania, Justin and Tamara Kennerly, Chris and Libby Kurz, Talia Leyva, Willow Liroff, Meggan O'Connell, Evan and Tammy Ohs, Leny and Frank Riebli, Leah Scheibe, Diane Sherman, Bruce Sievers, Luan Stauss, Tom and Heather Tewksbury, Catherine Topping, Josh and Gillian Viers, Julie and Malachi Weng-Gutierrez, and Kyung Yu.

Within Nolo, colleagues who lent a hand in researching everything from 50-state legal matters to fun facts, included Cathy Caputo, Lexi Elmore, Jessica Gillespie, Stan Jacobsen, Terry McGinley, Kathleen Michon, Stephen Stine, Leah Tuisavalalo, Charles Walmann, and Jo Warner. Sandy Coury and Sigrid Metson helped line up advisory board members. Particularly heartfelt thanks go to the late Steve Elias, whose energy and expertise on foreclosure matters are sorely missed by everyone at Nolo.

Big thanks to our colleagues in the editorial department, who supported us through the (long) process of writing this comprehensive (and yet fun!) text. Kudos to Susan Putney in Nolo's Production Department who took a challenging compilation of information and turned it into a beautifully designed book.

Thanks also to Nolo founder Jake Warner, who championed this book idea for years.

Our basements may be cluttered, our gardens may need weeding, and our floors may need a good scrubbing—but we love our homes. Thanks to the people who helped us get there—professionals (some who taught us what to do, others who taught us what not to do!) and our families, who share the joy of homeownership with us.

About the Authors

Ilona Bray is an attorney, author, and legal editor at Nolo. Her other real estate books include *The Essential Guide for First-Time Homeowners* and *Selling Your Home: Nolo's Essential Guide*. Her working background includes solo practice, nonprofit, and corporate stints. She sold her first home at a profit—despite being in the middle of a real estate downturn—and bought a larger home. Her fantasy house would be a Greene & Greene mansion like the Gamble House in Pasadena, with a large sun porch and lots of surrounding trees.

Ann O'Connell is an attorney, real estate broker, and legal editor at Nolo. She's a sucker for punishment, having passed bar exams in three states and the real estate broker exam in Colorado. Ann is a California native who bought her first house at the height of the real estate boom, only to become one of the first people she knew to not make barrels of money from Bay Area real estate. She now lives in Colorado, and recently bought a tiny cabin needing big renovations. Her dream house is somewhere on a swimmable lake. Through her own experiences or by helping others buy, sell, and litigate, she's seen it all: pulled survey pins, tenants who won't leave, strange things people keep in their garages, and—best of all—cabins with more moose than people for neighbors.

Marcia Stewart is the author or editor of many Nolo real estate books, including the best-selling *Every Landlord's Legal Guide*. Years ago, she found the perfect "starter" house in one of her favorite neighborhoods. As her family started to grow, so did the house, with a new second story and deck. Most recently she (finally!) remodeled her 1950s kitchen. Her fantasy house would be a Queen Anne Victorian with a home theater and a beautiful garden and pool.

Table of Contents

Your Homebuying Companion

· ·

Buying your first house might be one of the first certifiably grown-up things you ever do. And no matter how ready you feel, taking a major step like this—particularly one where there are so many zeros on the price tag—can make you want to just close your eyes and *get it over with*.

But if you're going to invest your time and money, you want to make sure you don't find just any house—you want to find the *right* house, at the *right* price, with the *right* loan. A house you're happy to stay in for a long time, no matter what the market does. To do that, you need more information than for practically any other type of purchase.

This book is full of nuts-and-bolts information about the home-buying process. But it's also got anecdotes and advice that we hope will remind you to enjoy this exciting, if sometimes frustrating or nerve-wracking process. Keep in mind what you're aiming for: your own home, where you're free to pound nails in the wall, get a cat, or paint your bedroom any color you want, without asking the landlord!

By the time you've read the key information here (don't worry, you won't have to read every chapter or every section), you'll truly be ready. We'll show you how to:

- choose the appropriate house in the best possible neighborhood, whether it's an old bungalow on a tree-lined street, a condo in the city center, or a custom-built home in a new development
- narrow in on a realistic price range based on your budget, and strategize ways to afford more
- select from a variety of financing options, from a 30-year fixed rate mortgage (like the one Mom and Dad got) to a private loan from a relative or friend
- pick a great real estate agent, mortgage broker, home inspector, and other professionals
- negotiate and sign an agreement to buy a house (find out what's important in all that fine print)

- wrap up your financing, get inspections, and take care of other last tasks, and finally
- close the deal, arrange your move, and settle into your new home.

You're going to benefit from the expertise of a team of 15 advisers from around the country who have reviewed this book and added the kinds of insights you usually get only in personal conversations. For instance, you'll meet a mortgage broker who explains why you should not let rejection by one lender stop you from trying another; a real estate agent who explains why writing an offer on a house that's already in escrow can put you in a strategic #2 position; a closing expert with straightforward advice on why you should care about things like "easements" and title insurance; and a lawyer who suggests how to save on attorneys' fees.

With this book comes special access to electronic materials on Nolo's website. There you'll find a Homebuyer's Toolkit with over two dozen checklists and letters to help keep you organized and on track during every stage of the process. Whether it's a "Dream List" that prompts you to set out your priorities, checklists to carry when you tour a house or condo, or a set of interview questions for potential real estate agents, you'll find it there.

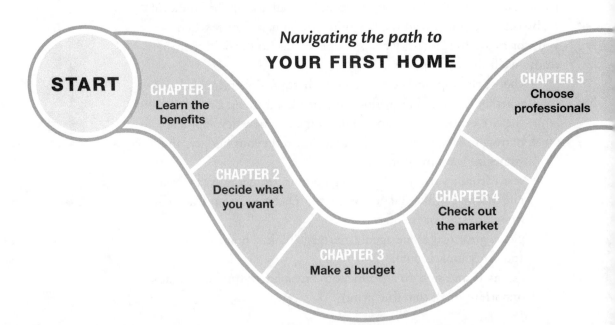

Navigating the path to
YOUR FIRST HOME

START

CHAPTER 1
Learn the benefits

CHAPTER 2
Decide what you want

CHAPTER 3
Make a budget

CHAPTER 4
Check out the market

CHAPTER 5
Choose professionals

The three authors of this book, Ilona, Ann, and Marcia, bring not only years of legal and real estate expertise, but also different first-time homebuying perspectives of our own. One of us bought with the help of family members and got probably the lowest mortgage payment on the block in one of the city's up-and-coming neighborhoods. Another bought a modest starter home with a hybrid adjustable rate mortgage, fixed it up, and managed to ride out the down market until she could sell. And the third learned the hard way that real estate does not always go up in value!

Our varied experiences help us understand that everyone has different objectives when buying and special challenges when buying for the first time. You might just be looking for a place—any place—to get started, you might want the challenge of a fixer-upper, or you might need the convenience of a low-maintenance condo. We know that you might be doing this alone, with your spouse or partner, or even with a friend. No matter who you are or what your goals and objectives may be, we hope you recognize yourself in some of the stories and experiences reflected in this book.

So hang on tight—to this book, that is. It will be your companion, providing advice, information, and inspiration all along the path to your new front door.

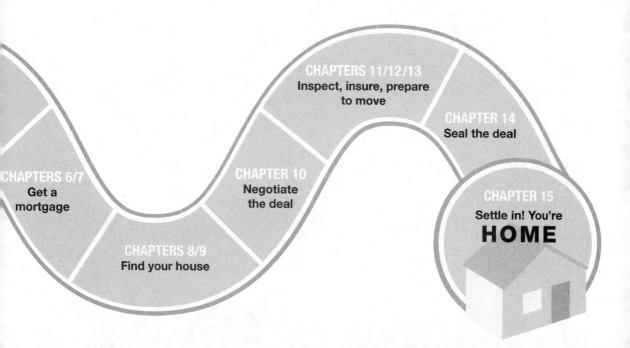

CHAPTERS 11/12/13
Inspect, insure, prepare to move

CHAPTER 14
Seal the deal

CHAPTERS 6/7
Get a mortgage

CHAPTER 10
Negotiate the deal

CHAPTER 15
Settle in! You're
HOME

CHAPTERS 8/9
Find your house

Get Updates, Worksheets, and More at This Book's Companion Page on Nolo.com

When there are important changes to the information in this book, we'll post updates online, on a dedicated page:

www.nolo.com/back-of-book/HTBH.html

And if you notice a useful sample form in this book, such as a letter or checklist, you'll have access to a digital version via the same companion page. See the appendix for a full list of forms on Nolo's website.

What's So Great About Buying a House?

Meet Your Adviser

Daniel Stea, broker/owner/attorney at Stea Realty Group, in Oakland, California (www.stearealtygroup.com).

What he does

"I (and members of my team) spend a great deal of time educating our clients about the purchase and sale process. We're always evaluating properties for them by running 'comps' (recent sales of comparable properties). Buyers want to make sure they're not paying too much; sellers want to make sure they're not receiving too little. Zillow and related websites provide only rough estimates, primarily based on price per square foot. It takes a human who has actually walked through all of those properties to start adding and subtracting for the various attributes, such as location, condition, schools, and so forth. That's one of the values that brokers bring to the table. As long as buyers and sellers can benefit from education, brokers' services will be necessary."

First house

"It was an adorable English Tudor in the Oakland hills, full of character. It had a leaking roof, which caused nearly $100,000 of dry rot. While buyers overlooked it as a giant headache, I saw the potential. Dry rot is a straightforward, routine repair. Other than that, it just needed a new roof, interior and exterior paint, and refinishing on the hardwood floors. We eventually updated the kitchen and bathrooms. When it came time to purchase a home closer to my office in Berkeley, I sold it for many times what I had invested in it."

Fantasy house

"Like many buyers in the San Francisco Bay Area, I'd love to have a place that's highly walkable to everything urban, yet far enough up in the hills to have a view of the San Francisco Bay. Only a few homes exist in that sweet spot. And they receive multiple offers and sell for a premium price. Style-wise, I see something to appreciate in almost every type of house: from the old ones that need a lot of work to the modern ones with walls of glass and high ceilings."

Likes best about his work

"Educating clients about the process in order to erase their confusion, alleviate their stress, and build their confidence. Buyers show up full of questions, 'How can I make my offer as competitive as possible without overspending?' 'Are certain contingencies more important for me to withhold than others?' and 'Which of a seller's hundreds of disclosure documents deserve my heightened attention?' Once they are educated about the process as well as about the current state of the market, we're ready to begin shopping and submitting purchase offers. The advocacy begins!"

Top tip for first-time homebuyers

"Be patient. A lot of people come to us in a panic, saying something like, 'We just got into town, we don't want to waste our precious money on these exorbitant rents, and we need to buy something right away.' But the process will go much smoother if you give yourself some time—ideally, six months to a year—to get to know the market, walk the neighborhoods, and learn about the homebuying process. In fact, if you're relocating here from Washington, DC, New York, or Boston, like many of our buyers do, I'd say rent first! It's very difficult to unpack your luggage in a new city and know where you want to live. Begin working with a Realtor long before you're ready to make your first purchase offer. We earn the same commission whether our buyers purchase now or a year from now. It's more important for them to be fully educated and relaxed so they have a good experience buying their home and thereafter refer us to their family, friends, and coworkers."

Picking up a book on homebuying for some light reading? We're guessing not. If you're reading this, you're probably seriously interested in buying a house. But before we launch into how, let's explore why—just in case you've got any lingering doubts about whether it's a good idea. This chapter will preview some of the primary financial and personal benefits to buying a home (and you'll find details on many of the subjects covered, such as tax benefits, in later chapters). Then we'll talk about some common myths and fears, and how to get over them.

⭐ **Best thing I ever did**

Buy my first home. Although Leah was happy with her rental place, she says, "I wanted a place that I could call my own, with a backyard for my cats, and space for an office so I could work at home full time. After three weeks of looking, I found it! And after a year, some of the best parts of homeownership are things I wasn't even expecting—like having already gotten to know more neighbors than I did during a whole six years in my apartment. Plus, although I've never thought of myself as domestic, I've had a surge of interest in decorating—I put up Roman blinds, have been picking out paint colors, and just bought my first Christmas tree!"

Investment Value: Get What You Pay For ... And Then Some

You've probably heard people talk about real estate as a great investment. But what exactly do you get out of the deal? Well, a few things: You'll build equity instead of spending cash on rent, you gain immediate benefits (a place to live!), and you'll eventually have full ownership of an asset that—at least over the long term—has a good chance of appreciating in value.

Leverage

Buying a home is one of those rare instances where you can control a very large and potentially appreciating asset with a comparatively small initial cash investment (your down payment). Better yet, notes adviser Daniel Stea, "You're using the proverbial 'OPM' (other people's money) for the balance of the investment, and that money is being lent to you at comparatively low cost given the historically low interest rates we've experienced these past few years. Yet you get to enjoy the appreciation on the full value of the investment, not just your cash component. It almost doesn't seem right!"

Equity, Baby

Over time, as you patiently pay your mortgage, two things might start happening—your principal loan balance will go down, and the house's market value may go up. Both of these mean that you're accruing *equity*. Equity is the difference between the market value of a house (what it's currently worth) and the claims against it (what you have left to pay on any mortgages or loans you've taken out against it). You'd be hard-pressed to find another investment where you can borrow a large amount of money, pay a modest interest rate, and reap every bit of the gain yourself.

> **EXAMPLE:** Hugo buys a home for $300,000 with a $60,000 down payment (20%) and a $240,000 mortgage. If the market value of the house is $300,000, Hugo's current equity in the home is $60,000 (market value minus mortgage debt). A few years later, Hugo has reduced the principal on the mortgage by $5,000, to $235,000. Meanwhile, the house's value has risen to $310,000. Hugo now has $75,000 in equity ($310,000 minus $235,000). That's $15,000 more than he originally invested.

Of course, the value of a property doesn't always increase: It can also decrease, sometimes dramatically. Fortunately, houses rarely drop in value permanently. And after some precipitous value drops in the early 2000s, home appreciation in 2019 averages around 4–5%, according to the S&P/CoreLogic Case-Shiller U.S. National Home Price indexes.

It Beats Paying Rent

A good chunk of the money you'll use to finance your home is money you're already spending on rent. When you buy a house, your rent money becomes investment money.

You Can Live in Your Investment

Some people like to call a mortgage a forced savings plan, because it makes you sock a little cash away every month in the form of a mortgage payment—money you will, with any luck, get back when you sell the place. On the other hand, you might call it a smart investment plan, because it gives you both a roof over your head *and* a way to convert your cash into a potentially appreciating asset.

You Can Borrow on Your Investment

Eventually, as your equity in your home builds, you can borrow against it at relatively low interest rates, using a home equity loan or a HELOC (home equity line of credit). These are also commonly referred to as "second mortgages."

The interest rates on these tend to be higher than on primary mortgages, but lower than on the typical credit card. The money borrowed can be used for any number of purposes, such as home improvements, college tuition, or a car.

Of course, there are risks—if you default and your house goes into foreclosure, the lender is second in line to be paid from the proceeds of the sale of your house, after the primary mortgage holder.

My, You're Looking Creditworthy!

We hear so much about people who ruined their credit score by getting foreclosed on that it's hard to remember the reverse side of the picture: A mortgage is seen as "good debt." When you successfully pay it down, credit-reporting companies view that as a sign that you're responsible and able to handle a large loan.

"This can do wonders for your credit rating," says adviser Daniel Stea. "It makes you a much better credit risk (statistically speaking), which becomes especially useful if you decide to apply for an auto loan, a small-business loan, a student loan for your kid's college tuition, and so on."

That House Is *Yours*

One benefit to buying a house is kind of obvious … you're becoming a home*owner*, and when the loan is paid off, you won't have to pay for a place to live. You could keep renting the same place you're in now for 50 years, and at the end of that time you'll still have to pay monthly rent checks to your landlord.

Tax Breaks: Benefits From Uncle Sam

You'll get to claim various federal tax deductions and credits for home-related expenses. For some, these can add up to some serious savings.

Tax Deductions Versus Tax Credits

Be careful not to confuse a tax deduction with a tax credit. A tax deduction is an amount that taxpayers who don't take the standard deduction, but instead "itemize" their deductions, subtract from their gross income (all the money earned during the year) to figure out how much of their income is subject to tax. For example, if your gross income is $80,000, and you have a $2,000 tax deduction, and you don't take the standard deduction, your taxable income is reduced to $78,000. Read "Will You Itemize Your Deductions?" later in this chapter to learn more.

A tax credit, by contrast, is a dollar-for-dollar reduction in your tax liability. If your taxable income is $80,000, and you qualify for a $2,000 tax credit, your taxable income is still $80,000, but you get to reduce the amount of tax you ultimately owe by $2,000.

Tax Credits

As a new homeowner, you might be entitled to certain tax credits:

- **Tax credit for first-time homebuyers.** At the time this book went to print, all the tax credits for first-time homebuyers had expired—but keep an eye on the news and www.irs.gov for anything new that might come along.

- **Tax credits for energy efficiency.** Homeowners who install solar, geothermal, fuel cell, or wind systems to generate electricity, or in some cases hot water, are eligible for a tax credit if the system is placed in service before January 1, 2022. There is no dollar limit on solar, geothermal, or wind system credits, but fuel cell system credits are capped at $500 per half kilowatt (kW) of power capacity. The credit value decreases over the next few years. It's 30% of the cost of the systems placed in service through December 31, 2019; then goes down to 26% for systems placed in service after December 31, 2019 and before January 1, 2021; then reduces to 22% for systems placed in service after December 31, 2020 and before January 1, 2022. It officially expires on December 31, 2021.

  Taxpayers can claim such credits using IRS Form 5695 *Residential Energy Credits*. For more about the credit, as well as the latest information on eligibility and expiration dates, see the Energy Star website at EnergyStar.gov.

Will You Itemize Your Deductions?

To take advantage of house-related tax deductions, you'll need to *itemize* your tax deductions, rather than take the standard deduction (for 2019 tax returns $12,200 for individuals and $24,400 for marrieds filing jointly). For most people, homeowners included, taking the standard deduction is the more beneficial approach under the latest iteration of the U.S. Tax Code. You'll want to run the numbers to see whether your itemized deductions exceed the standard deduction amount. If you do end up itemizing, you'll find that it involves a step up from the good old 1040EZ, but it's not all that complicated.

CHECK IT OUT

Go straight to the source. See IRS Publication 530, *Tax Information for Homeowners*, available at www.irs.gov. This publication will give you more detailed information about the tax benefits of buying a home.

TIP

Keep good records. If itemizing deductions is the right approach for you, be prepared to prove them to the IRS—all of them, not just the house-related ones. Keep a file of receipts for the more common deductions, such as unreimbursed business expenses (office equipment and travel); educational expenses (tuition and books); charitable contributions; and unreimbursed medical expenses. Consider getting help—even the cost of meeting with a tax professional might be tax deductible!

Mortgage Interest Deduction

One of the biggest potential deductions from your taxable income, if you itemize, will be the interest you pay on your home mortgage (available for mortgages of up to $750,000 for individuals and married couples filing jointly and $375,000 for marrieds filing separately). This one can be particularly advantageous during the first few years of a fixed rate mortgage, when most of your payment will be put toward interest.

Until the end of 2017, home-owning families with an adjusted gross income of $100,000 or less were able to fully deduct the cost of their mortgage insurance premiums (PMI). (PMI protects the lender's investment if it needs to foreclose—lenders require borrowers to purchase PMI if their down payment is less than 20% of the purchase price.) Although the PMI deduction has since expired, a bill to create a permanent PMI deduction was introduced in early 2019 (H.R. 284—116th Congress: Mortgage Insurance Tax Deduction Act of 2019), so it's possible that homeowners who itemize might be able to again use this deduction in the future. Check IRS.gov/Schedule A for the latest information before you file your taxes.

Other Tax-Deductible Expenses

Taxpayers who itemize can also deduct certain other expenses from their taxable income, such as:

- **Property taxes.** While the amount varies between states and localities, most people pay around 1% of the home's value each year in state property tax. You can deduct from your federal taxable income up to $10,000 of what you pay *collectively* for state, local, and property taxes.

- **Points.** Points are additional one-time (and usually optional) fees you pay to reduce your mortgage's interest rate. They're tax deductible in the year you pay them.

- **Interest on a home improvement loan.** If you take out a loan to make improvements that increase your home's value, prolong its life, or adapt its use—for example, by adding a deck or a new bathroom— you can deduct the interest on loans up to $750,000. But you can't deduct interest on loans used to make normal repairs, such as repainting the kitchen or fixing a broken window, and definitely not if you take out a loan secured by your home for some unrelated purpose, such as medical bills.

- **Home office expenses.** If you use part of your home exclusively and regularly for a home-based business, you might be able to deduct a portion of the related expenses—including the costs of some home repairs, or even things like landscaping if your home's appearance will be important to visiting clients.

Capital Gains Tax Relief When You Sell

While it might be too soon for you to imagine selling your first home, another important benefit is available if and when you do. Thanks to the Taxpayer Relief Act of 1997, you don't pay capital gains tax (usually 15%) on the first $250,000 you make when you sell. Double that to $500,000 if you're married and filing jointly, or to $250,000 per person if you co-own the place.

To qualify, you must (with a few exceptions) have lived in the home two out of the previous five years before selling. Many first-time buyers use this tax break to move from modest starter homes to roomier homes that cost more. Be sure to keep the receipts from all your home improvements while you live in the house—these expenses can increase your cost basis in the house, decreasing the amount that the IRS considers your gain when you sell.

Personality and Pizzazz: Your Home Is Your Castle

If you've always been a renter, you know the drill: Things stay the way they were when you moved in. White walls stay white, ugly carpeting stays ugly, and the funky bathroom light fixture stays funky.

When it's your home, you get to make your mark. There's just no way to quantify the psychological advantage of personalizing your space. Even people who've never taken an interest in home decorating, repair, or gardening find themselves hooked on the creativity and self-expression possible with home projects.

No More Landlord: Say Goodbye to Renting

Expressing your personality isn't the only advantage to leaving rental living behind. Say goodbye to things like waiting around for things to get fixed, wondering whether the landlord will raise your rent or kick you out, and being surprised by landlords who stop by at their own convenience.

Even reasonable landlords who make prompt and thorough repairs and never raise the rent can pull surprises or sell the property. Owning your own house reduces the stress and

---

The Future's So ... Expensive!

If you pay $1,000 in monthly rent now, approximately how much will you be paying in 40 years, assuming average inflation (3% per year) and no rent control?

a. $2,500   b. $4,400   c. $3,262

d. None of the above, because I'll own a home.

Answer: c or d.

uncertainty of renting. You're in charge of when you move on, who comes in the front door, and when and what gets done to the place. While that means you've got some extra responsibilities, you've definitely got some extra security and benefits, too.

Best thing I ever did

Make monthly payments to myself, not the landlord.

At age 25, Talia had only toyed with the idea of buying a house—she'd thought that, despite her full-time job, it was financially impossible. But then her landlord raised the rent. Talia says, "I looked into loan options—and to my surprise, I qualified. Within two months, I bought a converted first-floor apartment with a little patio, in a safe neighborhood. I love not having to share a washer and dryer with other people anymore. But even better is the feeling of independence of having my own place: Because I'm building equity, I like to think I'm making those mortgage checks to myself—and they're not that much higher than my rent checks were, plus I can claim some significant tax deductions."

You Can Do It … If You Want To

Are you still on the fence about homebuying? Some people just don't feel ready to take the plunge. Below are a list of common "I can't do it because …" excuses. Don't get us wrong: Not every excuse is a *bad* excuse. You just need to know whether yours are based on solid facts rather than plain old fear.

"But … I Like Renting"

Maybe you're thinking, *I really love my apartment* or *I'm getting such a good deal*. But even if your current rent seems cheap, cheap is never as good as free. Yes, we're aware that buying a house isn't free. But at some point, you won't be paying a mortgage anymore. That will *never* be true if you rent.

CHECK IT OUT

Run your own numbers. These calculators compare the costs of renting and buying:

- www.nytimes.com (search for "Is it better to buy or rent?"), and
- Nolo.com/legal-calculators (click "Should I rent or buy?").

While you'll need to guess how much you'll spend on a home to use these calculators, the result will at least give you a rough comparison. Revisit the calculators after you've looked at Chapters 3 and 6 (covering the financial details of buying a house).

All that being said, renting might be best in the following situations:

- **You plan on moving from the area within the next few years.** Buying is a long-term strategy, with significant up-front costs. Plus, it's easier to move out of a rental than a home you own—selling is almost as complicated as buying.

- **You need flexibility.** Buying is best for people whose lives are fairly stable. If your first priority is being able to quit your job any time a friend proposes a round-the-world sailing trip, maybe homeownership will feel more like a trap than a positive step. (Then again, we've met travelers who've sublet their house and supported their travels with the rent payments!)

- **You expect your income to decrease soon.** If you're planning to return to school or quit your 9 to 5 to pursue an acting career, you might not want to lock yourself into a mortgage. Still, you may be a potential homebuyer if you can afford something more modest within your anticipated future income or can pay the mortgage by co-owning the property or taking in renters.

- **It will cost you far more to buy than to rent.** Run those numbers, using calculators like the ones listed above. In a few markets, you can still rent for less than you can buy. If so, you might be better off renting and investing elsewhere—or simply renting a bigger and better place than you could hope to buy.

"But ... I Can't Afford It"

Maybe your main reservation about buying a home is that you simply can't afford one. Scraping together a 20% down payment can be a big task when you've got your plate full with student loans and other bills. Or perhaps you're afraid you won't qualify for the gigantic loan you'll need or won't be able to pay it once you get it.

⭐ **B**est thing we ever did

Focus on the spaghetti. Caryn and her husband Alec were stretching to their financial limits to buy a house, and Caryn says, "We were nervous, but our agent told us, 'You'll just need to eat spaghetti for about a year, and then things will even out.' For some reason, that image stuck in my head, and I thought, okay, I can handle eating spaghetti for a while. In fact, that's about the way it worked. The first year, we depleted our savings, not only with the house closing but with repainting and buying furniture. Now we've settled in, and owning a home doesn't feel like such a big load on our shoulders anymore."

Small Can Be Beautiful

If you think living in a small space means you'll be cramped, uncomfortable, and aesthetically disappointed, check out ApartmentTherapy.com. Under "Tours," you'll find several examples of tiny spaces other people have transformed into fabulous homes. Be inspired!

If you're struggling to come up with a down payment, don't lose heart. There are alternatives: For example, you might be able to augment your down payment with a loan from a family member, or even enter into a cobuying arrangement with a friend.

As for the mortgage payment, people who think they can't afford it often focus only on the big number—the five-, six-, or even seven-digit figure that says what a house is going to cost. But a mortgage allows you to spread that number out over a big portion of your life.

Finally, let's not forget that the first home you buy isn't necessarily going to be the one you'll live in forever. By remaining flexible, and starting with a not-quite-perfect house, you can break into the housing market. That's why they call it a "starter" house—it's only the beginning. The equity that you accrue might very well help you get into that next place.

"But ... I'm Single"

Some people are reluctant to buy a house because they're single now, but hope to be part of a couple before long. But did you know that nearly one-fifth of homebuyers today are single women? Obviously they have figured out that there's no secret rule that says only couples get to buy houses.

Best thing I ever did

Invest in my present as well as my future. Real estate agent Joanna knows about not wanting to buy a house as a single woman—she's seen it in many of her clients. But, says Joanna, "The problem with waiting to do something the traditional way is, what do you lose during that waiting period? I was in my early 30s and ready to have a place of my own. Plus, it makes sense to spend the money and get a tax write-off rather than pour it into rent. This isn't to say that buying alone wasn't stressful—I stretched financially to make it work. But since buying, my house has gone up in value."

Maybe you're worried that you'll have to move as soon as you meet Mr. or Ms. Right. While that admittedly is possible, it's also possible that in the meantime, the increased value of your place will help, not hinder, your happily-ever-after. If the value of your home increases and you pay down the mortgage, the two of you will have equity you can use to buy a place together. Besides—a house that's perfect for one might accommodate two just fine.

Best thing we ever did

Combine our homes. Hannah says, "I was a young professional and *very* single when I bought a condo. Two years later, I met Chad, who also owned a small home. Before I knew it, we were married and living in the house, renting out the condo. Then we had kids, and the house was just too small. We sold my place and Chad's, using the equity to buy a house big enough to accommodate our kids. It's nice to have a place that we chose together, with our family in mind."

"But … It's Too Much Responsibility!"

For some, the idea of owning a home just seems like too much to handle. Admittedly, renting is much simpler than owning. You write a rent check, and you're covered for the month. And in many rental arrangements, you can leave with just a month's notice—perfect for those with wanderlust.

Telling yourself that renting doesn't involve responsibility isn't really true, though. After all, what happens if you don't pay the rent? You get evicted—and then where do you go? Back to Mom and Dad's? Most people would rather do whatever it takes to make that monthly payment happen.

So if you've already lived away from home, you're familiar with what's needed to make monthly payments and handle monthly finances. Of course, when you buy you'll have other responsibilities, like taking care of your yard or doing repairs, but you're in charge of prioritizing what happens when. If you decide you don't want to repair the creaky stairwell until you've redone your kitchen cabinets, that's up to you.

"But … Maybe Prices Will Go Down!"

Trying to time the real estate market? Timing is definitely important, but it's not easy to get into the market at the perfect moment. Even experienced real estate pundits get it wrong. If prices look to be stable and you're just waiting until you can afford to get in, that's one thing. But if you're trying to out-clever the real estate market, you're likely to find that by the time you notice a trend everyone else will have, too; and prices may jump up before you know it.

So if you've watched your local market and economic news carefully, and have a solid sense of what's ahead, perhaps waiting for a price drop makes sense. But don't put your life on hold. That's particularly true if you're getting married, having a baby, downsizing for retirement, or doing something else that comes with its own timing demands.

"But ... I'm Still Scared!"

Buying a home can seem overwhelming, even if you've always wanted to do it. The process is unfamiliar, there's a lot of money at stake, and you might fear getting swept up into buying a place you don't even like or that will drop in value. But fear shouldn't stop you from realizing your homebuying dreams. To help calm the butterflies, take constructive steps such as these:

- **Know your strengths and weaknesses going in.** Then find ways to address them, for example with self-education or by hiring professionals.
- **Learn what you can expect from professionals.** Understand what real estate agents, mortgage brokers, home inspectors, and other professionals do, and put them to work for you, saving time and money.
- **Observe your local real estate market.** We'll show you how to research the trends in your area, in order to reassure yourself that you're buying an asset that is unlikely to drop in value, and that has long-term appreciation potential.
- **Understand the process.** Read up on all steps of the homebuying process now, so that you won't be confused—or need to do any late-night remedial study—when the process inevitably kicks into high gear.
- **Get organized.** Use all the worksheets and checklists in the Homebuyer's Toolkit on the Nolo website to stay on top of key tasks, such as choosing a real estate agent or inspector or pulling together financial papers for the lender.

This book will help you accomplish all those goals. It will tell you where you are at every step, so that you can breathe, get your bearings, and proceed with confidence. Get the facts, and you'll be ready.

What's Next?

Once you've decided you're ready to buy, it's time to figure out what's important to you. In the next chapter, we'll discuss how to examine and settle on your priorities regarding types of houses and neighborhoods.

What Do You Want?
Figuring Out Your Homebuying Needs

Meet Your Adviser

Paul Grucza, CMCA, AMS, PCAM, a community association expert and educator, author, and association strategist located in Seattle, Washington.

What he does

With 37-plus years of real estate-related experience (including as a licensed real estate broker and property manager), Paul is now an active lecturer and consultant, and faculty member for (and past president of) the Community Associations Institute (CAI, at www.caionline.org). CAI provides nationwide training, guidance, and resources to the volunteer homeowners who govern community associations. Paul received CAI's 1999–2000 "Educator of the Year" award. He established and hosted an award-winning community association issues television program for the Dallas-Fort Worth market which is viewed by well over one million people per week. He's also the director of education and client engagement for The CWD Group, Inc. AAMC® in Seattle, Washington (www.cwdgroup.com), which provides professional management and consultant services for a variety of condominiums and planned communities.

First house

"It was an absolutely rundown but beautiful Mission-style bungalow built around 1922, in one of the first incorporated subdivisions outside Buffalo, New York. The house was the builder's model for that subdivision, so it had all the features, including inlaid floors, woodwork, and leaded glass. I spent the next 11 or so years lovingly restoring it—regrouting the bathroom tile, refinishing the woodwork, rebronzing the heat duct covers, replacing the modernized light fixtures through a restoration company, and much more. It turned out to be the most beautiful home I've ever owned."

Fantasy house	"My true fantasy house would be a comfortably sized home situated on a bluff that overlooks Puget Sound and the mountains. Living in Seattle affords the opportunity to evaluate lots of wonderful properties, but since working with an architect, my fantasy will become a 'fantasy retirement home,' one that meets the need for views and accessibility. A redo of a midcentury rambler would be nice, but a built-from-the-ground-up is not bad, either."

Likes best about his work	"My daily interaction with a wide variety of people. Solving homeowner issues. Training and speaking to a variety of groups. They include homeowners, developers, service professionals, managers, and board members. This brings me more joy than anything—and after nearly 33 years, I'd better enjoy my work!"

Top tip for first-time homebuyers	"Regardless of the type of property you're looking for—whether a house, a condo, a cabin, a doublewide, or whatever—leave your emotions at home. Look at the property and its practical application in your life, and at what it will cost to turn it into your home."

You know you're ready to buy but are probably wondering, "Where do I start?" There's a lot to think about, like what kind of home or neighborhood you want, and what features you can't live without. This chapter will help you:

- identify neighborhood characteristics that fit your personality and that maximize house resale value
- understand how your lifestyle and plans should play into your choice of house
- learn the benefits and drawbacks of different types of properties (single-family houses, condominiums, or co-ops, plus new or old places), and finally
- create a Dream List, describing and organizing your priorities, to use when house shopping.

Later chapters will teach you how to do the looking, how to figure out whether you can afford what you want, and what to do once you've found a place. For now, focus on organizing your thoughts and priorities.

Know Your Ideal Neighborhood: Why Location Matters

If you're a lifetime renter, you've probably always thought about location in the short term, knowing you could move at the end of your lease. Buying is different: You're committing yourself to a location for at least a few years, and you'll probably feel a sense of investment in your community that you didn't while renting. So get serious about identifying your location preferences, then make sure these preferences won't mean buying a house with low resale prospects.

Neighborhood Features for Daily Living

Not everyone wants the same features in a neighborhood, and you're the one who's got to live there. Before letting anyone else tell you what the best neighborhoods are, consider your own preferences and priorities regarding:

- **Character and community.** For some, the uniformity of well-planned developments is pleasing; others enjoy the variety of older, one-of-a-kind homes. Visualize your ideal neighborhood: Does it, for example, feature trees and parks or restaurants and bars?

- **Safety.** While most everyone prefers less crime, safety often comes with a trade-off. For example, a rural neighborhood might be safe, but a city's resources and nightlife will be very far away.

- **Resources and accessibility.** Think about where the important places and resources in your life are, like your workplace, child's school or day care, pet care and boarding, grocery stores, health care providers, public transportation or major roadways, cultural amenities, and more. How much time are you willing to spend traveling to those places?

- **Schools.** If you're planning on sending children to public schools, consider the quality of the ones serving the neighborhoods you're considering.

- **Zoning and other restrictions on owners.** If you want the freedom to remodel your home, you'll have to be in an area that allows that. Or, if you appreciate community uniformity, you'll like living somewhere that limits the changes owners can make to their houses or property.

This isn't a complete list, and you should think about features that are unique to your needs. For example, adviser Bert Sperling notes, "If you're lucky enough to be a stay-at-home parent, you may find yourself lonely during the day if you have to travel a considerable distance to find some community for you and your youngsters."

They Call That a House?

You won't believe what people live in! Here are a few creative houses:

- The Golden Pyramid House in Wadsworth, Illinois: The largest 24-karat gold-plated object ever created.

- The Shoe House in Hellam, Pennsylvania: Just what it sounds like—in the shape of a work boot, made of light-colored stucco and featuring shoe-themed stained-glass windows in every room.

- A live-in water tower in Sunset Beach, California: Built in the 1940s, converted to a three-story house.

Neighborhood Features That Boost Resale Value

When it comes to the long-term value of your home, location really *does* matter. If you have a desirable piece of property that's also in a desirable location, more people will want to buy it. That keeps its value relatively high compared to nearby homes in less sought-after locations (which people may buy partly because they can't afford anything else).

Not surprisingly, many of the features that attract first-time homebuyers —like high-quality schools, low crime rates, convenient amenities, and neighborhood character and community—boost resale value as well.

Another major factor affecting resale value is conformity. Buying a house that's much bigger than the houses around it is usually a bad idea. Your house will appreciate at a slower rate, because buyers drawn to a neighborhood of smaller homes won't be able to afford the larger home, and buyers drawn to larger homes won't be drawn to that neighborhood. And if a house is just too unique—because the owner has customized it too much—it's going to stick out like a sore thumb.

Finally, try to get an idea of whether a neighborhood is up and coming. You can tell by looking at whether there seems to be a lot of remodeling, new landscaping, or trendy-looking shops. Bert Sperling adds, "If you read the signs correctly, you could get in on the ground floor of the next hot new neighborhood."

Know Yourself: How Your Lifestyle, Plans, and Values Affect Your House Priorities

Later in this chapter, we'll show you how to prepare a Dream List to help you find the right house. Before making your list, reflect on what you want the house for. (To live in, duh, we got that.) Although it might be hard to imagine where your life will be in a few years, do your best to consider:

- **Who is going to live in the home?** You may be on your own now, but in the future, might you bring in a roommate, significant other, child, elderly parent, or pet? If so, factor this into your priorities and adjust things like number of bedrooms, quality of the school district, number of floors, or availability of outdoor space.

*L*esson learned the hard way **Climbing stairs is easier before you've had kids.**
According to Bonnie, "My husband and I bought a two-bedroom cooperative apartment on the second floor of a New York building without an elevator. Happiness! A plus was that no one was living above us to make noise. Being young, we hardly thought about the flight of steps as an issue. After two years, we had a son. Now we had to go up and down the steps with a baby carriage, baby, and packages. And then we had a daughter, thus doubling the load. We're looking for another place now."

- **What do you plan to do in the home?** If you plan to work at home, spend a lot of time in the kitchen, or entertain frequently, plan adequate space for that. Conversely, consider whether you really need to spend extra for a huge gourmet kitchen if you eat takeout every night.
- **What does your lifestyle require?** If you travel for business, you might want the convenience of a condo with easy airport access. Or if you're into nightlife, you might want to be able to stroll home and crash at 2 a.m.
- **How do you like to spend your time at home?** Do you love the idea of remodeling an old home or creating a beautiful garden? Are you scared to death of anything that hints at the word "handy"? If you'd rather be throwing a cocktail party than mowing the lawn, the big house in the suburbs might not really be right for you.

*B*est thing I ever did **Looked for a house that sparked my artistic side.**
A graphic designer and yoga teacher, Diane had wanted to buy a house for years—but knew it would be a financial challenge. She says, "I scraped together enough to buy a small cottage, with a disastrous backyard—and I turned it into my art project. I painted those white walls celery green, brick red, and tan. I spent all winter pulling weeds, then put in flagstone and flowers. And eventually I sold it for a large profit—enough to buy a duplex, so now I'm a property investor!"

"Where *Could* I Be in Five Years?"

Instead of planning where you think you'll be in five years, why not play "Where *could* I be in five years?" Try it with a friend or partner over a glass of wine, or while walking in the park. You'll have to be a little realistic (do you *really* think you'll win the lottery?), but optimistic, too. You might see yourself finding a better job in another city, or having your first baby. Imagining the possibilities can help you not only define your housebuying objectives, but see how those goals fit into your life's priorities.

Know Your Ideal House: Old Bungalows, New Condos, and More

You probably have a vision in your mind of the house you want, whether it's a cozy cottage with fruit trees; an elegant brick townhouse with no yard; or a modern, glass-enclosed loft with views of the city. For an overview of your options, read on. (And when you're reading the bios of our advisers in this book, take a peek at their fantasy houses!)

Isn't my house classic? The columns date all the way back to 1972.

Cher, *Clueless*

Of course, where you live will play a huge role in what you can buy. For example, in Chicago or New York City, most of the properties available might be in high-rise buildings, while in less urban areas, most of the homes might be single-story ranch houses or newly built homes within developments.

Would You Like Land With That? Single-Family Houses

You wouldn't think we'd have to define "house," would you? But there are many different house types available, so let's be clear about what each one is. Technically speaking, a "house" is a detached, single-family dwelling. When you own a house, you own both the structure and the property that it sits on, all by yourself. Your house won't be attached to the next one, and you won't be cursing an upstairs neighbor for stumbling across the floor at 3 a.m.

Even if you know you want a house, however, an important question remains—new or previously lived in? Each has its own benefits and headaches.

 CHECK IT OUT

Interested in house styles? To decide whether you prefer a "Colonial," a "Victorian," or an "Italian Renaissance," look online at sites such as:

- ThoughtCo.com (search for "architecture")
- OldHouses.com (click "Old House Style Guide"), and
- Wikipedia.org (search for "List of house styles").

Old (or Not-So-New) Houses: Benefits and Drawbacks

If you're in an uber-urban area or your price range dictates it, older houses might be all that's available to you. Or maybe you just prefer a touch of historical charm. Either way, you'll likely get all these benefits:

- **Affordability.** Older homes tend to cost less to purchase than new, customized homes. (Though this isn't a universal rule—in large cities, where the majority of new home construction is far outside the city, it can be the reverse.)
- **Established neighborhood.** Instead of looking at mounds of dirt while perusing architectural drawings, you'll be able to get a feel for the neighborhood by taking a stroll.
- **Established landscaping.** You're not likely to find a tree-lined street, or a wisteria arbor over your front gate, in a new development.
- **Construction.** Older homes are often built with high-quality materials such as thick beams, solid-wood doors, and heavy fixtures.
- **Character.** Crown molding and built-in cabinetry are just a few of the fun features found in older homes—but rarely in newer homes.

There are also drawbacks to previously loved homes, including:

- **Lower resale value.** In some areas, older homes sell for less than their newer counterparts.

- **Replacement costs.** The years take a toll on appliances, water heaters, and roofs—and replacing them isn't cheap.
- **Efficiency.** Older houses tend to be less energy efficient than newer ones.
- **Style.** Although you can probably switch out the former owner's unique style choices (like magenta bathroom tile), it might require a fair amount of sweat equity (meaning *your* sweat builds equity).
- **Layout.** Older houses were built for another era … an era before plasma screen TVs and home offices. Rooms may be smaller and laid out differently than you'd like, with too few electrical outlets. And forget about the walk-in closet or large bathrooms.

Of course, not every used home is *old*. If you buy one that was built only a few years ago, some of the drawbacks described above will be eliminated. Likewise, you'll lose some of the benefits.

Newly Built Houses: Benefits and Drawbacks

Over three-quarters of a million new homes are built in the United States each year, often in planned communities or developments. (Of course, you can always buy a piece of land and build a custom home—but that's a different book, with its own unique set of issues.) No surprise—buying a new home has benefits, including:

- **It's mine! It's new!** A new house is a blank slate, clean and virtually untouched.
- **It's custom-built.** Although most builders offer a limited choice of floor plans, many allow buyers to choose details like paint colors, flooring, and fixtures (though good taste comes at a price).
- **Suited to modern tastes and needs.** New houses are built for today's lifestyles and trends, so you'll be able to find features like induction cooktops, a mud room, large closets, a two-sink master bathroom, and lots of natural light. Also, you shouldn't have to worry about replacing a water heater or roof anytime soon.
- **Livin' green.** New houses tend to be more energy efficient than older homes, so per square foot, you'll probably spend less money on

things like heating and cooling. With some searching, you might find a "green builder" who uses environmentally friendly building techniques and materials (see the U.S. Green Building Council's website at www.usgbc.org) or is even constructing "zero-energy" homes (which produce as much energy as they consume, using on-site renewable energy).

- **Community uniformity and planning.** Many new homes are built in planned unit developments (PUDs). Like condominiums, PUDs often have rules to maintain neighborhood aesthetics, and amenities like swimming pools and community centers.

But buying new can also have these drawbacks:

- **It will cost HOW much?** New houses' costs tend to mount quickly as you customize them to your wishes. Developers often offer unique financing alternatives (discussed in Chapter 7), which might make the purchase more affordable.

- **Who's this guy?!** You might have to deal with the developer's salesperson or representative, without the benefit of your own real estate agent to protect you. If you hope to use an agent, be sure to bring him or her along on your first visit—otherwise, you might lose your chance.

- **Not time-tested.** While it's exciting to get a brand-new home, you'll be the first to discover whether all the lights work, the dishwasher runs, the water heater heats, the pipes are connected, and more.

- **It will be done *when*?!** Developers don't always finish houses when they expect to, and often don't compensate purchasers for the delay. Instead, the fine print might release them of liability. Worse yet, financially unstable builders have been known to go bankrupt before houses are finished, or before adding amenities such as a golf course or swimming pool.

- **More rules?** As we'll discuss when we get to condos, some PUDs require all owners to live by a set of written rules. Short of selling, there's often little you can do to get out of these rules if you don't like them. Adviser Paul Grucza emphasizes, "Make sure you read everything before you take the plunge into a home located in a PUD."

Sharing the Joy, Sharing the Pain: Condos and Other Common Interest Properties

Maybe a traditional house isn't for you—perhaps it's out of your price range, you're looking to avoid all the maintenance, or you want to live in an area that just doesn't have many regular houses. If this sounds like you, consider an alternative, like a condominium ("condo") or co-op.

These types of properties are often referred to as common interest developments (CIDs), because they involve shared ownership or responsibility for common areas like hallways, recreation rooms, or playgrounds. How a place looks physically doesn't really make a difference—a CID might look like an apartment, flat, loft, or townhouse; be old or new; or be in the city or the country. (Detached houses in PUDs count too, but since we've already covered those, we won't include them in this section.)

Are you picturing yourself out on the roof with a hammer, doing your share for the common good? Don't worry, you most likely won't have to perform repairs or fix elevators. But you *will* have to become a member of a community association (often called a "homeowners' association," or an HOA), which makes sure those things are done. Your monthly membership fee (formally called a "maintenance assessment" or "regular assessment") will help keep common areas in good shape and provide a cash reserve for unanticipated or larger projects like replacing a roof. If you want to actively participate in the association, you can attend meetings and voice your opinion—or even get yourself elected to the board of directors. If you don't, you just write the check and hope the more active owners are like-minded.

There are three types of community associations: planned community associations (for PUDs, detached family homes, and townhouses), condominium associations, and co-op associations. We'll point out any significant differences among them as we go.

TIP

What the association leaders do. Every CID homeowner must join the community association, but it's the board of directors that handles the day-to-day work and decision making, such as coordinating repairs and collective services like trash pickup; managing amenities such as swimming pools, playgrounds, and tennis courts; enforcing the rules; preparing annual budgets; and conducting meetings.

Condominiums: Benefits and Drawbacks

When you buy a condo, you buy the interior space of your home. Your walls, ceiling, and floors define your boundaries instead of fences and sidewalks. As for the remaining "common space," the whole community owns and is financially responsible for it—be it stairwells, swimming pools, sidewalks, or gardens. Some of the benefits of condo life include:

- **Affordability.** A condo often costs less to buy than a house (although in major metropolitan or resort areas, the opposite is sometimes true). Maintaining a condo can also be less expensive, since costs that otherwise might be duplicated—like landscaping, roofing, and some insurance—are shared.
- **Convenience.** If you aren't into maintenance, you'll appreciate that the condo association—particularly in a larger community—is likely to hire a management company to take care of the landscaping and common areas. You might also get valuable on-site amenities like a gym or pool.
- **Community.** Because you're all part of the same community association, you'll get the opportunity to know your neighbors, whether you wish to or not.

Every rose has its thorns. Some of the drawbacks to condo living include:

- **Rules, rules, rules.** You'll be subject to a document called the master deed or Declaration of Covenants, Conditions, and Restrictions (CC&Rs). This sets forth not only rules for the community association board to follow, but rules governing all owners. You'll be told what you can do in the common space, and there will likely be restrictions on what you can do with or within your own unit. The CC&Rs can dictate everything from the color of your curtains or blinds to the type of flowers you can plant or pets you can adopt.
- **Buy for less, sell for less.** Condos generally appreciate at a slower rate than houses. And some have gotten into serious financial trouble in recent years, leaving homeowners unable to sell at all.
- **Privacy.** Since you'll be sharing common areas and usually walls or ceilings, too, you'll be giving up some privacy. Also, if having a large outdoor space to garden, entertain, or keep a pet is important, you might be frustrated by the outdoor spaces, which are usually either miniscule or communal (though reserving a "community building" or conference room might be an option).

Diet-Time for Fido?

What kinds of things do CC&Rs limit? Common examples are:

- whether you can have a dog, cat, bird, or other pet, and if so, its maximum height or weight
- whether you'll get a parking space, or whether your guests can park in the lot
- whether you can change the color or style of your window treatments or paint the outside of your unit
- the location or appearance of things like your mailbox, clothesline, satellite dish, flags, outdoor potted or hanging plants, and wreaths
- how long visitors can stay with you and whether they can use the amenities
- whether you can rent your unit to someone else, and
- whether you can smoke in your unit.

- **You share all costs, whether you want to or not.** It can be frustrating to see your monthly membership dues spent on things you never use, like the swimming pool. And if you're the kind of person who can live without a repair until you have spare cash, tough luck—you'll be forced to pay your share on the association's schedule, sometimes in excess of your regular fees. If you get behind on paying your assessments, your condo association might have the power to foreclose on you (even if you're up to date on your mortgage)!
- **New costs can sneak up on you.** In addition to your monthly membership or maintenance assessments (which can themselves be several hundred dollars), you might have to pay additional fees called "special assessments." These are one-time fees collected for major purchases the association can't afford to make with its current reserves (for example, to replace the roof). Do your research: In recent years, with many new buildings not fully occupied, the few owners in some CIDs have found their special assessments very high.

TIP

Size matters in condo developments. Your experience will be a lot different in a Boca Raton megaplex than in a Brooklyn brownstone. In a building with fewer units, you might find the rules less constricting—but you might also be more responsible for day-to-day operations and costs.

Townhouses and Duplexes: Benefits and Drawbacks

One compromise between a single-family dwelling and a traditional condo is a townhouse. Townhouses are usually built in rows and share at least one common wall (also called "row houses"). Like single-family houses, each townhouse owner has title to the building and the land it sits on. Like condos, townhouses might share some common areas, governed by a community association (but unlike condos, the community association usually owns the common area). Duplexes have similar characteristics, but share only one wall.

CAUTION

Be sure you know what type of property you're actually looking at. If a careless ad or agent calls a property a townhouse, but it's really a condo, you'd own a little less personally (because the land isn't yours, nor is the outside of your unit) and you should pay less accordingly.

Co-ops: Benefits and Drawbacks

Co-ops sound so glamorous, don't they? But what are they, other than swanky apartments in New York City for the rich and famous?

Celebrities Who've Owned Co-ops

Among the big names who've made a co-op home (or maybe one of their homes) are Glenn Close, Jimmy Fallon, Chloe Sevigny, Sean Combs (a.k.a. Diddy), Matthew Perry, and Kelis.

Like condos, co-ops (short for housing cooperatives) are defined by their ownership structure. When you own a house or condo, you own a piece of physical property. When you own a co-op, however, you own shares in a corporation.

The corporation, in turn, owns the building you live in, and you get a proprietary lease to live in a specific unit within the building. The lease allows you to live there as long as you own your shares and spells out any restrictions on your use of the unit.

As with any corporation, your shares also give you voting rights. Shareholders elect the board of directors, who make most of the decisions and manage daily operations or hire staff to do so. The shareholders pay a monthly "maintenance fee" to cover these and other costs. Usually, the more desirable the unit a shareholder has, the higher the maintenance fee.

Because of your limited ownership and other financial issues (discussed in Chapter 6), co-ops are sometimes difficult for the average first-time homebuyer to afford. The limitations also mean that co-ops tend to be quite slow to appreciate in value.

Factory Made: Modular and Manufactured Homes

Buying a prefabricated home no longer means living in an insubstantial-looking box. In fact, it's a creative option that's gaining in popularity. Now known as "modular homes," these are built in sections in factories and transported to their permanent lots. There, they're fully assembled to comply with local building codes. If you decide to buy a vacant property and build a home on it, a modular home might be a relatively low-cost option. It's especially suitable in areas where the weather is harsh and labor costs high.

Buying vacant property involves a number of issues that we don't explore in detail within this book. For example:

- You'll want to have it surveyed to find out about any hidden surprises, such a public path running through it (an "easement") or any encroachments by neighboring properties or other boundary issues.
- You'll want to pay particular attention to where your drinking and other water will come from, if it's available at all. If the land isn't served by a public water source or a community well, you might

need to dig your own well or install a cistern. And even if there is a public source, having the connections built can be costly.

- The lot might not be connected to the municipal sewer line. Creating this connection could be costly—or impossible. If you can't hook up to the city line, you're going to have to install a septic system. That's an expensive project that will be subject to many rules and regulations.

- You will need to investigate how the property is zoned; hopefully "residential," if you plan to live there. The zoning rules will also tell you exactly what uses are allowed under the assigned designation (for example, whether you can also open a home business or keep farm animals).

Million-Dollar Mobile Homes?

Yes, you'll find them in Malibu: Even the rich and famous (like Minnie Driver) sometimes retreat to manufactured home communities.

- Getting an environmental assessment done before you buy would also be smart, to make sure the property doesn't come with toxic soils or another serious environmental or clean-up problem. Also, if you will be building in or near wetlands, rivers, coastlines, or other water resources, you might run into a complex web of federal, state, and local regulations, which can severely restrict the area upon which you can build.

You'll also have to consider additional expenses resulting from the above-described issues and more, like transporting the home; getting the proper permits and access to utilities and sewer lines; hiring a builder to assemble the prefab parts and professionals for installations; and adding features like landscaping, driveways, or fences. A local contractor can give you a brief overview of the costs, players, and timeline.

Hiring a real estate broker with experience in vacant properties would be wise; many agencies don't handle these transactions. (Don't just call the number on the seller's sign! You'd then likely end up without your own, buyer's broker by your side to help negotiate and conclude the sale.)

CHECK IT OUT

Check out modular home styles, from the traditional to the ultramodern, at:

- ModularHomeowners.com
- ModularToday.com, and
- LinwoodHomes.com.

Another potentially low-cost option is the manufactured house, once commonly referred to as a mobile home. These too have come a long way and aren't always as mobile as their former name would suggest. Manufactured homes comply with federal building standards but aren't restricted by local or state building codes.

> *Ooh! I forgot about the washer and dryer! I've been dreaming about that my whole New York life!*
>
> Carrie, *Sex and the City*

Manufactured homes are typically built in a factory, then transported to communities of other, similar homes, and the owners lease the land the homes sit on. If the lease is terminated or the land is sold, the owners can be required to leave and take their homes with them. Another issue arises if and when you want to sell your manufactured home. Your buyer will likely wish to remain on the same land (given the difficulties of moving the structure); but the landlord typically has the power to refuse a particular buyer's entry into the community. Since a lot of the value of a home is in the land, these homes tend to *lose* value over time, and moving one could cost more than it's worth.

Manufactured homes are often more difficult to finance, too. The bottom line is that they're low-cost options to more permanent properties but don't usually offer the same equity-building advantages.

Putting It All Together: Your Dream List

Now it's time to fill out what we call your "Dream List." This is a handy worksheet where you'll write down your "must haves," such as number of bedrooms, size or type of house, neighborhood, maximum price, and anything else you consider a minimum requirement in a home, such as a garden. There's also space to note your "would likes," features you'd prefer but could live without or possibly add later (such as a deck).

Dream List

Address: 43 Belvedere Road, Oakland, CA   **Date visited:** March 3, 20xx

Contact: Tom Macht, Hills Realty, 510-555-3479

General Features	Must Have	Would Like	This House
Type (house, condo, etc.) or Style (Colonial, loft, etc.)	Single-family house in good shape with few stairs from the street	Ranch style or layout with bedroom on 1st floor, accessible for elderly parents	80 years old, but seemingly in great shape. Two-story. Den on first floor could be used as guest room.
Upper price limit	$900,000	$ 750,000	$ 850,000 list price
Age above/below	Less than 75 years old	Less than 50 years old	80 years old
Min. square footage	1,500	2,000	1,750
Min. lot size	2,500 square ft.	3,500 square ft.	3,000 square ft.
Number of bedrooms	3	4	3 (plus den that could double as guest room)
Number of bathrooms	2 full baths	3 full baths	2.5 (half-bath off of kitchen and full bath in master bedroom)
___ car garage	1-car garage	Large attached 2-car garage	No garage
Parking	Driveway parking, not on an incline	Same	Driveway parking close to house, level surface
Fireplace	Not a deal breaker	A gas fireplace	Nonworking fireplace
Flooring	Hardwood, at least in living room and dining room	Hardwood floors in good shape, in entire house	Hardwood floors in living room and dining room, but covered by wall-to-wall carpet. Floors need refinishing.
Other	Good separation from neighbors' houses	Lots of privacy, especially in backyard	Houses are fairly close, but trees provide some privacy on 1st floor

Dream List, continued

Floor Plan	Must Have	Would Like	This House
Formal living/ dining	Separate living and dining rooms	Large living room for entertaining	Small living and dining rooms, open on to each other
Great room	Don't care	Don't care	No
Number of floors	2	1	2 (short flight of stairs)
Basement/attic	Clean, dry basement for storage; no flooding problems	Large finished basement for kids' playroom plus storage, half-bath	Basement in good shape; could be divided into kids' play space and storage area. No bathroom.
Other			

Kitchen	Must Have	Would Like	This House
The basics	Large sunny kitchen, lots of counter space and storage	Gourmet kitchen with beautiful cabinets, walk-in pantry, natural lighting plus recessed lighting, hardwood floors	Decent-size kitchen, good light, adequate storage. Cabinets need resurfacing. Linoleum floor will need replacing. Lighting fixtures outdated.
Dishwasher	Built-in dishwasher	Same	Only portable dishwasher, but could add a built-in one
Other appliances	Gas stove, large refrigerator in good shape	New stainless steel appliances, including commercial stove	Refrigerator and oven don't match, but are only a few years old
Eat-in	Space for small table for four, or breakfast counter	Breakfast nook opening on to deck	Breakfast nook! Now to add the deck ...
Other			

Dream List, continued

Other Rooms	Must Have	Would Like	This House
Laundry	Washing machine and dryer	Separate laundry room on 1st floor, with space to hang clothes and iron	Washing machine and dryer in basement. Bare bones.
Family	Space for kids to hang out, separate from living room	Large finished playroom in basement	No separate playroom, but kids' rooms are large, and extra space in basement
Den/study	A room suited for office, with space for two desks, bookcases, and file cabinets	Two separate offices with built-in bookcases would be fantastic!	Den on first floor could double as guest room/ office. Master bedroom nook could be made into small office.
Other			

Outside	Must Have	Would Like	This House
Deck/patio	Sunny deck off of kitchen or ability to easily add one	Large deck plus patio in garden	Small deck off of second floor master bedroom; would be easy to build deck off kitchen
Garden	Sunny yard for garden	Established garden, fruit trees, good soil, underground watering system. Mainly sunny, with a few shade trees.	Back yard needs work. A few rose bushes and succulents, but potential. Completely open (no shade). No drip system.
Fenced yard	Yes—need for dog	Beautiful hardwood fence and large secure backyard	Fence in bad shape. Will need to replace, or fill in some areas with holes.
Pool/hot tub	Not necessary	Not necessary	No
Other			

Dream List, continued

Structure	Must Have	Would Like	This House
Central heat/air	Central heat	Central heat and AC	Central heat
Insulation	Throughout house and attic	Throughout house and attic	Only attic is insulated
Upgraded plumbing	A must	Copper plumbing	Not sure about the material, but plumbing, water pressure, etc. seem fine
Other			

Storage	Must Have	Would Like	This House
The basics	Good storage a must in entryway, bedrooms, kitchen, basement, bathrooms, and other rooms	Custom built-in closets in all rooms, lots of shelves, drawers, cupboards (especially in kitchen)	Adequate coat closet in entryway. All closets need updating, except for large walk-in closet in master bedroom.
Linen closet	Linen closet near bathroom	2 large linen closets, 1 near bedrooms, other bath	Small linen closet on 2nd floor only, outside of bathroom
Other			

Convenience	Must Have	Would Like	This House
Work within ___ miles/minutes	1 hour tops by car	15 minutes by car (one can dream)	30-minute drive to city (45-60 minutes in rush hour). Alternative = good public transport
Church/place of worship within ___ miles/minutes	N/A	N/A	N/A
Other			

Dream List, continued

Neighborhood	Must Have	Would Like	This House
Quiet street	Residential area; no speeding cars, walking distance to grocery, other shops	Same	Street a little noisy (dog next door), basically okay. Only a few blocks to lake and great shopping area!
Safe neighborhood	A must!	Same	Seems safe; need to talk with neighbors, check crime stats
Good schools	A must!	Lake Hills school district, schools within walking distance	Lake Hills school district! Elementary school is short (15-minute) walk from home
Rules/restrictions	N/A (we don't want to live in community association)	N/A	N/A
Community association fees	N/A	N/A	N/A
Accessible public transport	Short walk or drive to BART, and close bus stop	Short walk or drive to BART. Bus stop at corner	10-minute drive to BART, bus stop a 5-minute walk
Other			

Absolute No Ways Under Any Condition

Bad schools, high-crime area, fixer-upper.

Notes

This house is definitely a possibility—especially because of schools and location. We may be able to get it for less than list price—enough to cover some changes we'd like, such as refinishing/replacing floors, resurfacing kitchen cabinets, adding a built-in dishwasher, repairing backyard fence. May even be able to swing adding a deck off the kitchen!

Of course, expressing your preferences doesn't mean you'll get all of them. But later, when you're out househunting, reviewing a copy of your Dream List will help you keep your priorities straight.

The Dream List also includes a section for things you absolutely won't accept, under any condition, such as a dark kitchen with few windows. You might need this reminder one day, when you find a house that's perfect in every other respect.

TIP

Check in with your partner. If you're buying the house with another person, make sure you assess your priorities and complete the Dream List *together*. It won't help to make a list of priorities, only to find out they're in direct conflict with your fellow buyer's.

Best thing I ever did

Put my practical needs as a single woman first. Hope thought she was looking for a cute Craftsman with wainscoting, high ceilings, and a yard. "In fact," she says, "I almost bought a house that fit my supposed ideal. But at the last minute, I realized it wasn't going to work. My work hours don't leave time for home maintenance, and my safety was an issue in that neighborhood. So I switched gears and bought a late '80s townhouse with a drive-in garage with direct access to the house, in a nicer neighborhood. It's architecturally boring, but I'm comfortable there, the homeowners' association deals with most of the maintenance, and I haven't had a moment's regret."

ONLINE TOOLKIT

The "Dream List" can be found in the Homebuyer's Toolkit on the Nolo website. (See the appendix for the link.) A filled-in sample is shown above.

Dream List Directions

This Dream List includes the more common features found in many homes, but you can add others to this list (perhaps a must-have hillside location with a view) or delete some features. Add as many details as you want in the left-hand column ("General Features").

At the end of the Dream List, there's a section for those things you absolutely will not accept, under any condition. There's also a section at the end for notes, such as comments about a particular house or neighborhood—something you want to be sure to remember, such as a quiet location at the end of a cul de sac.

Fill in the "Must Have" column with your minimum requirements and the "Would Like" column with features you'd prefer but could live without. For example, for the "Number of Bedrooms" feature, you might write "3" in the "Must Have" column and "4" in the "Would Like" column. In some cases, you'll add additional information: For example, you might put a checkmark indicating that a house meets your upper price limit, and then note the actual price of the house. If a "Must Have" can be added when you move in, such as a deck or second bathroom, you can also note this.

If you fill out the left columns of the Dream List now and print more copies, you can use this sheet over and over again. Each time you visit a house, simply write in the address and note how it compares in the right-hand column ("This House"). Save copies for homes that seem like good possibilities.

What's Next?

Now that you know what features you're looking for, it's time to figure out whether you can afford them all. In Chapter 3, we'll explain how a lender is going to evaluate your finances and what you should do to evaluate them yourself.

Does This Mean I Have to Balance My Checkbook? Figuring Out What You Can Afford

Meet Your Adviser

Sydney W. Andrews, a 23-year veteran of the mortgage industry (NMLS #47982), owner of the mortgage company Loanenvy.com, and a licensed real estate broker.

What he does

"I work with individual homebuyers or homeowners, often through their financial planners or real estate agents, to help get them the right mortgage for their needs. This involves more background work than some realize, starting with evaluating the buyers' income, other financials, and credit report, and asking the right questions so as to learn about their long-term plans and financial goals. I help determine whether the buyers can afford a home at all, and if so at what price. An important next step, particularly here in the hot L.A. market, is arranging for a preapproval or prequalification letter. In a multiple-offer situation, it's key for them to show this type of financial readiness."

First house

"My wife and I purchased it in 2003, a single-family home here in Los Angeles, about 1,700 square feet. The look is very historic: It was built in 1926, Spanish style. At the time, property values were on the rise. Having already been outbid on a few other places, we knew we were going to have to bid over the list price of $750,000. We also knew that, two years prior, the owner had bought the place for $450,000, so the owner was going to make a good profit no matter what! We bid $40,000 over the list price, and wrote a letter about how much we loved home and were planning on starting a family here. It all worked out great. We've since added a second story, to make more room for family and friends. (That was a huge project: We rented an apartment for a year during the construction.)"

Fantasy house	"It would be on the ocean somewhere, maybe Kauai. It would have a big deck, and French doors, all overlooking the water. I grew up on Cape Cod, so I like to be near water. And let's include a pool for my wife, who is less eager than I to jump straight into the ocean."
Likes best about his work	"I'm frugal at heart, so I like saving people money. Let's say, for instance, they already have a loan, but can refi to a better one, perhaps a 15-year one that pays off more principal and puts them on a path to good retirement without a huge mortgage. That's why I like working with financial planners; they're focused on getting that client into a loan that meets long term goals down the road. It's a collaboration between the two of us. Or, for a first-time buyer, if they really plan to stay in the home for 30 years, then a 30-year fixed rate mortgage might be okay, but if it's simply a starter home, then maybe an ARM with a lower rate would make more sense for those first few years. It's also a good feeling when a first-time homebuyer comes in, nervous, thinking they might not really be able to afford a home, and we can put them through the process and make their dream come true."
Top tip for first-time homebuyers	"Try to find out how much you can really afford before going out and looking at homes. Speak to someone who can give you the right advice, and run your credit. (That's the first thing every mortgage lender looks at.) Also control your debt; don't buy a Tesla and then go look for a home loan! If you want a car in a few years, or have other planned major expenditures, factor that in to what amount you borrow, so as not to strap yourself to your loan."

U p to this point, we've been able to focus on the fun stuff—finding out all the great reasons to buy a house and imagining what the new place will look like. Now it's time to take a step into the world of finance—nothing that will require an accounting degree, fortunately. You might be wondering why we're even bringing up boring money stuff before you've started seriously househunting. That's what a mortgage broker is for, isn't it?

But wouldn't it be horrible to make an offer on a house and begin shopping for a loan, only to discover that you couldn't qualify for the amount you needed or the terms you expected? Even worse, what if you were able to get a loan, but discovered after moving into your new home that you'd borrowed more than you could handle—at least, without moonlighting?

Don't Play the Multiplication Game

You might have heard of a formula where you multiply your household's gross annual income by two and a half to find out how much you can afford to spend on a house. This might be fun and easy, but it won't help you draw realistic conclusions. It fails to factor in important things like how much debt you currently have, the terms of your mortgage, or how much you already have saved for a down payment. If you really want to guess how much you can spend before reading this chapter, you're better off using a reliable online affordability calculator like the one at Nolo.com/legal-calculators.

Getting familiar with your finances before there's a prospective property in sight—even if you just sit down for an hour or two—will help you estimate how much you can realistically afford to spend and prepare you to choose the best possible loan. This chapter will help you by:

- explaining the costs of purchasing a house
- demystifying the process mortgage lenders use to decide how much you can borrow

- providing simple ways to calculate what you can *really* afford based on your lifestyle and finances
- showing you how to boost your financial profile, and
- explaining what it means to get preapproved for a loan and why you should do so.

If you've already found a place and are trying to figure out how to pay for it, don't skip this chapter. A quick look at your finances will still help you decide whether your prospective home's cost is within your budget and whether you're likely to get the loan terms you're counting on.

Beyond the Purchase Price: The Costs of Buying and Owning a Home

Buying a house means some new expenses beyond the purchase price. A first-time homebuyer should plan to drop some cash for:

- the down payment
- the loan principal, loan interest, state and local taxes, and homeowners' insurance
- up-front costs, such as to conduct inspections and take other steps to close the deal, and
- recurring ownership costs.

The exact dollar figures will depend on you, the house you buy and where you buy it, and the type of mortgage you get. But even if you can't predict precise amounts, understanding these expenses and what drives them will save you some sticker shock.

Why Interest Rates Are a Big Deal

If you pay just half a percent more than you could have if you'd done some research—say, 4.5% instead of 4.0%, on a 30-year, fixed-rate mortgage for $200,000—you could end up (in this example) paying almost $21,000 more in interest over the life of the loan.

Down Payment

You may be plunking down a hefty chunk of change, in the form of a down payment, to buy your home. Down payments are traditionally calculated as a percentage of the purchase price. Although most lenders tightened lending practices after the 2007/2008 financial crisis and began requiring down payments of 20%, many are relaxing standards once again. If you have excellent credit (with a minimum FICO score of 620 for a conventional loan and 580 for an FHA loan), you should be able to qualify for a mortgage with between 3.5% and 10% down.

> **Tick, Tick, Tick**
>
> Finding the house you want to buy might not take as long as you think. According to the National Association of Realtors®, the typical homebuyer spent ten weeks searching before settling on a house.

Nevertheless, there are many benefits to making a large down payment:

- **No PMI.** If you pay 20% of your purchase price, you don't have to pay private mortgage insurance, or PMI, which lenders routinely require of homebuyers who borrow more than 80% of the home's value. Its purpose is to protect the lender if you default.
- **Smaller monthly mortgage payments.** If you borrow less money, you'll have less to pay back, leaving you more cash for other uses.
- **Less interest overall.** If you borrow less, you'll owe less in total interest over the life of the loan.
- **It's like money in the bank.** No matter what the stock market does, putting cash into your home is a low-risk way to use it.
- **Lower interest rate.** Borrowers who take out mortgages for more than a certain amount ($484,350 in most places in 2019, but higher in expensive areas, such as Alaska and Hawaii—up to $726,525 in 2019) get what are called "jumbo" loans, with higher interest rates. If making a down payment will lower your loan to below that amount, your interest rate will probably drop, too. Likewise, if you're a borrower with poor credit, you might be able to obtain better loan

terms if you fork over more cash at the beginning—the lender figures you've got more incentive to keep paying if you stand to lose your down payment when the lender forecloses.

Where Will I Get Down Payment Money?

If you're interested in making a down payment but haven't saved the cash, here are some alternative sources:

- **A gift or loan from family or friends.** A loved one with available cash might be willing to give you a low-interest loan, or even a gift.

- **Withdrawal from your IRA.** You can withdraw up to $10,000, penalty free, from an individual retirement account (IRA) to purchase (or build) your first home. Your spouse or cobuyer can do the same. That's a lifetime limit, however, and you will owe income tax on it. For more information, see IRS Publication 590-B, *Distributions From Individual Retirement Arrangements (IRAs)*, available at www.irs.gov.

- **Borrow from your 401(k).** Check with your employer or plan administrator about whether you can borrow from your 401(k) plan. Also ask how much you can borrow (usually $50,000 at most). But be warned: Lenders may factor the monthly 401(k) loan repayment amount into your mortgage qualification ratio. For more information, see IRS Publication 575, *Pension and Annuity Income*, available at www.irs.gov.

- **Current assets.** If you have other investments, like stocks or bonds, consider cashing them out—but be sure to factor in the taxes you'll owe. You might be also able to sell an asset like a car or valuable musical instrument. Be sure to keep a paper trail of the transaction.

- **Don't have a big wedding!** Okay, we're half joking here. But you wouldn't believe the number of couples we've met who said that, in retrospect, they wish they'd kept the wedding small and put that money toward a house.

Best thing we ever did

Make a 30% down payment. According to Nigel, "When Olivia and I decided to buy a house together, we were earning nonprofit salaries (low). But our parents were excited to see us settle down and gave us generous gifts. Between that and emptying our savings account, we had about 30% to put down—which convinced the seller to choose our bid from among the many others, because we'd obviously have no trouble financing the rest. Now we have absurdly low monthly payments—less than we'd be paying in rent—and the house has appreciated in value. Also, we're in a position to help our parents out financially, if they need it."

Principal, Interest, Taxes, and Insurance

Ever heard of PITI (pronounced "pity")? It stands for principal, interest, taxes, and insurance, all of which must be factored into your homebuying plans. Here's the breakdown on these expense items:

- **Principal.** The amount you borrow from the lender and must pay back, month by month.
- **Interest.** A percentage of the overall borrowed amount that the lender charges you to use its money. The exact rate varies widely.
- **Property taxes.** Taxes vary by state and sometimes by local area, but expect to pay somewhere between .5% and 2.5% of the house purchase price each year.
- **Insurance.** Coverage for theft, fire, and other damage to the property (required by your lender) and (usually) to cover your liability to people injured on your property or by you. Average rates run upwards of $600 per year, and around $2,000 annually in many locations. Private mortgage insurance or PMI also factors in here. If a homebuyer puts down less than 20%, the annual PMI cost can range from ½% to 1.5% of the loan amount.

Worst states for property taxes?

The five with highest rates nationwide in 2019 are:

#1 New Jersey

#2 Illinois

#3 New Hampshire

#4 Connecticut, and

#5 Wisconsin.

(Source: WalletHub.com)

It makes sense that these four items have their own acronym, PITI, because for some homebuyers (usually those whose down payment is less than 20%), all four must be paid into an escrow account managed by the mortgage lender each month. In fact, the lender will require that some portion of the PITI payments be made in advance at the closing, including one year's homeowners' insurance and several months' tax payments. The lender turns around and pays the appropriate party. The lender's rationale is that if you don't pay these bills (or your mortgage) and the lender forecloses and gets the property, it doesn't want to get stuck with your tax or insurance bill, too.

> **TIP**
> **PITI is paid differently when you buy a condo or co-op.** Instead of paying the lender, you might have to pay your community association or co-op board for your portion of the mortgage and real estate taxes (on a co-op), or for insurance on the jointly owned parts of the property (on either a condo or a co-op).

Added together, your total PITI might come to a lot more than your current monthly rent. That makes owning a home look like an expensive proposition. But it's not an apples-to-apples comparison. First, remember that your mortgage payments typically reduce your loan principal, so your payment is building equity, not just going into a black hole. Second, your interest payments (on indebtedness up to $750,000 if single or married filing jointly or $375,000 if married filing separately) and property taxes (on indebtedness, up to a total of $10,000 for all state and local taxes) are tax deductible if you itemize.

Up-Front Costs

Until now, we've been talking about costs associated with the house itself. But you'll also have to spend some pretty serious cash at the beginning to make the sale happen. (Sort of like paying first and last month's rent.) Particularly if you're trying to save up for a decent-sized down payment, you'll need to plan for the following additional up-front costs:

- **Closing costs.** An array of miscellaneous charges—for everything from couriers to loan points (discussed below) to insurance premiums—are lumped into a category called "closing costs." These vary across the country, but are usually around $3,700.
- **Home inspection cost.** You'll need to be ready to pay the inspector from whom you commission a report on the home BEFORE the closing; the amount will likely be between $300 and $600.
- **Appraisal.** You are also responsible for paying to have the lender-required appraisal done on the home. Budget around $425 to $625 for this.
- **Points.** Borrowers sometimes agree to pay a "loan origination fee" or "points" to obtain a specific loan. Each point is 1% of the loan principal (so one point on a $100,000 loan is $1,000). Paying points can lower your interest rate, so you pay less in the long term. But you'll probably need to pay the cash up front.

> ### The Best Metro Areas for First-Time Homebuyers
>
> According to Zillow, the top ten metro areas for first timers in 2019, taking into account median home values, appreciation forecasts, inventory-to-household ratios, and share of listings with a price cut, are: #1 Tampa, #2 Las Vegas, #3 Phoenix, #4 Atlanta, #5 Orlando, #6 Miami, #7 Detroit, #8 Dallas, #9 Nashville, and #10 Charlotte.

- **Moving costs.** How high these will go depends on how far you're moving, how much stuff you have, and whether you use a professional moving company.
- **Service setup costs.** You might have to pay fees to set up cable and Internet, a security system, and similar services in your new home.
- **Emergency fund.** It's a good idea (and sometimes a lender requirement) to have a couple months' worth of PITI payments saved, in case something goes unexpectedly awry.
- **Remodeling costs.** If you buy a fixer-upper or a planned remodel, you might need thousands of dollars in cash early on, just to make the place livable. Estimate high for these expenses—they're almost always more than anyone expected.

Recurring Costs

Yes, there's more. Whether new or old, your house will need regular maintenance—gutters cleaned and trees trimmed regularly, a paint job every few years, new appliances when the old ones die, and so on. If you buy in a common interest development, your personal maintenance costs might be lower, but you'll have to pay monthly dues and sometimes special assessments for unanticipated projects like resurfacing a damaged parking lot. While not part of your PITI, all of these expenses will affect your monthly cash flow.

> **TIP**
>
> **Adjust your payroll deductions.** Once you know the details of your mortgage, work with a financial professional to change your withholdings to account for your lower tax liability, freeing up more money for other expenses.

Spend Much?
How Lenders Use Your Debt-to-Income Ratio

Once you understand what you'll be paying for, and that you'll probably need a mortgage to make it happen, the obvious question is, how much can you borrow? To know that, you need to understand how lenders think. Just as you're trying to get the best loan, lenders are looking for the best borrowers.

Without knowing you personally, lenders need some criteria to figure out how risky it is to lend you money. If you make your payments, they'll turn a profit, either in interest or by selling your loan on the secondary market (more on that in Chapter 6). If you don't, they'll have to chase you down for the cash or sell the property to try to get it.

One of the criteria that lenders use is the comparison between your income and your debt load, called your "debt-to-income" ratio. They also look at your track record for paying previous debts, or your credit history, discussed below.

The concept of debt-to-income ratio isn't as complicated as it sounds. The lender simply looks at your household's gross monthly income, then makes sure that your combined minimum debt payments—for your PITI (including any community association fees), credit card, car, student loan, personal loan, 401(k) loan, and others—don't eat up more than a certain percentage of that amount. The idea is to make sure you have enough cash left over for your mortgage payment.

Maximum Acceptable Ratio: The 43% Rule

How high can your debt-to-income ratio go? Your overall debt shouldn't exceed 43% of your gross monthly income. (Gross monthly income means the amount you earn before taxes and other monthly withdrawals, plus income from all other sources, like royalties, interest, alimony, or investments.)

> EXAMPLE: Fernando and Luz have a gross annual income of $90,000 ($7,500 per month) and a minimal amount of existing debt. If they plan to spend 43% of their gross monthly income on PITI, they'll pay $3,225 each month. Assuming they spend about $652 of that on taxes and insurance, they can borrow about $530,000 using a 30-year, fixed rate loan at 4% interest.

CHECK IT OUT

Ready to run some numbers? Online affordability calculators show how a traditional lender will use your debt-to-income ratio to set your maximum monthly mortgage payment. Find such calculators at Nolo.com/legal-calculators, HSH.com, Bankrate.com, and Interest.com. Make sure any calculator you use factors in the amount of your down payment, your income and your debts, and your estimated taxes and insurance.

All you need to figure out your own debt-to-income ratios is your combined gross monthly income figure (including that of anyone buying with you). If you're self-employed, the calculation changes; you'll need to plug in your adjusted gross income amount, most likely using the average over the last two years.

Simply multiply your total monthly income by .43 to find out approximately how much a lender will say you can afford to spend each month on a mortgage payment.

Blasts From the Past: How Your Credit History Factors In

Aside from your available income, your lender's main preoccupation will be with your credit history. Most lenders want to know whom they'll be competing with to get your monthly dollars, how much you're borrowing from those various sources, and how good you've been about paying money back in the past. You've probably undergone credit history checks before, like when you applied for a car loan or rented a new apartment.

Managing Your Money Is So Easy!

You just use your credit cards! You pay your American Express with your Discover, your Discover with your Visa, your Visa with your MasterCard. Before they catch up with you, you're buried in a glorious crypt in Bel-Air!

Camilla, character on TV series *The Naked Truth*

Credit reporting bureaus exist to keep track of your borrowing habits. The three major companies are Equifax (Equifax.com), Experian (Experian.com), and TransUnion (TransUnion.com). They use a formula compiled by the Fair Isaac Corporation to calculate your "FICO" score (which we'll call your "credit score"; but beware when you see this term other places, because anyone can compile a number and call it a "credit" score).

In 2012, FICO introduced something called the FICO Mortgage Score. Some lenders use this instead of, or in addition to, your regular FICO score. The FICO Mortgage Score is computed by evaluating even more information than the regular FICO score, such as your history of child support payments, rental payments, and more (all gleaned from public records).

How Lenders Use Credit Scores

Lenders use your credit score to decide whether to lend you money and, if so, how much and on what terms. If you'll be financing your home jointly with others, the lender will look at each person's credit score. Unfortunately, that means that if one of you has a low score, it will probably affect the terms of the loan offered to all of you. If any of you has serious skeletons in the financial closet, either clear out the closet, reconsider the joint purchase, or get creative with your financing strategies.

Getting Your Own Credit Report and Score

The best way to know exactly what prospective lenders will be looking at is to look at it yourself first. Federal law requires each of the three major consumer reporting companies (named above) to provide you with a free copy of your credit report once every 12 months.

CHECK IT OUT

The only authorized source for free credit reports: Go to AnnualCreditReport.com. Other websites may advertise a "free report" but try to sell you something in the process. This site also links you directly to the websites for the big three reporting bureaus.

It's a good idea to ask all three agencies for your credit report. They sometimes have different information, and your lender might be looking at all three reports. You can do this simultaneously, but it means that you won't be able to get another free report from any of them for another full year.

𝓛esson learned the hard way — **Being financially responsible left me with no credit history!** When Willow decided to buy her first house, she didn't expect her lack of debt to create a problem. Willow explains, "I'd worked my way through school and taken out a student loan that I paid off almost immediately. And I'd always used a debit card instead of a credit card. As a result, I had to jump through all sorts of extra hoops, providing a letter from my old landlord showing that I paid the rent on time; showing records of my payments of phone bills and cable bills; and even having my parents add my name to their credit card account. (That last strategy worked faster than I expected—within one month, my credit score was the same as theirs.) Here I thought I'd been so good at controlling my finances, yet I discovered I'd been completely naïve when it came to creating a record of debt payments."

Federal law doesn't require the agencies to give you your credit *score*, which is different from your report and can vary by company. You'll probably have to pay extra to get the score (unless you live in a state like California that requires that consumers be given their scores for free when getting a mortgage). You can get your credit score either from the individual consumer reporting company websites or by going to MyFICO.com.

What Your Credit Score Means

When you get your credit score, it will be a number somewhere between 300 and 850—the higher the better. If your score is above 720, it's considered pretty strong. Most people are in the 600s or 700s. A higher number tells the lender you pay your debts on time, have limited sources of revolving credit, and have an established record of using credit prudently, making you a good credit risk. A lower number (below around 620 for conventional mortgages and 580 for FHA mortgages) means you look more risky—perhaps because you have enough revolving credit that if you maxed it all out you couldn't pay all your bills plus a mortgage; you've missed payments in the past; or you've never used any credit source, so the lender doesn't know what to make of you.

A low score will make it difficult to find a willing lender. And any lender you do find will expect you to pay more for the privilege of borrowing, probably in the form of higher interest. (If your credit is less than perfect, you might be able to clean it up, as we'll discuss below.)

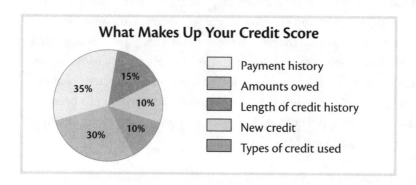

CHECK IT OUT

What makes up a FICO score? It includes your payment history (35% of the score), how much you currently owe (30%), how long you've been a borrower (15%), whether you have any new credit accounts (10%), and the types of credit you use (10%). To learn more, go to myFICO.com, a Fair Isaac website for consumers.

Understanding Your Credit Report

Get ready: Your credit report may go on for *literally* pages and pages. Focus on making sure the most critical information is mistake free, particularly these bits of data:

- **Name, Social Security number, and addresses.** You might have multiple aliases, especially if you have a common name. And an address you don't recognize may mean someone with the same name is incorrectly listed on your report.

- **Creditors.** Make sure you actually borrowed money from the creditors that appear, and that the amounts borrowed are accurate. Keep in mind that some types of loans, like student loans, can be sold or transferred. In that case, all creditors that have held the loan will appear, but the pretransferred or sold accounts should no longer be designated "open."
- **Open credit lines.** Make sure any lines of credit you've closed are no longer shown as open. Different reporting companies use different terminology, so if you're not sure, call to clarify.
- **Collections and judgments.** Make sure any collection actions or judgments are reflected accurately.
- **Late payments.** These notations will usually indicate a late payment of 30, 60, or 90 days. Make sure they're accurate.

Correcting Credit Errors

Credit reporting mistakes happen frequently. Inaccuracies in the report affect your score, and if your score drops, so does the likelihood of your getting the best possible loan. You'll want to spot and correct any errors and resolve any disputes before a lender sees your report, not after you've applied for a loan and been rejected.

All manner of mistakes are possible—from bits of credit history that aren't yours to a false claim that you paid a bill late. To correct such errors, contact the reporting agency in writing. If all three agencies misreported the information, you'll have to contact all three. Each agency might have a different procedure and forms to use for disputing the report. When you discuss issues over the phone, make sure to document conversations, including the date and name of the person you spoke with. Finally, if you have any documentation that supports your claim, send a copy with an explanatory cover letter.

The credit reporting agency has 30 days to investigate your complaint and give you its findings. If it can't verify that its version of events is correct, the agency is supposed to remove the information from your file. If it won't, you have the right to place a statement in your file giving your version of what happened.

Sometimes you can also work directly with your current and former creditors to correct inaccuracies or solve problems. If you're willing to pay the disputed amount, or the creditor is willing to settle for a lesser amount—which it sometimes is—the creditor might also agree to clear the item from your credit history. Likewise if you have proof of an error, it might be faster to go directly through the creditor than to correct it through the reporting bureau.

CHECK IT OUT

Need help patching up your credit? See *Credit Repair*, by Attorneys Amy Loftsgordon and Cara O'Neill (Nolo). It offers plain-English explanations and over 30 forms and letters to help you negotiate with creditors, get positive information added to your credit record, and build a financial cushion. Also, the Debt Management section of Nolo.com includes dozens of useful articles on credit repair.

Repairing Your Credit

Rome wasn't built in a day, and credit history can't be repaired in one, either. If you or a coborrower have a poor credit history, Fair Isaac suggests you start cleaning it up six to 12 months before applying for a loan. If your credit history is really messy, it might take even longer.

But here's some good news: Even if you have a long, ugly credit history, your score will be weighted in favor of your latest performance. Turn over a new leaf by following these strategies:

- **Pay on time from now on.** Don't miss due dates for credit cards and other bills. Setting up automatic payment plans can help, and your lender may reduce your interest rate in return.
- **Pay the worst first.** Start by paying off high-interest debt, like on credit cards. Also, keep your balances low on revolving lines of credit. Don't just move the debt around—that won't fool the credit scorers, nor will it free up cash for a mortgage payment.

- **Don't cancel credit cards.** Paying a balance down to zero but keeping the card active is typically much better for your credit score than actually cancelling the card.

> **TIP**
> **Check out FHA-backed loans.** Some low down payment federal loan programs are less strict about credit background. See Chapter 7 for details.

What's Your Monthly Budget? Understanding Your Finances

Now that you've seen what lenders look at to decide how much you can spend, it's time to think about what *you* believe you can spend. The point is to avoid taking on so much debt that you lose sleep or have to give up sushi for ramen noodles.

> **Lesson learned the hard way**
>
> **Should've budgeted for furniture!** According to adviser and real estate broker Tara Waggoner (whom you'll meet in Chapter 15), "I know a couple who, for the first nine months living in their first home, literally had almost no furniture beyond a card table and a futon. They'd rented a much smaller place before. In working out their budget, they forgot to take into account that they'd have to furnish all the rooms that they were so excited about in their new home: a media room, an office, and five bedrooms (they had kids). They laugh about it now."

In fact, if you look closer at that debt-to-income ratio, you'll realize that it has a built-in problem. It's based on your *gross* income—the amount you theoretically make before your paycheck gets eaten by taxes and other withdrawals. Your mortgage payment could, depending on your lifestyle, end up exceeding what actually remains.

The easiest way to understand your current spending and savings pattern is to do a budget worksheet. You can do this using either budgeting software, a spreadsheet like *Excel*, or with old-fashioned pencil and paper. List all your expenses, including food, entertainment, clothing, transportation and car-related expenses, health and dental care, child and pet care, student loans, and utilities. Hold onto your receipts, and if you use an ATM card or make electronic payments, look at your bank statement to see where it's all going each month. Include automatic monthly withdrawals on your budget worksheet—for things like a phone contract and gym membership. Of course, you can leave your current rent and any rental-related expenses out of your calculations.

 CHECK IT OUT

These websites have free budget worksheets you can print and fill out, or budgeting software to purchase:

- Mint.com

- Vertex42.com, and

- Quicken.com.

Next, compare your monthly expense total to your monthly net income —what comes home, not what you make before taxes and the rest. The difference between that take-home pay and your expenses is the amount of disposable income that you can use for new-house-related expenses.

CAUTION

Self-employed? Expect some frustration in qualifying for a loan. Lenders typically require you to have been self-employed for at least two years, and calculate self-employment income based on an average of the most recent 24 months. So, for example, if you've been self-employed for only 14 months, your income—no matter how high—might be excluded for loan qualification purposes. Similarly, if your first 12 months' self-employment income was only $12,000 but the next 12 months yielded $120,000, your 24-month average would be only $5,500 per month.

Don't Go Overboard Trying to Simplify Your Finances!

You can, according to mortgage banker Ken McCoy of Petaluma Home Loans, actually oversimplify your finances to the point that it hurts your credit rating and your ability to qualify for a mortgage at the lowest interest rate and on the most advantageous terms.

Let's start with your job. If the pay isn't great, you might be inclined to look for something better before buying a home. But, warns McCoy, "Changing your job can be a bad thing if it's in a different line of work. The lender wants to see at least two years' history in the same occupation, basically as a sign that you're going to stay in that job for the long haul."

Next, there's the matter of your assets. Like many people, you might have a checking account at one bank, a savings account at another, and a CD somewhere else. Consolidation would certainly make it easier to know what you've got; but, says Ken, "You'll be creating more, not less paperwork. Lenders want to be able to trace where all the money you're using to buy a home came from, and you'll end up having to supply statements from the accounts you closed, just to show the paper trail."

Finally, there's the all-important matter of your existing debt, including credit cards. McCoy says, "Prospective homebuyers tend to think about paying off their credit cards or getting rid of debt altogether. But realize that you might qualify for a mortgage with some existing debt; and if you pay it all off, you've just taken valuable money you needed for the home purchase transaction. What's more, you can actually hurt your credit score by having no existing credit, or by closing credit cards you've had for years."

Of course, nothing is cut and dried in this arena. There are certainly circumstances in which, for instance, taking a new job that pays much more would make sense. But how are you to know for sure? "Six months before you want to start looking for a home, sitting down with a mortgage professional would be smart," says McCoy.

Most people try to modify their spending habits if their disposable income isn't enough to cover the PITI. Having all your expenses in front of you helps you decide where to make such cuts. It also prepares you to draw the line if a lender or mortgage broker encourages you to pay more than your true budget allows. Remember, the lender mainly cares that you can pay back the money you borrow—not that you do it while living the life you want. If Zumba classes or Friday happy hours are important to you, then stick by your own budget and plan.

> **CAUTION**
>
> **Not to scare you, but ...** A lender can dip into your finances if you ultimately fail to make payments on your mortgage. The U.S. is divided into "recourse states" (the majority) and "nonrecourse states." In a recourse state, if the value of the home drops and you stop making mortgage payments, the lender may not only sell the home in a foreclosure sale, but also hit you with a deficiency judgment for the remainder of the mortgage debt. In other words, the lender can go after assets of yours other than the house securing the mortgage.

Getting Creative: Tips for Overcoming Financial Roadblocks

After running the numbers, you might feel that you can't afford a decent house, or maybe any house. But no matter your financial woes, there are steps you can take to ease them, including:

- **Reduce your debt.** This will free up cash for monthly house payments and reduce your debt-to-income ratio.
- **Make a new budget.** Revise your monthly budget, keeping your homebuying goals in mind. If you have targets, you're more likely to control your spending habits to meet them.

- **Reduce spending.** You might be able to get a roommate until you're ready to buy a place, apply an expected work bonus toward your fund, go back to basic cable, or shop more at thrift shops. Check out local freecycle groups (www.freecycle.org) for free items.
- **Borrow from a nontraditional source.** Consider different and creative options for borrowing money, from your family to the seller of the house you buy. For details, see Chapter 7.
- **Get a buying partner.** Perhaps you know someone who has cash and would be interested in jointly owning a property. Keep in mind that owning together doesn't have to mean living together, or even owning equal shares.
- **Cash out other investments.** Consider cashing out money invested in stocks, bonds, mutual funds, or other property to come up with a down payment, thus also reducing your monthly payment.
- **Sell an asset to raise down payment cash or reduce monthly spending.** Mortgage expert Russell Straub explains, "I've frequently encountered homebuyers with high-end cars and huge car loan payments. They often either had equity in the car or were paying so much per month on the car loan that it made their debt ratio too high. By selling the car (and maybe replacing it with a more modest vehicle or using public transport, car sharing with a service like Zipcar, or ride-sharing with Uber or Lyft), they were able to qualify for a bigger house payment."
- **Consider other home types, sizes, conditions, or locations.** Remember that condominiums are often cheaper than houses and old houses are generally cheaper than new.
- **Wait.** If you expect prices and interest rates to remain stable, your income to increase, and to save more money, you might delay your house purchase. With increased income, you might be able to borrow more; with an increased down payment, you might not need more.

The Power of Paper: Getting Preapproved for a Loan

Knowing what house-related costs will be laid at your feet, roughly how much a lender will let you borrow, and how much you'll really want to spend based on your income, lifestyle, and other factors, you can think about getting *preapproved* for a loan. Preapproval means you get a letter from a bank or lender committing to lend you a certain amount. It's often expressed as a monthly amount, because interest rates may vary, but the amount you can afford to pay each month does not.

> **CAUTION**
>
> **Preapproval is not a guarantee.** The bank hasn't really fully processed your request, and will place several conditions on your final approval. In fact, you'll need to comply with a host of requests for information. Lenders have become more prone to declining final approval than ever before, so be prepared. But it still helps you ....

Preapproval does two important things: It gives you some certainty that you can afford the houses you're considering, and it makes you more attractive to sellers. You'll know exactly how much you can borrow, and sellers will know that if you've put an offer on their place, you can actually (subject to the bank's final approval) come through with the cash.

> **TIP**
>
> **You don't have to use the lender that preapproves you.** It would make matters easier if you did, but there's no need to feel bound. You (or your mortgage broker) might find a better deal by the time you've chosen a house.

Why Preapproval Is Better Than Prequalification

You might have heard of loan *prequalification*, but don't confuse it with preapproval. When you get prequalified, you give a lender some basic information about your income and debts, and the lender estimates what you'll likely be able to borrow. But the lender doesn't commit to lending you that money, so prequalification mainly helps you ballpark the price range you should be looking at and readjust your expectations if need be.

Prequalification certainly won't wow any sellers. On the plus side, prequalification is easy to do (in person, over the phone, or on the Internet). Adviser Sydney Andrews notes, "I can draft a prequalification letter that will be pretty persuasive to the seller's agent reading it, explaining why the person is in a strong financial position, and closing with an invitation to call me with any questions."

Preapproval is a more involved process, and involves a check on your credit history. But preapproval will also give you more—a lender's written commitment to lend you money. That gives you more clout with sellers. Don't accept a verbal preapproval.

Of course, the lender will attach a few conditions to its commitment. If, for example, you lose your job, the bargain is off. And make sure your preapproval letter doesn't contain too many conditions. For example, if the letter conditions the loan on a credit check, it means the lender hasn't really done its homework, and you're not really preapproved.

What You Need to Show for Preapproval

To get preapproved, you'll need to provide the lender with some financial data. This is actually a blessing in disguise—it's all stuff you'll need to dig up to get a loan anyway, and it's about the last thing you'll want to be thinking about later, when you've found a place to buy and are juggling other tasks.

Here's what you'll need to pull together and photocopy. If you're buying with someone else, both of you will need to give the lender every item on the list:

- pay stubs for the last 30 days
- two years' W-2s and potentially two years of personal and business tax returns (likely more if you're self-employed)
- proof of other income
- proof of other assets (such as stocks or pension funds)
- three months of bank records (all pages) for every account you have

- source of your down payment (for example, bank records from you and anyone gifting you money)
- names, addresses, and phone numbers of employers for the last two years
- names, addresses, and phone numbers of landlords for the last two years
- information about your current debts, including account numbers, monthly payment amounts, and so on, and
- any other records and documents that you believe might be helpful for a lender trying to understand your financial situation.

ONLINE TOOLKIT

Use the "Financial Information for Lenders" checklist in the Homebuyer's Toolkit on the Nolo website. (See the appendix for the link.) It will help you keep track of all the items listed above, which you'll need for loan preapproval (and later, final loan approval).

You'll also need to fill out an application—if you're working with a mortgage broker, you'll probably get help with it, and can draw much of the information straight from the documents listed above. The lender will ask you for additional information once you've selected a property—that is, if you use that lender. If you switch lenders, you'll have to give the new one the whole works. The additional material includes:

- a property appraisal (you'll have to pay for that, usually about $425–$625—the lender will set it up once you've selected a property), and
- proof that you've obtained homeowners' insurance.

Where to Go for Preapproval

Your options for getting preapproved include working with a mortgage broker, going directly to a local bank or institutional lender, or using an Internet aggregator—a website that compiles loan information from a lot of different lenders into one place. For more on how to research mortgages, see Chapter 6.

If you haven't yet found a mortgage broker, there's no harm in going straight to a lender for preapproval. First, make sure the lender is willing to do two things: give you the up-front letter stating that you're preapproved up to a certain amount, and then give you another letter later, when you actually bid on a home. This second letter will reflect a preapproval amount equal to the amount you're offering to pay for the property. The second letter is important because when you give a preapproval to a seller, the seller doesn't need to know that you can afford to pay more. That kind of revelation can hurt your bargaining position.

Preapproval is usually a quick process. If documents are transmitted electronically, you could be preapproved within hours. At its longest, it should take only a few days.

CAUTION

If you initially told your lender you planned to buy a single-family home, but then change plans and decide to buy a condo, townhouse, or other home within an association, tell your lender ASAP. As adviser Paul Grucza explains, "I've seen people lose their ability to get a mortgage because either the lender forgot to factor in the regular and special assessments owing on this type of property, or the buyer forgot to mention them. This can be enough to push buyers right over the margin, so that they no longer qualify for a mortgage in the amount they were preapproved for."

What's Next?

Confident that you're not going to break your personal bank or end up without a home loan, you can now start checking out the housing market. We'll show you how in Chapter 4.

Stepping Out:
What's on the Market and at What Price

Meet Your Adviser

Colette Herwitt, associate broker and Realtor at Berkshire Hathaway HomeServices Rocky Mountain, REALTORS in Boulder, Colorado

What she does "I find perfect joy in helping my clients realize the dream of purchasing and owning a house that they truly love. When I work with sellers, my objective is to get them the absolute best possible return on their investment. I am honored by the loyalty and friendship of hundreds of clients. I enjoy being a member of the board of a fabulous local theatrical company and also spoiling to the brink my three grandchildren."

First house "Serendipity! We thought that we were happy in our rental of the second floor of a perfectly lovely Victorian home in Englewood, New Jersey. Never mind that my first child was sleeping in what doubled as the dining room. An afternoon stroll down a neighboring street and a newly placed "for sale" sign in front of a stunning brick Georgian Colonial changed all that! After my first step into the foyer, I knew it was meant to be. I loved living in that house—wonderful neighbors, nearby shops, good restaurants and an actual dining room sans the crib made for a perfect first home."

Fantasy house "I grew up in Chicago surrounded by some of the best architecture in the world. Early on, I gained a strong appreciation for the sleek lines of the amazingly wonderful mid-century buildings that the city had to offer. I'm fortunate that I am totally content living within the walls of my Boulder 1970s bi-level home—an abundance of light and my unobstructed views of the mountains never cease to amaze me. My fantasy house would incorporate both worlds: a mid-century masterpiece on my current lot."

Likes best about her work	"I am amazed and honored by how many clients have told me I've had a lasting, positive impact on their lives. This is an extremely personal business that I take very seriously. Hearing from clients years after the purchase or sale of their home, letting me know how instrumental they felt that I had been in their lives, brings tears to my eyes. There is no better feeling. Turning clients into friends for life—it doesn't get better than that!"
Top tip for first-time homebuyers	"Don't go above your budget. Make a long list of must haves and be prepared to pare down, realizing that some of the 'must haves' are okay to let go of. (You probably won't even remember it was a 'must have'! As a personal example, I desperately wanted a fireplace in my first home and never used it even once.) I am often asked by clients if a given home is a good investment. In my 26+ years of experience, I have found that a home purchased out of true love is almost always a good investment. Have patience! Your home is definitely out there."

Visualizing your perfect nest, and calculating what your budget will allow, was important. But now it's time to step out and see what the market really has to offer—before you turn into a serious house shopper, and possibly even before you find a real estate agent. This background work may take only a few weeks. Or, you might find that exploring new places is so much fun you want to make it a way of life for a while, like adviser Colette Herwitt did before she found a place to settle down in. In any case, your efforts will likely be worth it, helping you to know when to leap at a house and what price to offer. You'll want to:

- get a feel for the communities where you might want to live (if you don't already know)
- look at the houses already on the market, possibly including houses still under construction
- research prices other buyers have recently paid for houses like the one you want, and
- gauge whether the local market is kinder to buyers or to sellers.

TIP

Eager to skip all this and just start shopping? It's possible to check out the market and keep an eye out for your dream house simultaneously—but it's harder. Without a sense of the market, you might waste your time, for example rushing to turn in a too-low bid in a hot market. Or you might waste your money, for example by bidding too high in a cool market. Give yourself time to explore and be open to changing your mind about what you want.

What's the Buzz? Checking Out Neighborhoods From Your Chair

Use the tips below to help you either find the right neighborhood for you, confirm your feelings about one you've already chosen, or open your mind to new possibilities.

Where Do You Begin?

Most people have a good idea of where they want to live, sometimes right down to the street. But if you're moving from far away, you might not know your new town's uptown from its downtown, much less the names of neighborhoods. And even if you're already a local, there are probably places on your map you haven't explored.

Starting with a blank slate lets you play tourist in your new hometown- (or neighborhood-) to-be and begin making friends and contacts. Here are some effective strategies:

- **Talk to friends, colleagues, and relatives about where they live.** Ask what they like best and least about the area—you're sure to uncover surprises.
- **Out-of-towners: Start with whatever or whoever drew you to that town.** If it's a new job, ask your employer for staff contacts who'd be willing to share their experiences. The best people to talk to are those who've moved from far away themselves.
- **Look into where like-minded folks congregate.** Perhaps you have a particular interest or hobby, such as yoga, cooking, or music. Contact some related shops or businesses (or follow them on social media) to find out about the local scene. Their owners or employees can share insights on where things are happening and how to join in.
- **Check websites of local real estate agents.** Many include detailed community and neighborhood information. Even if you haven't hired an agent yet, you can call one and ask for information— the agent will probably jump at the chance to display knowledge to a potential client. Most agents know a lot about different neighborhoods, or at least about one neighborhood, since many of them specialize.

What's the Neighborhood Like?

One of your biggest questions will be about the character of your prospective neighborhood. Is it a place where you walk to get tapas or drive to pick up cheeseburgers? Will the local hotspot be a sports bar or a blues bar?

The character of any given community is one of the hardest issues to research (especially if you're completely new to the area), but these resources will get you started:

- **StreetAdvisor.com.** Search based on various filters (price, personality, things to do, and so on) or enter a street address and see how the locals describe their area. You can also ask questions.
- **Official website of the city or county where you're house hunting.** These typically provide helpful information for new residents, such as demographics, crime statistics, and contact information for police departments, post offices, public libraries, hospitals, parks and recreation centers, and more.
- **BestPlaces.net.** BestPlaces is known for its "best of" lists. It reveals the best and worst towns for everything from affordable housing to getting a good night's sleep to enjoying a cozy environment per the Danish concept of "Hygge." The site also gives statistical information. Find out, for example, the cost of living in a certain area; average temperatures; local home characteristics; and more. You can also compare the stats of your current hometown with those of your potential new one.
- **NeighborhoodScout.com.** This site's search tool provides reports on neighborhood residents' ethnicity, wealth, educational background, and other characteristics.
- **City-Data.com.** This site compiles scads of information about specific cities and neighborhoods (cost of living, home prices, and local transportation and amenities, attractions, history of natural disasters, and news stories). Photos, too!
- **Foursquare and Yelp.** Even if you check out only the reviews on restaurants or nightlife, you'll start getting a good sense of the neighborhood. But there's much more to be found, including neighborhood reviews on Yelp.
- **Neighborhood-specific Facebook pages, Twitter accounts, or websites.** These are usually set up to alert locals to events happening nearby.
- **Wikipedia.** Don't forget this popular site, which often provides interesting information on a city's or locality's history, geography, demographics, arts, education, and resources.

- **Your own, custom online search.** You can play detective! Think about defining characteristics of and landmarks around the neighborhood, such as parks, tourist sites, subdivisions, schools, natural features, shopping centers, and community centers. Search for the name itself or preface the name with "review of," and sit back as the search engine presents page after page of incredibly useful insights, opinions, comments, and facts.

What Will the Local Environment Be Like in 50 Years?

In 2018 alone, the U.S. was hit with 14 separate billion-dollar disaster events, according to the National Oceanic and Atmospheric Administration (NOAA). These included severe storms, tropical cyclones, and wildfires. Most experts agree that the number of major climate-related disasters is only going to increase over time.

If so, homeowners will experience more than just skyrocketing insurance premiums. The cost of heating and cooling a house will increase, as will the costs of defending a house against extreme weather (think: specialized roofing in hail-prone areas, grading and sea walls in flood-prone or coastal areas, and fire-retardant siding in drought-prone areas). In a worst-case scenario, homeowners will face displacement, massive repair costs, and even complete destruction of their property.

No one has a crystal ball to tell you how changing weather might affect your area. But The University of Maryland's Center for Environmental Science offers what might be the next best thing: an interactive map forecasting the climate in 60 years (https://fitzlab.shinyapps.io/cityapp). Pop in your city or click on the map to see what might be ahead.

 TIP

Short-term home rentals let you give the neighborhood a "test drive." Particularly if you're coming from out of town, why stay in a hotel when online services like HomeAway, VRBO, HomeStay, Tripping, and Airbnb let you experience life like a local? Owners often make themselves available for questions and can provide valuable insights about the neighborhood and city.

How Safe Is It?

If you're planning to live in your new home for a long time, make sure you feel secure there. NeighborhoodScout's 2019 report on the safest cities in the U.S. notes that although the safest cities might not be big, they're still usually located just minutes from some of the largest cities in the United States. Crime statistics for cities are available at City-Data.com. For an estimate of neighborhood crime risk, check out BestPlaces.net, which offers crime-risk indices down to the zip code level.

The most accurate source for neighborhood crime stats is from the local police department. Most larger cities put local crime reports online, often on a city map. Realtor Colette Herwitt notes that smaller towns still often put crime stats in local newspapers. These "police blotters" are often also posted online (and can sometimes be an entertaining read!).

Safest Cities in the U.S.

These cities have the fewest violent and property crimes per capita, according NeighborhoodScout's 2019 report:

1. Lake in the Hills, Illinois
2. Franklin, Massachusetts
3. Shrewsbury, Massachusetts
4. Bergenfield, New Jersey
5. Pleasant Grove, Utah
6. Marshfield, Massachusetts
7. North Ridgeville, Ohio
8. Florence, Arizona
9. Bartlett, Illinois
10. Buffalo Grove, Illinois

Best thing I ever did

Not assume an okay-looking neighborhood had low crime. Before buying her first house, Talia says, "I came close to buying a place in another neighborhood. It had looked fine when I was driving around. But my agent suggested I contact the local police station. I did and discovered that because this neighborhood was surrounded by areas where crime was much higher, it actually got its own share of break-ins and assaults. The crime rate was too high for me to feel comfortable living alone. I shifted focus to another area, where I now live and feel safe."

One can also research registered sex offenders online. Nearly every state has passed a law, usually called "Megan's Law" (after a young victim of abduction and sexual assault), requiring state governments to distribute information about sex offenders living in different communities. Many states have websites giving offenders' addresses. The U.S. Department of Justice maintains a searchable nationwide database (includes information from U.S. state, territorial, and tribal governments) at NSOPW.gov; or do a search for "Megan's Law" and the name of your state. But take the information you find with a grain of salt—not all state websites are regularly updated, and some contain inaccuracies or misleading information.

Will the Services You Need Be Nearby?

The existence or proximity of schools, parks, shopping, and more could make or break your neighborhood decision. Check out websites such as:

- **WalkScore.com.** Shows the proximity of local restaurants, shops, schools, and other amenities and calculates the time it takes to get there by walking, biking, or using mass transit. Also delivers a "Walk Score" for each neighborhood or city.

- **Google.com/maps.** To estimate your commute drive time and distance, enter your work address and an address from the neighborhood where you might live. You'll receive a drive time estimate for the most direct route and possibly alternate routes.

- **Yelp.com.** Use Yelp to find nearby restaurants and businesses, and check out their reviews.

- **Health.usnews.com/best-hospitals.** This list of America's best medical centers comes from *U.S. News & World Report*. Medicare.gov also lets you compare hospitals and get care statistics through its Hospital Compare feature (search for "Hospital Compare" on the homepage).

Is It Zoned for How You Want to Use It?

After liberating yourself from your landlord's rules, you might be less than excited to discover that the home business you'd always dreamed of starting is prohibited, or that you can't turn the garage into an in-law cottage or add a second story. Local zoning rules or other city regulations (even criminal laws) are usually to blame. It's also worth knowing what general uses the neighbors are allowed.

First, find out the zoning category of each neighborhood you're interested in from the municipal planning and building department. A classification called single-family residential is the norm. But beware: Some neighborhoods with ordinary-looking houses might actually be zoned for multifamily residential, transitional, or a mixed use, such as residential plus commercial. One of these other classifications might be good for you. For example, if a home business is in your plans, mixed commercial and residential might be perfect. But these alternate classifications can also be a problem, particularly when it comes to your neighbors' future plans. Multifamily zoning, for example, might mean the house next door could be replaced with an apartment building.

Also realize that zoning ordinances usually deal with more than how the property can be used. They typically dictate the allowable square footage of a home, its maximum height, and where it can be placed on the property. A home might have to be set back a certain distance from the street and be a certain distance away from neighboring homes. This can affect your plans to add an extra room or a deck.

Research the zoning and other municipal rules further—ideally with the help of your real estate agent or attorney—if any of the following are true:

- **You intend to operate a home business.** In an area zoned residential, take a careful look at the local rules—they don't always give a clear thumbs up or down. Some, for example, prohibit home businesses in general but allow exceptions, such as for writers, artists, accountants, consultants, and other businesses that are unlikely to cause noise or traffic problems. Even then, a city ordinance could prohibit you from employing anyone onsite who doesn't actually live in your home. To find out local rules that might apply to your business, contact the planning or zoning department for the city or county where you plan to live. Finally, if you're buying a condo, co-op, or similar property, be sure to check any restrictions the governing association has placed on home businesses. Also talk to other local home business owners about the restrictions, and whether their neighbors have raised any fuss.

RESOURCE

Planning on starting a home business? Check out the articles in the "Business Formation" and "Taxes" sections of Nolo.com. And for detailed information, including more tips on zoning, see the Nolo books *Legal Guide for Starting & Running a Small Business*, by Attorney Fred Steingold (or the *Women's Small Business Start-Up Kit*, by Peri Pakroo, J.D.). Also check out *Home Business Tax Deductions: Keep What You Earn*, by Stephen Fishman, J.D. (Nolo), which discusses issues like when you can deduct general home maintenance.

- **You plan to remodel the house or garage or add other structures (even a fence, pool, tiny house, or child's tree house).** Rules for changing an existing house or adding structures to the property can be sticky and require permits. In towns with a lot of historic properties or notable natural features, Colette Herwitt has observed that doing a legal remodel can be especially fraught with red tape: Local ordinances might restrict height to preserve the view or impose strict guidelines for remodeling older homes—even if they're not designated "historic." Consider talking to a local architect about your plans—they're used to dealing with, or getting around, the rules.
- **You plan to park a boat, an RV, or a large vehicle in your driveway.** Some city planners have decided this doesn't look so good.
- **The house has historic landmark status, or looks like it should.** Once a house is designated as historic, any remodeling—even basic things like a new paint job—might be subject to rules on style and color. Still, owning a historic home can be personally satisfying and offer high resale value if you restore it.
- **You plan to cut down a large tree.** Yes, your landscaping might be a topic of separate regulation.

- **You have any other special plans for the property.** Local rules are limited only by the imagination of the local government. Bizarre ones sometimes pop up in response to a sole homeowner's inappropriate actions, like having put up too many holiday lights.
- **Vacant lots are widespread in the neighborhood, or you see a lot of new construction.** You'll want to know what might legally be built there.
- **You plan on keeping any farm animals, such as roosters or a goat.** They may well be prohibited.

Which celebrities keep chickens?

The likes of Barbra Streisand, Tori Spelling, John Cleese, Reese Witherspoon, Jennifer Aniston, and Rachel Weisz are reported to share their properties with feathered, egg-laying friends.

Thinking of raising chickens in your backyard? Check out BackYardChickens.com, which includes everything from links to local laws to reviews of different types of breeds. Or, if you're planning on becoming an amateur beekeeper, know that some cities prohibit bees, while some allow them if immediate neighbors provide written permission. One place to start your search is the Apiary Inspectors of America website, www.apiaryinspectors.org.

Is It a Planned Community, With Restrictions on Homeowners?

If you move into a community interest development (CID), you may find your choice of house paint colors limited to white, white, or white—and that's just for starters. The homeowners' associations that oversee such communities often regulate how individual homeowners can alter, maintain, and use their property (such as fence style in a detached house or curtain color in a condo or co-op). A home located in a traditional subdivision consisting of lots might also be controlled by restrictions.

For now, just realize that these sorts of restrictions exist, and plan to research them further if you look at a CID.

How Are the Local Schools?

If you have children, or plan to, then the quality of the local school district is probably high on your list. Even if you don't plan to have children, you should be concerned with school quality, because the *next* family that buys your home might have or want children. And they'll pay more if the local schools are great.

To get statistical information about school performance, check your state's department of education website, usually accessible from its main webpage. Also see GreatSchools.org, a national, independent nonprofit organization, which helps parents choose schools and support their children's education.

Best thing I ever did

Visit local public schools. Violet says of her family's move from Connecticut to Pennsylvania, "Our criteria for choosing a neighborhood were: school district, school district, and school district. We'd heard there were two excellent districts close to my husband's new job. So I took my son and daughter to visit the principals and teachers and watch classrooms in action. The school in one of the neighborhoods had great classroom morale, lots of activities, and ethnic diversity. Wouldn't you know it, the houses in that neighborhood were mostly million-dollar-plus McMansions. But we found a fixer-upper we could afford. It was worth the hard work to make it livable—the kids love their school."

See for Yourself: Driving Through Neighborhoods

You can tell a lot about an area by cruising through it. When you get a real estate agent, he or she might drive you around, but it's good to go on your own first, free to explore. You might find yourself thinking, "I could live here," or "Get me out, fast."

First, open a map (online or off), and locate the areas where you might like to live. Even if you're normally all-digital, it can be good to print out some maps to give you the big picture while you're driving around. Plus, you can make notes for later reference. Pay special attention to places on the map you've never been to that are close to or within your highlighted area. Then systematically drive up and down the streets, imagining yourself living there. (The character of a neighborhood can change in the space of a city block, or right after a natural divider such as a freeway, park, or large housing complex.)

Look beyond the houses and think about whether the local features fit your lifestyle—would you, in fact, walk to the bus stop, garden in the front yard, or jog at the local track? Focus on questions like:

- **How well are the homes maintained?** Neat homes and yards are signs that homeowners feel invested in their properties.

- **How's the traffic?** Are people driving sanely or zooming around with music blasting? Does the major street leading to the neighborhood become a noisy parking lot during rush hour?

- **What types of local businesses are around?** Franchise chains, funky coffee shops, and upscale restaurants could become your favorite hangouts—or you could be in for frustration if your favorite cuisine is nowhere to be found or there's no dry cleaner nearby.

- **Look for indicators of future growth.** Is a light rail line being built nearby? Are there bike lanes, or nearby transit stops? Also look for new "infill" housing, small apartment buildings, and mixed-use structures (with shops on the bottom, apartments above)—new development might indicate that investors don't expect to see a downturn in the neighborhood any time soon.

- **Check the signs.** Literally. If you see lots of "For Sale" signs, it *could* mean people are moving out, and you'd want to know why—a new factory or mini-mall being built nearby? Rising sea levels leading to frequent flooding? You'll either have a greater chance of snagging a bargain, or you might decide to look elsewhere. On the other hand, a lot of homes for sale could also mean the neighborhood is hot, hot, hot!

If you like what you see, you might even add another color highlighter to the map, showing your favorite streets (useful for cross-referencing with later home sale ads). You're guaranteed to find a surprise or two.

Lesson learned the hard way **The grill's going every night!** Barry is a committed vegetarian, while his girlfriend Ann is not. After a long search, the couple found an adorable house near a commercial street dominated by restaurants. Barry says, "We carefully had the house inspected and talked to the neighbors about safety. But we'd visited the house only in daylight. Our first evening after we moved in, we noticed a cloud of aromatic smoke coming from a nearby BBQ joint. I was horrified, and Ann started mischievously suggesting sneaking out for a bite. We love the house, but it took a while to get used to the permanently meat-scented night air."

On Foot: Talking to the Natives

There's probably no better way to find out what a certain neighborhood is like than talking to people who already live there. Pick a day when you're feeling relaxed (preferably not open-house day). Then walk around, paying attention to smells and sounds. (Cocooned in your car, you might not notice odors coming from a nearby brewery, airplane or freeway noise, the buzzing from a local generator, or rowdiness at a nearby commercial strip.)

Talking to people in neighborhoods still under construction is obviously harder—but it might be possible if you're not the first to buy. Or, you can visit surrounding developments to get a general feel for what to expect.

Look for people out gardening or walking their dogs. It might feel funny to strike up a conversation with a stranger, but complimenting said garden or dog is a pretty reliable conversation starter. Explain that you're thinking of buying, and ask questions like:
- What do you like most and least about this area?
- Which streets are quietest? Busiest?
- Do you feel okay about walking outside at night?
- Do you have kids? Do they go to public school here?
- Are there any changes planned that will make the neighborhood better or worse (such as a new development, changed policing system, or pending school initiative)?

Coffee shops and local restaurants are also good places to meet people, including the businesses' owners. And even on open-house days, you can meet a lot of locals and talk to real estate agents about community issues.

Sunrise, Sunset: Getting Day and Night Perspectives

There's a reason open houses are usually scheduled on Sunday afternoons: The sun is high in the sky, the neighborhood is quiet, and no one's working. Life couldn't be better! To plug back into reality, though, try visiting a neighborhood at different times of the day or week. Neighborhoods near schools can sound like a parade is passing every weekday around 3:00—and then the insanely bright floodlights at the football fields click on after dark. Neighborhoods located in lovely little gulches or valleys can seem dull by early afternoon, when they lose their daily dose of sunshine. Visit late at night to assess how comfortable you feel, how many people are out and about, and how well-lit (or not) the area is.

Best thing we ever did **Drive through the neighborhood at night.** Sam and Kari were looking to buy when the market was crazy and their options limited. They got excited when they saw a nice, affordable house right on the border of a neighborhood they liked. On a whim, they drove back to take a look later that night. To their dismay, they discovered a side of the neighborhood that wasn't apparent during the day: Groups of partiers stood around smoking and drinking. According to Sam, when an elderly neighbor saw their bewildered looks, she "asked whether we were lost, then advised us, 'Don't buy here; it's not safe. I'd get out if I could.' We took her advice and are so glad we took that evening drive."

Got Houses?
Finding Out What's Locally Available

By now, you've probably narrowed down your search to specific neighborhoods. So, you're probably curious about what's for sale there right this minute. It's the easiest research task you'll ever take on, thanks to resources like:

- **Realtor.com.** This is the granddaddy: the MLS database of homes for sale kept by Realtors nationwide. It has a direct feed to current listings. Or, try searching online for "MLS" and the name of your state or city. (The homes won't change much, but the formatting will.)

- **Trulia.com.** This well-designed search engine allows you to search properties based on various criteria, such as type of house, foreclosures, and price reductions. Its colorful maps show neighborhood features, demographics, and prices. Trulia's app allows you to quickly locate nearby homes for sale and open houses.

- **Zillow.com.** The website offers extensive listings of homes for sale, including FSBOs and foreclosures. And with its award-winning app, you can not only pull up a map showing homes for sale near your exact location, but save your favorites and sign up for notifications of when new listings hit the market or old listings drop their prices.

TIP

The farther you get from the original MLS, the greater the possibility for inaccuracies. Although many websites draw data from the MLS, they're not always as quick to update the listings—for example, when a sale is pending. So you might fall in love with a home on-screen only to discover that it's no longer available.

- **Real estate sections of city or community newspapers.** City papers often have online classifieds, but don't forget tiny community papers—they sometimes have the best classifieds, because they're devoted to a limited geographical area.
- **ForSaleByOwner.com.** This site lists homes (so-called "FSBOs") being sold without help from real estate agents, so they might not appear in the MLS. Also try FSBO.com. For more on buying a FSBO, see Chapter 9.
- **Websites sponsored by local real estate brokers.** Some broker sites provide photos, neighborhood information, and advice. Try local Berkshire Hathaway, RE/MAX, or Sotheby's International Realty websites, for example. Or, just enter a search phrase such as, "Chicago real estate," and you'll find both big and small real estate firms specializing in the area you enter.
- **Looking for a newly built home?** Check out NewHomeSource.com, where you can refine your search with criteria such as "Green Features" or "Pool."

And you can always do a general search, such as "houses for sale in Ithaca, New York," to make sure you haven't missed anything.

How Much Did That One Go For? Researching "Comparable" Sales

All the houses you see advertised come with a price tag—but the price might have little to do with reality. How much a buyer actually pays often varies from the list price, up or down, by thousands or even tens of thousands of dollars. In a cool market, many sellers have an inflated idea of what their house is worth, and eventually sell for less. In hot markets, some sellers set an artificially low list price in hopes of attracting a large pool of potential buyers who will compete for the house with outrageously high bids.

There's no sense in choosing—or eliminating—a neighborhood or an area based on price until you find out how much houses there are *really* selling for. (Later, such knowledge will ensure you don't pay too much or offer too little for a particular house.)

Look at final sale prices of houses comparable to the type you're interested in, or "comps." The most accurate comps come from houses that sold recently (preferably within the last six months) within the same general area (what's considered the "general area" varies, but in most urban areas is about six blocks—or less, in case of major boundaries such as a freeway) and with the same basic features as the house you hope to buy (like number of bedrooms, square footage, garage, neighborhood, lot size, general condition and construction quality, and landscaping).

You'll never find two exactly comparable houses, so do your best to take a sort of average. Your agent, once you're working with one, will also be able to give you this type of information, with even more recent data. And when you're ready to bid on a particular house, the agent may draw up a report on the comps. But for quick and dirty comp data, use the websites listed below.

CHECK IT OUT

Here's where to get comparable sales data. A number of online services track home sales. Two cautions apply, however: One, the listings might be out of date, and estimates can be wacky if they're generated by a computer. Two, beware of signing up to be contacted by an agent. Check out:

- Zillow.com (using the "Zestimate" feature), and
- Trulia.com (under "Discover a place you'll love," click "Sold" and enter search information such as a zip code or a neighborhood name and city).

EXAMPLE: Paul and Leslie want to buy a three-bedroom house in Ardmore, Pennsylvania. They take the address of one such local home and pop it into one of the websites above. The closest matches are a three-bedroom, one-bath house that sold for $350,000 three months ago; a three-bedroom, 1½-bath house that sold for $375,000 five months ago; and a three-bedroom, one-bath that sold for $328,000 six months ago. Without looking at the actual houses, they project that they'll need to pay somewhere in the mid- to high $300,000s for the house they want. They might also posit that prices are rising, that the house currently for sale could be overpriced, or that adding a one-half bath can measurably raise the value of a house. Unfortunately, websites don't tell you about details such as house style, condition, landscaping, or charm. As Paul and Leslie start visiting actual houses and working with a knowledgeable agent, they'll have a chance to sharpen their understanding of local house values.

Eventually, your knowledge of sale prices will turn you into a sort of amateur appraiser and help you decide on the appropriate price for houses you're looking at. Don't discount the value of your own research and intuition: House values depend partly on buyers' subjective responses to them, and you're a buyer. Placing an exact market value on a house is an inexact science (though appraisers, real estate agents, and sellers do their best to come close).

Hot or Cold? Take the Market's Temp

To figure out home values, you also need to know whether you're in a market that's hot, cold, transitional, or balanced. At local open houses, do you have to wait in line just to squeeze up the stairs, or do you find yourself all alone with a chatty seller's agent? When talking with friends and neighbors about homebuying, do they tell stories of how being outbid on houses drove them to couples' counseling, or how they're plotting how to get a bargain from a seller whose house has languished on the market for weeks? These are just a few of the more extreme indicators of whether the local—emphasis on the word "local"—housing market is hot or cold.

A hot market means there are more buyers than sellers, or not enough houses on the market to satisfy demand. As soon as a house is listed for sale, it's snapped up, and sellers can be inflexible about the price and buyers' attempts to negotiate. In the hottest markets, you might be competing against other buyers to offer the highest price, the shortest closing period, and the smoothest transaction.

A cold market means there are more sellers than buyers, and houses might remain on the market for months at a time, waiting for a buyer. If, as happened several years back, this is coupled with a major economic downturn, foreclosures can flood the market and bring down prices. This gives the buyer leverage when negotiating, because the longer a seller has waited, the more desperate he or she may be to unload the place. Mean- while, sellers know that you have other options.

> **TIP**
>
> **Markets can be lukewarm or mixed, too.** As Realtor Mark Nash notes, "Hot or cold is a generalization. For example, in some markets, starter single-family homes could be hot, and penthouse condos could be cold."

The urgency of your house search, and your approach to sellers, will all be shaped by knowing whether you're in a market that's hot, cold, transitional, or balanced in the middle. It's not hard to figure out the basic "hot or cold?" question—as long as you focus in at the neighborhood level and aren't fooled by general headlines. The more difficult part is gauging where the market is going—a market can move up or down in a matter of weeks.

The housing market can be affected by the local and national economy, mortgage interest rates, the availability and cost of housing (including rentals), the supply of and demand for homes (which can vary by time of year), and more. Scads of real estate commentators make their living trying to predict what's next, but none know for sure. Nor do they specialize in the corner of the world you're looking at, which might have its own mini hot and cold regions.

You'll develop a sense of where your local market is going once you start seriously house hunting. If, after several weeks, you find yourself able to predict the asking prices of newly offered homes, the market is probably pretty stable. If, on the other hand, you notice open house or "price reduced" signs on houses you looked at a few weeks ago, the market is probably plateauing or cooling. And if you've been outbid on a house or two and notice that the list prices of similar houses seem to be inching out of your range, the market is heating up and you'll need to act quickly. A real estate agent can also tell you about trends, based on the increasing number of listings in the MLS database and the average time that houses stay on the market.

TIP

Don't put your life on hold trying to predict the future. For every person who waited for the market to drop and got a good price, there's another one who watched it pass them by. Just find a house you want at a price that's fair and affordable at the time. If you're planning to stay there for more than a few years, you'll weather any downturns.

Lesson learned the hard way

Waiting for the downturn that never came. Eva, an artist, says, "At one point, I thought I'd never marry and decided to buy my own house. I began looking, accompanied by my dad, who'd offered to pitch in on the down payment. But every time I found a place I liked, my dad said, 'That's way too much, prices will come down soon.' He said that first about houses in the $200,000 range. Then I watched as similar houses started selling for $300,000, then $400,000. I bought a tiny place soon after, which fortunately has since risen in value. But it kills me that I could have had it for much less a couple years earlier—or could have had a bigger house that would fit my, guess what, husband and new baby!"

Just Looking: The Open House Tour

Visiting open houses—where sellers throw the doors open to just about any interested party—is educational, free, and fun. For now, don't look only at houses that are smack dab in your price range. By looking at too-expensive and too-cheap houses, you'll get a feel for what various house features—like another bedroom or an updated kitchen—are worth.

As you visit open houses, compare their features to your Dream List, to get a sense of which items will or won't be easy to find. Now's a good time to refine your list, too, if you realize that "a fenced yard would be great," or "I can't live next to an apartment complex."

Remember, unless you're ready to read the rest of the chapters and ramp up your activities in a hurry, don't fall in love with a house yet. You're still getting to know what's out there. In later chapters, we'll discuss how to take a hard look at a particular house—evaluate its physical condition, whether it's priced appropriately, and whether it meets your long- and short-term needs—as well as how to prepare an appropriate offer.

If a house really does look perfect, and you can't resist, at least heed this final warning: Don't sign anything on the spot. You might meet an oh-so-friendly agent who says, "I can write up your offer, no problem!" That agent represents the seller, whose interests, including getting the highest price and the most advantageous terms, will be put first. Go home, take a deep breath, look at later chapters of this book, and do some quick shopping for a buyer's agent—if you really want to buy that house.

Best thing we ever did **Just start looking.** Fiona was more convinced than her girlfriend that they could handle the financial commitment of a house. Fiona says, "Even after we'd done our research, had a mortgage broker evaluate our finances, and asked our parents to pitch in on a down payment, she resisted going to open houses. According to her stressed-out logic, we weren't *really* ready, so it was a waste of everyone's time. Finally I got her out looking, and it was great—seeing open houses suddenly made the process fun. Of course, it was also a reality check, since we realized we could afford less than we'd thought. But we ended up finding a wonderful house, with great neighbors."

Nothing to Look at Yet?
Finding Your Dream Development

If you're thinking of buying a newly built home, your community-to-be might look like a large sandbox. But that doesn't mean you can't do advance research. Your most important task will be to choose the best-quality developer before you go any further. Why? Well, as with any other product, different house manufacturers make different quality products, or have different track records for reliability. You don't want to even go near a house built by a developer at the low end of the quality spectrum, or who's teetering on the edge of bankruptcy, no matter how affordable it seems.

Figure out which developers are working in your area, which are worth buying from, and whether they offer the types of houses you want. To find developers, use the websites listed under "Got Houses? Finding Out What's Locally Available," above. Then use the following tips to research them:

- **Talk to people.** This includes others who have purchased from a particular developer, local contractors, real estate professionals, appraisers, and city planning staff. Don't stop until you've gathered information about each local builder's reputation from a variety of sources.

- **Ask tough questions of the developer and others.** You'll want to find out how long the developer has been in business; how well funded the business is; whether it's ever been sued and for what; and the credentials of the developer, its employees, and contractors. Don't just take the developer's word for it—double-check with your state's licensing board and the local building office.

- **Search online.** To hear feedback from other consumers, try searching Internet blogs, local newspaper websites, and homeowner-run websites such as HomeOwners for Better Building (HOBB.org). Also search for local news stories about the builder or developer to see whether complaints have arisen about the quality of the homes or other sensitive issues.

- **Call your local Better Business Bureau.** It's often the first place that people turn to with complaints about local developers. Visit www.BBB.org for more information.

What's Next?

You've hopefully gotten a sense of which neighborhoods not only have a character you like, but offer the safety, schools, or other amenities you need. You've also gotten a sense of the local market and whether it offers houses you might want at a price you can afford. You're almost ready to do some serious house shopping. But first, let's figure out who's going to help you do it.

Select Your Players: The Real Estate Team

Meet Your Adviser

Greg Nino, associate Realtor at RE/MAX Compass in Houston, Texas (www.everydaysold.com).

What he does
"Looking 'behind-the scenes' at my work as a Realtor, I'd say I spend the majority of my time answering questions, putting out fires (of the metaphorical sort), driving around, explaining the process, and helping clients overcome their anxieties and feel good about what they're doing. Anxiety is common among homebuyers, regardless of age, level of education, or income. And no wonder: They're trying to juggle their life while dealing with the major decisions and changes that a real estate transaction involves. I do my best to make it easy and offer reassurance."

First house
"It was a newly constructed home. I had only just gotten my real estate license, and made every mistake in the book—the very mistakes I've warned readers against in this book! We signed up for the first home to be built in the development, which was problematic because we couldn't see or compare our place with any of the others. We had far too much fun picking out all the features and amenities; style of countertop, carpet, and so on. We paid dearly for all that—in fact, we overpaid for the neighborhood in general. Although we loved the house, we felt we had no choice but to sell it a couple of years later when prices began dropping."

Fantasy house	"I would love a small, functional house in an awesome neighborhood near a lake, with rolling hills and land—but close to a major city. Two thousand square feet would be fine. My priority would be getting out and enjoying the land and lake."
Likes best about his work	"Not sitting behind a desk all day! Being a Realtor is a great career for someone who likes multitasking, change, and not being in a monotonous relationship with an office. I get a new set of bosses every few months, with the new clients who come in the door."
Top tip for first-time homebuyers	"Surround yourself with professionals who know what they're doing, and who have lots of hands-on experience in the area where you're buying. The Internet is useful, and yes, it's worth consulting, but relying solely on advice you find there is like trying to diagnose an illness solely using WebMD. Remember, a Realtor does more than unlock doors and collect a commission: You can ask your Realtor as many questions as you want. Be ready to listen to the answers, too."

B uying a first home is a complex process, and there's no reason to do it alone. You can bring together a team of experts who've seen it all before (many times!). They'll not only help you understand what you need to do but also perform key tasks themselves. Your real estate team will most likely include:

- a real estate agent, who will help you find, negotiate for, and complete the purchase of your home
- a mortgage broker, mortgage banker, or loan officer, who will help locate the best financing
- a real estate attorney (in several but not all states), who will make sure the deal is properly and fairly drafted and that the seller has good title to the property
- one or more professional inspectors, who will examine the property for pests and defects, and
- a closing or escrow agent, who will help ensure that the transfer happens smoothly and on time.

Unlike a sports team, these players might not work together directly. But even if they never meet, they share a common goal: to help you purchase your house on the best possible terms. Still, you're the boss (and the checkbook), so you'll want to be confident about your players and their abilities. In this chapter, we'll explain each person's role and how to select top players.

Your Team Captain: The Real Estate Agent

Your real estate agent has the broadest role of any team member: You'll work together from start to finish.

Who Real Estate Agents Are

You've probably heard different names—broker, agent, or Realtor—used to describe real estate agents. These convey different levels of experience, training, and knowledge:

- **Agents.** A "real estate agent" is the most basic and generic of the choices. Agents must be licensed in the state where they work. This usually means completing 180 hours of classroom instruction, passing an exam, and renewing their licenses every one to three years. When we use the term "agent" in this book, it's in the broadest sense of the word. Recognize, however, that someone who hasn't sought professional affiliations or qualifications beyond being a licensed agent may be limited in expertise, connections, and ethical obligations. (Keep reading to find out why.)

- **Brokers.** A real estate broker is, in most states, one step up from an agent, with more real-estate-related education and experience. In fact, explains adviser Greg Nino, "Brokers typically manage offices and agents, and if the buyer has problems the agent can't resolve, the broker will handle them." In smaller, independent agencies (or "brokerages"), the buyer might work directly with a broker. And a few states blend the terms, allowing all real estate agents to use the word "broker" in their title, for example as a "designated broker" versus a "managing broker" in Washington state. Bottom line: Ask agents you might hire for the details on their licensing designation and what role they play in the office (or will play in handling your sale), and check your state's department of real estate licensing for confirmation and more information.

> ### Real Estate Agents on the Silver Screen
>
> - Annette Bening plays Carolyn Burnham in *American Beauty*.
> - Jack Lemmon, Kevin Spacey, Alan Arkin, and Ed Harris play competing agents in *Glengarry Glen Ross*.
> - Julianne Moore plays Marlene Craven in *The Hand That Rocks the Cradle*.
> - Craig T. Nelson plays Steven Freeling in *Poltergeist*.
> - Silvia Miles played a real estate agent in *Wall Street*.

- **Realtors.** Most licensed agents are members of the National Association of Realtors® (NAR), a trade association. Joining does cost money. (Realtors join at the local level, which gives them automatic membership in the state and national organization. That's important for you to know mainly because certain NAR practices vary state by state.) NAR members can use the designation "Realtor." In some states, only Realtors have access to the MLS. Realtors must comply with the NAR's standards of practice and Code of Ethics. Better yet for you as a consumer, NAR enforces its ethics rules. If you have an ethics complaint regarding your Realtor, you can file it with NAR and it might help with mediation, or take enforcement action— including issuing a fine or cancelling the Realtor's membership. Membership also suggests that the agent is up-to-date on real estate issues (because NAR provides training—required, in some instances —member newsletters, and other resources) and has a network of contacts through the organization.

- Realtors might also have advanced designations/certifications through the NAR and its affiliate organizations. You're particularly interested in the Accredited Buyer Representative (ABR) or Accredited Buyer Representative Manager (ABRM) designations, given to Realtors or brokers specializing in representing buyers.

What Your Agent Does for You

As your team captain, your real estate agent answers to you but coordinates other players and handles multiple tasks. Expect your agent to:

- **Suggest neighborhoods.** Although this book helps you look for the right neighborhood, your agent should be able to pinpoint possible locations. Ideally, your agent will live in or around the area you're interested in and give you an insider's perspective.
- **Show you comparable sales data.** To help you gauge the market value of any house you're interested in, your agent should compile a written report (called a comparative market analysis, or CMA) of comparable properties ("comps") that are currently listed or have sold within the last three to six months. (If prepared by a broker, the same report may be called a "broker's price opinion," or BPO.) "In addition," says Greg Nino, "your agent should discuss past and potential trends of the community you're looking to buy in."
- **Find prospective homes that meet your needs.** You'll tell your agent how much you want to spend, what physical characteristics are important to you, and what type of neighborhood you're looking for. A good agent will search for properties that meet your criteria and show them to you as soon as they're available. Or, if you're considering buying a newly built home, your agent should help you find builders with excellent reputations and negotiate builder

incentives, concessions, upgrades, homeowner association dues, and so on. Any competent agent knows that this task might take one day or one year—in either case, the agent will patiently help you find what you're looking for.

- **Walk through prospective properties with you.** Your agent will set up appointments to visit properties for sale, and will accompany you on these showings. Your agent acts as another set of eyes on the house and the lot it sits on, helping you think about practicalities

> ### Who's the typical Realtor?
>
> According to the National Association of Realtors®, most of its agent members:
>
> - earn about $41,800 per year
> - have been in the field for about 8 years, and
> - are approximately 52 years old.

(like whether the house provides enough storage space or has an impractical floor plan), and spotting potential problems (like a water stain on the ceiling indicating a possible leaky roof, or an old plumbing system in a sparkling new kitchen). The agent might also suggest easy-to-make improvements, such as converting an unused nook into a home office space. The agent will coordinate a second and even third showing, if needed. "And don't forget that you might sell one day," adds Greg Nino. "A good agent will warn you about any issues the house might present when that time comes."

- **Draft a written offer and negotiate the sale.** In the majority of states, your agent will help you draft an offer or other written statement that includes your offer price and terms. In other states, a lawyer will do this. (The offer process will be discussed in detail in Chapter 10.) The agent will also ensure you receive any legally required disclosures about the property. After your offer is accepted, the agent will handle all communications with the seller as your representative, negotiating over issues that come up, such as repair needs or price changes. Adviser Daniel Stea urges, "Make sure your agent has the ability and commitment to negotiate the best price on your behalf. Too many are so eager to get into contract or to move the deal to the next step that they push less hard than they could have."

- **Explain the process.** Your agent should (beginning at your first meeting) be able to summarize the process of and timeline for searching for homes, writing an offer, and everything else up to closing the deal.

- **Open escrow.** Your agent should open escrow for you (help begin the process of finalizing your purchase) or give you recommendations for a reputable escrow, title, or closing company or real estate attorney (depending on what state you're buying in). While sellers cannot mandate that you use a specific escrow officer or title company, buyers often use the listing agent's preferred title company if they're expecting the sellers to pay for an owner's title policy (OTP).

- **Manage day-to-day activities leading up to and including the closing.** Once the seller accepts your offer, you have a lot to do: scheduling home inspections, finalizing your loan or other financing, getting insurance, and so on. Your agent should guide you through each step, either handling the tasks directly or working with the appropriate professionals. And if your sales contract contains contingency clauses, your agent can help make sure that you comply with the deadlines for contingency removals. The real estate agent should also either attend your closing or send a substitute with sufficient training to assist you.

Will You See More of the Agent or an Assistant?

Experienced, busy agents often serve a number of clients simultaneously. They might not, for instance, be available to walk through a home with you on a moment's notice. Such agents might work with a team of fellow agents or assistants and ask one of them to step in for matters such as this—then return to your side for important matters such as negotiations. Adviser Greg Nino notes that many agents have a "working partner"—another Realtor who steps in to show a property or help in other ways when an agent is on vacation or otherwise unavailable.

Should you be worried about getting "pushed off" onto an assistant? As with many things, it depends on the quality of the agent. An excellent agent will have a well-trained team, every member of which you can trust to give you the help you need. You should perhaps be just as worried about hiring an inexperienced agent who has all the time in the world to help you.

Still, when establishing your relationship with the agent, it's worth asking who exactly you'll be working with and how accessible you can expect your agent to be.

Make Sure Your Real Estate Agent Plays for You

Real estate agents make a living representing one of two parties: the buyer or the seller. Most agents have several clients—both buyers and sellers—at any given time.

Usually, it's not a problem for an agent to represent both buyers and sellers. However, it can become one when the agent who is selling a house for one client has—or takes—another client who wants to *buy* it. This "dual agency" (also known as an "intermediary relationship") is allowed in some states, and has the potential to create problems for buyers.

Dual agency frequently arises when a prospective buyer visits an open house, expresses interest, and the seller's listing agent says, "Don't worry that you don't have an agent yet; I'll write the deal up for you." Adviser and Realtor Daniel Stea says, "Buyers too often think this might save them money—which it likely won't. The listing agent might even imply that the buyers might have a better shot at getting their offer accepted this way. In reality, the listing agent might simply be attempting to generate a second commission by representing the buyer."

You can imagine the potential problems when one agent represents two parties with opposite interests: While the buyer wants to buy the place for as little as possible, the seller wants to sell for as much as possible.

Most states require agents who wish to be dual agents to obtain written consent from both the buyers and the sellers. But it's not usually a good idea to consent to this. You want someone who is on your team all the way. As Greg Nino notes, "A dual agent is not even permitted to give you advice and opinion! That said, every market is different, and for short sales, HUD purchases, and foreclosures, you'll find that dual

Real-Estate Fiction

- *Death by Real Estate*, by Maggie MacLeod (Daybreak Publishing): Barb Parker is a mystery-solving real estate agent.
- *Closing Costs*, by Seth Margolis (St. Martin's Press): Five couples try to survive the cutthroat Manhattan real estate market.
- *Good Faith*, by Jane Smiley (Anchor): A divorced real estate agent is lured into a development deal by a newcomer to his small town.

agency happens almost routinely, because the processes are typically more complicated and the details mostly in the hands of the listing agent. Or, if there's a *hot* listing and you *really* want the house and don't mind paying top dollar, you might rely on the strategy of using the listing agent (thus hoping that agent will favor your offer in order to make twice the commission). Ethical? Not always. A true reality? Sometimes!" In more routine transactions, however, your safest bet is to get your own, buyer's, agent—one contractually bound to represent only you (though your agent must still be fair and honest with the seller).

In a similar situation called a designated agency, you're represented by one agent, and the seller is represented by another agent who works in the same brokerage. In states where designated agency is allowed, all parties must normally agree to it in writing. The risk of divided loyalties is much less than with a dual agency. Still, you'll want to be confident that your agent is trustworthy, and be careful about what you disclose.

Finally, on the other side of the table sits the seller's agent, often called the "listing agent." The seller's agent is hired by the seller. While the seller's agent is ethically and even legally bound to be fair and honest toward you, this agent focuses on representing the seller's best interests. You want the seller's agent to remain where he or she belongs—on the other side of the table.

How Real Estate Agents Are Paid

After hearing about what a good agent can do for you, you might start mentally calculating whether you can fit one into your budget. The good news is, your agent is one person in this process you *won't* have to hand money to. The seller ordinarily pays the entire commission (averaging 5% to 6%), which is split between the seller's agent and yours (usually, 2½% to 3% each). You do end up indirectly paying for your agent's services, though, because the seller will probably factor the cost of paying both agents into the purchase price of the home.

Some people will tell you that agents are mainly out to make buckets of money—maximizing their commission and minimizing the amount of time they spend with you. They caution you that agents will show you only properties above your price range, push you to offer too much, or rush you into a purchase.

It's true that the more you spend, the higher the agent's commission goes. However, to say that agents are solely motivated by money is an overgeneralization—in fact, it's often not in the agent's own interests to behave this way. If, for example, you're pushed to offer an extra $10,000 on a home, and then don't qualify for the mortgage, the agent will have wasted a lot of time. Or what if you pay the extra $10,000, then feel the agent trapped you into it? You'll never use that agent again and will tell your friends not to, either. Neither prospect will appeal to the professional, experienced agent you'll be choosing—not to mention the fact that an extra $10,000 on the sales price adds up to only about $150 in increased commission.

To avoid a possible misunderstanding about how your agent gets paid, make sure there's a written agreement between the two of you. This should spell out the extent of the agent's expected services and your financial obligations, and deal with other matters such as whether you'll go to mediation in the event of a dispute (mandatory in most states). No need to sign this immediately—many agents will wait until you're ready to submit your first offer (at which time such an agreement is required in some states and by some real estate companies).

 CAUTION

Only sign up with an agent you intend to work exclusively with. You'll likely encounter a lot of agents during the homebuying process, and many will vie for your business. Be straightforward with agents you talk to by letting them know you're still trying to decide who will represent you or that you've already decided to work with someone. Don't let an agent work for you when you intend to work with someone else—it's just not fair!

Using an Agent When Buying a Newly Constructed House

When buying a new house from a developer, or having one built for you, you can be represented by your own real estate agent. However, the agent usually needs to be with you on your very first visit or the developer won't allow the agent to collect the commission or referral fee.

Builders Exert Pressure to Keep the Whole Transaction In-House

In order to understand the full scope of why a new-home builder might make things harder if you don't use its in-house salesperson, you need to understand how builders tend to structure the transaction. Greg Nino explains, "Builders like to use their own, preferred lender, appraiser, title company, and of course Realtor. The builder will push the preferred lender the hardest, knowing that the lender will use the preferred appraisal management company (especially if the builder owns it). Spec homes (inventory homes that are already built), in particular tend to be priced very high."

If you use the company lender, the home will likely hit value and appraise for the amount you're planning to pay for it. If you use your own lender, however, there's a good chance the home will not 'hit value.' Knowing this, the builder might offer huge incentives if you don't bring your own agent (an agent who will likely encourage you to shop around for independent lenders). Often the builder will offer extra "built-in" financial incentives if you use its loan officer, such as 3% towards closing costs, plus perks such as furniture gift cards, flat screen televisions, and more. The builder wants total control. It might also refuse to pay for an Owner's Title Policy (about .8% of the sales price) if you don't use its lender. Meanwhile, most of these lenders are working a hundred files for the builder at a time, and the service is seriously lacking. Remember, NO buyer is required to use a particular Realtor. The builder-preferred Realtor is likely to act as a mouthpiece for the builder, and any savings you supposedly get by using the preferred Realtor will likely be far less than if you used an outside agent who can actually negotiate on your behalf (and may be willing to offer a discounted commission)."

Developers usually have salespeople, paid by and loyal to the developer, who they'd prefer to have you use for the tasks your agent would normally handle, such as drawing up written agreements. Of course, these usually favor the developer, for example, limiting the developer's responsibility for shoddy work or late completion. It's worth bringing your own agent to advocate on your behalf and help you negotiate a fair deal.

However, if you're represented by an outside agent, the developer might, as a way of recouping part of the commission or referral fee (particularly in a hot market), be less flexible about price or less willing to give special incentives or upgrades.

 TIP

Consider adding an attorney-review contingency to your contract. If bringing your own real estate agent appears unnecessary or impossible, at least insist that an attorney review your agreement. You can make this a condition of the sale (a "contingency"), as discussed in Chapter 10.

Getting the Best Agent Out There

It's worth putting some effort into finding an experienced real estate agent with whom you'll enjoy working. You could just walk into any real estate agency, but you'd probably end up with whoever had time to spare. Instead, start by getting recommendations from family members, friends, colleagues, or neighbors who've bought homes—particularly in the neighborhoods you're interested in. Ask the people recommending agents for as much detail as possible: what type of transaction the agent assisted with, what the agent's strong (and weak) points were, and so on. Personal recommendations are your best sources of objective information.

If you come up dry, you can search NAR's database of Realtors at www.realtor.com, and click "Find REALTORS®." Yelp, Zillow, and Trulia are also becoming rich sources of agent information and reviews. Your state association might also provide similar information (but keep in mind that this is a membership listing based on location and doesn't distinguish between good and bad agents).

CHECK IT OUT

Check their license. To make sure a prospective agent is currently licensed in your state, visit the website of your state's real estate commission or ARELLO.com, a searchable license verification database provided by the Association of Real Estate License Law Officials (ARELLO). ARELLO's main site, www.arrello.org, can also link you to relevant laws and regulations.

If It Doesn't Work Out: Firing an Agent

One common misconception is that once you've chosen an agent, you can't fire that person. Whether you can extricate yourself from the relationship (and what it will cost you to do so) will probably be determined by the terms of your agreement. If and when you and the agent sign an agreement regarding the agent's representation, try to insert a clause allowing you to release the agent with sufficient notice (usually, about 48 hours) if things aren't working out. Watch out for a clause that requires you to pay a cancellation fee if you dump your agent. And to give you more flexibility, try to limit the relationship to 30 or 45 days rather than, say, six months. "You can also make the agreement address specific," notes Greg Nino. "That way, if you might want to fire your agent, he or she is only permitted to represent you on *that* one house."

Even if your agreement doesn't specifically give you the right to fire your agent, if an agent isn't showing you appropriate properties, or isn't responding to your calls or inquiries, or you just don't like working with that person, you might want to move on. Of course, if the problem can be resolved by a simple conversation, it's wiser to try that first. But if that's fruitless and the agent isn't willing to walk away, you might need to discuss the issue with the managing broker (the agent's boss).

If you decide to end a working relationship, do it *before* you find a house you want to buy. It would be totally unethical—and risk a lawsuit—to try to get out of the relationship just to avoid letting the agent claim the commission.

Real Estate Agent Interview Questionnaire

Ask potential agents the following questions, as well as anything special to your transaction, like their experience helping buyers looking for fixer-uppers or newly constructed houses.

Name of real estate agent and contact information (phone, email, etc.):

Date of conversation:

1. Do you work full time as a real estate agent?

2. How long have you been in the real estate business? How many people work in your office?

3. Do you have additional certifications beyond your general real estate license? If so what are they?

4. What's your standard practice for presenting a purchase offer to the seller?

5. How many residential real estate transactions have you been a part of in the past year?

6. In how many of those transactions have you represented the buyer?

7. What was the price range of homes you helped clients buy within the last year? What was the average price?

8. Do you specialize in a certain type of property?

9. Do you specialize in a certain geographic area?

10. Do you partner with other agents or use assistants?

11. How will I reach you? Are there days or times you're unavailable, or do you have any vacations planned? What if you're on vacation when my house is closing?

12. Can you provide three names of recent clients who purchased homes with you, who will serve as references?

NOTES:

Real Estate Agent Interview Questionnaire Best Answers

1. Yes.

2. The longer the better, but at least three years. If the agent is still relatively new, definitely make sure he or she is part of a respected, vibrant office where agents share ideas and advice.

3. More certifications show a commitment by the agent. A Realtor ABR or ABRM designation indicates that the agent has significant experience working with buyers.

4. The best agents present offers to sellers or the sellers' agent in person or on the phone, rather than, say, emailing them in and hoping for the best.

5. Should be a minimum of ten.

6. Should be at least half, but experience with representing sellers is relevant, too. Most agents start out representing buyers, then begin representing sellers after they've gained experience and their happy clients come back ready to sell. Representing sellers also helps an agent develop a fuller sense of the whole transaction.

7. Should be about your price range.

8. Should be the type of property you're interested in, like a single-family house, condo, or co-op.

9. Should be the geographic area where you're looking to buy.

10. If so, find out who you'll be working with, what their real estate experience is, and what they'll be doing.

11. Make sure you can reach the agent when you need to. If you plan to buy soon, make sure the agent will be readily available (not on vacation).

12. Should be "Yes."

Once you've got a few names, choose a few agents to meet in person. Agents' websites often contain their photos and descriptions of their skills, services, or philosophies. You're looking for an agent who is knowledgeable about the area and the type of house you want to live in; experienced; easily reachable and responsive to your needs; ethical and honest; compatible; and loyal. If you're interested in checking out unusual types of deals (a house in foreclosure or a short sale, for example, as discussed in Chapter 9), ask the agent about his or her experience with such transactions.

At the interview, ask concrete questions about the agent's experience, certifications, and more, and how the agent's skills will be put to work for you. "A smart buyer," says Greg Nino, "will consider: 'Do I like this agent? Do I trust him or her? Can I work with this person? Does the agent know

Real Estate Agent Reference Questionnaire

Here are possible questions to ask the agent's referrals or your friends providing recommendations. You can choose the ones that seem most fitting (asking all of them could be a bit much) or add others that interest you, such as special issues if you're buying a foreclosure or a new house in a development.

Name of real estate agent:

Name of reference: Date:

1. How did you choose the agent? Did you know the agent before you worked together?

2. What kind of house did you buy?

3. Was the agent responsive? Did the agent return calls, texts, and email promptly, follow through on promises, and meet deadlines?

4. Did the agent take the time to find you the right property?

5. How long did you look?

6. How many houses did you look at before you bought? Did you make any previous offers that fell through, and if so, why?

7. Did the agent show you houses in your price range?

8. Are you happy with the house you bought, and the neighborhood it's in?

9. Did the agent help you coordinate other details of your purchase, like finding financing and working with the title company, inspectors, or insurance agents? If you bought a new home from a developer, were there some items that needed completion or adjustment after the closing? If so, did your agent help nudge the developer to get the work done?

10. Did the agent keep you up to date, and explain everything in terms you understood?

11. What was the best thing about working with this agent? The worst? Would you work with the agent again?

OTHER COMMENTS:

what he or she is talking about?" You might also request the names of three recent clients, as references. Even though references your agent provides likely won't have anything negative to say, talking with past clients might provide insight into whether the agent's personality and style of doing business will be a good fit. (Realize, however, that not all agents will be willing to provide this information, for privacy and liability reasons.)

ONLINE TOOLKIT

For a comprehensive set of questions for both the agent and his or her references: Use the "Real Estate Agent Interview Questionnaire" and the "Real Estate Agent Reference Questionnaire" in the Homebuyer's Toolkit on the Nolo website. (See the appendix for the link.) Samples of these forms are shown above.

Best thing we ever did

Got an agent who specialized in our neighborhood. Craig and Lorena had been looking for an affordable starter house in a much-desired neighborhood for months, with no luck. Lorena explains, "Although our agent specialized in our target neighborhood—she lived there—there just weren't many houses we liked at a price we could afford. We'd just about given up when she called us. A neighbor of hers was getting ready to sell and was willing to let us have first peek. We loved the place and immediately put in an offer, which was accepted. The place was never even advertised!"

TIP

Don't spill your beans. Wait to tell the agent your own objectives (where you want to live, how much you want to spend, and what type of property you're looking for) until your questions have been answered. You don't want the agent to feed you the answers you want to hear.

Who Does What

It's your agent's job to …	But it's still your job to …
Talk to you about your needs.	Research and choose the right agent, and negotiate the terms of the agency.
Research houses and neighborhoods that meet your needs and give you data on comparable properties.	Clearly explain and describe to the agent what you're looking for.
Show you houses with features that you want, in your price range.	Choose the right neighborhood.
Help you write up offers (except in states where attorneys do this).	Choose the best house for you.
Deliver your offer to the seller.	Choose your professionals, like the mortgage broker, inspector, and closing agent.
Notify you of counteroffers and help you negotiate with the seller.	Secure your financing.
Recommend professionals like brokers, inspectors, and closing agents; help you coordinate working with these people.	Respond promptly to your agent's questions.
Attend important events like inspections, appraisals, the final walk-through, and (usually) the closing.	Attend important events (like inspections) whenever possible.
Explain the process, timeline, and technical concepts.	Avoid, or at least knowingly consent to a dual or designated agency relationship, if the situation arises.
Respond promptly to your phone calls and inquiries.	Decide on the key terms of your offer.
Help with any snafus you encounter during the process.	Speak up if there is a problem.
Disclose a dual or designated agency.	Read all documents carefully.

Your Cash Cow: The Loan Officer, Mortgage Broker, or Mortgage Banker

Even in inexpensive housing markets, you'll likely be taking out a mortgage to finance your purchase. In the next chapter, we'll talk about how to research options, select the best loan, and actually apply for it. Here, we're going to talk about the people you'll work with to do that.

Most buyers get their loans through either a mortgage broker, loan officer, or mortgage banker—a professional who's in the business of compiling and filtering through the options for you. Your other primary alternative is to go directly to a bank, a credit union, or another commercial lender.

If you're buying a newly constructed home, the developer may line up financing for you—but it's definitely worth checking out other options.

> **TIP**
> **A "mortgage broker," "mortgage banker," and "loan officer" aren't the exact same thing.** A mortgage broker is the middleman who brings you and a lender together. A mortgage banker or loan officer represents a lender who actually lends you money. But we'll sometimes use the term "broker" generically in this chapter, to mean all of the above.

Your Personal Shopper: The Mortgage Broker, Banker, or Loan Officer

A mortgage broker acts as your agent to get you the best possible loan terms, given your financial situation and goals. All mortgage loan officers and brokers must be licensed by either the federal government or a state organization. This information is easily verified by using the National Mortgage Licensing System (NMLS) website at www.NMLSConsumer. org. Individual mortgage brokers are also sometimes certified by the National Association of Mortgage Brokers (NAMB). To be NAMB certified, brokers must show a certain amount of work experience and other qualifications, pass a written exam, and attend continuing education training. There are two types of NAMB certification: Certified Residential Mortgage Specialist (CRMS) and Certified Mortgage Consultant (CMC).

As for compensation, mortgage brokers and loan officers make most of their money by commission paid by the lender.

 TIP

Choose a loan officer or mortgage broker before you find a house. If you wait until you've found a property you want to buy, you'll have very little time to find the best professional.

Often, a homebuyer goes directly to a lender, rather than dealing with a mortgage broker. The buyer might like the personal aspect of walking into a local bank branch or even have found a better deal than is available through a broker. You can often find a lender's advertised rates on the Web or in your local newspaper—we'll talk about searching for that in Chapter 6.

If you decide to work with a lender, you'll probably still be dealing primarily with a person within the institution called a "mortgage banker" or "loan officer," as described above. This person performs the same duties (more or less) as a mortgage broker, except that instead of scouring the entire loan market, the loan officer will help you identify which of the bank's own portfolio of loan products suits your needs. In other words, you'll be limited to the loan packages offered by that institution.

The loan officer should help you fill out your application and handle necessary paperwork like obtaining your credit report and getting an appraisal. However, once you've chosen a bank, you won't be able to choose your loan officer as you would a broker—or your available choices will be limited.

How much personal contact you have with a specific loan officer depends on the lender. Lenders come in all shapes and sizes, from the behemoth bank to the local credit union.

Some operate almost entirely online, even having you apply online. Examples include Rocket Mortgage by Quicken Loans, loanDepot, and Better. Often, online lenders have some of the lowest fees and interest rates, likely because they've cut out the operating costs of the local office and can pass the savings on to you. If you work with online lenders, you'll have to rely more heavily on technology (you'll need reliable email and easy access to a scanner) to transmit documents. Also, you should be comfortable with the fact that you'll likely communicate with several different people during the transaction, and never meet any of them face to face.

What Your Broker or Loan Officer Does for You

To help you find the best loan possible, a good loan officer or broker will:

- Talk with you about your financial situation and goals.
- Find and explain financing options available to you.
- Work with you to get preapproved for a mortgage.
- Help you complete and assemble the documentation the lender needs. This might include your loan application, confirmation of employment and wages, financial information, and credit report.
- Once approved, review loan documents before you sign them. If the lender refuses to approve your loan, your broker or loan officer should explain what went wrong and help find alternative mortgage options.
- Coordinate the property appraisal.
- Order lender's title insurance.
- Continue to act as a liaison between you, your real estate agent, and the lender up through the closing day.

TIP
Run your own numbers. The mortgage broker's view of your finances will be much like the lender's—a measure of what you can qualify for based on your debt-to-income ratio. Don't look to the mortgage broker to tell you what you can comfortably afford: Conduct a personal evaluation of your finances, as explained in Chapter 3.

Getting the Best Mortgage Broker or Loan Officer Out There

Good mortgage loan officers and brokers possess many of the same traits as good real estate agents—integrity, professionalism, and experience. They should also be skilled (and patient) at explaining complicated financing concepts. In addition, good mortgage brokers stay informed about the policies, requirements, and products of various mortgage lenders, so as to provide you with up-to-date and accurate advice. Don't be afraid to ask brokers about their schedule. Most respond to clients' inquiries outside of normal working hours, and it's a good idea to work with someone you know will be available for any last-minute questions.

Who Does What	
It's your mortgage loan officer or broker's job to ...	**But it's still your job to ...**
Offer you loan products that meet your needs.	Give the mortgage broker all relevant information about your financial picture.
Explain financing concepts and loan products.	Provide personal financial documents.
Coordinate loan approval with the lender.	
Check your credit, help you fill out your application, arrange the appraisal, and verify your financial information.	Decide which loan you want.
	Negotiate the terms of the loan if you think the broker's markup is too high.
Before the deal closes, make sure all of the lender's underwriting conditions are met, coordinating with you and the lender, appraiser, credit report company, title company, flood insurance certificate provider (if applicable), and mortgage insurance provider.	Return your broker's calls and respond to inquiries.
	Read all documents.
Make sure all loan conditions are met and the cash is transferred for closing.	Double-check that you've gotten a rate-lock commitment in writing.

Mortgage Loan Officer or Broker Interview Questionnaire

To get the best mortgage broker on your team, ask the following questions, as well as any special to your situation (for example, concerning a credit history issue, your interest in an FHA or other government-backed loan, or the broker's experience with self-employed buyers).

Name of mortgage loan officer or broker and contact information (phone, email, NMLS number, etc.):

Date of conversation:

1. How long have you been in the residential mortgage business?

2. Do you work at it full time?

3. Are you licensed?

4. Are you certified by the National Association of Mortgage Brokers?

5. How many residential mortgages have you brokered in the past year?

6. How many of those transactions were with first-time homebuyers?

7. Can you describe a tricky deal you were able to successfully close?

8. Can you provide at least three names of recent clients who will serve as references, at least one of whom was a first-home buyer?

NOTES:

Best Answers:

1. The longer the better, but at least two years.
2. Yes.
3. Must be yes.
4. Certification is preferable.
5. Should be a minimum of ten.
6. The more the better, but should be at least five.

7. Hopefully, you'll hear about a tough situation that the broker handled well. A broker who has done only easy deals may not have the experience you need.
8. Only acceptable answer is "Yes."

Mortgage Loan Officer or Broker Reference Questionnaire

Here's what to ask the mortgage broker's references. You can add any other questions that interest you, for example, whether the person tried to negotiate the broker's fee down.

Name of mortgage loan officer broker:

Name of reference:

Date:

1. How did you choose the mortgage broker? Did you know the broker before you worked together?

2. What kind and size of loan did you get?

3. Was the broker responsive? Did the broker return calls and emails promptly, follow through on promises, and meet deadlines?

4. How long did you look?

5. Did the broker give you a variety of options?

6. Did the broker arrange for you to lock in your interest rate for either 30, 45, or 60 days prior to the closing?

7. Are you satisfied with the loan you got?

8. Did the broker help you coordinate other details of your purchase, like working with the title company or insurance agents?

9. Did the broker keep you up to date, and explain everything in terms you understood?

10. What was the best thing about working with this mortgage broker? The worst? Would you work with the broker again?

OTHER COMMENTS:

Get recommendations from friends, coworkers, and other home-owners. Your real estate agent is another good resource. A less reliable option is the "Find a Mortgage Professional" feature on the NAMB website, www.namb.org. NAMB membership is just a starting point: You'll want to learn more about each broker's education, experience, and philosophy. Ask whether the broker will tell you up front about every fee he or she will charge you (you might want to negotiate these fees, as we'll discuss in Chapter 6).

Next, interview two or three prospective mortgage brokers. Ask about their experience and certifications, plus any questions special to your situation (like whether they can provide help getting an FHA or other government-backed loan). Also ask for the names of three references, and follow up to check whether these folks enjoyed working with the broker and are still happy with the loan they got.

Although you can get a lot of good information about mortgages online, when it comes time to actually apply for your loan, Realtor Greg Nino advises that "Working with a local lender can reduce the chances of something going wrong. Even if the terms aren't quite as good as those online, paying a little more can be worth it for the personalized attention you'll receive." Greg also notes that local brokers are typically more accessible than those who work for big banks—they don't disappear when the clock hits 5 p.m., and they don't route you to customer service when you have questions. Another benefit is that getting a preapproval letter from a local lender is more likely to impress sellers (and their agents): Big banks are notorious for not doing in-depth due diligence when they produce preapproval letters, increasing the chance that the buyer will be denied a loan once the bank finally digs into the buyer's loan worthiness.

ONLINE TOOLKIT

For a handy set of questions to use in your interview and when checking references: Use the "Mortgage Loan Officer or Broker Interview Questionnaire" and the "Mortgage Loan Officer or Broker Reference Questionnaire" in the Homebuyer's Toolkit on the Nolo website. (See the appendix for the link.) Samples of these forms are shown above.

Your Fine-Print Reader: The Real Estate Attorney

In some states, such as New York and Massachussetts, real estate attorneys are a regular part of the homebuying process. Even in states where this isn't the case, you might need an attorney's assistance in a complex transaction. After all, if you don't use an attorney and the transaction later goes awry, you'll still have to hire one, at much greater time and cost. If there's anything legally unusual about your planned purchase, save yourself headaches by working with a lawyer to structure the deal, not salvage it.

What's legally unusual? It's wise to get an attorney involved in situations such as these:

- You'd like to rent the home for an extended period, such as a year, before you're obligated to buy it.
- You'd like to move some belongings into the home's garage or basement before the closing date.
- You'd like an escalation clause that gives you the right—within limits—to meet or exceed any competing offer.
- You'd like to make sure that a current tenant in the home will be moving out before closing.
- You're willing to let the seller retain possession of the home for a time beyond the closing, but you want to make sure the seller will pay you a fair rent.

Easements are another classic example of when a lawyer's help might be warranted. Adviser Daniel Stea recalls a transaction in which the seller and neighbors had a verbal easement allowing the neighbors to access their parking spot through the seller's driveway. "The buyers naturally wanted to have this arrangement reduced to writing—and that writing is the sort of thing a lawyer should really draft, to make sure nothing is left out." However, Stea also notes that, "I'd estimate that out of every 50 home sales that I handle in California, only a couple need a lawyer's assistance."

TIP

There's no substitute for your own attorney. Don't expect the seller's attorney, the closing agent (who might be an attorney), the real estate agent, the mortgage broker, or anyone else in the transaction to look after your legal interests. Then again, you might not need any attorney at all, particularly if you're in a state where they're not a traditional part of the transaction. Plenty of real estate sales go through just fine without an attorney's help.

Who Real Estate Attorneys Are

A real estate attorney is, by definition, one who focuses on real estate transactions. This may sounds obvious, but you don't want to get stuck working with an attorney whose main expertise is estate planning or corporate mergers. Ideally, your attorney will have several years of real estate law experience, at least some of it working directly with other, more experienced attorneys. Additionally, in most cases, you'll want an attorney who specializes in helping buyers with their residential real estate transactions: drawing up contracts, researching title, and the like. An attorney who specializes in litigating disputes is a better fit if you think you'll need to sue or you might be sued—but when structuring your deal, you'll be trying to avoid that result.

CHECK IT OUT

Are attorneys always involved in real estate transactions in your state? Any experienced real estate agent should be able to tell you this, or you can check with your state bar association. Find it through the American Bar Association's website, www.americanbar.org (search for "state and local bar associations").

What Your Real Estate Attorney Does for You

Depending on your needs and which state you're in, your attorney might become involved in one or more of the following: negotiating, creating, or reviewing the sales contract; overseeing the homebuying process to check for compliance with all terms and conditions of the contract; performing a title search or reviewing the title abstract or title insurance commitment (to determine whether there are any liens or encumbrances on the property); explaining the effect of any easements or use restrictions; negotiating or representing you in a contract dispute with the seller; reviewing the closing documents ahead of the closing; and representing you at the closing.

> **TIP**
>
> **Check your prepaid legal plan.** Such plans—perhaps provided by your employer—sometimes provide legal services for homebuyers, so if you have one, this might be the time to use it. However, make sure the plan truly offers the level of service you need. Make sure you'll be represented by the same attorney every step of the way, and won't be dealing primarily with a paralegal or secretary.

An attorney can also assist you in complex transactions, for example if:

- Legal claims have been made against your prospective house that must be satisfied by the time the property is sold—for example, a construction lien imposed by a contractor whom the seller hasn't paid yet for remodeling work. Your lawyer can make sure that the seller's lawyer addresses this issue.
- Problems show up with the title: For example, the driveway is shared by the house you want to buy and the neighboring house, but that isn't reflected in the home title. Your lawyer can prepare an agreement for you and the neighbor to sign that can become part of the title documents.
- You need help reviewing community interest development agreements and documents like CC&Rs, a co-op proprietary lease, or a new home contract drafted by the developer.
- You need to structure a private loan from a relative or friend to make the purchase.
- You are purchasing the house jointly with others and need to structure a cobuyer agreement and document how title will be held.
- A little later on, the seller tries to wiggle out of the deal, and you want your lawyer to inform the seller of the legal consequences for failing to perform.

"One of the most valuable things we do for our clients is simply to make sure that all discussions about seller repairs and the condition of property have been put into writing," says Massachusetts attorney Alicia Champagne. "The object is to avoid situations like one I had, where our client had been told by the seller's listing agent, as they talked in the house's basement, that the seller would extend a $1,500 escrow credit for replacing the hot water heater. Unfortunately, no one ever told any of the attorneys about this. We got to the closing, and the buyer said, 'Where's my $1,500?' The seller's attorney simply refused to authorize payment. And without any proof in writing, there was nothing we could do."

Getting the Best Attorney Out There

It's smarter to hire an attorney who's a real estate expert, even if it costs more. If you pay the attorney by the hour, the seasoned one won't need to spend time just researching real estate laws and learning about local practices.

Many, but not all, states require you to have a written fee agreement with your lawyer. It's worth doing, anyway. Your agreement establishes the terms of representation: what the lawyer is expected to do, how much you'll pay and on what basis (for example, hourly or a flat rate), and when the lawyer must be paid (in some areas, attorneys are paid at closing; in other areas, they're paid outside of closing). Often you'll have to pay some advance money, called a retainer—but the rest of the lawyer's fee will be paid later. Ask prospective attorneys about payment practices in your area.

TIP

Count the hours. If you have an hourly arrangement with your attorney, here's a way to keep costs in check: Ask that the attorney contact you before starting each discrete task (like reviewing condo CC&Rs) and give you an estimate of how long that task will take. If it sounds reasonable, say okay, but require the attorney to contact you if additional time is needed.

Attorney Interview Questionnaire

Ask the following questions, as well as any specific to your transaction—for example, regarding the attorney's experience with condo, co-op, or newly built house purchases.

Name of attorney and contact information (phone, email, etc.):

Date of conversation:

1. What percent of your time do you spend helping residential real estate buyers?

2. How many years have you been handling residential real estate legal matters? What are the typical services you provide?

3. Do you charge hourly rates (if so, at what rate) or flat fees for services?

4. Do you have an active license to practice law in your state?

5. Have you ever been subject to any disciplinary proceedings?

6. Have you ever been sued for malpractice? What was the result?

7. How many individual homebuying clients have you represented in the past year?

8. Can you provide the names of three recent clients who will serve as references?

NOTES:

Best Answers:

1. More than 50%.
2. The longer the better, but at least two years.
3. No one right answer—you'll want to compare fees between attorneys. But try not to base your decision solely on how high or low the fees are.
4. Only acceptable answer is "Yes."
5. Only acceptable answer is "No."
6. Only acceptable answer is "No," unless the suit was dismissed as baseless.
7. Should be a minimum of seven.
8. Not all attorneys will provide references, but if one does, it's worth your time to follow up.

Attorney Reference Questionnaire

Here's what to ask the attorney references. You can add any other questions that interest you—for example, whether the attorney knows about buying a co-op.

Name of attorney:

Name of reference:

Date:

1. How did you choose the attorney?

2. Did you know the attorney before you worked together?

3. What kind of legal services did the attorney provide?

4. Was the attorney responsive? Did the attorney return calls and emails promptly, follow through on promises, and meet deadlines?

5. How long did you work together?

6. Are you happy with the attorney's services?

7. Did the attorney keep you up to date, and explain everything in terms you understood?

8. What was the best thing about working with this attorney? The worst? Would you work with the attorney again?

OTHER COMMENTS:

To find potential attorneys, start by getting recommendations from friends, coworkers, and trusted real estate professionals. If that doesn't pan out, you can get names from professional organizations or use lawyer referral services (such as the Nolo lawyer directory, at Nolo.com).

Then interview three or four attorneys. Clarify in advance whether you must pay for this interview time. Some attorneys offer free consultations, others don't. It might be worth paying, though, to start your purchase off with a highly regarded attorney. At the interview, ask about not only the attorney's general legal skills, but also how much time he or she spends on transactions similar to yours—especially if you're buying a condo, co-op, or newly built house. Make sure the attorney is familiar with local real estate practices and relevant state and local rules that apply to your transaction.

If possible, get and check references for any attorney you plan to hire, especially if a substantial amount of legal work (and money) is involved. While some attorneys will be reluctant to provide names of clients (because of client confidentiality), it doesn't hurt to ask.

Who Does What	
It's your attorney's job to ...	**But it's still your job to ...**
Provide the services outlined in your agreement, such as drafting an offer or contract, reviewing the contract, or verifying title.	Give the attorney all relevant documents and information.
Tell you how much services will cost.	Return your attorney's calls and respond to inquiries.
Keep everything confidential.	Make all decisions affecting your transaction, such as whether to complete the sale if there is a cloud on title.
Explain problems, complications, and the meaning of legal documents or terms.	Decide how you want to take title.
Advocate on your behalf to make sure contract terms are legal, fair, and satisfactory to you.	
Explain your options for describing your method for taking ownership on the title, and the legal effect of each option.	

ONLINE TOOLKIT

For a handy set of questions to use in your interview and reference checks: Use the "Attorney Interview Questionnaire" and "Attorney Reference Questionnaire" in the Homebuyer's Toolkit on the Nolo website. (See the appendix for the link.) Samples of these forms are shown above.

TIP

You can look up an attorney's discipline record. Every state has an organization (such as a bar association or a disciplinary committee) responsible for disciplining attorneys who violate ethics rules. Try searching online for "attorney discipline records" and the name of your state.

Your Sharp Eye: The Property Inspector

Before you buy a home, you'll probably have it inspected at least once (per a contingency you'll put in your contract, as discussed in Chapter 10). The purpose is to make sure that you're getting what you pay for— namely, a house in as good a condition as it appears to be. Suppose you make an offer assuming a place is in tip-top shape, then discover that the foundation needs to be redone? The property's value suddenly plummets— you might not even want to buy it at all.

The traditional inspection contingency allows about two weeks (or ten working days) for inspections to be completed, and about three days after that for you to approve them. That's not much time—in some U.S. regions, market conditions may shorten the inspection period dramatically, and the better inspectors have a waiting list. So it's good to choose your inspector before agreeing to buy a house.

Who Inspectors Are

A general home inspector visually examines the home, inside and out, for mechanical and structural flaws that could affect performance or safety.

Then the inspector prepares a detailed written report summarizing the findings and ideally including photos of problem areas. Greg Nino explains, "It is their job to know a little bit about everything with the home." General inspectors usually have a background in general contracting, residential homebuilding, or engineering. Some states require home inspectors to pass a test and be licensed, while others do not.

The more specialized inspectors have other areas of expertise and backgrounds and may need a state license (licensing is fairly common for pest inspectors, for example).

What Your Inspector Does for You

A general home inspection is usually limited to areas that can be seen during one two-to-three-hour visit without disturbing or damaging the property, such as viewing the condition of the roof, visually inspecting the electrical system, and examining the foundation. This inspection could also reveal that more specialized inspections are needed, for example, of the chimney or foundation.

A structural pest inspection, which most lenders require in areas prone to pests, is more limited in scope. The inspector looks for any pests, such as fungi, termites, or beetles, that can damage the structure.

Getting the Best Inspector Out There

When choosing a general home inspector, look for one who's been in the business for many years and is not only licensed (if that's available in your state), but affiliated with a professional or trade organization, most notably the American Society of Home Inspectors (ASHI). Ideally, you also want someone who has been a residential homebuilder or contractor.

Many buyers use a home inspector recommended by their real estate agent. Be careful: Inspectors who rely too much on agent referrals might be reluctant to find problems that could end up scuttling the deal, thus disappointing the agent. That's why it's worth getting independent recommendations from your friends, coworkers, and recent homebuyers.

Home Inspector Interview Questionnaire

Ask potential inspectors the following questions, as well as anything specific to your situation, like whether the inspector has experience with historic or remodeled properties.

Name of inspector and contact information (phone, email, etc.):

Date of conversation:

1. Do you work full time as a home inspector?

2. How long have you been in the home inspection business?

3. Are you affiliated with ASHI?

4. How many home inspections have you done in the past year in this area? What types of houses?

5. What kind of inspection report do you provide? Can I see an example?

6. Do you have current, active errors and omissions insurance?

7. What did you do before you were a home inspector?

8. Can I accompany you on the inspection? Can I take photos or videos?

9. Can you provide at least three names of recent clients who'll serve as references?

NOTES:

Best Answers:

1. Yes.

2. The longer the better, but at least two years.

3. Only acceptable answer is "Yes." ASHI is the national organization with the most stringent professional standards.

4. Should be a minimum of 15.

5. Many inspectors have sample reports on their websites; you want as comprehensive a report as possible, versus a short checklist. And you definitely want to see a sample report if there isn't one on the inspector's website.

6. Only acceptable answer is "Yes."

7. Only acceptable answer is a building-related position, such as a contractor or building inspector.

8. Only acceptable answer is "Yes" to the question of whether you can accompany the inspector. But whether you'll be permitted to take photos or videos is a matter of the inspector's own preference.

9. Only acceptable answer is "Yes."

Home Inspector Reference Questionnaire

Here's what to ask the inspector's references:

Name of inspector:

Name of reference:

Date:

1. How did you choose the inspector?

2. Did you know the inspector before you worked together?

3. What kind of inspection did you get and how much did it cost?

4. Was the inspector responsive? Did the inspector return calls and emails promptly, follow through on promises, and meet deadlines?

5. Did the inspector take the time to explain everything to you?

6. Did you go along on the inspection?
   If not, why not?
   If so, how long did it take?

7. What kind of report did you get?

8. Are you happy with the home inspection services and report you got?

9. Did the inspector keep you up to date, and explain everything in terms you understood?

10. What was the best thing about working with this inspector? The worst? Would you work with the inspector again?

OTHER COMMENTS:

TIP

The general inspector shouldn't do the repairs. A general home (not pest) inspector evaluates problems and recommends solutions. But no ethical inspector would say, "And guess what, I can fix that for you, at this price." That's a conflict of interest, violates the standards of the main industry trade groups such as ASHI, and is prohibited by law in many states.

Unlike general home inspectors, pest inspectors traditionally are the ones who do the extermination and fix-up work. Yes, it's a potential conflict, but that's the way the industry works, and the good news is that they actually have an interest in finding problems. For that reason, it's safe to go with your agent's recommendation; the remainder of this section will focus on general, not pest, inspectors.

To find a general inspector who will give the house a thorough going-over, interview two or three, asking questions about their experience, price, and scope of services. Also ask any questions specific to your situation, like whether the inspector has experience with historic remodeled properties. (Also, Greg Nino notes, "Understand that inspectors may charge more for an older home, a home with more than one air-conditioning unit, or one on pier and beam or some other odd kind of foundation.") Then request the names of three recent references, and follow up to make sure they were impressed with the inspector's eye for defects and communication abilities—and haven't found subsequent problems!

ONLINE TOOLKIT

For a comprehensive set of questions for both the inspector and his or her references: Use the "Home Inspector Interview Questionnaire" and the "Home Inspector Reference Questionnaire" in the Homebuyer's Toolkit on the Nolo website. (See the appendix for the link.) Samples of these forms are shown above.

Who Does What	
It's your home inspector's job to ...	**But it's still your job to ...**
Inspect the house for defects.	Attend the inspection.
Write a summary report of the findings.	Read the inspector's report.
	Coordinate follow-up inspections.
Recommend repairs or further inspections, if necessary.	Negotiate with the seller over problems discovered during the inspection and arrange for or hire professionals to do follow-up inspections or make the necessary repairs.

Your Big Picture Planner: The Closing Agent

A lot has to happen between signing the agreement to buy a house and closing the deal—it's a process that usually takes at least a few weeks. You want to make sure that the house is in good shape, your financing is squared away, and that the seller doesn't pull any surprises. And on the closing day, a number of documents need to be signed, and money transferred back and forth.

To take care of the many details, it makes sense to have a third party—in many states, a completely neutral third party—to make sure both of you are doing what you promised. That's where the closing agent (sometimes called the "escrow agent," "escrow officer," "closing officer," or "title agent") comes in. Every state's requirements for who can serve in this role are different. In states where attorneys handle the closing (such as Massachusetts and New York), you might not have one neutral intermediary, but instead two attorneys, yours and the seller's, sharing the tasks.

Who Closing Agents Are

Even though we call a closing agent a member of "your" team, the agent is really looking out for both you and the seller (unless you're each using your own attorney). The closing agent acts as a check on both of you, to make sure you complete the transaction according to the terms of the purchase agreement. The agent usually works for a title or escrow company.

What Your Closing Agent Does for You

Although you may not meet your closing agent until you're far into the purchase process—possibly until closing day—the agent will be working behind the scenes long prior to that. (You can meet your closing agent before then, if you want to—and if you have questions or envision some hairy complications, it's a good idea to get in touch.) Expect your closing agent to:

- **Arrange your title insurance.** The closing agent will order or perform (if he or she already works for a title company or is an attorney) a title search and arrange for a title insurance commitment to be issued. The title search and title insurance commitment will show whether the seller is actually in a legal position to sell the property to you and whether any liens, easements, or other encumbrances affect ownership of the property (we'll translate that gobbledygook in later chapters). After the seller clears up any title defects and your purchase is closed, the closing agent will help make sure you're issued a title insurance policy.
- **Coordinate with lenders.** The closing agent is going to coordinate with two different sets of lenders: the seller's lender(s), assuming the seller hadn't already paid off the mortgage, and your mortgage lender(s). The closing agent will make sure the seller's lenders are paid in full when the property is sold to you.
- **Establish an escrow or trust account.** The closing agent will keep any money you deposit in a separate bank account, called an escrow or a trust account, until the closing date, when the money will be transferred to the seller. The seller might also agree to deposit money there for repairs (your lender or state law might prohibit

this, though, so check with your closing agent and your lender before deciding to hold funds in escrow for repairs). In states where both parties are represented by attorneys, the seller's attorney opens this account.

- **Prorate expenses.** The closing agent will figure out who, as between you and the seller, pays what proportion of any property tax, municipal assessments, and condo or association fees owing or paid during the time period around the sale.
- **Follow instructions.** The closing agent will follow written instructions prepared by you and the seller and make sure that all these tasks are accomplished by the date of closing—and sometimes even after the closing. For example, the closing agent may retain funds from the seller's check to assure that all utility bills get paid for service the seller received before the closing date.
- **Record the deed and pay the seller.** At the closing, the agent will transfer payment to the seller. Afterward, the closing agent will publicly record the new deed that transfers the property to you.

How You'll Pay the Closing Agent

The closing agent is paid a fee that's included in closing costs. In some locations, it's customary for the buyer to pay the fee; in other locations, the seller; and elsewhere, the fees are split. Your real estate agent should know the local custom, though you and the seller can negotiate something different. (The fees themselves are not negotiable.)

Getting the Best Closing Agent Out There

Who chooses the closing agent depends on local custom and how strongly you, as the buyer, feel about having a voice in the matter. The choice of a closing agent is usually made early on and spelled out in the purchase agreement. Often the closing agent is someone either the buyer's or seller's real estate agent knows, however. If you want to use a particular company or individual, mention it to your agent at the outset so it can be included in your offer.

Who Does What	
It's your closing agent's job to ...	But it's still your job to ...
Collect and coordinate paperwork, including financing and required disclosures.	Understand and sign off on the instructions that guide the agent's activities.
Obtain a title report and coordinate issuance of a title insurance policy.	Obtain homeowners' insurance and supply the closing agent with the details, including premium amount.
Prorate costs like taxes, insurance, and loan interest.	Read the preliminary title report and, with the help of your real estate agent or attorney, resolve any disputes.
Hold deposits of money in a separate account and transfer them as appropriate.	Arrange for a timely money transfer of whatever portion of the closing costs you agreed to pay (or arrange to have them paid through financing).
Pay recording fees and taxes.	
Transfer and record the deed.	Coordinate directly with other parties— inspector, real estate agent, or mortgage broker—to make sure everything is in order, including advising your agent when contingencies can be removed.
Transfer your payments to the seller.	
	Read all documents carefully before signing.

TIP

Choose a closing agent who's conveniently located. You'll have to drive there at least once, for the closing, and maybe more often, for example, to sign a power of attorney or deliver an old divorce decree.

To make sure you're choosing the best closing agent, get referrals from not only your agent, attorney, or mortgage broker, but from trusted family members, friends, neighbors, or colleagues. Adviser Sandy Gadow, author of *The Complete Guide to Your Real Estate Closing*, suggests making sure your referral source found the closing agent to be efficient, accurate, and able to handle the closing according to schedule.

Strength in Numbers: Other Team Members

Although we've covered the key players for most homebuyers' teams, there are a few other professionals whom you'll either want to consider bringing in or might interact with along the way. These include:

- **Tax professionals.** You might want to consult an accountant or other tax pro to make sure you're taking advantage of all the tax benefits of buying a home. This is particularly important in the year you buy, when many of your expenses may be deductible.

- **Insurance agents or brokers.** You're going to need to purchase homeowners' insurance for your house (the lender will require coverage of physical hazards, at a minimum, as described in Chapter 13). To do that, you'll probably work with an insurance broker. Your other option is to directly contact representatives of insurance agencies whose services come highly recommended.

- **Contractors.** If you're considering remodeling, or want to have someone lined up to handle any problems that an inspector's report identifies, it's worth getting recommendations for a good contractor early on. That way, you can have the contractor look at the house and tell you how much the remodel or repairs or repairs would cost, or whether it's worth buying in the first place.

What's Next?

With a team of professionals beside you, you're ready to really launch your home search. In the next chapter, we'll discuss one of the most important parts of homebuying: financing your mortgage.

Bring Home the Bacon: Getting a Mortgage

6

Meet Your Adviser

Lisa Shaffer, loan adviser at RPM Mortgage in Alamo, California (www.rpm-mtg.com).

What she does "I see my job as providing clients with an exceptional experience when they're purchasing or refinancing a home. Of course, this involves both work that the clients see and a lot of behind-the-scenes activity. My first step in working with a new client is to simply ask questions and listen. I like to find out what a client's needs and intentions are, for example, 'Where do you want to buy? Will this be your first home? How much can you feasibly put down? How long do you plan to stay in the home?' Through such conversations, I can assess what steps need to be taken before the client applies for a loan (for example, cleaning up credit) and which loan program will work best for the client's needs. Then I work with a team of in-house processors, underwriters, and assistants, and also with title companies, to ensure that the entire transaction happens seamlessly. All of this couldn't happen if I and my team weren't regularly monitoring interest rates, watching for changes in the real estate market and the economy in general, and so on."

Fantasy house "It wouldn't be far different from what we have now: a little bigger in square footage, same ranch-ish style, but surrounded by a lot of land. There's a beautiful ridge in our town, and it would be great to have a home nestled below it and surrounded by oak trees. There, the kids could run around, climb trees, and have open space with room to explore."

First house

"It's a three-bedroom that my husband and I bought when newly married, and still live in. The house has evolved with us. Its emotional aspects are, by now, as important as its physical ones. It's the house whose threshold we crossed when we were first married; the house we brought our newborn babies home to; and the house where our children took their first steps and experienced their first Christmases and birthday parties. I guess we can now say it's truly a 'home.' It's also in a great, family-oriented neighborhood. Three parks are within walking distance, the kids can get around by bike, and many of the neighbors have kids, too."

Likes best about her work

"I enjoy taking the time getting to know my clients, and finding personalized solutions for their financial issues and needs. It's especially satisfying when I can help get someone get into a home when they doubted they could afford one at all. Recently, for instance, I worked with a man who'd gone through a foreclosure. He was quite discouraged, thinking he might be out of the real estate game for good. We were able to help him find financing and buy another home. Other clients of ours have had a good income but not much saved up for a down payment, and we've been able to find them first-time buyer programs (either through the government or through niche programs offered by banks) to help them buy a home sooner than they'd thought possible."

Top tip for first-time homebuyers

"There's no timeline but your own. A lot people think, 'I need to hurry and buy, home prices are rising, and interest rates are low.' They don't want to miss out. But readiness to buy a home is an individual matter and difficult to rush. A lot needs to fall into line: your credit score, income, readiness to commit to homeownership, job stability, and so on. Take your time, and realize that opportunities will still be there when you're ready."

I f you're like most homebuyers, you simply won't have the cash on hand to buy a home outright. Thankfully, in spite of ever-tighter standards, there are still lenders willing to front you the money you'll probably need.

If you've already started researching mortgages, you might have been put off by all the numbers and fine print. People start out promising themselves, "I'm going to learn all about mortgages," and end up saying, "I'll take the first decent deal I find; I just want to buy this house."

But you don't need to swing to either extreme. With a little buyer's savvy, you can avoid a mortgage that's just plain wrong for you or costs more than it should. We'll show you how by looking at:

- the basics of mortgage financing—interest rates, points, and more
- different loan options—fixed rates, adjustable rates, and everything in between
- how much to borrow versus how much to put down
- where to research mortgages, and
- the mechanics of applying for and getting a loan.

Let's Talk Terms: The Basics of Mortgage Financing

Before you start mortgage shopping, let's cover the basics: what a mortgage is and how it works. A mortgage is a loan to purchase property, with the property as collateral. That means that if you buy your dream home, and you don't make the payments, the lender can recover what it's owed by foreclosing on the property—that is, taking possession of and selling it.

> The average home buyer spends double the time researching a car purchase as he or she does researching a mortgage.
>
> —*Zillow*

Naturally, the lender gets into this risky business to make money. It does that primarily by charging interest and points (one-time fees when you take out the loan). The variety of mortgage options means you can borrow the same amount of money but with different terms and end up paying very different amounts back. While interest rates and points look like tiny numbers and percentages in the beginning, they add up to real dollars later.

EXAMPLE: Rob and Amy have found their dream house but don't have a mortgage yet. The local bank offers them a $350,000, 30-year, fixed-rate mortgage at 4% interest, with no points. The monthly principal and interest payment would be about $1,671, and they'd pay about $251,543 in interest over the life of the loan.

Meanwhile, Jimmy and Devon are interested in the same house. They go to a broker to discuss their options. She finds them a $350,000, 30-year, fixed rate mortgage at 3.5% interest, with one point. The point will cost them $3,500, but their monthly payment will be about $1,572, and they'll pay about $215,797 in interest over the life of the loan: That's $35,796 less than Rob and Amy will ultimately shell out (assuming they both stay in the home for 30 years).

All About Interest Rates

Most of us have been borrowing long enough—either to buy a car, go to college, or get this season's fashion must-haves—to understand what interest rates are and that we don't like them. An interest rate is an amount charged by a lender, calculated as a percentage of the loan amount. Interest rates are usually high on credit cards (sometimes above 20%), but thankfully lower on other forms of credit, like mortgages. And as we discussed in Chapter 1, interest paid on your mortgage is tax deductible.

In the 2000s, home mortgage interest rates hit record lows and were still hovering at a mere 4% in 2019. When this book went to print, they looked unlikely to climb anywhere near early-1980s levels (15% and up) in the foreseeable future. Nevertheless, with the economy in flux, we should expect some volatility.

You're not stuck with your first mortgage for life. If you sell the house, you'll get a new mortgage when you buy your next one. And if you decide to stay put, you can refinance your mortgage (essentially, trade it in for a better one) if rates drop and the value of your house holds steady or climbs. Though you might pay fees to refinance, it could be well worth it. (If the value of your house drops, however, refinancing might not be an option. After the market crisis in 2008, homeowners in this situation who were counting on refinancing found themselves instead pushed into foreclosure.)

Monthly Payments for a $100,000 Fixed Rate Mortgage

This chart shows the variation among monthly payments for a 30-year, $100,000 fixed rate mortgage at different interest rates.

Interest Rate	Monthly Payment
3.0%	$422
3.5%	$449
4.0%	$477
4.5%	$507
5.0%	$537
5.5%	$568
6.0%	$600
6.5%	$632
7.0%	$665
7.5%	$699
8.0%	$734

What Those Percentages Really Mean

Unfortunately, mortgage interest rates aren't always as straightforward as they appear. For one thing, you might see them expressed two different ways: as a base rate and as an annual percentage rate (APR). Those two numbers aren't going to be the same. The base rate is the actual rate used to calculate your payment, while the APR is the total cost of taking out the loan, factored out over the life of the loan and taking into account any fees you pay, like appraisal fees and credit reports. Lenders provide the APR because they're legally required to.

The APR should be a good indicator of what a loan really costs, except that it factors the costs *over the life of the loan*—and the chances of living in the same place for the whole term of a mortgage, without refinancing, are pretty low. However, the APR can be informative—like when a loan is advertised at a very low interest rate, but a slew of additional fees increase the cost dramatically.

Why You Might Not Be Offered the Advertised Interest Rate

To complicate matters, the rates you see advertised aren't necessarily what you'll be offered personally. For starters, interest rates change daily, so if you're looking at them on a Sunday, by Monday they could be higher or lower. And the rates you're offered will depend on some factors unique to you, such as:

- **The type of mortgage you choose.** You'll typically be offered a lower initial interest rate on an adjustable rate mortgage (ARM) than on a fixed rate mortgage. Notice we said *initial*—stay tuned for more on that later in this chapter.
- **How risky you are as a borrower.** If you have a history of paying bills on time, a steady high salary or other significant income, low debt, plan to make a hefty down payment, and request a loan that isn't humongous relative to your overall financial situation, you'll probably be offered a comparatively low interest rate. If the opposite is true, your rate might be higher, to compensate the lender for the added risk.
- **The loan-to-value ratio.** A large down payment tells the lender that you're not likely to walk away from your investment. A small one, however, makes the lender nervous. If you default, the lender will spend time and money chasing you down and might have to initiate foreclosure proceedings. Also, the lender could lose money, if you owe more than the house is worth. It protects itself from such risks by charging you higher interest.
- **Whether the loan can be resold.** Lenders often resell loans on the secondary mortgage market, discussed below. That frees up the lender's capital to make more loans (meaning make more money). If your loan doesn't qualify for resale, it's less desirable for the lender. You'll pay a premium to make up for that.

The Secondary Mortgage Market and Jumbo Loans

A whole market exists in which original lenders sell loans to secondary lenders. Usually the original lender is paid a flat fee upon sale, and the new lender gets to collect the rest of your mortgage payments, including interest.

Why does this matter to you? Because the primary players in this secondary market, Fannie Mae (the Federal National Mortgage Association) and Freddie Mac (the Federal Home Loan Mortgage Corporation), buy only those loans that meet certain financial criteria, including that the mortgage doesn't exceed a certain amount (which varies by location and is regularly adjusted: for 2019, it was $484,350 in most places, but as high as $726,525 in high-cost areas for a one-unit home).

- **Whether the loan has points.** Loans with points (an optional up-front fee) will normally come with a lower interest rate.

You can't be certain of the interest rate and the exact terms of your mortgage until you've selected and applied for it. But knowing what affects the rate will help you view all options with a critical eye.

All About Points

No, this isn't some obscure score in the homebuying game. A point is a loan fee equal to 1% of the principal on the loan (so one point on a $100,000 mortgage is $1,000). Points are added to the up-front cost of some mortgages in exchange for a lower interest rate. You probably won't be offered more than two or three points on a loan, because the lender would have to significantly reduce your interest rate to make it financially beneficial to you.

Depending on how far the interest rate is lowered, it can, in theory, be smart to get a loan with points, particularly if you have the cash, are planning to stay in your place for a while, and don't plan to refinance soon.

Paying points might work for some buyers, but it's not for everyone. As adviser Lisa Shaffer explains, "If you plan to keep the loan for only a couple of years, buying down the interest rate might not make sense—you might not be able to recoup the cost of the points you pay." It's worth discussing your long-term plans with your mortgage broker before locking in an interest rate—your broker can help you decide whether points make sense in your situation.

You can also run some comparative numbers on the latest loan offerings (with and without points). The table below (which shows how long you'd need to stay in a house to make up for your points payment through a lowered interest rate) and online calculators will help you with these comparisons.

When to Pay Additional Points for a Lower Interest Rate

Use this chart to determine how many years you should stay in a house to recoup the cost of points.

Additional Points	Interest Rate Reduction							
	⅛%	¼%	⅜%	½%	⅝%	¾%	⅞%	1%
0.25	2.3 yrs.	1.1	0.7	0.5	0.4	0.3	0.3	0.3
0.5	5.3	2.3	1.5	1.1	0.8	0.7	0.6	0.5
0.75	10.0	3.7	2.2	1.6	1.3	1.1	0.9	0.8
1.0	23.5	5.3	3.1	2.3	1.8	1.4	1.2	1.1
1.25		7.2	4.2	2.9	2.3	1.8	1.6	1.3
1.5		10.0	5.3	3.6	2.8	2.3	1.9	1.6
1.75		13.5	6.5	4.4	3.3	2.7	2.3	2.0
2.0		21.0	8.0	5.3	3.9	3.2	2.6	2.3
2.25	No matter how long you plan to have the loan, don't pay the extra points.	9.8	6.2	4.6	3.6	3.0	2.6
2.5		12.0	7.2	5.3	4.1	3.4	2.9
2.75		15.0	8.5	6.0	4.7	3.8	3.3
3.0		21.0	9.8	6.8	5.2	4.3	3.6
3.25			11.4	7.7	5.9	4.7	4.0
3.5			13.5	8.7	6.5	5.2	4.4

CHECK IT OUT

Ready to run some numbers? Various websites have calculators that allow you to figure out whether a points or no-points loan works best for you, such as Realtor.com, www.rpm-mtg.com, and Dinkytown.net. Also check out calculator apps from QuickenLoans, Zillow, and others.

For taxpayers who itemize, one advantage to points is that they're deductible in the year paid. In slow markets, sellers sometimes pay for points as an incentive to the buyer, and you can even deduct those.

Who's Got the Cash? Where to Get a Mortgage

There are two major players in the mortgage game, and both can help you get the loan you need. You might work with a mortgage broker, who will help you find the best available mortgage from among a variety of lenders. Or you might go straight to a lender (through a mortgage banker or loan officer), which will probably mean fewer options, but possibly a better deal. For more information on choosing a mortgage broker or lender, look back at Chapter 5.

Narrowing the Field: Which Type of Mortgage Is Best for You?

Mortgages come in two basic flavors: fixed rate mortgages and adjustable rate mortgages (also called ARMs). There are variations on these two types, and some are better for certain kinds of buyers than others. Though you'll discuss your unique situation with your broker or lender, you can first educate yourself about the options.

CHECK IT OUT

Mortgages have their own lingo. For a glossary that will help you decode it, go to www.mtgprofessor.com (under "Other Tools," click "Glossary").

Fixed Rate Mortgages

If you like predictability and stability, you'll probably like fixed rate mortgages. The interest rate is set when you get the loan and never changes. If you borrow $250,000 at 4.5% interest, you'll continue to pay 4.5% interest until you've paid off the loan.

> **TIP**
> **Despite the fixed rate, you're not actually paying the same amount of interest each month.** That's because in the early years of your loan when the principal is at its largest, you technically owe more interest. But the lender calculates your payment so it's the same amount each month (the loan is "amortized"). The way amortization shakes out, the interest you owe makes up a greater portion of your early monthly payments. As you gradually start to reduce the principal, less interest accrues, and so more of your payment goes to reducing principal. So, for example, on a 30-year $200,000 loan, at 4% interest, your monthly payments of $955 would include $667 of interest in the first payment and $3 in the last.

Beyond buyers who crave predictability, fixed rate mortgages are good for those who want to stay put long term, particularly if interest rates are low. Even if interest rates go sky-high, you'll have a fixed rate you can live with. You pay a premium for this stability, because fixed rate mortgages usually have higher starting interest rates than ARMs. That protects lenders who are stuck giving you a nice low rate for the full term of the loan, even when interest rates increase and other buyers are paying them more.

The Gold Standard: 30-Year Fixed

The ultimate in predictability and stability tends to be the 30-year fixed rate loan. It allows borrowers to finance their home purchase at a preset interest rate and pay it off over a full 30 years. These loans make sense for people who plan to live in their homes for several years. (Of course, you don't have to stay in your house that long.)

The Saver's Special: 15-Year Fixed

If you're extremely disciplined and can afford it, you might consider a shorter-term fixed loan, most typically a 15-year mortgage. Like any fixed rate mortgage, these have stable interest rates and predictable terms. By paying more each month, you ultimately pay less interest overall. As an added plus, you probably get a relatively low interest rate.

You can see why they're not as popular, however: Paying money back faster means committing yourself to relatively high monthly payments.

> **EXAMPLE:** Adina wants to take out a loan for $150,000 to buy a new condo. She can choose between a 30-year, fixed rate mortgage with a 4.5% interest rate, and a 15-year fixed rate mortgage with a 3.5% interest rate. With the first loan, Adina will have a monthly principal and interest payment of around $760. After 30 years, she'll have paid about $123,610 in interest. If Adina takes the second loan, she'll have a significantly higher principal and interest payment, approximately $1,072 each month. However, at the end of 15 years, she'll have paid off her mortgage and spent about $43,018 on interest ($80,592 less than with the 30-year mortgage).

Shorter-term fixed rate loans free your income for other purposes earlier than longer-term mortgages do. If you know you're going to want money for something else—for example, to pay college tuition, purchase a second home, or retire—such a loan can act as a serious forced savings plan.

That doesn't necessarily make it the most financially savvy option, however—especially not if you can make money by investing elsewhere or reducing your higher-interest debt (like on credit cards). For example, if you commit to a 15-year mortgage instead of contributing your money to a retirement plan, you could end up house rich but cash poor—with a place to retire in, but not enough money to do so. A better way to accomplish your savings goals might be to take out a longer-term loan and contribute the cash you've freed up to a 401(k) or an IRA.

As a compromise, some people take out a 30-year fixed rate loan but then make higher-than-required monthly payments to the loan principal.

The more principal you pay, the less interest accrues, so if you make early payments, you also end up paying less interest overall. While this strategy won't save you quite as much money as a shorter-term fixed rate loan would (since your interest rate will probably be a little higher), you face less future risk. If someday you can't afford to make more than the minimum payment, you're not locked in.

TIP

Put it to principal. If you decide to make a prepayment, be sure to follow your lender's instructions on how to allocate a payment toward principal. If, for example, you pay your mortgage online, you might have to check a box directing the funds towards the principal. If you pay by check, you might have to make a note on the check itself. If you get this wrong, the lender might apply the payment toward the next one that's due, which will defeat your purpose.

Adjustable Rate Mortgages

As the name implies, the interest rate on an adjustable rate mortgage (ARM) can fluctuate during the loan term—and no one can predict with certainty where interest rates will go. For buyers who aren't put off by this risk, or see buying their first home as a short-term stepping-stone, the ARM might be an attractive option.

The relatively low initial interest rates are certainly eye-catching and have made ARMs a favorite among new buyers.

But what about those fluctuating interest rates? They're definitely the main risk factor in an ARM. After the starter rate runs out, the rate adjusts periodically at an agreed-upon term. This term (called the adjustment period) may vary from one month to several years. Buyers in previous years were lured by lenders offering ridiculously low initial interest rates, only to find their payments completely unaffordable once the rate adjusted (sometimes, as quickly as a month later). This contributed to the very problems in the mortgage market that make lenders more careful about offering ARMs today.

When you're looking at the loan description for an ARM, check out a number called an index: The lender will adjust your rate to equal the index plus an extra amount, so that it makes a profit. That bit of profit, calculated as either a set amount or percentage, is called a margin.

Luckily, your lender doesn't get to invent the index. It will draw on a particular published, market-driven number. Common indexes include the London Interbank Offered Rate (LIBOR), the 11th Federal Home Loan Bank District Cost of Funds (COFI), U.S. Treasury Bills, or certificates of deposit (CDs). The LIBOR is usually the most volatile, meaning it jumps up or down quickly and dramatically, while the COFI is less volatile. Also, an index that averages rates over the long term (a year or every six months) is preferable to one that moves up and down based on the weekly "spot" rate.

Another number to seek out when comparing ARMs is the life-of-the-loan cap. This is a maximum on the ARM's total interest rate, no matter how high the index rises. The lender usually allows a well-padded 5%–6% above the starting interest rate, which can affect your monthly payment by hundreds or even thousands of dollars. Still, it's far better than getting an ARM without a life-of-the-loan cap—that's downright dangerous.

In addition to a life-of-the-loan cap, most ARMs limit how much your interest rate can increase at any adjustment period. This number is called the periodic cap. It's also a floor, limiting the amount the rate can decrease at one time. Look for an ARM that doesn't change by more than 2%–3% at each adjustment period. Otherwise, your monthly payment could shoot up very rapidly.

> EXAMPLE: On a $200,000 loan, you're choosing between a 30-year, fixed rate mortgage with a 4.5% interest rate and an ARM with an initial 4% rate. The life-of-the-loan cap on the ARM is 6% over the initial rate (10%). Your monthly principal and interest payment on the fixed rate loan would be approximately $1,013 and never increase above that. Your monthly payment on the ARM would start at approximately $955. However, if your interest rate adjusts to the maximum 10%, your payment could go as high as $1,755—about $800 more.

Traditional ARMs

The traditional ARM works like this: The loan starts out at a below-market interest rate, called a teaser rate. This rate adjusts frequently, as frequently as every month in some cases. As we've seen, that adjustment can make a big difference in your monthly payment.

In the past, many people who chose a traditional ARM couldn't really afford the home that they were hoping to buy—if you can only afford the monthly payment in the first few months when the interest rate is artificially low, what are you going to do when it goes up? Failing to recognize the possibility of a raise in ARM payments down the line is exactly what put many homeowners into foreclosure in 2008 and the years immediately following. As a result, lenders will no longer let homebuyers qualify for a mortgage based on their ability to make the initial, low ARM payments. You'll have to also show that you can afford higher ongoing payments.

With the benefits of easy loan qualification gone, and interest rates still low (at the time this book went to print), adviser Lisa Shaffer says, "I usually don't recommend ARMs to my clients right now, with the exception of hybrid fixed and adjustable rate mortgages" (discussed below).

CHECK IT OUT

Interested in a traditional ARM? You'll need to know what maximum amounts you could owe each month. Your mortgage broker should be able to calculate this for you, or you can use an online ARM payment calculator, like the ones at www.nolo.com/legal-calculators, www.interest.com, or www.dinkytown.net.

Interest-Only ARMs

The interest-only variety of ARMs were once very common, but now less so, having acquired a bad rap during the mortgage crisis. This is, at least at the beginning, just what it sounds like: You start out paying only the interest that accrues on the loan principal, making for very low monthly payments. The downside is that you don't reduce the amount you borrowed (there's no "P" or principal in your PITI). And of course, you have to start paying off the principal at some point—usually between three and ten years later. At that time, you'll have to pay much higher monthly payments.

Interest-only loans are attractive when home prices are going up fast, with first-time buyers squeezing into the market. These buyers hope to make the low monthly payments long enough for their house to rise in value, then either sell without having to pay off the loan principal or refinance on better terms.

Judging an ARM Beauty Contest

If you decide to get an ARM, here's a summary of the features to examine:

- **Initial interest rate.** This should be significantly less than is available on a fixed rate mortgage, to balance the added risk of rate increases.

- **Adjustment period.** Look for annual or biannual (not monthly) adjustment periods.

- **Index.** A slow-changing index (such as the COFI) is preferable to a rapidly changing, volatile one.

- **Life-of-the-loan cap.** Don't agree to pay a maximum interest rate greater than 6% above the initial rate.

- **Periodic cap.** The interest rate should change only a reasonable amount at each adjustment period; 2% is about right on a one-year ARM.

- **Low margin.** The margin should be as low as possible; around 2.2% on a six-month ARM or 2.5% on a one-year ARM.

- **No prepayment penalty.** You will almost never see these anymore, but watch out if you do. You don't want to be charged extra for making early payments or refinancing.

But as the fairly recent crash in most real estate markets showed, this can be a dangerous strategy. Leading up to the crash, buyers counted on the value of the property increasing, especially because their interest-only payments didn't increase their equity. When the value of the property dropped, many buyers faced a serious loss, particularly when forced to sell sooner than planned (maybe due to a job transfer or because they couldn't afford their monthly payments after the interest rate increased). And the buyer would remain responsible for paying the difference between the amount the house can be sold for and the remaining loan balance.

Buyers who pay down principal are in a much better position to weather unexpected drops in home prices. Even if forced to sell, they'll owe less than their interest-only counterparts, because they'll have built up some equity by reducing principal.

Hybrid Loans

Hybrid loans, like hybrid cars, can save you money. While hybrid cars do it by eating less gas, hybrid loans do it through lower interest rates. They're a safer and more realistic option for many first-time buyers who want to break into the market but don't plan to be in their first homes forever.

Someday, you'll be able to paint your front door red!

That's what homeowners in Scotland reportedly do after they've paid off their mortgage.

Hybrids work like this: For a set period of time, you pay interest at a fixed rate—usually, below the market rate on a regular fixed mortgage—and after that, the rate becomes adjustable. The fixed-rate term is usually three, five, seven, or ten years. The frequency of the adjustment varies, but it's usually every six months or one year. (A "5/1," for example, means that the rate is fixed for five years, then adjusts every year.)

That means you want to know how long you'll be in your home before signing up for a hybrid ARM. If you're not sure or you want to maximize flexibility and reduce risk, select a hybrid with a longer fixed-rate term (such as ten years). You might have to pay a slightly higher interest rate, but you'll save the cost of a refinance, if you realize at the end of the shorter term that you're not ready to go. And you'll save yourself the stress of trying to predict where you—and interest rates—are going to be in ten years.

Will You Face Discrimination by Mortgage Lenders?

Decades have gone by since the federal Fair Housing Act prohibited discrimination in mortgage lending based on race, color, religion, national origin, sex, familial status, or disability. Yet various studies and news reports indicate that the problem has not gone away.

For example, after The Center for Investigative Reporting analyzed 31 million records of Americans trying to get conventional mortgages in 2015 and 2016, it concluded that racial disparities continue in 61 U.S. metro areas. Discrimination against African Americans was particularly common in the South.

Researchers at UC Berkeley found that not even online lending, which is increasingly prevalent, has prevented instances of racial discrimination. In a 2018 study, these researchers concluded that minorities had paid 5.3 basis points (one basis point equals .01% of the purchase price) more up front to obtain the same mortgage interest rate as nonminority mortgage applicants, faring only a little better than they would have with in-person applications.

And a 2019 study reported on in the journal *Proceedings of the National Academy of Sciences* found that same-sex couples applying for mortgages were 73% more likely to be denied than opposite-sex couples. (Mortgage applications don't actually ask about sexual orientation, but they do ask about the applicants' gender.)

Such news could easily lead one to conclude that antidiscrimination laws aren't making a difference. Still, counsels adviser Sylvia Gutierrez, "There's no point in letting fear of discrimination stop you from applying to banks or lenders of any size for prime loans." If your mortgage application is denied, or the terms you're offered seem unfair, ask the lender what it based its decision on. Accusing it of unfair dealing is less likely to yield results than simply pressing it on its own standards.

Then, Gutierrez suggests, "Ask what you can do to better prepare your application. Sometimes it turns out that a simple adjustment can turn a 'no' into a 'yes,' such as fixing an error on your credit report or providing a court order showing that your ex-spouse is responsible for a joint car payment."

If you're still having no luck, Gutierrez offers one more suggestion: "Because commonality in culture sometimes helps an applicant better connect with the loan officer, find one who looks like you."

Getting Your Cash Together: Common Down Payment and Financing Strategies

Talk to someone who bought their first home over a decade ago, and you might hear, "We put zero down!" or "We got two mortgages so we could avoid private mortgage insurance!" But with the market having done a huge turnaround, such methods have nearly dropped off the map.

The Traditional: 80/20

Lenders feel safe with buyers who pay 20% down and finance the rest. If you're willing to pay that much up front, the lender is relatively confident that you're not going to default: You've already shown you're a serious saver, and you'll have a lot on the line. Even if you default, the lender has a good chance of collecting what it's owed if it sells the house through foreclosure, because you have more equity in the property. In turn, the advantage to you of putting 20% down is that you avoid paying for private mortgage insurance (PMI), and you'll pay less interest overall.

Of course, if you're in a very hot market, you might not want to wait until you've scraped together a 20% down payment. That's especially true if increasing prices mean you'll later have to pay even more for a house (uh oh, that 20% amount just became a moving target). You could end up being priced right out of the market. What's more, if values are rising while you're saving, you won't reap the benefits of the increased value—instead, you'll pay for it down the road, when you're finally able to afford a place.

> ### Not a Recommended Strategy
>
> **Homer:** *Homer Simpson does not lie twice on the same form. He never has and he never will.*
> **Marge:** *You lied dozens of times on our mortgage application.*
> **Homer:** *Yeah, but they were all part of a single ball of lies.*
>
> —The Simpsons

The Golden Past: Little or Nothing Down

While 100% financing was all the rage some years ago, lenders today almost universally don't allow borrowers to use it. If the value of the property drops and you haven't paid off a significant portion of the mortgage, the lender stands to lose everything. Many lenders are no longer willing to take that risk. However, many states and local governments offer down payment assistance for struggling buyers. Adviser Lisa Shaffer recommends, "Ask your mortgage professional about what down payment assistance programs might be available to you."

> **TIP**
>
> **Want to make a low down payment?** Check out FHA mortgages, described in Chapter 7.

Where Do I Look? Researching Mortgages

Once you understand your loan options, you can start researching where to get the best deals. We advise exploring several research avenues—everything from talking in person with a mortgage broker to researching loans online. Then you'll have plenty to choose from, or at least come up with lots of questions to ask a mortgage broker.

As you research, organize your findings within one folder or file. You might create a worksheet or spreadsheet to compare different mortgage features like interest rates, fees, or other terms or requirements. There's also one available on the Federal Trade Commission website (search for "FTC Mortgage Shopping Worksheet"). No need to fill out your worksheet for every mortgage—just the few you're seriously considering.

Online Mortgage-Related Sites

In addition to sites operated by individual lenders, various sites aggregate lender information and allow you to compare different loan options.

At Bankrate.com, for example, you can compare rates based on your geographic location, the amount you want to borrow, and the terms you're seeking. Then you can contact the prospective lenders directly to get more information.

 CHECK IT OUT

Check out these sites to compare different lenders:

- Bankrate.com

- HSH.com

- Trulia.com, and

- CompareInterestRates.com.

Be careful, however, about any websites that require you to enter personal information like your name, Social Security number, or address. In the worst case, you can actually agree to purchase a mortgage online—not the smartest impulse buy. More likely, you'll be contacted by potential lenders, or they'll check your credit history (and multiple inquiries can affect your credit score, though all checks within a 14-day window are treated as one).

Banks and Other Direct Lenders

You can also research rates through banks and other direct lenders (such as savings and loans, credit unions, and investment firms). You can do this online, pick up printed information that's available in bank lobbies or sent in the mail, or talk to a loan officer. Your options range from large national lenders to small local ones: Don't assume a bigger bank means a better loan.

Mortgage Brokers

A mortgage broker is an obvious resource and should be able to give you detailed information and help you get preapproved when you find a good loan. For more information on choosing a broker, refer back to Chapter 5.

I'll Take That One! Applying for Your Loan

Assuming you get preapproved for a loan (described in Chapter 3), you'll have already dealt with most of the necessary loan paperwork and given a lender a laundry list of your relevant financial information. (Even if you decide to work with another lender, you'll still have all the documents in one place.) If you don't get preapproved, you'll probably apply for a loan after you've made an offer on a house, and you might be pressed for time. Your contract will probably give you a few days to find satisfactory financing. The lender is still going to want the documents listed in Chapter 3, as well as those below.

Assembling Your Documents

After preapproval, and after you've chosen a house, but before the loan is finalized, your lender will need:

- **A copy of the house purchase contract.** Your real estate agent should be able to provide this directly to the broker or lender.
- **A preliminary title report.** (Called a "title insurance commitment" in some parts of the United States.) The title company should give this directly to the lender or broker. The report tells the lender whether the seller owns the property free and clear and whether there are any financial, legal, or other encumbrances on the property.
- **A property appraisal.** The appraisal report (which the lender will arrange for) tells the lender whether you're asking to borrow more than the house is worth. If the actual value of the home is lower than the purchase price, then the lender is not well protected if it has to foreclose, and the loan won't meet its loan-to-equity standards. Let's say the purchase price for your home is $500,000 and the lender is willing to lend you 80% of the home's value ($400,000). Your 20% down payment would be $100,000. But if the appraiser says the home is worth only $450,000, the lender would be willing to lend you only $360,000 (0.80 x $450,000 = $360,000). You'd likely have to come up with a $140,000 down payment to close the deal (unless the seller agrees to lower the price).

It's also typical for the lender to ask permission to get more financial information about you, either from you directly, or by contacting different entities that have that data. This can include getting not only your credit history, but also your employment records (from current and past employers), bank records, and possibly even IRS tax records.

ONLINE TOOLKIT

The "Financial Information for Lenders" checklist in the Homebuyer's Toolkit on the Nolo website includes a complete list of the documents you need to apply for a loan. (See the appendix for the link.)

Lesson learned the hard way **The mortgage paperwork will be ridiculous.** "I thought we were in good shape," said Catherine, who bought a condo in San Francisco. "Both my husband and I had gotten job promotions, and we'd saved up for a 20% down payment. Still, we had to supply reams and reams of paper. I sent the lender something like 12 months' worth of my checking account statements, which it went through line by line, asking about various transactions. They wanted to know, for instance, why I was paying someone $365 a month. It was to our dog walker!"

Filling Out the Application

Many lenders use a standard mortgage application form called the Uniform Residential Loan Application (sometimes called "Form 1003"), mainly because it's used by Fannie Mae and Freddie Mac. You might want to take a peek at the form before it's given to you, at www.fanniemae.com (search for "Form 1003"). Although the form is quite long, a lot of the information is stuff you already know. The rest, the loan officer or mortgage broker should be able to help you with.

In recent years, lenders have developed apps to help streamline the loan application process. Rather than making you complete a loan application line by line, these apps ask targeted questions and use your responses to auto-populate a completed loan application. Ultimately, however, you're responsible for making sure the information is accurate, truthful, and complete, so review the form carefully before signing.

Adviser Lisa Shaffer notes that changes are coming to the Uniform Residential Loan Application. A new version designed by Fannie Mae and Freddie Mac will be required for all loans originated after February 1, 2020.

TIP

Play it straight. Think a little fib on your application is no big deal? Watch out: It's known as mortgage fraud, and as mortgage broker Russell Straub explains, "It's rarely prosecuted on the front end, but if a mortgage goes bad and ends up in foreclosure, a scapegoat is usually looked for. The original application is scrutinized, and in the worst cases—which I've seen—borrowers go to jail."

How About Locking in a Rate?

Interest rates change frequently. If you apply for a loan and rates go up before the sale is complete, the lender will require you to pay the higher rate.

To avoid that, you can ask for a "lock in" or "rate lock." It ensures you get the interest rate quoted to you. If interest rates are on the rise, this is a great thing, especially if you can't afford a higher rate.

There are some downsides: Lock-ins are usually tied to a specific property, and they're usually short term. Typically, you can get a lock for 30 to 60 days without much trouble, but you might have to pay for it, perhaps in the form of extra points or a slightly elevated interest rate.

What if you're planning to buy a short-sale property (as discussed in Chapter 9)? Realize that the seller's lender might take several months to issue a final approval—probably more time than you can get a rate lock for. You will, according to mortgage broker Russell Straub, "really need to get an actual purchase contract with a fairly firm closing date in order to lock in an interest rate."

If you get a lock-in, make sure it's in writing and specifies the interest rate, closing costs, and any points you'll pay on the mortgage.

No later than the third business day after receiving your application, and no later than the seventh business day before the loan is consummated (typically when the loan documents are signed), the lender must deliver something called a "Loan Estimate" to you (or place it in the mail). Read this estimate carefully. It's designed to help you understand the key features, costs, and risks of the loan for which you applied. (The form replaced ones previously known as the "Good-Faith Estimate" and the initial "Truth-in-Lending disclosure.") It might be revised over the course of the transaction, however. For example, adviser Lisa Shaffer explains, "If the lender issues you a Loan Estimate prior to your locking an interest rate, the lender will issue a revised Loan Estimate within three days after the rate is locked."

Getting an Appraisal

The final step in your loan application process is for the property you are buying to be appraised. Lenders today have to order appraisals through an appraisal management company. The idea is that the appraiser is an independent third party who will provide a written, objective evaluation of the home, thus assuring the lender that the buyer will have enough equity to meet its lending guidelines.

The appraiser will take a careful look at the property, inside and out, and take numerous pictures to show your lender the quality of the home. The appraiser will also consider how the local real estate market is doing and comparable sales data from nearby homes.

If the appraiser says your house is worth as much as or more than the amount you're paying for it, and everything else in your application looks good, your loan should be approved.

If—as is common—the appraisal report indicates your planned purchase price is higher than the market value for the home, however, you could be in for complications. The lender will use the lower of the appraised value or the contract value in determining how much money it's willing to lend on the property. If the value of the property comes in lower than the contract price, you might have an option to "appeal" the appraisal. You would most likely do this by providing comparable sales information that might previously have been overlooked.

Sample Loan Estimate (page 1)

FICUS BANK
4321 Random Boulevard · Somecity, ST 12340

Save this Loan Estimate to compare with your Closing Disclosure.

Loan Estimate

DATE ISSUED	2/15/2013	**LOAN TERM**	30 years
APPLICANTS	Michael Jones and Mary Stone	**PURPOSE**	Purchase
	123 Anywhere Street	**PRODUCT**	Fixed Rate
	Anytown, ST 12345	**LOAN TYPE**	☒ Conventional ☐FHA ☐VA ☐ _____
PROPERTY	456 Somewhere Avenue	**LOAN ID #**	123456789
	Anytown, ST 12345	**RATE LOCK**	☐ NO ☒ YES, until 4/16/2013 at 5:00 p.m. EDT
SALE PRICE	$180,000		*Before closing, your interest rate, points, and lender credits can change unless you lock the interest rate. All other estimated closing costs expire on 3/4/2013 at 5:00 p.m. EDT*

Loan Terms

		Can this amount increase after closing?
Loan Amount	$162,000	**NO**
Interest Rate	3.875%	**NO**
Monthly Principal & Interest *See Projected Payments below for your Estimated Total Monthly Payment*	$761.78	**NO**
		Does the loan have these features?
Prepayment Penalty		**YES** • As high as **$3,240** if you pay off the loan during the first 2 years
Balloon Payment		**NO**

Projected Payments

Payment Calculation		Years 1-7		Years 8-30
Principal & Interest		$761.78		$761.78
Mortgage Insurance	+	82	+	—
Estimated Escrow *Amount can increase over time*	+	206	+	206
Estimated Total Monthly Payment		**$1,050**		**$968**

		This estimate includes	In escrow?
Estimated Taxes, Insurance & Assessments *Amount can increase over time*	**$206** a month	☒ Property Taxes ☒ Homeowner's Insurance ☐ Other: *See Section G on page 2 for escrowed property costs. You must pay for other property costs separately.*	**YES** **YES**

Costs at Closing

Estimated Closing Costs	$8,054	Includes $5,672 in Loan Costs + $2,382 in Other Costs – $0 in Lender Credits. *See page 2 for details.*
Estimated Cash to Close	$16,054	Includes Closing Costs. *See Calculating Cash to Close on page 2 for details.*

Visit **www.consumerfinance.gov/mortgage-estimate** for general information and tools.

But think twice: What if you really did agree to pay an excessive price? Unless the property is uniquely valuable to you, you might not want to buy it at that price after all—or should at least commission an independent appraisal. (And you should be legally able to back out, based on your contract's "financing contingency," to be discussed in Chapter 10.)

Monitoring Your Loan Once You're Approved

After you're approved for the loan, you can focus your energy on other things. Trust us, plenty of other tasks will be competing for your attention. But realize that the loan isn't actually made until the day you close on the house. It's worth staying in touch with your broker or lender, particularly if you have continuing concerns about the terms of your loan or approval. Also be mindful of any date restrictions (for example, lock-in deadlines) as you finish the purchase process.

But before you forget about the details of your loan entirely, make sure you get a Loan Estimate from the lender. You're entitled to receive this document within three days of applying for your loan.

Lenders are required to give you a standard form that looks like the sample above. Read it carefully. It spells out some very important details about the loan you're getting—for example, the initial interest rate, the initial payment amount, whether the amount can rise, and whether the loan has a prepayment penalty or balloon payment.

 ONLINE TOOLKIT

The Homebuyer's Toolkit on the Nolo website contains a blank "Loan Estimate." (See the appendix for the link.) A partial sample is shown above.

New-Home Financing

If you're buying a newly constructed home, the developer is likely to offer you some unique financing alternatives. The usual possibilities include closing costs paid by the developer, mortgage subsidies (buydowns), or allowances for upgrades like higher-quality fixtures. All are more common when developers have large numbers of unsold properties and there's a large supply of new homes on the market. (And in particularly slow markets, developers might offer packages featuring everything from cruises to free fireplaces!)

Mortgage Rate Buydowns

To make its houses more affordable, a developer may offer to "buy down" your mortgage. That means subsidizing the interest rate you pay for the first two or three years by prepaying part of the mortgage interest. In a 2-1 buydown, for example, you pay a below-market interest rate (and make reduced mortgage payments) the first year of the loan, and a slightly higher (but still below-market) rate the second year, with the developer filling in the gaps. The two-year period is meant to cover the time when money is usually tightest for first-time homebuyers. The rate adjusts to market levels in its third year.

EXAMPLE:

Year	Interest rate you pay	Monthly payment on a $300,000 fixed rate, 30-year mortgage
1	2.5%	$1,185
2	3%	$1,265
3–30	3.5%	$1,347

Depending on the particular developer, you might be able to apply a buydown to a mortgage you find yourself. Other developers might limit buydowns to mortgages offered through their preferred lender. You usually need good credit to qualify for this type of program.

And as with any loan package, make sure the buydown works for you—will you really be able to pay the increased mortgage payments after the initial reduced-rate period? If there are any strings attached, such as high initial points or above-market interest rates after the buydown period ends, also consider how much you'll end up paying over the life of that loan. If you can afford higher monthly payments from the start, you might find a more competitive mortgage elsewhere. Use the mortgage calculators recommended in Chapter 6 to compare mortgage options.

TIP

Don't lock in your mortgage interest rate for an unrealistically short time if purchasing a newly constructed home. As Florida loan officer Sylvia M. Gutierrez cautions, "Construction delays are common, and interest-rate extension fees will cost you real money. Some lenders will offer you extended rate lock periods for an additional fee. If you don't have this, you might want to consider waiting to lock in your interest rate until the property has been issued the Certificate of Occupancy from the county or city. Only then can you have some real idea as to the expected settlement date."

Other Developer Financing Incentives

Many developers offer special financing deals to new homebuyers who use the developer's in-house or preferred lender. In some cases, the lender has done a blanket appraisal of all houses in the particular development, so you don't have to pay for a new appraisal. The lender will probably also offer special mortgage programs, often with faster or easier approval for creditworthy purchasers and simpler closing procedures. To seal the deal, developers might offer to pay closing costs or points; provide upgrades, such as better-quality carpet or countertops; even offer gift certificates for home design stores.

Although the developer might present its in-house financing as the world's greatest deal or even the only possible deal, don't cave to the pressure without doing your research. It might seem easier (time- and paper-wise) to go with the developer's recommendation, but that convenience likely comes at a price—namely, above-market interest rates. Particularly if the developer is anxious to sell, you might instead get a loan from another lender but negotiate with the developer for another benefit like a lower purchase price (a better deal than most financial incentives); a mortgage buydown; extra features, such as more closets or built-in bookshelves; or upgrades such as higher-quality lighting.

Unique Financial Considerations for Co-op Buyers

Much of the standard financial advice regarding homeownership doesn't apply to co-ops. Here's a summary of what's different:

- **Two-tiered financing.** Two loans are often involved with co-ops. First, the cooperative will take out a mortgage for its purchase of the property (which you'll probably help pay for, as part of your regular maintenance fees). Later, you'll probably need a loan to purchase your shares.
- **Higher down payment.** Co-op boards frequently require buyers to make large down payments—often upwards of 25% of the purchase price. Your co-owners have good reason for this: They want to make sure you're in sound financial shape and can afford your monthly maintenance payments.
- **Higher interest rates.** Some lenders are reluctant to finance co-op purchases, because if a buyer fails to pay on time, there's no house to foreclose on, only intangible shares in a corporation. Fewer willing lenders and greater risk translates into higher interest rates.
- **Tax deductions.** Tax deductions for co-op mortgage and maintenance payments are more complicated than for condo or single-family home payments. While the co-op management will help you calculate how much of the maintenance payment can be deducted (if you itemize), you might need to consult a tax professional.
- **Flip taxes.** A "flip tax" is a misnomer—it's really a transfer fee levied by the co-op when a member sells. It can be calculated different ways: for example, based on the number of shares the seller holds, a flat amount, or the sale price. Usually the seller is responsible for this fee, but the seller can pass it off to the buyer.

What's Next?

You've probably got a good idea of which traditional method for financing your home will work for you, if any. But before making your final decision, you might want to consider alternative financing methods, discussed in Chapter 7. It covers such methods as borrowing from family or friends or getting government-assisted or seller-backed financing.

Mom and Dad? The Seller? Uncle Sam? Loan Alternatives

Meet Your Adviser

Timothy Burke, founder and CEO of National Family Mortgage (www.nationalfamilymortgage.com), based in Waltham, Massachusetts. National Family Mortgage has facilitated over $1 billion in mortgage loans between relatives.

What he does "Despite what the 'CEO' title might suggest, I'm part of a small business (launched in late 2010) where everyone works as part of a team, each person doing a bit of everything. A good part of my time is spent interacting directly with clients; we've helped thousands of families across the U.S. properly document and manage over $1 billion in mortgage loans between relatives. I also deal with company finances, marketing, connecting with press, and more."

First house "In 2016, my wife and I purchased an old New England farmhouse built in 1770. The home has been renovated several times over the years and is in wonderful condition. In fact, it's such a great home that we were initially confused by what we felt was a very competitive listing price, given the size and location. Our Realtor explained that so many buyers in greater Boston are looking for new or recent construction, older properties turn away the majority of eligible buyers. As a result, the home was priced to sell, and its age worked to our advantage!"

Fantasy house "We're still loving our first home and feel grateful to be the stewards of such a special place. When my wife and I sit in our dining room, we often imagine the exciting dinner conversations that have occurred there over the last 250 years. Our house is older than the United States of America! The family that sold it to us maintained beautiful gardens on the one-acre grounds, and we've already enjoyed several relaxing evenings enjoying the natural beauty. Now, we have to learn to garden!"

Likes best about his work	"It's very rewarding when clients return to us to structure additional loans. That tells us that we're doing something right. And I do feel like National Family Mortgage is part of some exciting changes in the way people engage with financial services and handle their finances. Why pay a bank if you don't have to? The financial crisis of 2008 changed the way Americans handle their personal finances. It might sound cheesy, but I feel like we're helping make dreams come true, in a win-win transaction that hopefully benefits everyone."
Top tip for first-time homebuyers	"Don't focus solely on the purchase price and mortgage payments. You'll need to get ready for a host of new expenses that come with homeownership: like maintenance, property taxes, landscaping, furniture, and if you live in an area like mine, snow removal! I'd suggest doing a complete review of your spending habits, lifestyle goals, and ideally retirement plan (the earlier you start saving, the more effectively your nest egg will grow), in order to properly budget for a home you'll be able to afford over the long term."

With competing payment pressures from student loans and other bills, and the high cost of housing, it's hard—if not impossible—to come up with all the cash needed to buy a house. You might be struggling to get a down payment together or to qualify for a mortgage. Most traditional loans don't provide much flexibility, either, especially if down the road you want to make an adjustment to your payment schedule.

If this sounds familiar, we suggest you look into alternative, more flexible or affordable forms of financing. (Yes, this could mean your mother—but keep reading; it might be worth it.) We'll cover:

- gifts or loans from family members and friends
- financing directly from your house's seller
- low-down-payment loan programs available through federal, state, and local agencies, and
- special financing options available for new homes, such as direct financing from developers (buydowns).

No Wrapping Required: Gift Money From Relatives or Friends

Don't be shy: Many first-time homebuyers (around one-quarter of those age 38 and younger) get some gift money from a relative (usually their parents) or a friend, according to the National Association of Realtors 2019 Home Buyer and Seller Generational Trends report. If used for the down payment, such gifts help buyers reduce their monthly mortgage payments or increase the amount of house they can afford. Large gifts may even be used to finance the entire purchase. Some buyers also seek gifts for moving costs, home furnishings, and remodeling.

By making your home purchase possible, the giver gets not only emotional satisfaction, but possible financial and tax benefits. If someone is planning on leaving you money by inheritance anyway, a gift is a way to reduce the size of their taxable estate (very large gifts can be taxed, though the laws on this are continually in flux). Better yet, your parents or other gift givers can watch you enjoy the money during their lifetime, rather than watch you pay extra interest to a bank.

CAUTION

If you're expected to pay it back, it's not a "gift." Adviser Timothy Burke says, "That might sound obvious, but I notice that a lot of folks, especially young people; tend to think of a 'loan' as money coming exclusively from a bank, but view all financial help from family, even if there's an expectation of repayment, as a gift. If you represent to your primary mortgage lender that the money coming from your family is a gift when you actually have every intention of paying it back, you might—even if unwittingly—be committing mortgage fraud. The lender is keenly interested in the difference, as it will factor loans into your debt-to-income ratio for loan qualification purposes, while leaving gift money out of the equation."

For advice on approaching your parents or others for a cash gift, see the discussion below on borrowing money from family or friends.

How Gift Givers Can Avoid Owing Gift Tax

Believe it or not, the IRS attempts to keep track of cash gifts—and if someone makes total gifts over a certain amount during his or her lifetime, that person's estate can end up owing "gift tax," even though the recipients of the money don't! Fortunately, not every gift counts toward this total, and the gift giver has to give away quite a bit of money for it to apply. Anyone can give a tax-free gift up to $15,000 per year to another person (2019 figure; it's indexed to go up with inflation) without any tax implications. That means, for example, that every year, your mother and father can give you $30,000 (plus $30,000 to your spouse or partner, if you have one), without it counting against the lifetime tax-free limit.

> **EXAMPLE:** Leslie and Howard would like to buy a house for $300,000 and hope to raise a 20% down payment, or $60,000. If each set of parents gives Leslie and Howard $30,000, the couple have reached the needed amount, with no tax liability or reporting requirement for anyone.

If a relative or friend wishes to give you more than $15,000 during a single year, that person will need to file a gift tax return (Form 709) with the IRS. This doesn't mean the gift giver will have to pay gift taxes, because computing the gift tax debt is (as of recent years) put off until the giver's death. At that time, the first $11.4 million of all the gifts made over the person's lifetime will be exempt from the tax (2019 figure).

For more information, see IRS Publication 559, *Survivors, Executors, and Administrators*, available at www.irs.gov; and the Wills, Trusts & Probate section of Nolo.com. If a sizable amount of money is involved, your relative or other gift giver should consult an estate planning or tax attorney.

Why You Need—And How to Get—A Gift Letter

If you use gift money to buy your house (not just your furniture), your bank or mortgage lender will require written documentation from the gift giver stating that the money is in fact a gift, not a loan. Remember, the lender is carefully evaluating how heavy a debt load you'll have. It wants to make sure it's not competing with another creditor for your monthly payments.

The "gift letter" should specify the amount of the gift, your relationship to the gift giver, and the type of property (the exact address, if you've already selected a property) for which the money will be used. Most important, it should state that the money need not be repaid. Ask the gift giver for a letter or prepare your own for the giver's signature. Your lender might also have a gift letter form.

 ONLINE TOOLKIT

The Homebuyer's Toolkit on the Nolo website includes a "Gift Letter" you can tailor to your situation. A sample is shown below. (See the appendix for the link.)

If the gift money hasn't been transferred to your account yet, the lender might want verification that the money is available, including the name of the financial institution where the money is kept, the account number, and a signed statement giving the mortgage lender authority to verify the information.

Gift Letter

A relative or friend should prepare this gift letter for your bank or other lender. Before finalizing the letter, check with your lender to make sure that it includes all required information, such as evidence of the donor's ability to provide these gift funds.

Date: _____

To: _[name and address of bank or lender]_____:

I/We _____[name(s) of gift giver(s)]_____ intend to make a GIFT of
$ _[dollar amount of gift]_ to _____[name(s) of recipient(s)]_____,
my/our ___[relationship, such as daughter]___, to be applied toward the
purchase of property located at: __[address of the house you're buying,__
__if known]__.

There is no repayment expected or implied in this gift, either in the form
of cash or by future services, and no lien will be filed by me/us against the
property.

The SOURCE of this GIFT is: __[the account the gift is coming from]_____.

Signature of Donor(s):

_____

_____

Print or Type Name(s) of Donor(s):

_____

_____

Address of Donor(s): Street, City, State, Zip:

_____

Telephone Number of Donor(s):

_____

Preventing Emotional Fallout From Gift Money or Family Loans

To avoid family blow-ups, it's usually best if parents or relatives discuss the gift or loan with other close relatives (like your siblings). They might do well to make similar gifts or loans on the same terms to all children and document the transactions. Preferential treatment, or lack of documentation of intentions, are known to cause jealousy and conflict, especially if loans remain outstanding at the time of death and the children have differing recollections of the parents' intentions.

All in the Family: Loans From Relatives or Friends

Private loans are another popular way to finance a home: About 6% of homebuyers ages 38 or younger borrow money from family or friends, according to NAR. (And that's just for their down payment. It doesn't include those few lucky buyers whose parents lend them the entire purchase amount.)

Before you say, "Oh no, not my family," consider that the numbers probably wouldn't be this high unless there was something in it for the family member or friend, too. Take a look at the total amount of interest you're likely to pay before your mortgage is paid off—wouldn't it be better to keep that amount within the family?

This section will explore private (also called intrafamily) loans, including:

- different ways to structure a loan from family or friends
- the benefits for borrower and lender
- how to raise the issue with your family member or friend, and
- dealing with the legal and tax issues concerning private financing.

Structuring the Loan

You can use a loan from family or friends for your:

- **First mortgage.** You could sidestep the traditional lending industry and finance your entire purchase price with a mortgage loan from your relatives, friends, or others.

- **Second mortgage.** A private loan may also be used to supplement a bank mortgage. This would be a similar arrangement to what was once available from conventional lenders, called an "80/10/10" loan or "piggyback loan." It basically means making a down payment of less than 20% (10%, maybe), getting a conventional mortgage for the bulk of the purchase price (perhaps, but not necessarily, 80%), and then borrowing the remainder (say, 10%) elsewhere— or in your case, from friends or family. You'll end up making two payments each month: one on the primary, bank loan, and one on the secondary, family loan. A major advantage if you can't afford a 20% down payment is that this arrangement lets you avoid paying PMI. For its protection, your private lender will record the mortgage publicly, thus getting in line behind the bank for repayment if the house is foreclosed on. It's unwise to forgo this step unless the loan is relatively small (less than $10,000), for the reasons discussed below.

- **Down payment.** Borrowing from friends and family to help with your down payment is also a possibility. How would this differ from setting up a second mortgage, as described above? First off, if the loan amount is small enough, arranging all the paperwork for an actual secured mortgage might not be worthwhile for you or your family lender. Second, if you tell a conventional lender to which you're applying for a loan that you're "borrowing down payment money," it will likely get confused and insist that the friend or family member sign a gift letter. (The reasons are technical: To a lender, "down payment" means "equity," which is the very opposite of debt, end of story. But to further complicate matters, the FHA has no such hangups about use of loans to fund down payments—we'll discuss FHA loans later in this chapter.)

If you're borrowing part of the house's purchase price from an institutional lender, check whether it requires you to structure your private loan in a certain way or limits the amount you can privately borrow. For example, if you're borrowing down payment money, many institutional lenders require that at least 5% of the purchase price comes from your own funds.

Especially if a sizable amount of money is involved, you should get some advice on how to structure the loan from a real estate attorney.

Benefits of Intrafamily Loans to the Borrower

Some of the reasons that first-time homebuyers turn to family and friends for help financing their houses include:

- **Interest savings and tax deductions.** Family and friends often charge 1½% to 2% interest points less than conventional lenders, resulting in thousands of dollars in savings over the life of the loan. And, if you document the loan properly (as we describe below) and itemize your tax deductions, you should be able to deduct the mortgage interest charged, just as with a traditional mortgage.

- **Flexible repayment structures.** While a bank is probably going to require an unchanging monthly payment schedule, a private mortgage holder might be more flexible. For example, you might mutually agree that you'll make quarterly (not monthly) payments or delay all payments for the first few years. And if, down the road, you want to temporarily pause payments (perhaps to take unpaid leave from work after the birth of your first child), your parents or another private lender might agree to that. Good luck finding such a flexible institutional lender.

- **No points or loan fees.** Institutional lenders often charge thousands of dollars in loan application and other fees. Family and friends don't.

- **Easier qualifying.** Your relatives or friends probably won't require that you have a great credit score. You qualify as long as your lender trusts that you'll pay back the loan. Of course, a "yes" isn't automatic, but as adviser Timothy Burke points out, "Family members tend to have a better sense than anyone of whether their child or other relation can be counted on to honor their debt."

- **Saving on private mortgage insurance.** If you borrow more than 80% of the house purchase price from an institutional lender, you'll have to pay PMI. By borrowing privately, you can avoid this cost.

- **Minimal red tape.** To borrow from an institutional lender, you must fill out an application form and provide documentation verifying every item on the form, then wait for approval. Friends and family don't usually adopt this level of scrutiny.

- **Better deal on the house.** If you've arranged private financing in advance and can close quickly, sellers who are time pressured might accept a slightly lower offer.

- **No lender-required approval of house's physical condition.** Private lenders don't usually require that a house's major defects be repaired before closing, as some institutional lenders do. That would let you buy a fixer-upper and take care of its defects later. (Of course, you should still have the house professionally inspected.)

Benefits of Intrafamily Loans to the Lender

Here are a few ways that making a private loan can also benefit your family members or friends:

- **Competitive investment return.** You can offer to pay an interest rate that's higher than your lender could get on a comparable low-risk investment like a money market account or certificate of deposit (CD). (And you're still likely to pay less than you would to a bank.)
- **Ongoing source of income.** Some investments just sit there and gain in value or pay occasional dividends. With your private loan, your lender will receive regular payments from you, which can be reinvested.
- **A financially liquid asset.** Some investments, such as long-term CDs, are hard to cash out in an emergency. Don't worry; we're not saying your family lender can change his or her mind. But he or she can potentially sell your mortgage to someone else. (There is a secondary market for the purchase and sale of existing mortgages, or you might be able to refinance if your lender wants out.)
- **Low risk.** Your parents or other private lender can count on two things: first, your commitment to repay the loan, somehow, someday, even if the original repayment schedule needs to be rejiggered; and second, that your house offers collateral. If worse comes to worst, you can sell it and repay the loan. (Or your lender can foreclose on you, though few would ever do that.)
- **Estate planning protection.** If your family members were planning to leave you money anyway, this lets them get a head start. By leaving a clear paper trail, they reduce the possibility for complications and transfer of money outside the family in the event of a later divorce, death, or remarriage.
- **Emotional satisfaction.** Don't underestimate the sense of achievement that your loved ones get by watching you gain a foothold in the world, with their help.

If all this sounds unrealistically rosy, consider Timothy Burke's experience: "Not only do we see return customers, as I mentioned, but the default rate among our clients is very low—under 1%. When a borrower can't make the payments, it's usually due to a legitimate crisis, such as a medical emergency. In that case, the family lender is typically quite willing to restructure the loan in some way. As long as you go into this arrangement with clear expectations, and document it properly, it can create a sense of mutual support, not conflict."

Best thing I ever did

Borrow from Mom and Dad. When Amy decided to buy a 1904 farmhouse in Northampton, Massachusetts, she assumed she'd get her mortgage from a bank. Then, her mother made her an offer she couldn't refuse: Borrow $180,000 from Mom and Dad, at a (then-)competitive 5.75% interest rate. Her mother figured, "Why is my daughter paying the bank when she could be paying me?" In addition to helping their daughter, Amy's parents earned a decent yield on a low-risk investment, not easy in these days of low interest rates. "It's a little bit scary borrowing from your parents, but this is an official thing," says Amy. And her mother jokes, "The mortgage was actually $173,000, but she wanted a little extra for shoes."

Will Private Financing Work for You?

Still feeling hesitant? The following questions will help you decide whether private financing will work for part or all of your home financing:

- **How much money do you need?** If it's $5,000 or $10,000 to help with the down payment, that will probably be a lot easier to come by than $50,000 or $100,000.
- **How long do you need to borrow the money for?** Some private lenders may be fine with a ten- or 20-year repayment period (and for tax reasons, might actually prefer a longer term). But if your relative or friend wants the money completely repaid in a few years, make sure such an arrangement is financially feasible for you.
- **Do you have any other options?** Is your credit so bad that no bank will approve the loan (or you'll qualify only at really unfavorable terms)?

- **Does a close relative or friend have the money to lend for the amount and term you need?** If your parents are well-off but are going to need money soon for retirement or to pay your brother's college tuition, they might not be in a position to help.
- **What are the personal costs to you?** If you risk hurt or jealous feelings of siblings, cousins, or others; a sense of perpetual debt or guilt; or similar hazards, the loan might not be worth it.
- **What are the costs to set up a private loan?** Getting specialized help from an attorney and accountant to structure your private mortgage might run in the thousands. Companies like National Family Mortgage might be able to set up and manage the loan for much less. Or, just go back to your conventional lender, especially if the private loan would be fairly small (say, less than $10,000).
- **Does your family member or friend trust you?** Your lender wants assurance that you'll eventually pay the money back, so not only love, but trust, will be key. If you have a history of credit problems and debts, you'll need to show concrete evidence—to your lender and yourself—that you've learned how to responsibly handle debt.

How to Approach Mom, Dad, or Another Private Lender

Even people who are convinced that private loans are a win-win proposition might blanch at the thought of asking for one. But if you approach it like a business proposition, it's not so hard. You're offering a loan at a fair rate of interest, secured by a promissory note and a mortgage.

Unfortunately, family loans are enough of a business proposition that, in some cases, they may fall under the federal Dodd-Frank Act, which is implemented by the Consumer Financial Protection Bureau and governs mortgage lender licensing. Because of this, you might want to consult an attorney before getting too deep into proposing a loan to your family member—particularly if it's not a member of your immediate family (parent, child, spouse, sibling, grandparent, or grandchild).

Here's a little more on why Dodd-Frank might affect you: Although most state laws regarding mortgage transactions contain exemptions for loans made within the family, and indeed Dodd-Frank contains a similar exemption, it applies that exemption only to "immediate family." Aunts and uncles, for example, would be expected to comply with Dodd-Frank, as if they were a mortgage lending company. And just figuring out the compliance requirements could be a huge hassle—which, again, is why we suggest checking in with an attorney for help.

To present it this way, of course, you'll need to find the appropriate time and place. Never surprise a potential lender by blurting out a request at a social event or an informal occasion. Make an appointment, even if you see your parents (or brother or old roommate) regularly and the formality seems odd. Give them a general idea of what you want to talk about, but save the details. For example, you might say, "As you know, I'm actively house hunting now and looking for various ways to finance this. Rather than go into all the details now, I'd like to sit down and talk with you about this." If you sense resistance, back off gracefully.

If you get a positive response, schedule a specific time to meet. Be prepared to discuss your proposition logically and honestly. Ideally, you will have done a lot of homework trying to arrange a loan from a traditional lender, so you'll have all the numbers at your fingertips. Bring along photocopies of all relevant documents, such as the financial materials you pulled together for your bank or other lender.

Prepare a separate one-page list of key terms and issues you want to discuss with a relative or friend, including:

- the amount you want to borrow, at what interest rate and repayment schedule (see below for advice)
- the amount of money you have available for the down payment (the higher it is, the lower the lender's risk of loss)
- your financial ability to make monthly payments (even without setting rigid qualification rules, your lender will want to know)
- the financial protections you'll offer the lender (a promissory note and mortgage, as described below), and
- the financial benefits to the lender (how your proposed interest rate compares to money market and CD rates).

When you meet, give the potential lender ample time to ask questions, and don't expect a decision on the spot.

The Loan Amount and House Purchase Price

How much you'll ask for depends on how much you expect to pay for your house and how much you think your parents or other private lender can spare. Your intrafamily loan will most likely be a second mortgage, to supplement financing from a bank or another traditional lender. The terms "first" and "second" literally refer to who gets paid first if there's a foreclosure. Your bank or institutional lender will no doubt insist on being the first in line, regardless of the size of its loan.

Your house purchase price won't be exact unless you've already made an offer and had it accepted. If you're still looking, be prepared to show the potential lender a close estimate, based on the price range you're looking in. If your private lender wants to make sure the house you find will be worth what you plan to pay, offer to get it appraised prior to purchase (if you're not already doing that for an institutional lender).

The Interest Rate You Propose to Pay

For a private loan, the interest rate you and your lender pick can in theory be anything between 0% and the limit set by usury law in your state. But for practical as well as tax reasons, it's best to charge a rate that's higher than the Applicable Federal Rate (or AFR; more on that below) but lower than what you'd pay to an institutional lender. Propose paying a little less than half the difference between these two. For example, if fixed rate mortgages cost 3.5% and the AFR is at 2%, you might propose paying 2.75% interest.

Websites such as CompareInterestRates.com, Bankrate.com, and HSH.com will give you a sense of current institutional interest rates. A simple search for "IRS AFR" should bring you to the right page, or you can find it posted on www.nationalfamilymortgage.com. By the way, although the AFR and interest rates change month by month, your loan doesn't have to follow suit—it's fine to stick with the rate you settle on initially, in the month you sign the loan.

ONLINE TOOLKIT

Use the "Private Loan Terms Worksheet" in the Homebuyer's Toolkit on the Nolo website to organize your presentation to a parent or another private lender. (See the appendix for the link.)

Check the AFR: Too-Low Interest May Cause Your Lender Tax Problems

The IRS sets a minimum rate for private loans, called the Applicable Federal Rate (AFR), each month. The exact percentage varies but is usually less than bank mortgage rates and higher than money market account or CD rates. In mid-2019, the AFR averaged a little less than 3% for long-term loans (those lasting longer than nine years). For the current rate, search the IRS website at www.irs.gov.

What's the big deal if your private lender charges you less than the AFR —or even no interest at all? No problem for you (who wouldn't want a low interest rate?), but there might be tax ramifications for the lender. This is mainly an issue if you're borrowing a substantial amount of money from a relative or friend, or receiving a loan on top of a gift that exceeded the $15,000 annual exclusion. If the interest rate doesn't meet the AFR, the IRS will "impute" the interest to your lender—meaning it will act as though your lender really received the AFR-level interest on the loan. The question then becomes, where did the interest money go? Aha, reasons the IRS, your lender gave it right back to you, as a gift. Then the IRS can demand that the private lender file a gift tax return for any amount over the annual gift tax exclusion.

Also, even if your private lender charges you less than the "imputed" interest rate, the IRS requires him or her to report interest income at the imputed rate. If the lender doesn't and is audited, and the IRS discovers the omission (unlikely), the IRS will readjust the lender's income using the imputed interest rate and charge the tax owed on the readjusted income plus a penalty. Theoretically, the IRS could zap the giver under both income and gift tax rules.

TIP

Is your family reluctant to charge you that much? Tell them they can always decide later to "forgive" you some or all of your payments, of not only interest but principal. For tax reasons, they should write you a letter referencing the loan and stating the amount they're forgiving. They'll also have to factor this decision into their gift tax obligations—forgiven loan payments are considered gifts. And it's best not to structure the whole loan with the assumption you'll never repay—the IRS sees this as a fraudulent way of avoiding gift tax, by stretching a one-time gift out over several years.

Other Proposed Loan Terms

You don't need to go into your discussion with a completely drafted loan agreement—after all, part of your objective will be to negotiate those details with the lender. Still, you can show that you've thought carefully about how to structure the loan profitably for both of you, by suggesting a:

- repayment schedule (such as monthly or quarterly)
- mortgage term (length)
- payment amount, and
- the plan if things go wrong, such as late payments and fees you will owe, what constitutes loan default, and loan restructuring options.

Again, be sure to run these by your institutional lender, if any, before finalizing your loan agreement with a relative or friend, to make sure you won't be undermining your qualification for institutional financing.

Gracias, Arigato, Merci

Find a way to show your thanks for a gift or loan—a card, lunch at your new house, and maybe more. But be aware that, depending on your relationship with your relatives, they might also expect frequent stays in your new guest room, your rapt attention as they give decorating advice, or that they can comment on your spending habits. Then again, some might act like this without having contributed to your house purchase!

Creating Your Loan Documents

If your relative or friend agrees to lend you money, you'll need to finalize the loan with the proper legal paperwork. A handshake isn't good enough for anyone. For one thing, it's easy to misunderstand something you've only talked about. Clarifying and writing your agreement down now avoids disputes, as well as memory lapses down the line. For another, failing to record your lender's mortgage on the property leaves that person out in the cold if some other lender or creditor forecloses on your house—they wouldn't be entitled to any of the proceeds, some of which might go to a creditor who came along later (like a home contractor, whom you haven't yet repaid and who files a lien). And finally, written proof that you're paying mortgage interest might allow you to deduct it at tax time.

To make your agreement legally binding, you'll need these two documents:

- **Promissory note.** You'll need to sign a note for the amount of the loan, including the rate of interest, repayment schedule, and other terms, such as penalties for late payments. Nolo sells an online promissory note on its website (Nolo.com). If you're borrowing only a few thousand dollars or less, a promissory note might be all you need. But for most intrafamily loans, it makes legal and financial sense to also prepare a mortgage.
- **Mortgage (or "deed of trust," in some states).** A mortgage gives your lender an interest in your property to secure repayment of your debt (per the promissory note). It needs to be recorded with a public authority, such as the registry of deeds.

Unless you're experienced in real estate transactions, we recommend you get an expert's help with preparing and recording a mortgage and related legal documents. Ask your lender or closing agent for advice, or check out a company like National Family Mortgage. We'll let adviser Timothy Burke explain the advantages of working with such a company: "It makes the process easy. Our intrafamily mortgage payment processing platform issues a monthly statement to borrowers and lenders, collects and credits loan payments, and provides year-end tax forms. We even offer a way for borrowers to have their monthly insurance and property tax premiums put into a separate escrow account, just like you'd get with a bank mortgage."

A One-Person Bank: Seller Financing

Surprisingly, the seller can be one of the most flexible sources of financing for your new house. Seem counterintuitive? There are several ways that sellers can help—admittedly not that common, but keep your eyes open for situations where:

- The seller is having difficulty finding a qualified buyer or is anxious to move a house that's been on the market a long time.
- The seller would prefer to be paid over time at a favorable interest rate rather than receive all the equity at the time of sale, perhaps to supply a regular income for upcoming retirement.
- The seller can justify a higher price by helping with the financing.
- The seller's house has substantially appreciated in value over the years, so that the seller will owe a high amount of capital gains tax when it's sold. By essentially selling the house to you over time, the seller can reduce the tax hit.

Here's a brief overview of the various forms of seller financing. As with loans from family and friends, be sure to consult with your primary lender to find out how seller financing will affect your eligibility, and get expert help for documenting and recording the mortgage.

Getting a Mortgage From the Seller

A form of seller financing often called a "seller carryback" allows the seller to essentially sell you the house on an installment plan. The seller transfers ownership of the house to you at the closing, but in return receives a promissory note entitling him or her to scheduled payments and a mortgage, providing a lien on the property until the loan is repaid. It's often structured so that the buyer has a balloon payment after a few years, at which point you'd either refinance or move out of the house. This kind of arrangement works best for a seller who already owns the house free and clear and won't have to turn around and pay off a bank loan upon sale.

You can also use seller financing to cover a second mortgage, when the amount you've saved for a down payment plus your bank loan doesn't quite add up to the sales price. Experts say you can save 1% or 2% by offering to accept a seller-financed arrangement rather than taking out a second bank loan.

If seller financing looks like an option, approach the seller in an organized way (see our suggestions, above, for approaching family and friends). Be prepared to provide detailed information about your income, credit, and employment history, plus references—more information than you'd need for a close relative. As with other private loans, seller financing can be flexible and creative. You might ask the seller for:

- a competitive interest rate (less than you'd pay for a fixed rate mortgage)
- low initial payments (unless you can easily afford high ones)
- a mortgage rate buydown (as described below)
- no prepayment penalty
- no large balloon payment for at least five years, plus the right to extend the loan at a reasonable interest rate if market conditions make it impossible to refinance or pay the balloon payment in full, and
- the right to have a creditworthy buyer assume the second mortgage if you sell the house.

This is a hard bargain, so be prepared to give up on the less important terms.

Assuming the Seller's Mortgage

Another option might be to assume the seller's mortgage: You would take the seller's place with the seller's bank or mortgage holder, subject to all the conditions the seller agreed to. This type of financing makes most sense when the interest rate on the seller's mortgage is lower than the current market rate. It's all aboveboard, done with the lender's consent (unlike something called a "wraparound," where you pay the seller and the seller pays the unwitting bank—not recommended).

One problem with assumable mortgages is that you'll probably have to pay much more for the property than the seller owes on his or her mortgage and will either need a very large down payment or a second mortgage to cover the difference. Since second mortgages are usually at a higher interest rate, you won't want to assume a seller's mortgage if the savings on the assumed mortgage will be cancelled out by the higher rate on the second mortgage.

Another potential problem is that usually only adjustable rate mortgages (plus FHA and VA loans, with some conditions) are assumable, so the interest rate probably won't stay where it is. Examine how high it might go using the suggestions in Chapter 6.

Finally, the seller usually wants something out of the deal, too: often, a higher asking price. That's because the seller is still on the hook for the mortgage if you default.

Backed by Uncle Sam: Government-Assisted Loans

The government thinks homeownership is a good thing—in fact, the federal Department of Housing and Urban Development (HUD) declares that its mission includes the creation of quality affordable homes for all. That might translate into some financial help for you, depending on where you live and whether you meet the eligibility requirements for programs administered by the:

- Federal Housing Administration (FHA)
- U.S. Department of Veterans Affairs (VA), or
- state and local housing finance programs.

We provide a brief overview of government low-down-payment and insured mortgage programs below, with contact information so you can check the latest offerings and eligibility requirements.

The application process for many government loan programs is similar to applying for a conventional loan. Your mortgage broker or lender can tell you what's available, which lenders participate, and whether or not you qualify based on your income and other eligibility requirements (such as your veteran status) and the price of the house you want to buy.

TIP

All types of homes qualify. Government loans are often available for loans for new houses, condominiums, co-ops, and manufactured homes—although there will be a few more hoops to jump through in terms of inspections, warranties, and other requirements.

CHECK IT OUT

Looking for a list of all government housing loan programs? Check out www.govloans.gov. In addition, be sure to see the sites mentioned below for FHA, VA, and state and local housing finance programs.

FHA Financing

The Federal Housing Administration, or FHA (an agency of HUD), helps people get into a home using a low down payment and with low closing costs. The FHA itself doesn't provide financing, but it does provide government insurance for a variety of fixed and adjustable rate mortgages issued through FHA-approved lenders. The insurance means that if you default and the lender forecloses, the FHA reimburses the lender for its losses. This reduces the lender's risk and increases the lender's willingness to offer low-down-payment plans.

The FHA's most popular program (Section 203(b)) requires a low down payment—usually a minimum 3.5% of the sales price. This, coupled with higher loan limits, makes FHA financing more popular with homebuyers now than in previous years. (Maximum loan limits vary by area, but in 2019 are generally between $314,827 and $726,525 for single-family homes in the continental U.S. and up to $1,089,787 for properties in Alaska, Guam, and Hawaii.) FHA loans are assumable by qualified buyers, which might make your house easier to sell when the time comes. Also, there is no prepayment penalty, should you decide to refinance or pay off your loan early.

FHA loans are a particularly good option for buyers with less than stellar credit histories (including bankruptcy), because they're typically easier to qualify for than conventional loans.

Another important benefit to FHA loans, according to adviser Lisa Shaffer, is that, "Unlike with other loans, you're allowed to get the entire down payment, as well as the closing costs, gifted to you. And family members are allowed to cosign on the loan to assist you in qualifying."

Not only gifts, but loans from family members are permitted by the FHA, Timothy Burke notes, "on a secured or unsecured basis, up to 100% of the borrower's required funds to close. This may include the down payment, closing costs, prepaid expenses, and discount points."

Sound good? Unfortunately, FHA loans don't work for all buyers, because of:

- **Fees.** Like all loans, FHA loans might include a loan origination fee (though some have dropped them), which you must pay at closing. FHA loans also require purchasing upfront mortgage insurance, which you can pay for out of pocket or finance into the loan. This is in addition to buying monthly mortgage insurance. Loan officer Lisa Shaffer notes, "It's also important to realize that when you have an FHA loan, you will have to maintain mortgage insurance for the entire life of the loan, regardless of the loan-to-value ratio."

- **Appraisals.** The lender must have an appraisal of the house you want to buy done by an FHA-approved appraiser. If the appraised value is less than what you pay for the house, you must make up the difference in cash (not with the FHA loan).

- **Ineligibility of major fixer-uppers.** Standard FHA loan programs won't help you buy properties needing significant repairs; any work recommended by the appraisers must be done before the sale closes. (If you're buying a serious fixer-upper or foreclosure home, check out the FHA's Rehabilitation Mortgage Program, known as Section 203(k).)

If you're planning to buy a condominium, particularly stringent FHA requirements might affect you. Lenders will be able to obtain FHA-backed loans only if the development meets a number of criteria, such as being mostly owner-occupied, having a certain level of insurance coverage, and being in good financial standing. If you're considering using an FHA-backed loan and have found a condominium you're interested in, it's a good idea to check with your lender to find out if it meets the FHA's requirements before you invest too much time and energy in making an offer. Also be aware that some lenders have been known to adhere to the FHA requirements even when the borrower is seeking a regular, non-FHA loan.

VA Loans

The VA provides access to competitive loans, usually with no down payment and no PMI, and no prepayment penalty, for men and women currently in military service and to veterans with an honorable discharge. Specific eligibility rules primarily relate to the length of service. For example, service personnel now on active duty are eligible after serving 90 continuous days, regardless of when the service began.

Eligible veterans must have a good credit history and proof of sufficient income.

The VA doesn't actually make these loans but, similar to the FHA, guarantees repayment to the lender of certain loans (available from participating private lenders, such as mortgage companies, banks, and savings and loans). The most common offerings are 30-year fixed rate mortgages or ARMs.

Technically, the VA itself doesn't set a maximum loan amount, but its rules effectively set limits in line with the FHA's.

You must pay the VA an administrative ("funding") fee for the loan, typically ranging from 1.5% to 3.3% of the total borrowed (depending on the amount of the down payment). Also, the VA places certain limits on what closing costs you may be charged for.

To avoid making a cash down payment, your loan must be at or below the VA's appraised value for the house. Of course, despite the VA providing backup, you're still expected to repay the whole loan.

CHECK IT OUT

To apply for the VA's "Certificate of Eligibility" (which may take several weeks) and see lists of participating lenders, contact the VA. See its website, www.va.gov (under "VA Benefits and Health Care," click "Housing Assistance"), or call 844-698-2311. Regional VA offices (listed on the main VA site) may also provide loan information.

State and Local Programs

Your state or local housing financing agency might sponsor special home financing programs at competitive rates and with low-down-payment options for first-time homebuyers. Also look for other local benefits, such as down payment assistance or local tax credits.

CHECK IT OUT

Looking for more information on state and local homebuyer programs? See the HUD website, at www.hud.gov/buying/localbuying.

What's Next?

Now that you understand all your financing options, you're ready to get out there and buy a house. Chapter 8 gives some suggestions on how to make the most of your house search.

I Love It! It's Perfect!
Looking for the Right House

Meet Your Adviser

Mark Daya, owner of Sac Platinum Realty, a team of experienced real estate agents in the Sacramento, California metro area. He's in the top 1% of Realtors in Sacramento County, and focuses on representing clients in the town of Rancho Cordova.

What he does

"I am obsessed with finding ways to make life easier for my clients when it's time for them to buy or sell a house. I've been licensed since 2005, so I've experienced hot markets, cold markets, and everything in between. Having ridden out these ups and downs, I've fine-tuned negotiation strategies to suit the market's mood and achieve the best outcome for my clients. I also focus on a specific geographic area, which really helps me evaluate prospective homes for clients—in-depth area knowledge makes it easier to spot good deals and know when to hold off on a property. When I'm not out helping my own clients, I'm building and supporting my team."

First house

"A few years before I became a licensed real estate agent, I was visiting a friend at his new house and I started thinking I should buy one, too. I decided to check out homes in his subdivision, and when I walked into the first model home I knew in about five seconds that it was "the one." It had an open floor plan that I loved (this was in 2002 when open floor plans were just starting to gain popularity), and I jumped on it. I'm glad I didn't hesitate, because shortly after my offer was accepted the development became so popular the builder had to start a lottery to choose buyers."

Likes best about his work	"I love the people side of my job. I'm thankful to have the opportunity to help clients achieve their homeownership dreams. I get a lot of satisfaction from knowing that I've made the process as smooth and painless as possible. There's nothing better than the sense of accomplishment I feel when I know my client is happy after a successful closing."
Fantasy house	"It's all about a water view—could be a lake, river, or ocean. My must-have is a stacking sliding glass door—the kind that disappears into the wall, turning an indoor space into an outdoor space, so I can enjoy the view year-round. The house would be a modern design, with lots of space for entertaining. And, of course, it has to have an open floor plan!"
Top tip for first-time homebuyers	"If you can, try to decide what neighborhood appeals to you the most before you begin your house search. Once you've decided where to focus, hire an agent who specializes in that neighborhood. An area specialist can warn you about aspects of the neighborhood that aren't apparent from the MLS or a drive-by, such as a development known for having faulty plumbing or being in a noisy flight path. Don't hire your friend's friend who just got a license—experience really does matter."

The brakes are off, and you're ready to visit houses that seem to match your Dream List, and choose one.

But first, breathe deeply and cultivate some nonattachment. "Most first-time buyers will ultimately have to make compromises," says adviser Mark Daya. Sellers of beautiful houses usually know they've got a gem and price it accordingly.

Meanwhile, the market contains its share of duds: houses with dark rooms, weird layouts, and repair nightmares. "But don't lose sight of your dreams. With a knowledgeable agent and some luck, you might find a house that's pretty close to perfect," adds Mark. So to make your search productive, we'll show you how to:

- get help from your real estate agent, friends, and neighbors
- compare each house with your Dream List, looking past the fancy furniture or staging, the need for fixing up, or the shininess of a recent remodel
- see whether you can live with the layout
- review disclosure and other information you receive from the seller
- do your own, informal inspection for repair issues, and
- understand how to approach buying a not-yet-constructed house, or one in a common interest development (CID).

Survey Says:

The average homeowner spends 124 hours searching for a house and looks at ten to 12 houses before buying one. Some must be looking at a lot more than that, so don't sweat it if you're one of them! One of this book's coauthors looked at over 200 houses before buying (she had a *very* patient agent).

How Your Agent Can Help

While you should take an active role in househunting, your agent's expertise will be invaluable in several ways.

> **TIP**
>
> **Take a photo with your smartphone, get instant info about the house.** The award-winning (not to mention addictive) Homesnap app brings up data about price (if the house is currently on the market) or estimated value (if it's not), school district, tax assessments, size, and more. (Inputting an old-fashioned street address works, too, but who can resist trying the photo function?) And while you're at it, try the Walk Score app to find out how easily you can hoof it from the house to nearby restaurants, shops, schools, and more.

Diving deep into the Multiple Listing Service (MLS). Your agent can use the MLS's database to access information about properties that isn't available to the general public. Not only does the MLS provide basic information about the house's price, features, and current status ("active," "under contract," "sale pending," or "closed"), but it also allows agents to check out a home's complete market history (how long it's been for sale, previous offers, offers that fell through, and so forth). For example, an active listing might say that the house has been on the market for only 64 days. But deeper within the MLS's database, an agent can see that the sellers have put the property on the market multiple times over the past two years—which could signal to the agent that the property is overpriced, that the sellers are motivated, or that there's something wrong with the property requiring more investigation.

> **TIP**
>
> **No need for embarrassment; your agent has heard it all.** Some agents' stories might as easily have come from a therapist: homebuyers they've counseled about whether to have children or couples whose divorces they predicted. Get used to your agent knowing your private concerns, but try to work out issues on your own. A house visit isn't the place to argue about whether you need an extra bedroom for your mother-in-law to live in.

Knowing the inside scoop. Apart from the MLS, the agent has been watching the market for longer than you and might hear about houses coming up for sale long before they're advertised—don't be surprised to hear your agent say, "If you can wait another week, that house will be on the market." If your agent is connected and involved in the community, it's more likely you'll find out about homes for sale before they're listed on the MLS.

Identifying reasonable sellers. Experienced agents recognize the signs of sellers who, for example, are unrealistic about pricing or have already had deals fall through because they were difficult. Your agent might be able to weed out which houses' sellers are worth negotiating with—and which ones aren't.

Arranging showings. Part of your agent's job is to set up appointments to tour homes you are (or might be) interested in. If you'd like to visit the same home more than once, don't be shy—just ask your agent to schedule another showing.

Helping evaluate houses. Another set of eyes can be a great help when visiting houses. Your agent might point out defects that you missed or possibilities you hadn't imagined. Just don't let your agent's judgment overtake your own. If you feel like you need some "alone time" when touring a home, don't hesitate to ask your agent for some space.

And more. Some agents find creative ways to help. For example, homebuyers visiting from out of town might find their agent is willing to pick them up at the airport and make hotel reservations. "Don't be afraid to ask your agent if you need assistance with something out of the ordinary—if your agent can't help, it's likely he or she knows someone who can," says Realtor Mark Daya. And agents regularly work evenings and weekends, showing you houses, reporting back on houses they've previewed, and more.

Best thing we ever did

Visit open houses without our Realtor. Although Pat and her husband loved their Realtor (their second one, after they'd fired the first), she was extremely busy. And, says Pat, "We knew finding an affordable house in a good school district, with yard space for our children, wasn't going to be easy—so we spent Sundays looking at every open house we could.

By a stroke of luck, an agent at an open house told us that a nearby house would be up for sale soon. Its owner lived out of state and needed to sell in a hurry. Our Realtor made some calls, and we put in a bid. On Christmas Eve, we found out that our bid had been accepted, and we got the house!"

What's Better? Open House or Individual Appointment?

The answer might actually be "both." Open houses are great for scoping out the possibilities quickly and anonymously, particularly on an action-packed Sunday. Visiting open houses unaccompanied by your agent can be nice for gauging your own reactions with no outside influence. But a quick visit is never enough—if a house looks promising, ask your agent to schedule an individual showing.

The Rumor Mill: Getting House Tips From Friends

People planning to sell their house don't usually make a big secret out of it—they tell friends and neighbors, long before they formally list the house. If you can tap into the same network (most likely if you already live nearby), you might find out about a house before it's up for sale.

Mention that you're house hunting to friends, neighbors, your hair stylist, the florist, your dentist, and more. Many home seekers blast out exactly what they're looking for via social media, email, or even letters, and some go so far as to promise a treat or reward to anyone who helps them find a house.

Luke: *Maybe one place wasn't so bad.*

Lorelai: *Oh good, describe it to me.*

Luke: *I don't know. It had walls with a kind of a floor with a light.*

Lorelai: *Okay, hold on there, mister. If you tell me it's got a roof, I'm stealing that baby out from under you.*

—From the TV series *Gilmore Girls*, 2000

Keeping Track of New Listings

One of the most difficult parts of buying a home can be simply finding an acceptable one that's up for sale! Although the real estate market has improved in recent years, it's still true that fewer homes come on the market than is considered "normal." That means that in many areas of the U.S., buyers pounce on new homes as soon as they come up for sale.

This requires a proactive approach to house hunting. As discussed, your agent can be a good inside source of information. Another good strategy is to sign up for new-listing alerts from real estate websites, such as Realtor.com or Zillow.

Planning Ahead for House Visits

Don't get too ambitious—most buyers find that visiting between four and eight houses per day is all they can handle before their brains fry. To make the most of your visits, do some prep work. Make sure you've got not only the complete list of houses you want to visit and have consulted a map about what order you'll visit them in, but have packed all the items on the House Visit Checklist shown below.

ONLINE TOOLKIT
You'll find a blank version of the "House Visit Checklist" on the Homebuyer's Toolkit on the Nolo website. (See the appendix for the link.)

In some markets, the sellers and their agent might be present while you're touring a house (awkward!). Assume that they are evaluating you. Dress comfortably but professionally, without overdoing it—a lot of bling might signal you can afford to pay full price (or more!). However, adviser Mark Daya notes that "it's pretty unusual for sellers to be there when you visit the property. If they are, be polite and friendly, but if you need some time alone to look around, you or your agent can respectfully ask them to hang back."

TIP

If the house has a rental unit, never tell existing tenants what you will or won't do as owner. For instance, saying "I'll keep the rent low" could create false expectations, leading to later arguments. But be friendly, and ask tenants for information concerning roof leaks, sewer backups, break-ins, and more. Tenants might reveal things you'd never learn any other way.

Unless your child is small enough to carry in a sling or backpack, leave the kids at home for the first visit. Most parents can focus better without chasing a toddler or hearing choruses of "This will be *my* bedroom"/"No, *mine!*" You can (and should) get your kids' okay later. And this should go without saying, but don't bring pets along on house visits.

House Visit Checklist

Tuck the following into your bag:

- ☐ your Dream List (from Chapter 2)
- ☐ your list of Questions for the Seller or Condo/Co-op Checklist (from later in this chapter)
- ☐ your First-Look Home Inspection Checklist (from later in this chapter)
- ☐ something for taking notes
- ☐ binoculars (handy for examining the roof)
- ☐ camera, camcorder, or charged-up smartphone, to remind yourself of what you saw, and
- ☐ tape measure and notes on the type and size of your furniture.

Come on In: What to Expect as You Enter

Okay, your feet are crossing the welcome mat, and you're getting your first peek inside. The seller's agent might be in one of the front rooms, happy to greet you and to answer questions. If you've made an appointment, either the seller's agent will let you and your agent in, or your agent will get a key from a lockbox. In rare cases (and with FSBOs), the seller will be there as well.

> **TIP**
>
> **If it's *really* awful, you can leave!** No need to be polite and do the full tour. While some aspects of a house can be changed, such as filthy blinds or old cabinets, trust your instincts and don't waste your time.

Picking Up the Paperwork

Your first task is to see what paperwork the sellers have made available to you. This might include a property fact sheet, with basic information like the house's size and amenities; a disclosure form that details what the seller personally knows about the condition of the house's structure, features, appliances, and environment; and/or a pest report and possibly a general inspection report, including details discovered by a professional.

You probably won't get all three of these—you might get none, or only the basic fact sheet or a flyer. How much information a seller is *legally* required to give potential buyers varies from state to state (though some sellers give more than is required).

> **TIP**
>
> **"As-is" on a fact sheet equals red flag.** It normally means the seller wants you to buy the house without requesting payment for any repairs, perhaps without even doing a home inspection. Ask what it means to *this* seller, because there's no official definition of "as-is" in many markets.

Questions for Seller Worksheet

Here are some basic questions you and your agent will want to ask about a particular house, in terms of repair needs, utility costs, and neighbors. Add anything else to this list of interest—for example, if you have specific questions about the garden.

1. How long has the house been on the market?

2. What repairs or improvements have been done in the last few years?

   What are the house's major or most immediate repair needs?

3. Does the seller use a particular repairperson, plumber, electrician, or pest control person? If so, please provide their names:

4. How much money does the owner pay for monthly utilities (gas, garbage, electricity, water, cable, or satellite)?
   Are there any other ongoing costs?

5. Has the owner had any problems with water or dampness in the basement or any other part of the house?

6. Is there a furnace and a central A/C system, and if so, when was it installed?

7. How are the neighbors? Are there issues regarding fences, trees, or property lines?

8. Is there any kind of organized neighborhood association?

NOTES:

Questions for Seller Worksheet (continued)

How to evaluate the answers:

1. If it's more than a few weeks (depending on how fast houses are moving in your market), ask whether there's been a price drop and whether any offers have fallen through and why. Maybe it's overpriced and ripe for you to make a lower bid on.

2. Some of these repair problems may be stated in the disclosures or inspection report, but it's helpful to have the agent summarize them for you. Don't hesitate to be direct and ask things like "Have there been any roof leaks?"

3. Any use of repairpeople can reveal repair issues the seller didn't mention when answering Question #2. The information will also be useful if and when you move in!

4. If you're stretching just to buy the house, make sure it doesn't come with unusually high ongoing costs.

5. The basement and attic are likely suspects here. Moisture problems are hard to repair and hard to insure.

6. Installing a new furnace or A/C can be another major expense—and one that's important to deal with soon, for the sake of your personal comfort.

7. Difficult neighbors can't be repaired, while a community that works together can enhance livability. Specifically ask about the level of noise; cooperation regarding fence, tree, or parking issues; and any behavioral problems or oddities.

8. Consider whether living within a planned community is for you and exactly what rules and restrictions that entails.

First Questions to Ask

If the house looks promising, you and your agent should ask some basic questions concerning repair needs, utility costs, neighbors, because there's no official definition of "as-is" in many markets. You'll most likely ask these of the seller's agent, but if the seller is there, or is selling without an agent, ask the seller directly.

ONLINE TOOLKIT

Use the "Questions for Seller Worksheet" in the Homebuyer's Toolkit on the Nolo website. (See the appendix for the link.) A sample is shown above. Tailor this worksheet to your interests, for example, adding a question on whether there's hardwood flooring under any carpets. (Also, if you're buying a condo or co-op, the Toolkit contains a separate checklist for you.)

Do We Have a Match? Using Your Dream List

Even the "right" house probably won't be just as you imagined. Carrying your Dream List (with the first two columns filled out) will help you stay organized and avoid getting distracted—for example, being so impressed with stainless steel appliances that you forget that one bathroom won't be enough. Fill out your Dream List before leaving each house. At the end of a day's househunting, when you can barely remember your own name, it will answer questions like, "Was it the brick house that had the patio?"

TIP

Get organized. Keep a file for each house that seems like a possible match. Include your filled-out Dream List, property fact sheet, and other paperwork.

All the World's Been Staged: Looking Past the Glitter

In the old days, you'd see houses for sale pretty much as the sellers lived in them—with their furniture, dishes, and clutter. But in many parts of the U.S., the real estate industry has learned that by emptying out and then gussying up a place with rented furniture, flowers, curtains, artwork, and more, buyers will be wowed into paying more—often tens of thousands more—for a home.

The resulting makeover job goes by the trade name "staging." And it's your job to look past it, to see whether the house has good bones or is just wearing a lot of cosmetics and concealer. To avoid being hypnotized:

- **Figure out whether each room has all the furniture it needs.** Stagers usually remove most of the owner's furniture and then bring in a select few pieces—some smaller than normal. As you look at a bedroom, for example, picture it with your queen-sized bed, nightstands, and bureau, not the twin bed and delicate side table.

- **Notice where flowers and knickknacks have replaced functional objects.** In a normal laundry room, for example, you'd expect to find detergent, laundry baskets, and a drying rack. Not in a staged house—you're more likely to see a wicker basket filled with fluffy, lavender-scented towels.

- **Observe what your eyes are being led toward—and therefore away from.** If the entry hallway is small and dark, you can bet you'll see a glorious display of flowers on a nearby table.

- **See whether your stuff will fit into the closets and cabinets.** With the owners having moved out their clutter, you might not immediately notice that there's no hall closet, linen closet, medicine cabinet, basement, or attic.

- **Figure out what style the house is without the staging.** Stagers can make a ranch house look like a Victorian, or a 1950s drab home look like an Arts and Crafts bungalow.

- **Try turning on all lights, including table lamps.** Stagers often set lamps next to beds or couches, even though there's no electrical outlet. A lack of outlets is a common defect in older homes. Also, check that kitchen and laundry appliances actually have a source of power and other connections needed for operation.

- **Turn off all lights.** Many sellers turn on lights for showings. Turn off lights to see how much natural light is in the home. (Be a good visitor and turn the same lights back on when you go, unless the seller asks otherwise.)
- **Smell that apple pie!** If the house smells dreamy or the music sounds divine—well, someone made it that way. And they don't come with the house.

Staging isn't all trickery—if it's well done, you might pick up some ideas for how you'd do up the place yourself. Just don't pay more than the house is worth simply because it looked gorgeous after the staging job.

Recent Remodels: What to Watch Out For

If you can afford a house that someone else has fixed up, great—you can save a lot of effort and ongoing maintenance. But not all sellers have good motives, judgment, or taste. In particular, watch out for houses where the seller has:

- **Never lived there, but fixed it up to make a profit.** This is called "flipping." Unfortunately, because the seller had no personal stake in the house, you can't count on quality materials or workmanship. If you get as far as making an offer, you'll of course hire an inspector. But before things get that serious, save yourself a heap of trouble by making sure the necessary permits were issued and getting an independent appraisal before relying on appraisal reports the seller shows you. Fraud cases involving flipping are surprisingly common, where the appraiser is in cahoots with a seller and overvalues the house based on superficial or low-quality improvements.

> **Donkey:** *Whoa. Look at that. Who'd wanna live in a place like that?*
>
> **Shrek:** *That would be my home.*
>
> **Donkey:** *Oh and it is LOVELY. You know, you're really quite a decorator. It's amazing what you've done with such a modest budget. I like that boulder. That is a NICE boulder.*
>
> From the movie *Shrek*, 2001.

- **Customized for unique tastes.** Overcustomizing can be detrimental to a house's value, like if the seller was a sports fan who did the whole house in team colors. If you and the seller are kindred spirits, great—but good luck finding the next buyer.
- **Overimproved the house.** A property can actually be made so fabulous that it's no longer comparable to surrounding homes. Unfortunately, surrounding homes set the standard for home values in that area. You might enjoy the house while you live there, but be prepared for slow rises in value and difficulty reselling.

Feng Shui Tips

The Chinese practice of feng shui (pronounced "fung shway")is based on a simple truth: Your exterior and interior surroundings can influence your life. Even if you don't believe in it, a house with good feng shui might have greater appeal to buyers. According to feng shui consultant and author Kartar Diamond (www.fengshuisolutions.net), "Every house has what I call an energetic blueprint. This can either enhance or undermine your health, well-being, and career." Though some feng shui issues can be fixed, Diamond recommends homebuyers avoid the following problems:

Exteriors

- lots of cracks in the outdoor pavement
- a triangular-shaped lot or one that narrows in the back
- a corner house on a busy street
- a house at the bottom of a cul-de-sac or below street level
- trees that appear to be leaning away from the property (like they're trying to escape!)
- a house within view of a cemetery, church, hospital, fire station, ugly eyesore, or place that makes a lot of noise, like an auto repair shop or bar.

Interiors

- chronically dark rooms or tight, congested spaces
- uneven floors
- big exposed beams in the bedrooms
- front door aligned directly with back door or window
- toilet or kitchen in center of house, and
- stairs right behind entrance door.

Walk the Walk: Layout and Floor Plan

The physical layout of a house can make a huge difference in whether you're comfortable living there. When visiting a house, imagine going through your daily activities. For example, "I'm opening the refrigerator—it bumps the oven door, and I'll have to chop vegetables on this tiny countertop across from the sink."

Best thing I ever did **Not buy the house with the weirdly placed bathroom.** Kurt, an avid gardener, was close to bidding on a two-bedroom Victorian. He says, "It was on a corner, with a lot of garden space around it. I was already visualizing planting roses. The problem was, the one and only bathroom was stuck right between one bedroom and the kitchen. It had a door on each side. Imagine being a guest and having to worry about locking both doors! I'm hugely relieved I held off."

What Do They Know? Reviewing Seller Disclosure Reports

One of the most important pieces of paper in this process is the disclosure report, which most—but not all—states' laws require sellers to give prospective buyers. (Exceptions are sometimes made for certain properties, such as those in probate, where the original owner has died.) And it has become a standard practice even in states where the laws don't require it.

Most seller disclosures are made using a standard form, upon which the seller will check off features of the property and rate or describe their condition. If the house hasn't yet been built, the developer obviously won't have much to disclose—but might still need to tell you about things like the type of soil; previous uses of the property; possible future uses of surrounding land; and the developer's intentions regarding existing trees, streams, and natural areas.

What you read could affect your decision whether to make an offer. To find out more about a topic mentioned in the form, ask for it in writing. And if you receive the disclosure form *after* making an offer, you can cancel the sale if you don't like what you read. Even after the sale has closed, if a problem pops up that you believe the seller knew about and didn't disclose, you can sue the seller on that basis.

Exactly *when* you're given the seller's disclosures varies by state. In a few states, such as Alaska, Kentucky, and New Hampshire, sellers must give you disclosures before you've made an offer. But most states don't require the seller to do this until *after* you've made an offer, often just before the two of you sign the purchase agreement.

What's in a Typical Disclosure Report

The typical disclosure form is a few pages long and describes features like appliances; the roof, foundation, and other structural components; electrical, water, sewer, heating, and other mechanical systems; trees and natural hazards (earthquakes, flooding, hurricanes); environmental hazards (lead, asbestos, mold, radon, or contamination by use as a meth lab); and zoning.

Some disclosure forms also cover legal issues, such as ownership problems, legal disputes concerning the property, or community association fees. Strange but true: The forms might also require information about suicides, murders, and other deaths on the property; nearby criminal activity; or other factors, such as excessive neighborhood noise.

Understanding Your State's Disclosure Requirements

Disclosure requirements vary among states, and some sellers try to wiggle out of the requirement altogether. Your agent should make sure the seller complies with the law—but the question will remain, how much did the law require the seller to tell you about in the first place? If the standard form doesn't mention past flooding, the seller doesn't have to, either (but shouldn't lie if asked). You might want to read your state's law, or at least the form, to look for holes.

Even in nondisclosure states, buyers can negotiate to make seller disclosures a part of their purchase—or might get them without asking. Law or no law, your state Realtor's association has probably created a standard disclosure form for sellers to use. Some agents include the sellers' completed disclosure in the MLS listing, while others let buyers know that the seller will provide a disclosure form once they accept an offer. Most sellers know that if they don't provide disclosures, the buyers will think they've got something to hide. Beyond these possibilities, "It's buyer beware," says New York attorney Richard Leshnower.

And the Prize Goes to Arizona

... for the most interesting creatures listed on its seller's disclosure statement. The form asks sellers whether they've seen any scorpions, rabid animals, bee swarms, rodents, reptiles, or bed bugs on their property.

To find your state's law, talk to your real estate agent or state regulatory agency. You can find yours at www.arello.org (under "Resources" click "Regulatory Agencies"). Or you can search online for "real estate disclosure," "disclosure form," or "disclosure statement" and the name of your state. The Real Estate section of Nolo.com includes articles on seller disclosure requirements for several states.

TIP

Buying a house built pre-1978? By federal law, the seller should, before you buy, give you a form disclosing whether the seller knows of lead-based paint in the home and a pamphlet called "Protect Your Family From Lead in Your Home." For more on lead hazards, see www.epa.gov/lead.

Penalties for Sellers Who Fail to Disclose

Most states put some teeth into their disclosure laws, by allowing buyers to cancel the sale if the seller doesn't provide the disclosure form or doesn't fill it out completely and honestly. Some states also charge monetary penalties to sellers who violate the law, or punish sellers' real estate agents for failing to disclose problems that they observed or were told of by their clients, the sellers.

And, if you find out after the sale that the seller didn't disclose something material, you might be able to claim reimbursement or sue.

CAUTION

Fraud happens. "One of the most blatant cases I've seen," says Massachusetts attorney Ken Goldstein, "was one where, a couple of weeks after the sale, the new owners heard a crash from the basement. The ceiling—one of those drop structures with a metal framework and tiles fitting in the grid—had just collapsed. The tiles were all soaking wet. Suspiciously, an old kitchen pot was sitting within the wreckage. It turns out there was a leaking pipe up there, and the sneaky seller had apparently removed a tile and put in the pot. That worked to hide the problem through the closing date—but then the pot overfilled."

Can You Trust the Disclosures?

Now comes the question of how much to believe of what the seller discloses. There's no nice way to put it: Sellers are just people, and some of them lie. Even upright citizens have been known to lie, after rationalizations like, "The basement hasn't flooded in years (never mind the drought)." And a less-than-honorable seller—for example, someone who's been running a methamphetamine lab within the home—is hardly going to admit it on the disclosure form. (The toxicity levels created by meth manufacturing are enough to make the home unsaleable.) If meth seems like a possible concern, ask the neighbors what they've observed, and get a separate inspection.

Will They Tell You If It's Haunted?

If plates fly around your prospective home's kitchen, houseguests flee the back bedroom screaming, or a bloodstain reappears nightly on the staircase, you want to know about it, right? But don't expect to see a "haunted" box on any state's disclosure form. Nevertheless, sellers are, in many states, obligated to disclose things that affect a house's marketability, which the oddities described above certainly could. Smart sellers would describe exactly what they've observed, without drawing conclusions.

Lying isn't the only problem, either. Even honest sellers might be allowed to keep quiet about something they only suspect. Some state's forms might offer handy escape hatches, like a box saying "don't know," or "no representation." In Oregon, for example, sellers need only disclose problems of which they have "actual knowledge."

That can lead to situations like one described by Oregon broker Debbie Stevens: "A buyer I represented moved into a house where, within one month, the water line from the street failed. Of course, we immediately wondered whether the seller had failed to disclose something. It turned out the seller's neighbors had had repairs done on their water line, and the repairperson had actually told our seller, 'Your water line is old, too; I can fix it while I'm in here.' But the repairperson couldn't predict when the seller's water line would fail, and the seller didn't want to pay for repairs. Unfortunately, we had to conclude that the seller wasn't necessarily wrong to say nothing, since he didn't know how close the water line was to failing."

Also, in most states, sellers aren't required to poke around for problems—just to tell you what they already know. A house's owners can remain blissfully unaware of many serious problems—a cracked foundation, termites deep in the walls, or a roof on the verge of leaking—and won't be held responsible.

Reviewing the Seller's Inspection Reports (If Any)

Some sellers voluntarily provide copies of inspection reports they've commissioned themselves, either pest reports (common in California) or general inspections. In theory, this is no mere subjective opinion—the report was drafted by a trained professional, right? The answer is a not-so-resounding "maybe." The quality of home inspectors varies widely, and are you going to gamble on the seller having chosen the most nitpicky one in town?

That's not to say the seller is trying to pull a fast one. But inspectors who are regularly hired by sellers describe feeling pressured not to be "deal-breakers," but rather to downplay problems they find. They tend to use fuzzy words in their reports like "worn" or "serviceable."

First-Look Home Inspection Checklist

Here's what to look for in your initial house visit.

☐ **Examine the roof.** If the roofline is sagging, be prepared for foundation problems. Ask how old the roof is. A roof ten years old or older will probably need replacing soon; a $10,000-plus job. Loose, curling, or missing tiles or shingles also indicate a new roof is needed, as do shafts of light in the attic. Complex roofs with lots of gables, intersecting surfaces, and multiple roofing materials are difficult to maintain and expensive to replace. Some older roofs contain asbestos, making replacement even more expensive.

☐ **Listen for squeaks when you walk.** Squeaks are caused by loose nails, often loosened by sagging or movement in the structure, which might mean settling problems.

☐ **Take cues from your feet.** They'll tell you whether the flooring feels unstable, or the house has started to settle unevenly. As you walk up stairs, make sure the heights feel uniform. And step close to the toilet and tub. If the floor feels soft, leakage might be occurring, possibly caused by the owner's failure to change the seals on the toilet or caulk the wall tiles.

☐ **Use your nose.** At worst, fusty odors or your sudden sniffling might mean a mold problem. Other odors, such as cat urine or cigarette smoke, are also a bother to get rid of and reduce the value of the house. (Or maybe you'll just smell a lot of air freshener, which should make you wonder what's being covered up.)

☐ **Turn on the faucets.** What does the water look like? If you see rust particles or discoloration, the pipes might be rusted, and need replacement. What do you hear? Knocking sounds might mean old, leak-prone pipes. Try turning the faucet to its maximum. If the underlying problem turns out to be low water pressure, this is tough to solve—but needs to be fixed if you plan on enjoying your showers. Also make sure the hot water arrives within a reasonable length of time.

☐ **Open windows and doors.** If they don't open easily or lock completely, they'll need to be repaired for safety as well as convenience.

☐ **Look for signs of water damage.** Look for stains or puddles on the ceiling, around the window frames, by the water heater, under the sink, and all over the floor of the basement (if there is one). Not only are these repairs costly, but because of scares over toxic mold, they can make a house expensive to insure.

☐ **Find the electrical panel.** Is it an old-style one, small, and with fuses rather than circuit breakers? That's a several-thousand-dollar upgrade. If you suspect old wiring, look at the plugs near the bathroom and kitchen sinks. If they've been modernized at all, you'll see special plugs with little rectangular "TEST" and "RESET" buttons (these help protect you from water-related electrocution).

First-Look Home Inspection Checklist, continued

☐ **Take note of peeling paint.** A paint job is an easy, cosmetic repair—but nevertheless can cost several thousand dollars. And peeling paint can be especially problematic if it's old and lead-based or contains asbestos texturing material.

☐ **Turn light switches on and off, or try turning on many lights and appliances at once.** If the lights flicker, or the electricity goes, there might be a bad connection or a circuit overload. These aren't expensive fixes, but are safety priorities.

☐ **Examine the appliances.** Ask whether the refrigerator, stove, dishwasher, washer and dryer, and other appliances come with the house. Then look to see whether they add value or will require a trip to the dump. Test to make sure they're functional; open the refrigerator door, and light the stove's burners.

☐ **Ask whether the house has a furnace or air conditioner.** Many houses still operate on small units that work in only a few rooms. Ask that the furnace or A/C be turned on.

☐ **Look for unprofessional repairs or upgrades.** If the house has been in the hands of unqualified do-it-yourselfers, some work might have to be redone.

Item or Area	Okay	Problem
Roof		
Flooring		
Odors		
Water and plumbing		
Windows		
Doors		
Electrical		
Paint and walls		
Appliances		
Furnace		
Air conditioning		
Exterior		
Other		

NOTES:

SEE AN EXPERT

Go to the source: Call the inspector directly. There's no law saying you have to rely solely on the inspector's written words. If you're seriously thinking about making an offer, consider calling and asking the seller's inspector for details and for information about his or her background. Better yet, ask the inspector to come back and do a walk-through with you. The fee for this shouldn't be high, given that the inspector has already viewed the property.

So, if you've got a report in front of you, how do you evaluate its worth? Start by reading it carefully, following the advice on understanding inspection reports provided in Chapter 11. Also check whether the inspector is a member of ASHI (the American Society of Home Inspectors). And you can ask your real estate agent about the reputation of the inspection company—and of the seller's agent, who probably selected the company.

Best thing I ever did

Learn to decipher the pest report. Abby was looking for a fixer-upper, so she knew her future house would have problems. But when the seller gave her the pest report, she says, "I almost called off the deal—the fix-up was going to cost almost half of what I'd be paying for the house. Then I took a closer look. The report said things like, 'cellulose fiber near foundation—$200 to repair.' It turned out that just meant there was a big piece of wood leaning on the foundation—all I had to do was brave the spiders and drag it away. I found a lot of items that weren't as major as they'd seemed."

Finally, no matter how reputable the seller's inspector, if the report was written more than a few months ago, it's too old. New problems can crop up in a day. And the seller might have already tried to repair some of the problems—for better or for worse. A professional inspection is important, but it's best to rely on the one you'll commission yourself, later.

Poking Around: Doing Your Own Initial Inspection

From the first moment you look at a house, you should be taking stock of its physical condition. If there's a chance you might make an offer, you'll want a clear idea of how much the house is worth, which is based partly on its state of repair.

ONLINE TOOLKIT

Bring along the "First-Look Home Inspection Checklist," found in the Homebuyer's Toolkit on the Nolo website. (See the appendix for the link.) A sample is shown above. It details both the easiest and most important issues to look for.

The checklist won't lead you through an in-depth inspection. But there's a lot you can spot during an ordinary open house visit, like sagging rooflines and leaking pipes. It might be more polite to wait for an individual appointment to do things like turning on heat and stove burners. Again, if you're really interested in the place, you should hire a professional inspector, normally after making an offer.

When you get really serious about a house, adviser Mark Daya recommends testing the property in two other ways before making an offer:

- **Test the commute.** "Try driving from your house to your workplace, at the same times of day you'd normally leave and return if you lived there. If the drive would make life miserable, you'll want to know this before you close the deal."
- **Visit the neighborhood at odd times.** "Most people tour houses on the weekends, which might not represent the feel of the neighborhood on the other five days of the week. What if parking on weekdays is a nightmare due to a popular business nearby? Or what if the house is downwind from a smelly factory that operates only on weekdays? These are the types of things you won't experience on the weekends."

CHECK IT OUT

Eager to take on more-difficult inspection tasks? Get guidance from:

- The American Society of Home Inspectors website at www.ashi.org. Click the "Homebuyers/Sellers" tab, then "Home Inspection Virtual Tour" to get a fun visual tour of what your inspector will eventually examine.

- Local community colleges, adult schools, and home improvement stores, many of which offer excellent and inexpensive classes in home repair.

Hey, Nice Dirt Pile! Choosing a Not-Yet-Built House

You'll have a lot of choices if you're buying a new home from a developer: which lot you want, which type of model house you like, and which upgrades you'd like inside. All of this requires imagination if you're buying before the house is built (though some developments are nearly fully built in advance).

CAUTION

Bring your agent along on the first visit! If you show up unrepresented, the developer might take the position that the agent should not be able to take credit for or be involved in the sale.

Choosing Which Lot Your House Will Be Built On

Even if all the lots look identical on the subdivision map, walk around the building site, and examine the map for the following:

- **Likely water flow.** Poor drainage is a common complaint in new developments. It's caused by improper grading and is difficult to fix, so avoid lots located at low spots or the bottom of a hill. A lot on a creek might sound nice but could end up flooded by next year's "100-year storm." Also look for concrete-lined drain channels in hillsides above your lot—many are poorly maintained, which could lead to flooding or even a landslide.

- **Noise.** If your house will be next to a major traffic artery, railroad tracks, or airport, expect extra noise (and possibly commuting delays).
- **Services.** While it's convenient to have services close by, being immediately adjacent to a grocery store, fire station, or school can raise levels of traffic, litter, and noise.
- **Lot size and position of neighbor's houses.** How big is the lot in relation to the size of your house-to-be? In many new communities, homes are built so tightly together that owners can hear their neighbors' televisions or see in their windows.
- **Location.** You'll pay more for a house that sits on a lakefront and less for one that backs up against the freeway. The more desirable the location, the less negotiable the price.
- **View.** If a view is an important asset on your lot, find out whether you have a right to prevent downhill neighbors from blocking it with new homes, additions, or trees. Many trees grow fast enough to block a scenic vista within five to ten years.
- **Remaining undeveloped land.** If there's a big, open field nearby, find out from the local zoning or planning department what it's zoned for and what kind of development is planned. Unless it's an established park, you can be sure that something will be built there eventually.
- **Orientation.** South-facing homes typically receive more light (and heat), so consider how this might affect your use of the lot. For example, in areas where it snows, you might want your driveway to face south so the snow melts faster.

Choosing Your House Design and Upgrades

For the house itself, you might be choosing which model type you want and whether you want upgrades. This is where that low, advertised price can change dramatically. The modest-sized model might look tiny compared to the model mansion next door, and the simple, standard kitchen may look shoddy next to the glossy custom cabinets. To help rein in your choices, consider:

TIP

It's possible to negotiate for free upgrades, especially in slower markets. Because it doesn't cost the developer nearly as much to make the upgrades as you'd probably be charged, they use them as incentives.

- **What the model home includes.** Some contain the upgrades, so that buyers mistakenly think that's what the final house will look like. Try asking how much the model house would cost with everything you see in it. Other model homes might contain cheap and tacky basics, to steer you toward the upgrades. Either way, look closely at the quality of woodwork, flooring, appliances, and more; decide which you're willing to pay to upgrade; and get the developer's promises in writing.
- **What was NOT on your Dream List.** If you'd never thought about needing a wood-burning fireplace or an outdoor barbecue, why add (and pay for) them now?
- **What construction shortcuts the developer uses.** Watch out for so-called "value engineering," in which developers maintain the luxury look of a house without the actual quality—for example, by installing windows that don't actually open, or decorative beams that are made of foam, not wood. Examine the model home carefully, and ask lots of questions.
- **Retail cost of possible upgrades.** No need to pay a developer more to add high-quality materials than you'd pay for them yourself. Double-check the cost of big-ticket items like cabinetry or floor coverings at your local home improvement store. Then negotiate with the developer to bring the price down, or plan to hire a local contractor for upgrades.
- **What upgrades will add resale value.** If you ever sell your home, the less flashy, more practical upgrades will attract the most buyers. For example, swimming pools don't always add value to a house, while extra office or storage space will. Other practical, valuable upgrades include more electrical outlets, a fenced-in backyard,

storm windows, and whole-house air conditioning. In adviser Mark Daya's market, buyers value upgrades such as energy-saving features and future-proof technology—tech systems that won't need a lot of work to update as technology advances.

- **Tax impact of your house size and upgrades.** You might have seen a property tax estimate in the seller's written materials. If the house hasn't yet been built and assessed, however, that figure means nothing more than the value of the land. Call your local tax board for information.

Don't Fall for the Hype!

Watch out for these common sales tactics developers use to encourage impulse buys and create a sense of urgency:

- **The luxury tour.** You might be whisked around lovely house models by an attractive professional, maybe even with tasty treats or drinks along the way.

- **The "now or never."** You might be told that a building or development is almost sold out—or is sold out. Whaddya know, you receive a call a few days later saying that a deal has fallen through, and a unit or house is now available.

- **The moment of silence.** If you're buying with someone else and find yourselves alone in an office, resist the temptation to do what the seller wants: namely, talk about what you just saw, and whether it's a good idea to buy it right that minute. You might be overheard.

- **The "today and today only."** "Today only, upgraded granite counter-tops," or "We'll pay your closing costs." We can't say such strategies don't represent the truth, but it's a favorite sales tactic.

- **The freebies.** As if buying a house weren't enough, some developers throw in motorbikes, cruise trips, and flat screen TVs. Try to remember that these are minor extras compared to what you'll be paying to buy the property.

CAUTION

If you back out, your upgrades won't be refunded—you pay for them up front. "I've seen people lose $50,000 in upgrades because of a job transfer," says Realtor Mark Nash. "The reason for this policy is that the property is less marketable with your personal choices stamped on it—it's more like a resale." Plan ahead!

Buying a New or Old Condo or Co-op? Research the Community

If you're buying a property in a common interest development, such as a condo, co-op, townhouse, or planned unit development (PUD), its physical state shouldn't be the only thing on your mind. You should also be asking, "How stable is this organization, how much power will the community association have over my life, and will it exercise that power?"

Although the term "community association" might sound like a social club, the reality is that you're relying on all of your neighbors to do important things like pay their monthly assessments (also called dues) and follow community rules. A few of your neighbors—whom you might not like or agree with—will serve in leadership roles. They'll make important decisions about your living environment. Some associations are responsible minigovernments, but many are more like dysfunctional families. So, it's well worth your time to:

- obtain and read all the paperwork regarding the association, and
- ask questions of the sellers, the neighbors, and the governing body.

Read the Large and Fine Print

Community associations normally put their main rules into documents called the "bylaws" and "master deed" or "Declaration of Covenants, Conditions, and Restrictions" (CC&Rs). As soon as you're seriously interested, get a copy of these, as well as of this year's budget, and read them carefully (at the least, you can make receiving these documents a contingency of your purchase offer, as described in Chapter 10). If you're buying a newly built home, the builder might include these as part of your disclosures.

You'll learn about things like the permission process if you want to add on to your house, what color you can paint your fencing or exterior, limits on pets, types of allowable landscaping, how high the monthly dues (maintenance assessments) are, when the association can decide to charge you special assessments for projects affecting the entire community (like the pool or common room), whether the builder will charge you a transfer fee when you sell (a new and noxious clause), and more. This isn't abstract stuff—it will have a real, direct impact on your daily life and finances.

You might find that the association owners don't want to cough up these documents until you've made a purchase offer. For condos, however, in most areas, anyone can go to the county recorder's office and get a copy of the CC&Rs. (They're part of the deed that's recorded to publicly show who owns the property.)

Unless you're buying into a completely new development, these documents are just the beginning. You'll also want to research what the association or board has been up to lately. Ask for minutes from meetings (ideally up to three years' worth), and review these for signs of internal disputes, financial troubles, or planned new projects.

CAUTION

Signs of association money troubles: Ask further questions and think twice about buying if you spot evidence that:

- more than 15% of the units are in foreclosure or have been on the market for several weeks and remain unsold

- more than 15% of owners are overdue on their homeowners' fees (known as the "delinquency rate")

- the association's reserve account is almost empty, or

- major litigation is pending.

Condo/Co-op Worksheet

Here are some basic questions you'll want to ask the seller, seller's agent, and neighbors about a particular condo or co-op. Tailor this list according to the particular property (Hawaii homebuyers can delete the question about snow removal!), and add other questions of interest—for example, if you have specific questions about waste disposal or want more details about restrictions on use of a community pool.

1. Do you enjoy living here? What are the best and worst things about it?

2. What percentage of the properties are rented out to tenants?

3. Are you happy with the community association and management? Are there any particular problems? What do you wish it would do differently?

4. What exactly is included in your monthly association or maintenance fee? (Some might include heating, parking, storage facilities, and use of the clubhouse, while others charge separately for these services, if they're available at all.)

5. Where is your parking? Indoor? Outdoor? Reserved? Private garage? How many spaces am I allotted? Is there parking for guests or disabled persons? Do you offer electric charging stations for hybrid vehicles?

6. How strictly does the board or management enforce rules?

7. What amenities are included in your membership (for example, a clubhouse or laundry room)? Are there any waiting lists?

8. Are there any waiting lists for things such as parking spots or storage lockers?

9. Are any special assessments planned? When was the last one? What was it for?

10. What taxes can you expect—for example, local school taxes?

11. For co-ops: How much is the mortgage on the property itself? (This might affect your monthly maintenance fees and whether they are deductible because they pay the underlying mortgage.)

Condo/Co-op Worksheet, continued

12. In the event of snow, by what time of day can you expect it to be shoveled or plowed? Does this include parking areas?

13. Are there any annual surcharges, such as for fuel?

14. How high is the reserve fund (of emergency money)?

15. Who determines how much is spent on various projects?

16. Are meetings of the board or association open or closed? How do members or shareholders contribute to decision making (for example, by submitting questions in advance of meetings)? Have you attended meetings, and if so, would you describe what they're like?

17. If people will be living above you, is there a rule saying the floor must be carpeted? Are the walls well insulated?

18. Are any of the neighbors difficult or inconsiderate?

17. How are package deliveries handled in the building if there's no doorman?

18. Do owners have a right to rent out their unit? Are owners allowed to offer short-term rentals, such as through Airbnb or VRBO?

19. Are there many vacancies in the building or development? How long does it take for the average unit to sell—are they in demand, or does it take a while?

20. When are workpeople allowed to enter and work on a unit? Saturdays, Sundays, evenings? Must they be licensed? Do they need association approval for access, or to register to gain entry?

21. What kind of repair or construction work can be done without the approval of the association or board? What's the procedure for approval? How long does approval usually take?

22. Does the management keep up with its repair and maintenance obligations? How long does it take for needed repairs to be made?

According to adviser Paul Grucza, "Stagnant hourly wages have seriously impacted people's ability to pay their dues and assessments. A delinquency rate of between 5% and 7% is average and realistic, but I've heard of associations where up to 70% of the homeowners can't pay what they owe. That puts a huge burden on the other homeowners—they'll likely either have to pay more themselves or watch the property decline. Several associations that I know of have even had to file for bankruptcy protection."

Also check on the ratio of units that are, or are allowed to be, rented out (the "rental cap"). The more units that are owner-occupied, the better the community usually is at attending to details like the budget and maintenance. Lenders also consider owner occupancy levels when approving buyers' loans, and might decline to offer some loan products if too many units are occupied by renters. Also, in a down market, rental property investors are often the first to go into foreclosure.

Why so much research? First, if there are restrictions you can't stomach, or common sources of major disgruntlement among fellow owners, you'll know the place isn't for you. Don't assume that the rules will change, or that an exception will be made! Second, you want to know how well funded the association is. If cash reserves are low, your monthly dues might go up, you might have to pay special assessments, or your property's value might plummet because neighboring homes are in foreclosure or sitting vacant.

Ask Lots of Questions

As with any neighborhood, it's worth finding out how people like living there, and who your neighbors will be. But you should also ask more-targeted questions, from your first interaction with the seller or seller's agent, and continuing on with people you meet within the community. Ask about everything from governance policies to package delivery to the neighbors' characters.

ONLINE TOOLKIT

Use the "Condo/Co-Op Worksheet" in the Homebuyer's Toolkit on the Nolo website for suggested questions. (See the appendix for the link.) A sample is shown above.

CHECK IT OUT

For more about community living: See the Community Associations Institute (CAI, www.caionline.org). Also, your state's website should link you to the relevant law. And search online for local organizations serving community association members.

What's Next?

Still having a hard time finding the right house at the right price? Look to Chapter 9 for alternatives. Or if you've already got your eye on a place, skip to Chapter 10, which discusses how to make an offer.

Plan B: Fixer-Uppers, FSBOs, Foreclosures, and More

Meet Your Adviser

Rob Jensen, broker/president, Rob Jensen Company, Las Vegas, Nevada (www.robjensen.com).

What he does

"I'm the broker of a firm that specializes in guard-gated communities in Summerlin, Las Vegas, and Henderson, Nevada. Our clients often seek a country club lifestyle, so we generally work in golf course communities with spectacular views, high-end amenities, and the peace of mind that comes with having a guard 24/7. My typical day involves negotiating deals, meeting with clients, and sharing expert advice on buying and selling luxury homes."

First house

"I bought several homes in 2004 that steadily increased in value until the market completely crashed. Since then, I've learned a lot by studying history, cycles, and market conditions. This knowledge has been invaluable in advising my clients and helping them understand how to navigate the market."

Fantasy house

"My dream home would definitely be in Spain, as close to world-class rock climbing as possible. It would have glass walls to capture extraordinary views of the landscape, a climate-controlled wine cellar, and a resort-style infinity pool."

Likes best about his work	"As a luxury real estate broker, I've had the opportunity to meet and work with incredible people across multiple industries, from gaming to entertainment. It feels great to help these people buy and sell extraordinary homes. In some cases, new friendships develop during these interactions, which is always a plus!"
Top tip for first-time homebuyers	"Interview a few agents—I'd suggest three to five—before deciding whom you want to work with. So many buyers stumble into their agent relationship, or keep a number of agents on the hook. But the sooner you can strike up a relationship and have an agent that you are loyal to, the sooner that agent will provide you all the possible benefits of his or her services, sending mailers on your behalf, looking at prospective homes, and so on. Also look at each agent's track record, responsiveness, availability, personality type, and any other criteria that are important to you. You'll be spending lots of time together."

You're already frequenting the open-house circuit, and you've got a good agent. But maybe the perfect house hasn't yet appeared, or at least not at a price you can afford. It's not hopeless! Check out some creative alternatives, including:

- houses that have stalled on the market
- houses that aren't on the market yet
- starter houses
- potential remodels and fixer-uppers
- space that can be shared with a co-owner or renter
- FSBOs (houses "For Sale by Owner," without a seller's agent), and
- foreclosures and probate sales.

As Ira Serkes, a Berkeley Realtor with Pacific Union, counsels, "The house you want, at the price you want to pay, might not actually exist. But it's important not to compromise on essential features such as neighborhood safety and number of bedrooms. Once you've gotten to know current market realities, and adjusted your expectations accordingly, finding a house you're happy with will happen much faster."

Castoffs: Searching for Overlooked Houses

In every market, a few houses have been on sale for so long that buyers have moved on and lost interest—which gives you a chance to step in and offer a lower price. Houses get overlooked for a broad variety of reasons: Maybe they're priced too high, have structural or cosmetic problems, or are unattractive to most buyers (because of a bad layout or a location on a busy street). They might even be "stigmatized properties," meaning they were the site of a crime, suicide or other death, rumored environmental dangers, haunting, or some other occurrence that gives buyers the creeps (and lowers the house's market value).

We haven't exactly made such houses sound appealing—but whether you should be interested at all comes down to two questions:

- If the house was simply overpriced, is the seller ready to sell it for what it's really worth?
- If the house has other problems, do they happen to be ones you can live with or feasibly change?

For example, when Realtor Carol Neil was helping her daughter house hunt in the always-competitive San Francisco market, she found they were getting outbid, and couldn't locate anything suitable for an acceptable price. So Carol went into the MLS and searched for listings tagged "expired" or "price reduction." Carol says, "It's wise to watch price reductions and visit the properties to see what the original 'flaw' was: cosmetics, price, or the property itself."

Carol's search led to a house with a view of the ocean and within walking distance of the elementary school that her grandsons attended. The problem? It was overpriced, because it smelled of cigarette smoke and was badly decorated, with tacky pink curtains and carpets—totally fixable, but hard for buyers to look beyond. The seller had rejected the only bid, expecting multiple, higher offers. When Carol's daughter came in four months later offering a price that accounted for the house's problems, the seller at last became realistic and accepted.

Your agent can help you with searches like Carol's and offer insights as to why a house hasn't yet sold. "I also like to look for homes listed as 'withdrawn' and 'leased,'" says adviser Rob Jensen. "The property might have been withdrawn because the seller was just tired of it being on the market without any solid offers. By reaching out to the listing agent, I can find out the back story. Sometimes, it's just been withdrawn temporarily, perhaps for the holidays. For whatever reason,

How'd They Sell That House?

Houses where infamous murders occurred don't fare well on the real estate market:

- Nicole Brown Simpson's 3,400-square-foot condo languished on the market for two years before selling for $200,000 below the asking price. The buyers changed the address and remodeled.
- Jeffrey Dahmer's Milwaukee apartment building was so stigmatized by his series of gruesome murders that the entire neighborhood's occupancy rates went from 80% to 20%. The building itself was demolished by developers.
- In 2004, the Boulder, Colorado, mansion where JonBenét Ramsey's body was found sold for $1.05 million ($345,000 under asking). Since that sale, the house has been listed seven times with an asking price ranging from $1.7 to $2.7 million. Despite the passage of many years and an address change, the house still attracts lookie-loos—but no serious buyers.

it might still be available upon inquiry. Or, if the property is being rented, it might come back on the market soon."

If the problem is serious, or the seller appears extremely unrealistic, cross the place off your list. But some overlooked houses might still remain prospects to pick up at an affordable price. In fact, says Rob Jensen, "Some buyers just don't want to deal with sellers who are unrealistic about their price. That might make your offer one of the few the seller will receive!" You might be a unique match for a particular property—for example, if you're unfazed by a house's criminal history. Also, some stigmas are more rumor than fact—maybe the former occupant actually died in the hospital, or an inspection turns up a logical reason for the spooky clanking noises.

Steer Clear of Meth Lab Houses

The highly toxic substances used to manufacture the illegal drugs known as methamphetamines can permeate various parts of the house, from carpets to drywall to countertops to air ducts. The health results haven't been fully studied yet, but include respiratory illnesses, migraines, cancer, and more.

Decontamination costs anywhere from $5,000 to $100,000, depending on the size of the home and other factors. If you hear any rumors that a house you're interested in used to be the local "drug house," have it checked. (And don't trust the seller's disclosures!)

TIP

Newly constructed home seekers: You too can find castoffs. Try looking at what's available in recently built developments. Sometimes, deals fall through or houses remain unsold even after construction ends on a development. At that point, developers are typically eager to sell the remaining homes quickly so they can move on to the next project. They don't like having their capital tied up in homes that haven't closed yet, so they might offer a discount or incentives to keep production moving. You might see these homes advertised as "builder closeouts." Though you won't get to choose the upgrades and finishes, buying a brand new builder closeout can be a great opportunity. Just make sure to stay away from closeouts where the builder is in bankruptcy or financial distress.

Houses Not Yet on the Market

If you're really coming up dry in your home search, and you know the neighborhood and type of home you're seriously interested in, be proactive. You—or more likely your agent—can knock on doors, talk to locals, and even mail a personalized letter to specific homes that match the criteria on your list. Chances are, some local homeowners are in the early phases of getting ready to sell, and might appreciate being saved the trouble of preparing and listing the property.

Adviser Rob Jensen suggests, "Work closely with your agent to send out a letter that includes a photo of you and your family, as well as a description of why it's so important for you to live in that neighborhood."

Another possibility is to go to Zillow.com, and see whether the seller of a property that has caught your eye has entered a "Make Me Move" price. This means the property isn't currently on the market, but that the owner might just be willing to sell for the "dream" price listed. Your agent can follow up.

Look What's Back on the Market!

Many houses go under contract only to have the deal fall through because the buyers didn't qualify for financing. And sometimes, buyers walk away for other reasons, whether personal or related to the house. That can put a home's sellers in a tough position—they've moved on with their lives and might be paying another mortgage, making them less than interested in going through yet another round of advertising and open houses.

If you keep your eyes open for such properties, you might be able to snag a bargain. According to attorney Alicia Champagne, "I see a lot of #2 buyers get the house."

"In fact," adds adviser Rob Jensen, "If there's a house you're particularly interested in that's in escrow, write an offer now! That way, if the deal hits a bump—say, the buyer needs a three-week extension to finalize the loan—the seller might just turn to you."

A Foot in the Door: Buying a Starter House

Every buyer's Dream List starts out ambitious—that's what dreams are for. Now that you've explored the market, you might have found you need to scale down your dreams concerning size, location, amenities, or something else. Perhaps you can get by without an office, or the kids can share a room (hey, the *Home Improvement* kids did it!). Or maybe you'll find a neighborhood that's up and coming. (Watch where the artists go! They are often the brave souls who turn a dicey neighborhood into a desirable one.)

With a starter house, you get your foot in the door of the real estate market, start building equity, and save enough to buy a bigger or better place in the not-too-distant future. It's a particularly solid strategy if you can expect increases in your income—for example, you or your partner will be graduating from school and getting a job soon. But even without saving, increases in the house's value and your equity can help launch you into the next house.

A few cautions apply to buying a starter house, however:

- **Transition ain't cheap.** You're going to have significant transaction costs each time you move: closing costs, agent commissions, and moving expenses. A seller can pay up to 7% of the overall price to sell the house, when you factor in the traditional 6% commission and approximately 1% in closing costs.
- **Tiny isn't as cheap as you'd think.** Even if the house is matchbox sized, you have to pay a reasonable amount for the land it sits on, particularly in a nice neighborhood.

- **Your possible short-term timeline should be factored into your choice of mortgage.** Run the numbers carefully before you pay points on a loan, for example, because you might not recoup their cost if you move within a few years.
- **Plan for the risk of a drop in real estate values in the next few years.** If the value of your home drops, you won't be building much equity and might have to sell at a loss. That could make it tough for you to afford a bigger or better home.

Don't be scared by the number of cautions. Many homebuyers adopt this starter-home strategy. It allows you to start enjoying the benefits of homeownership right away, learn the ropes of being a homeowner, and develop a realistic sense of when and how you can move to your next place.

Have It Your Way: Buying a Fixer-Upper or House You Can Add on To

Buying a house that needs a major overhaul, or will support an addition, is a great strategy for some buyers. The advantages are obvious: Pay less, and exercise your own excellent taste to produce a house you'll love living in and might sell at a profit. Plus, if the place is livable now, you can make these changes later, when you have more cash or equity (which you can borrow against).

Best thing we ever did

Buy a house we could add on to. Erica and Carl had recently married and planned to have kids. But, says Erica, "All the houses in our price range were too small, too far from our offices, or had no usable backyard space—and we had an image of hanging out with family and friends on a back deck. After a year's searching, we decided to buy small and add on. We found a well-priced two-bedroom, to which we added a second bathroom and a deck. That depleted our savings, but five years later, right before our second child, the house had gone up in value enough for us to qualify for a home equity loan and add another bedroom."

Sisters Are Fixing It for Themselves

Who says home repairs are "man's work"? Anyone who's repair-challenged can take advantage of fix-it resources, such as PrettyHandyGirl.com and AnikasDIYLife.com, with tutorials, message boards, and DIY videos. Or try these books:

- *Dare to Repair: A Do-It-Herself Guide to Fixing (Almost) Anything in the Home*, by Julie Sussman and Stephanie Glakas-Tenet (Storey Publishing). With its Rosie the Riveter cover, it's easy to spot and teaches tasks from unclogging sinks to patching drywall.
- *Chix Can Fix: 100 Home-Improvement Projects and True Tales From the Diva of Do-It-Yourself*, by Norma Vally (Studio). Seen her on the Discovery Channel? Now you can read her lively instructions and stories about dealing with plumbing, electricity, walls, floors, doors, and windows.
- *The Tuff Chix Guide to Easy Home Improvement*, by Paige Hemmis (Plume). Another star author, from "Extreme Makeover." This book focuses on home repair advice for novices.

How Much Fixing-Up Can You Handle?

Ideally, you'd like a house where the fix-ups are minor—like getting rid of the paisley wallpaper and mustard linoleum. Unfortunately, other homebuyers and investors are also looking for easy fixers, so huge bargains are sometimes hard to find. Nevertheless, a certain number of cosmetic fixers will remain overlooked, particularly if they look unappealing from the street (some potential buyers won't even get out of their car).

At the other end of the spectrum are major remodels, requiring structural upgrades, adding or removing walls or rooms, and more. Unless you've got a contractor in the family or can get a 203(k) loan (discussed below), we suggest avoiding these—especially if they contain health hazards (such as toxic forms of mold) or are virtually unlivable (perhaps with big holes in the floor or roof). Here's why:

- The bank could refuse to approve your loan until a certain amount of repairs are done, and neither the seller nor you might be able to pay for or complete these repairs.

- Major repairs can drain your bank account. You're looking for a fixer-upper because the perfect house doesn't seem to be in your price range, right? Also, construction surprises are inevitable, and usually expensive.
- Dealing with large-scale improvements can disrupt your life and strain your personal relationships. If this is your first home, you might not be ready to hire contractors; take time off work to supervise the maelstrom of activity; and deal with delays, no-shows, or cost overruns—especially if you're living in the house.

The best bargain is usually a fixer-upper somewhere in the middle: one that can be made livable with a manageable amount of your own work or professional help. Think new paint, new flooring, and new windows rather than a new foundation and roof. When you find one that looks promising, be sure to:

- Check whether your plans are actually feasible. This almost certainly means contacting your city building department regarding height limits, requirements to bring old wiring and other systems up to code, setback rules, view ordinances, or parking restrictions.
- Ask architects, contractors, and engineers about the costs and feasibility of any plans, from minor ones, such as carpet and paint, to major structural changes like adding a second story or a room.
- Have a serious conversation with anyone buying with you about the stress this project might cause. Discuss how you'll cope without a functional kitchen or bathroom, or who would deal with the many different contractors and workers.

Now, about those 203(k) loans alluded to earlier. These are federally (HUD-) backed mortgage loans, which provide home financing, at a long-term fixed or adjustable rate, to cover not only purchase costs but property rehabilitation work. The lender will take into account both the cost of the work and the projected value of the property with the work completed. The property must be a house or condominium unit that has been completed for at least one year. Many buyers use 203(k) loans, particularly because these might be the only choice when buying a foreclosure home that's in such bad shape that no lender will otherwise fund the loan. For more information, search www.hud.gov for "203(k) rehab mortgage insurance."

Expect the unexpected. Noemi and Hugo bought a rundown house on a street where many young couples were buying and remodeling. Hugo explains, "Our plan was to live there through the remodel, stick around a few years, and then move into a bigger place. But almost immediately, we ran into complications. First, after the roof was torn off, we were told we'd need a special beam to get the raised ceiling we wanted. Meanwhile, rain poured in on our hardwood floors, which had to be replaced. This resulted in a trickle-down effect (literally), with one delay after another. We ended up staying in our old apartment through the ten months of remodeling, paying both rent and a mortgage. We love our house, but we're no longer planning on moving soon!"

 CHECK IT OUT

Sometimes, tearing down and starting over might be easier: Check out RemodelingCalculator.org, which has a calculator to help you estimate the cost of replacing an entire house (look under the "Remodel Calc" menu).

Will You Make Money When You Sell?

Although eventually profiting on the sale of your remodeled or fixed-up house might not be your first priority, it's worth considering. Not all upgrades excite buyers enough to make them pay more—a new furnace, for example, rarely raises eyebrows. To check whether your planned changes will lead to profits, start with the websites below and then talk to a real estate agent. "Kitchens and master bathrooms are big selling points," says Rob Jensen, "and modern design is especially popular right now. Modern remodels done in the kitchen and master bathroom have been reaping big dividends in Las Vegas. I suggest having a conversation with your Realtor about what upgrades buyers are looking for in your market."

CHECK IT OUT

Estimate your remodeling costs, see cost-to-value ratios, or get general remodeling advice at:

- www.remodelingcalculators.com
- www.nari.org (the National Association of the Remodeling Industry), and
- www.remodeling.hw.net (click "Cost vs. Value").

Cobuyer Discussion Worksheet

To make sure you will be compatible, discuss the following issues before buying a place with someone else. Add anything else important to this list—for example, whether or not you want a dog or cat. Jot down notes and then draft a co-ownership agreement (with an attorney's help or using one of the contracts in Living Together: A Legal Guide for Unmarried Couples, *by Attorneys Frederick Hertz and Lina Guillen (Nolo)).*

1. How long you plan to stay in the house (and possible reasons that this could change, like moving to take care of an ill parent or getting married).

2. How you'll each be able to afford mortgage payments and other costs, and what happens if one of you falls on hard times.

3. Rules for sharing space (for example, cleaning up, dividing the costs of utilities and house supplies, limiting music volume levels, and overnight guests (short- or long-term)).

4. How much repair, improvement, or decorating the house could use, and how you'll budget for these.

5. How much of the property each of you will own, and how you will take title.

6. What will happen if one of you dies—for example, whether the deceased's interest in the house will go directly to the other owner, or go to an heir.

7. What will happen if one of you wants to move out or sell the house sooner than the other would like to. (Many buyers include what's called a "right of first refusal" in their co-ownership agreement, giving the nondeparting owner first crack at buying the other owner's share of the property, at a specified value, usually either the original purchase price or the currently appraised value.)

8. How you will handle disputes.

OTHER:

Share Your Space: Buying Jointly

Ask around: You're probably not the only person in your circle of friends or family who'd like to buy a house but can't quite make the finances work. You might find an interested, compatible cobuyer (or two). If you're living with roommates now, it won't be a big change.

Consider looking for a structure containing separate units, such as a duplex, which would allow you each to have your own entrance, kitchen, and more. But your lives wouldn't be completely separate—you'd still need to agree on major issues concerning your shared ownership.

Best thing I ever did

Buy a home with my sister. Meggan and her sister had both finished college and were looking to rent apartments in Worcester, Massachusetts. "But," says Meggan, "the two of us got to talking. For the amount we'd each pay to rent separate apartments, why not just join forces and buy a multiunit house? Eventually we found a three-family home, built in the 1920s, with beautiful woodwork and built-ins. We split all the costs 50/50 (the mortgage, the expenses, right down to the lawnmower), and each took one floor. Some tenants were already living on the third floor—a dependable family— and they stayed on. Everything worked out great, and three years later, after my sister and I had both married, we sold the place for double what we'd paid for it."

The cheaper alternative is usually to buy a single dwelling and share the entire space jointly, meaning you'd have less autonomy. With some looking around, you might be able to find a place with a layout conducive to independent lives, such as bedrooms in opposite wings.

You'll have to make some major decisions in advance about the financial and other aspects of your shared ownership. The biggest financial question will be how you split the down payment and monthly expenses—an even split, or a percentage split based on a factor such as the amount of money you each put in or the size of your bedrooms? Keep in mind that how you split ownership dictates how you can claim any related tax benefits.

Another major question involves who gets the property if one of you is no longer in the picture? If one of you dies, will the other person automatically own the whole house, or will someone named in the deceased owner's will inherit it? And in a less dire scenario, if one of you wants to move out, can that person rent his or her portion of the place, sell to any buyer, force the whole property to be sold, or be obligated to offer the other owner a chance to buy the "property interest" (that's legalese for an ownership share)?

Think about these issues before buying, because the manner in which you describe your ownership on the property deed (in legalese, "take title") will legally determine the answer to some of them. For example, joint tenancy almost always involves a 50/50 split (depending on state law; see Chapter 11).

Cobuying is a huge commitment, and it's crucial you choose the right person to share the responsibilities of homeownership and discuss issues like how often to mow the lawn or clean the house. Sit down with your potential co-owner to discuss such issues.

Then, no matter how compatible you two seem to be, put your agreement in writing, preferably with an attorney's help. "Frankly," says adviser Rob Jensen, "Cobuying is such a risky business that I'd recommend you consider renting out a bedroom to help with expenses, in lieu of bringing in a cobuyer—that keeps you in control."

 ONLINE TOOLKIT

Make sure your discussion covers all the bases: Use the "Cobuyer Discussion Worksheet" included in the Homebuyer's Toolkit on the Nolo website. (See the appendix for the link.) A sample is shown above.

 CHECK IT OUT

Looking for details on buying a home with someone other than a spouse? If you and your cobuyer are a couple, you'll find useful information and sample forms in either *Living Together: A Legal Guide for Unmarried Couples*, by Attorneys Frederick Hertz and Lina Guillen (Nolo); or *A Legal Guide for Lesbian & Gay Couples*, by Attorneys Frederick Hertz and Emily Doskow (Nolo).

Subdivide Your Space: Renting Out a Room

If total privacy is a luxury you can sacrifice, at least in the short term, it might help you afford a home. In fact, if you've already got a roommate whom you enjoy living with, that person might be content writing the rent checks to you, instead of to your current landlord.

You can often charge almost as much as what renters would pay for an apartment and set down rules regarding which rooms they can use, kitchen cleanliness, and more—it's still *your* place. The rent will help you pay the mortgage, and you can charge for a portion of the common costs, like utilities. Of course, you'll want to protect yourself with good tenant screening and a written rental agreement.

If you can't face the thought of a stranger having your front door key, look for a duplex, a place with a casita in the back or a basement apartment, or another multiunit building.

CHECK IT OUT

Planning to be a landlord? Check the terms of your mortgage. Some loans, such as VA or FHA loans, might prohibit using the property as a hotel or for "transient" purposes. These restrictions could prevent you from renting rooms or offering short-term rentals. Also look into state and local laws that might impact your plans or guide your actions. Attorney Alicia Champagne warns, "Some town ordinances set a maximum on the number of non-blood-related individuals who can live in a house." Your homeowners' association (HOA) or governing body of your common interest community might also have strict rules and restrictions—or a flat-out prohibition—regarding rentals. Get help on legal matters from *First-Time Landlord: Your Guide to Renting Out a Single-Family Home*, by Janet Portman, Ilona Bray, and Marcia Stewart (Nolo). And if you're considering short-term rentals, such as through Airbnb or Vrbo, there might be additional city regulations for you to take into account.

Hey, Where's Their Agent?
Looking for FSBOs (For Sale by Owners)

Another way to broaden your search is to visit FSBOs, that is, houses sold by owners not working with agents. Just how many sellers go the FSBO route is impossible to say, but most estimates put it at close to 8% of all U.S. houses. That's a lot of houses an ordinary real estate agent might not be showing you. (It's financially risky for the agent, because collecting a commission can be challenging for various reasons when dealing with FSBOs.) If you want an agent to include FSBOs in the home search, this is something to talk about early on.

Sometimes, FSBOs can save you money. The seller might have underpriced the house or be willing to share the commission savings with you. But don't count on savings—sellers going through the effort of advertising and showing their houses aren't always interested in parting with any of their earnings.

In fact, warns retired Realtor Nancy Atwood, "Many FSBO sellers I encountered were near or underwater on their mortgage, trying to save every cent and avoid the stigma of foreclosure or a short sale. A good listing agent would tell them to just go to their lender and work out a short sale!" Attorney Alicia Champagne adds, "I see a lot of these deals fall apart, because the seller didn't research seller closing costs and remains short of funds."

Your Agent's Role in Buying a FSBO

Most agents don't routinely search for FSBOs. They find that most FSBOs are improperly priced, thus saddling the agent with the problems that arise from dealing with a seller who has little idea how to sell real estate or what's legally involved.

So, you'll need to work out in advance whether you want your agent to show you FSBOs. One option is to do the searching yourself, using the resources listed in the next section. If you see an ad for a FSBO that looks interesting, the appropriate next step is to tell your agent about it before visiting the house.

That lets the agent deal with the next important issue—getting paid. Your agent will call and ask whether the FSBO seller will "cooperate" regarding the commission (that means paying the portion of the commission that the seller's agent would normally hand over, usually about 2½% of the sale price). Don't be surprised if the answer is no. Your agent will then come back to you and discuss the commission, to see whether you're willing to pay it. You should agree on the rate in advance.

Finding FSBO Houses

Because FSBO sellers aren't represented by real estate brokers, they don't have access to the MLS database (unless they've made a special effort to find and pay a broker for the discrete task of listing the house). That means you'll find most FSBOs either listed on independent websites (like those below) or advertised by alternative means (craigslist, local newspapers, or yard signs).

 CHECK IT OUT

Your best bets for finding FSBOs on the Web are:

- ForSaleByOwner.com

- FSBO.com, and

- Zillow.com (click on the "Buy" menu, then choose "By Owner" under "Listing Type").

Dealing With FSBO Sellers' Varying Personalities and Skill Levels

Sellers without agents might not know much about the real estate market, and they're negotiating with buyers without an agent acting as a buffer. That means that the success of buying a particular FSBO house—from setting a price to closing the deal—depends largely on the seller's own personality, real estate knowledge, and skill set.

In the best-case scenario, you might find a FSBO seller who is a fair-minded lawyer or retired real estate professional, who sees no reason to enlist extra help for a familiar process. In the worst case, you might find a seller who is a skinflint curmudgeon know-it-all or a total flake, who overprices the house, refuses to discuss commissions, and cancels the sale the minute you bring up inspections or repairs. And even the most expert sellers' judgment can be affected by emotions when they're trying to sell their own house.

Best thing we ever did

Get to know our FSBO seller. Maria and her husband had been keeping their eyes open for a house that would not only fit them and their two girls, but include an in-law unit for an elderly parent. "We knew such a house would be hard to find," says Maria, "so when we heard that my husband's sister's best friend's mom's house was sitting empty—she'd recently moved into an assisted-living center—we contacted the family to sound them out. They'd just begun thinking about selling and were intimidated by the amount of work it would take to clear out the place (the mother was a packrat) and to fix it up (it desperately needed a new roof, not to mention cosmetic fixes like replacing the orange shag carpet). But after my family and I saw the house—which was just what we wanted—I talked to the mother directly, and we hit it off. In fact, eventually she told her daughter that selling the house to us was almost like keeping it in the family. We agreed to buy it without an agent, at a price that was reasonable given all the fix-ups and the commission savings. The whole arrangement was mutually beneficial in many ways—including when we began picking up the seller at her assisted-living center and driving her to the house so she could sort through the lifetime of possessions."

Buying a FSBO Without an Agent

If you don't have or want an agent yet, you can buy a FSBO on your own—but be prepared for a steep learning curve. Often, FSBO deals occur between friends or acquaintances, which hopefully means the transaction will be cordial. But beware the canny seller—acquaintance or stranger—who might try to take advantage of you. And any deal can get mired in disagreements. No matter what your relationship with the seller is, you'll need a standard, written sales agreement to protect both of you.

If saving money is a key concern, consider hiring an attorney for limited parts of the transaction. (In a few states, you'll have to use an attorney for certain tasks, anyway.) A few hours' advice can save you from later heartache and expense and still cost you thousands less than an agent's commission. One option might be to hire a lawyer to serve as your coach. Ask the lawyer to give you a purchase agreement form that's widely used in your community and that fairly protects both you and the seller. The lawyer can also explain how to complete the form yourself, and then review your handiwork.

You could also negotiate a flat fee with an agent to handle the transaction. Realtors have access to state forms and all the preferred vendors that you might need.

Whatever you do, don't go without the services of an escrow and title company, which might operate as one and the same, to help guide you toward the closing, as described in Chapter 11.

 TIP

If no agent is involved in a FSBO, some states don't require seller disclosures. In that case, it becomes doubly important to bring in the most thorough professional home inspectors you can find to assess the property's physical condition.

Buying a Short Sale Property

A "short sale" is real estate lingo for a house that's being put up for sale for less than the homeowner owes on the mortgage and where the homeowner is unable or unwilling to come up with the difference—usually, a home-owner in financial distress who is trying to avoid foreclosure. Sometimes, but not always, the seller has already defaulted on the loan. That makes it potentially affordable but with some major risks, as discussed below.

The traditional way that a short sale works is for the seller to find a willing buyer, and then present the lender with the buyer's offer, often on a preprinted application form, and accompanied by an appraisal showing the property's estimated market value. The hope is that the lender will agree to forgive what remains on the loan and let the sale go forward, as a way to get rid of a mortgage that it would probably never have been able to fully collect on anyway. Lenders sometimes also reach out to sellers who are behind on their home payments, offering them relocation money and a path toward preapproval for a short sale. The lender will, as part of this process, order a BPO (broker-price opinion) analysis, showing what amount the house could sell for.

No matter what, the need for the seller's lender to approve the sale adds a major potential hurdle—not to mention time delay—to the process. Even if you offer the preapproved BPO amount, the lender will still need to conduct various investigations, take action on paperwork, and run the numbers, trying to balance the amount that would be lost on the loan against the probable loss (and cost and hassle) if the property continued on into foreclosure. "One issue on the lender's mind is potential fraud," says adviser Rob Jensen. "The lender wants to make sure you're not, for example, buying your sister's place in order to sell it back to her a couple of months later. I had one home-selling client where the lender just wouldn't approve the short sale, and we found out it was because long before, when my client had owned shoe stores, the buyer had been among the store's vendors. The lender saw that as a sign that this might not be an arms' length transaction."

TIP

"'Short' doesn't mean 'quick'!" The term "short" comes from the fact that the seller is short on paying the bank back in full. According to attorney Alicia Champagne, "Many buyers come to me thinking a short sale is like a fire sale, and expecting to close the next week. This is the opposite of the truth. Some banks won't return phone calls for literally weeks. Short sales are best for buyers who can wait."

A short sale might have an alluringly low price—especially in comparison to what the seller owes—but that doesn't necessarily make it a good deal. The seller might have overpaid to begin with, or the market might have fallen significantly. And as we'll explain below, as the buyer you may be responsible for significant additional costs that aren't accounted for in the selling price.

You also run the very real risk that the lender will—after you've probably waited two months or more—say no. This is particularly likely if the seller has advertised the property for much less than is owed on it, desperately fishing for any offer.

Making an Offer on a Short Sale

If you're interested in a short sale property, choose an agent who's dealt with them before. Some agents won't deal with them at all, fearing the uncertainty of the process. "That's unfortunate," says attorney Alicia Champagne, "because there are buyers for whom short sales can be a good deal. The key is that they have the time to wait for approval and a place to live in the meantime. Whatever you do, don't give notice to your landlord, lock in a mortgage interest rate, or buy furniture, until you've received approval from the short sale owners' lender!"

TIP

In the meantime, keep looking! Adviser Rob Jensen says, "Even though the short sale might get approved, there's no need to put all your eggs in one basket. If you find another house to buy, you can withdraw your offer on the short sale property."

It's helpful to know whether the homeowner has more than one loan. If so, you'll need the approval of all lenders to make the sale. The more lenders there are, the harder it is to get approval, because each lender must agree to taking a smaller piece of the pie. Ask your agent to research this for you.

Beyond this, there's not much point in trying to play detective. The lender has various behind-the-scenes concerns that you can't readily find out about, much less strategize around, such as whether it wants to take more losses on its balance sheet this quarter. Also, make sure your agent talks with the seller's agent about what kind of legwork has already been done. Banks will approve a short sale only if the seller is in financial distress. Make sure the seller has at least contacted the bank and gotten confirmation that the bank will consider a short sale. Unless you're not in any particular hurry to buy a place, you don't want to waste your time waiting for a bank to respond to an offer that you're fairly certain will just be rejected anyway.

What to Expect With a Short Sale

If you decide, after obtaining the information above, that you still want to buy a short sale, expect it to differ from a regular sale in a few ways:

- **First in line is best.** Short-sale sellers will often approach the lender with the first offer received, even if it's on the extremely low side. Why? Because once they've started the long process of gaining bank approval, they don't want to derail it by bringing in an alternate offer; nor do they want to give the bank any ideas about how they could actually get more for the house than the offer on the table.

- **The seller has no profit motive with regard to the home sale.** By the very nature of the deal, a home seller is not allowed to profit on a real estate short sale. So if you're in a multiple offer situation, and want your offer to stand out, upping your offer price might not help. One thing that savvy offerors have done, however, is to include a request to buy some of the seller's *personal* property— perhaps at a premium price. (If, for example, you suggest buying the seller's patio chairs and barbeque grill for $3,000, you might just find that the seller prefers your offer over the others.)

- **You're somewhat at the mercy of the sellers and their listing agent.** Both might be competent and have the ability to move things along—or not. The agent in particular will have a lot of work to do: There's a lot of paperwork to submit and agents must closely monitor the bank's progress and responses. You, too, will need to be attentive, and make sure you're getting things in on time. There can be a lot of hurrying up and waiting.

- **Lower commissions paid by the seller to your agent.** The lender, who is ultimately paying the real estate agent commissions, might negotiate them down with the seller's agent, and your agent will get paid less as a result. If you agreed to pay your agent more in a buyer's brokerage agreement, you'll have to make up the difference out of your own pocket or renegotiate the agreement.

- **The property will be sold "as is."** Lenders offer the property in its present condition, with no reductions for repair needs. To make sure you know what state things are in, be certain you have an inspection contingency in the contract, allowing you to have the property professionally inspected and back out of the deal if you're not satisfied with the results. (We discuss inspections in greater detail in Chapter 12.) Just don't expect to negotiate any of the repairs with the bank—though you can try.
- **You might have to pay all or most of the closing costs.** These fees are, in a normal transaction, usually split with the seller, but the bank might (in some states) refuse to pay. Check into what's customarily paid by both parties in a short sale in your state.
- **The transaction will take longer.** You might spend months waiting for your offer to be approved or rejected by the bank. While you'd think the bank would take more of an interest, it might by now be acting as a mere servicer, collecting payments on behalf of a secondary investor to which it has already sold the owner's mortgage. Make sure your offer terminates at some realistic point in the future. How can you even choose a closing date to write into your offer in such circumstances? "Approximately three months out is the norm," says adviser Rob Jensen. "You might need to update that along the way. But keep on top of the approaching date—I remember one prospective short sale that the lender closed out in its system on the closing date, because we had passed the close date."
- **Last-minute unhappy surprises.** When the lender finally approves your offer and sends the seller the paperwork to finalize the deal, it's not uncommon for the seller to discover that the lender has inserted language saying that even after releasing the mortgage, the lender can come after the seller for the difference in what is owed—which, for the seller, defeats the purpose of the short sale and might make the deal fall through. (In fact, the seller might have asked you to sign an addendum allowing it to cancel the deal if the lender won't release it from liability for this deficiency.)

As you can see, short sales are extra work and hassle. Unless you're going to get a property at a deep discount—even after adding up the costs of your real estate agent's commission, repairs, and closing costs—and you have enough time to wait around for the bank to respond to your offer, you're probably better off buying a house that isn't conditioned on an unusual form of bank approval.

Buying a Foreclosure Property

Foreclosure occurs when a homeowner can't pay back a mortgage loan, and the lender exercises its legal right to force a sale. They became especially common after meltdowns in the bank and mortgage industries, but they can occur in any market, giving rise to interest by bargain-hunting homebuyers.

Before you even consider going the foreclosure-home route, it's important to understand that foreclosure is a more varied and complex process than it might sound like. Foreclosures happen at every price point, from the highest-end houses to the lowest. The bank or lender doesn't usually foreclose right away—they give borrowers a grace period first. When a lender does move toward foreclosure it creates opportunities for new buyers at three stages of the process:

1. **Preforeclosure.** The property is still owned by the homeowner, and if there's no equity, their only other way out is a short sale.

2. **At a public sale or auction.** This typically means you're handing over cashier's checks on auction day. It's cash only, and you have no opportunity for due diligence unless you can find a way to inspect the house prior to the auction.

3. **Buying directly from the bank (called real-estate-owned, or REO).** These sales still appear in the MLS. Buyers can pay cash or obtain financing.

> **TIP**
>
> **Step aside, investors!** Regular buyers who plan to live in the homes themselves get a "first look" at some government-owned foreclosures. Investors need to wait before putting in a bid—20 days for FHA-owned properties and 30 days for HUD homes.

States Where Most Foreclosures Happen

The five U.S. states with the largest percentages of homes foreclosed upon in mid-2019 were:

- Delaware
- Florida
- Illinois
- Maryland
- New Jersey

Source: www.RealtyTrac.com

The main advantage in buying a foreclosure is price—you're likely to get some sort of a discount no matter what stage you buy at. The main disadvantages to buying foreclosure properties are:

- **Accepting risk.** As we'll explain further below, you might have to forgo at least some of the normal protections available in a typical transaction; for example if you're buying at auction, you might not get to see (much less inspect) the property before you buy, have to accept it "as is," and have to go without title insurance.

- **Waiting to make sure the owner is protected.** All states have laws to make sure banks can't rip properties out from under late-paying owners on a moment's notice. For buyers, that means deadlines, delays, court rules, and uncertainty—particularly in the many states that allow the former owner to "redeem" or buy back the property within a certain period of time after it was sold in foreclosure (usually from ten days to one year after the foreclosure sale, and usually before you've moved in). Of course, if that happens, your money will be refunded. But do you really want to be held in limbo, unsure of whether you'll ever be able to occupy the house?

- **Competition from experienced real estate investors.** If there are good deals to be had, you can bet real estate investors will be lined up in front of you.

- **Risks of undisclosed repair needs, tax liens, or other issues with the property.** Remember, these homeowners were probably financially stressed for a while. They might have held back on maintenance, gotten behind on their taxes, or used the house as collateral for other debts.

- **Lack of leverage.** If you're buying at auction, attorney Ken Goldstein counsels, "This isn't like buying from a nice couple who've lived in the house for 40 years. You'll be dealing with corporate America; and you won't exactly be on an even footing."

- **Ravages of time.** Any time a house sits empty for a while—as a foreclosure often does—it deteriorates. As attorney Viviane Shammas says, "Almost half the foreclosed homes I see here in Michigan have water damage and mold—the inevitable result of pipes bursting during winter. I've also come across critters, squatters, drug dealers, bugs, spiders, a sewage gas smell, rotted gaskets that spring leaks, stolen appliances, and other damage from break-ins."

In some cases, when you estimate the repairs a foreclosed home will need, it becomes clear that the privately owned and maintained home down the street is actually a better buy.

Preforeclosure or redemption period sales are especially dangerous territory unless you have a knowledgeable lawyer. And even if you want to look only at foreclosures that are already bank owned, find an agent who specializes in them—most don't handle them at all, while some go so far as to arrange bus tours of local foreclosures. A good source is www.reonetwork.com.

If you still have a regular real estate agent (as well as a specialized foreclosure agent), explain to both what you're doing, so that you can agree on each agent's limited role. And hire a real estate attorney to help navigate this somewhat touchy area.

Buying a House in Preforeclosure

When a house is in preforeclosure, the owners who have fallen behind on their payments have received a notice of default from their lender, or the lender has filed a lawsuit to start foreclosure proceedings. The lender will typically give the homeowner a set period of time (depending on their state's law; 90 days is common) to either sell the house for enough to pay off the loan, catch up paying all late mortgage payments and fees, or work out some other agreement (such as a loan modification or short sale).

Preforeclosure listings are publicly available even if the homeowner hasn't listed the property for sale. Online services like Foreclosure.com or RealtyTrac.com compile this information from public records.

Some aggressive homebuyers or investors use this information to find homes in preforeclosure and then approach the defaulting homeowners to make an offer. Of course, they'll be mainly interested in properties that are worth more than the homeowners owe, so that they can offer less than market value but still help the homeowners get out from under the mortgage. (If the seller owes more than the property is worth and can't make up the difference or negotiate an agreement with the lender, the main alternative short of foreclosure is a short sale, discussed above.)

Whether a homeowner will appreciate this, if you attempt it, is questionable. Some might feel that you're circling like a predator. Others might be grateful that you're helping them get out of a tough predicament. A homeowner who is being approached by impersonal investors who are scooping up multiple homes at a time might, however, actually appreciate receiving a handwritten note from you saying something like, "I understand you're going through a rough time, and my family would like to get into your neighborhood but can't afford anything we've seen yet, so maybe we can work something out."

If you were to find a homeowner ready to sell, you could negotiate just as you would any other transaction (though you'd absolutely want to get a lawyer's help). But you'd probably be very pressed for time. Depending on the state you're in, the homeowner could have as little as a few weeks from the time the lender files a "Notice of Default" to catch up on the mortgage (meaning you'll have to close the deal by then), or the lender will put the house up for auction. Once the auction takes place, the house is considered "foreclosed."

Buying a Foreclosure at Public Sale or Auction

If the seller doesn't pay what's owed and the lender forecloses, the property will be sold at a public sale or auction. This is rarely a good time for a first time homebuyer to get a good deal, for several reasons.

First of all, the lender will probably make the first bid on the house, for the amount owed on the mortgage. Unless the amount owed is low in relation to the home's value (rarely the case), you won't want to bid any higher. And if the price is right and you want to bid, you'll be competing with savvy real estate investors. Even if you're the highest bidder, you have another giant hurdle to overcome: You'll be expected to have come with cash in hand, without a traditional loan or financing, which is rarely a realistic option for first-time buyers.

Add to this the fact that you'll know very little about the house itself. You might never have even seen the place, and you'll have to take it "as is," without the benefit of an inspection. (Though if it's tenant occupied, you might be able to talk your way in for a look.) It isn't uncommon for disgruntled homeowners to trash their former homes or to strip them of all valuable assets when foreclosure happens (light fixtures, appliances, even copper wires). Or if the house has sat vacant for a long time, thieves might have done the same thing. Even worse, you might have to go without title insurance, leaving you open to the risk of an unpaid lien or a later claim to title.

When you buy a foreclosure, you aren't working directly with the homeowner. But that doesn't mean the homeowner isn't involved. If a stubborn homeowner or tenant hasn't moved out, you will likely have to proceed with an eviction action or exchange "cash for keys"—that is, give them some money to vacate the place, to avoid the hassle and expense of the eviction.

Buying a Bank-Owned House

If no one else buys the property at the foreclosure sale, the bank will then own it (as an REO) and likely try to sell it, usually by listing it with a local real estate agent. You might come across these deals if you browse standard MLS listings.

At this point, the bank might be willing to sell the house for less than the seller owed, while still hoping to get as close to market value as possible. What's more, says attorney Ken Goldstein, "As sellers, banks are far less motivated or willing to compromise than you'd expect. In a 'normal' home transaction, the seller wants to sell as badly as the buyer wants to purchase. But banks might be flooded with property transactions, so that no one deal among the thousands claims a prominent place on their radar screen."

Even if the price is a little lower than you'd find on a house that isn't bank owned, a bank-owned property comes with additional complications. By the time the bank gets to selling it—which can be a long time—it might have been vacant for months. Banks usually do little more than pick up debris and do a basic cleanup, so you won't see any expert staging here, and you might find that the lower price is balanced by the hard work you'll have to put in to make the house liveable.

Best thing we ever did **Buy a bank-owned home.** Anjanelle and Alan were looking to buy a house in the Sacramento, California, area. "When a wave of bank-owned properties flooded the market at rock bottom prices, we thought it might finally be affordable," says Anjanelle. "But it was an uphill battle, and it took several months." They bid on three houses before striking a deal, offering a little above the asking price to avoid being outbid. But then the house didn't appraise for the amount of their offered price. "We thought the deal was going to fall apart, but the bank was so anxious to get rid of the place, and we already had a deal on the table, so they dropped the price. It worked out great for us, and then we had enough cash to do some of the major repair work the house needed, like painting the smoke-damaged walls and having the worn-out hardwood floors refinished."

Also, banks usually sell properties "as is." At this stage, you'll at least have the benefit of an inspection contingency (discussed in more detail in Chapter 11). That means that while you can't expect the bank to do anything about needed repairs, you'll at least be able to have the property professionally inspected, and back out of the deal if you don't like what you see.

If you do find a good deal on a bank-owned home, chances are you're not the only one. It isn't unheard of for well-priced bank-owned properties to garner ten to 20 offers. (Your real estate agent should be able to find out this type of detail on properties you're interested in, with a little legwork.) To make your offer stand out, you might have to pay more than other bidders. You'll definitely want to be preapproved for a loan, and not just a token preapproval, but one where the lender has done all the underwriting processing. It could help if your preapproval letter

Housebuying Fantasies

For when reality hasn't yet delivered the house of your dreams, here are some fantasies to indulge in:

- **Buy an island.** Whether you'd fancy an Irish island with a castle or a coral reef atoll in Belize, they're listed, with photos, at www.vladi-private-islands.de.

- **Buy an airplane.** A California woman paid $100,000 for a 747; disassembled it; and turned it into a curvy, eco-friendly cottage. (The plane's nose was used as a meditation temple.) Look for "The 747 Wing House," in *Architectural Record*, at www.architecturalrecord.com.

- **Build a treehouse.** You can buy plans—including for a treehouse that's 64 square feet and requires two trees to support it—at TreehouseGuides.com.

- **Convert a caboose.** They're available at Cabooses4sale.com.

- **Live on a houseboat.** You provide the boat, and lease the dock or slip. But first, visit Amsterdam's Houseboat Museum: www.houseboatmuseum.nl.

Okay, now get back to reality.

comes from the selling lender (some sellers even require this)—they'll trust their own assessment of your finances better than anyone else's.

Houses Sold at Tax Sales

When a homeowner fails to pay property taxes, the state may take title to the property, then sell its claim (its "lien") at auction. The buyer of the lien will have to allow the current owner a legally specified amount of time to pay off the lien and reclaim the property before stepping in to claim title. The procedural requirements are complex and definitely not recommended for first-time buyers.

CHECK IT OUT

For information on foreclosures, see the following sites:

- RealtyTtrac.com (for a monthly fee)
- https://HomeSales.gov (for listings of houses foreclosed upon by HUD, USDA, and the VA), and
- Foreclosure.com.

Regular Sellers Are Also Trying Auctions

Some ordinary home sellers are deciding that auctions—either live or online (but NOT in foreclosure)—are the fastest, most profitable way to sell. Live auctions are usually handled by professionals who let potential buyers visit an open house first and hire inspectors before making a bid. The buyer pays the company a premium, usually 7%–10% of the house price.

Online auctions are usually handled on sites like Auction.com and eBay, and the procedures vary depending on the sellers: Horror stories have emerged of naïve buyers who purchased houses sight unseen. The bottom line is you might get an auction bargain, but there are unusual up-front costs and risks.

Buying a House in Probate

Usually if a homeowner dies, and either left a will or didn't leave any instructions at all, the property must be "probated." A court reviews the case, orders a division of assets, and more. Without getting too deep into the legal details, some properties end up being sold, usually at a court-supervised public sale or auction. This is the classic "probate sale." Another variation on this theme is that the estate's executor, administrator, or personal representative might sell the house privately, with or without a broker, so that cash can be distributed to the heirs.

It's possible to get a bargain on a house in probate whether it's sold at auction or through negotiation. If it's sold at auction, a minimum bid is set based on its appraised value, and you might be the only bidder. Even if you're not, California real estate agent Annemarie Kurpinsky points out that, "Unlike competing for nonprobate properties, you know exactly how high the other bidders are willing to go, and you therefore have no feeling of having overpaid." And with a negotiated purchase, you might benefit from the heirs' desire for a quick sale—they might regard any money that they get as a windfall.

But the disadvantages of buying a probate property include:

- **Legal and procedural hassles.** Court procedures vary by state but almost always involve paperwork and deadlines—and often a trip to court to bid on the house.
- **Risks of undisclosed repair needs.** You're waiting for a property whose physical condition may be going from bad to worse. And many states lift their disclosure rules for houses in probate. (After all, the whole point of a disclosure form is for the seller to share knowledge of the property gained from years spent living there—but the seller in this case is dead.) Worse yet, in many probate sales you must buy the property "as is," without making the sale conditional on the results of inspections.

If you're interested in probate houses, find an agent who specializes in them. Or, if you happen to know about a person who has died, there's nothing wrong with checking the probate court records to find out who's administering the estate and contacting that person. The executor (or "administrator" or "personal representative") is probably an amateur—a relative of the deceased—and might be grateful for a way to liquidate the real estate without the expense of a commission or the hassles of an auction."

What's Next?

Your home search might continue for a while, but that's all right. Don't settle for anything less than a home that meets your minimum requirements (even if those had to be adjusted), and where you'll be happy living for long enough to strategize your next move. Once you find the right house, things will move quickly: Your first step will be to make an offer to the seller, as described next.

Show Them the Money: From Offer to Purchase Agreement

Meet Your Adviser

Richard Leshnower, a New York-based attorney with specialized experience in real estate.

What he does	Helps buyers and sellers negotiate and close on the purchase of co-ops and houses in New York City and surrounding areas. Richard not only represents people at the front end of property sales, but helps some who come to him with postsale problems—for example, a buyer who didn't understand what she was signing and discovered that she'd bought a house without buying its side yard.

. . . .

First house	"I bought it in 1974, a beautiful colonial in Woodmere, New York. I asked my boss (another attorney) to represent me at the closing. Closings in 1974 involved a lot fewer documents than you'll encounter today! But what I remember most about the closing was the behavior of the husband seller, who was retiring and moving out of state. He flipped out under the pressure of the moment. He stood up, grabbed the table and threw it over. Papers went flying all over the floor. His wife jumped on him to calm him down. The good news is that he returned to his gentlemanly self, and the deal closed—and I lived in that house for 30 years."

. . . .

Likes best about his work	"Helping people who are otherwise intelligent and cautious find their way out of a tough situation—for example, afford a home when they thought they couldn't qualify for a mortgage. And nothing thrills me more than when I get a call out of the blue from a client who's moved elsewhere, to tell me how he or she is doing."

. . . .

Fantasy house	"A majestic house with an ocean view, like you might find in Big Sur, California. In addition to the usual rooms, I'd like a small hideaway room where I can read, view television, and use the computer. And let's pack the house full of other good stuff like a game room, swimming pools (outdoor and indoor), bowling alley, gym, movie theatre, and a slip for a boat. Not that I really 'need' all of this—my wife Karyn and I are empty nesters and already have a house we love in Boca Raton, Florida, and a co-op apartment in Hewlett, New York."
Top tip for first-time homebuyers	"Pick good advisers who you know are on your side and will be available to you for consultation. Don't let anyone tell you that something is too difficult for you to understand—you don't have to read every word of every document, but ask your advisers to educate you on their meaning. Also, walk the property and look at every nook and cranny yourself. That avoids situations like one where some buyers (whom I didn't represent) bought a big house on a large area of land one summer but didn't walk beyond the thick shrubbery in the backyard. After moving in, they heard trains rumbling—and sure enough, there was a train track right behind the rear property line, which came into full view that autumn, when the leaves fell off the trees."

Y ou've found it, the place you love, the home you want. Now all you have to do is tell the seller you'll take it, sign a few papers, and move in, right?

Not quite. First, you'll need to decide on the terms of your offer, and that involves more than whether you'll offer the asking price. This is also your chance to, say, ask the seller for a short closing period so you can move in soon or request that the custom-built kitchen table be left with the house. You'll figure out whether you and the seller can agree on such terms once you start negotiating. In this chapter, we'll explain how to:

- submit an offer, negotiate with the seller, and reach an agreement
- decipher the typical language in a standard home purchase contract
- decide on the contract's basic terms like price, contingencies to protect your interests, and deposit
- make your offer the best it can be, given the market you're in, and
- work with a developer to buy a new home.

Start to Finish: Negotiating and Forming a Contract

Buying a house is nothing like most of the financial transactions we make—for one thing, the price and other terms are largely negotiable. As adviser Richard Leshnower says, "This isn't like putting a dollar into a vending machine and getting a can of soda."

To understand the options and get the best deal—and to know what input to give your agent or attorney—it's good to know how the process works before you begin. (This description applies primarily to purchases of existing homes—we'll discuss buying a new home later in the chapter.)

Submitting an Offer

Once you say, "This is the house!" your real estate agent will probably suggest preparing an offer. (In a few states, however, your attorney will do the drafting, or the opening offer may be verbal.) You'd normally go back to your agent or attorney's office, but if there's time pressure, perhaps from competing buyers, drafting an offer in the agent's car is not unheard of.

In fact, because most real estate paperwork can be handled digitally (with the help of electronic signing technology), you and your agent don't even have to be in the same place to preparing an offer. Says adviser and real estate broker Tara Waggoner (whom you'll meet in Chapter 15), "We can often prepare and submit an offer within the hour—which has become especially important as multiple-offer situations become the norm."

Seriously, Are You Ready?

Use this checklist to decide whether you're ready to make an offer on a specific house, or whether you should do more legwork first:

☐ I've hired or am already working with a real estate agent, mortgage broker or lender, and/or attorney.

☐ I've done my research and learned about what to expect from the homebuying process in my area.

☐ This house is in my price range, and I have my down payment cash available.

☐ I'm preapproved for a mortgage, and I know what kind of mortgage I want—or the seller is willing to provide financing.

☐ I'm ready to devote much of my time over the next several weeks to closing the deal and preparing to move (unless it's a yet-to-be constructed house, in which case the time period may be longer).

In many states, a buyer's initial offer eventually serves as the complete contract, after both the buyer and seller have approved and signed it. Such offers are written in great detail, including not only a proposed price, but what conditions (contingencies) must be met for the deal to finalize, how disputes would be resolved, and who will pay what fees. It might be accompanied by a sum of money called an earnest money or good-faith deposit.

In other states, the offer is a very short document or is not written down at all—the point is just to communicate to the seller that you'd like to buy the house. It might contain some basic terms, such as the price, closing date, and a list of contingencies—most likely including an inspection and that the buyer and seller reach a "mutually satisfactory purchase and sale agreement." The full contract is written later, sometimes with the seller's attorney creating the first draft—in which case, you should read it extra carefully! You will likely be asked to sign first and then to return the contract to the seller for signature. "If you're worried that a better offer might come along in the meantime, don't allow any lag time," urges adviser Richard Leshnower. Give the sellers a short time to sign. Or, if you live in a state where attorneys draft contracts, Richard suggests scheduling a sit-down contract signing as soon as possible. At a sit-down signing, all the parties and their attorneys meet to draw up and sign the contract so there's no possibility of another buyer swooping in with a better offer. Don't depend upon mere binders or correspondence—you want to be "in contract."

TIP

Ask your agent to explain the standard contract ahead of time. Says Illinois Realtor Mark Nash, "When working with first-time buyers, I show them the standard form and all required disclosures before we even start looking at properties. I answer questions they have about what each clause and phrase means, and I encourage them to read it over and make sure they really understand it. That way, when it comes time to actually write up the contract, they're less overwhelmed—they're dealing with the specific terms they want in the agreement, not the basic meaning of the contract language itself."

Presenting Your Offer

Once you have an offer together, someone (usually your agent) must present it to the seller. A great agent can present your offer in the best possible light. Perhaps your offer isn't as high as the seller would like, but you're preapproved for a mortgage and aren't requiring many contingencies that could slow the process. It's your agent's job to highlight and "sell" your offer's strengths.

Ideally, your agent will contact the seller's agent and arrange for a time to meet and present the offer. The seller might come to this meeting, too. Sometimes the seller will hear multiple offers from several potential buyers on the same day. In hot markets where time is of the essence, though, your agent might call the seller's agent to announce that the offer is coming via email, and discuss the highlights of the offer during that call. Make sure that your agent receives confirmation from the seller's agent of having received the offer.

Sellers might specifically request that offers be sent by email or an e-contract platform (a popular one is CTM eContracts). In that case, you might (depending on local practice) include a personal cover letter outlining your qualifications and the strengths of your offer.

The Seller Responds

After you've submitted your offer, you'll probably be on pins and needles, wondering how the seller will react. The seller is eventually going to do one of three things: (1) accept, (2) reject, or (3) make a counteroffer.

 CAUTION

In some situations, the seller might not respond right away. Particularly if you're offering to buy a house sold in a short sale (requiring bank approval) or making an offer on a bank-owned property, it could be weeks or even months before you hear back from the seller. If you're patient, you can wait for the response and maybe get a good deal. If you're in a hurry to move, however, you might have to withdraw your offer and look elsewhere. Or, it can't hurt to request that a response be made within a certain time frame—giving the seller a deadline (even one you don't expect will be met) gives you an excuse to contact the seller and hopefully get a status update.

The Seller Accepts Your Offer

If the seller accepts your offer in writing, you might, depending on which state you're in and what form your offer took, be in contract. Then again, you might have a mere verbal acceptance of your offer, or an agreement to negotiate, neither of which means much.

"Until you, as the buyer, have your hands on a contract of sale with both the seller's and your signatures, don't get overly excited—you're not yet in contract," says adviser Richard Leshnower. "A lot depends on the seller's good faith at this point. I know of situations where sellers have entered into a contract with a buyer before they'd received the returned contract sent to another prospective buyer."

Once you have an actual purchase and sale agreement that both you and the seller have signed, you and the seller can begin to perform all the tasks that take you up to the closing, as described in Chapter 11.

The Seller Rejects Your Offer

Sometimes, the seller will flatly reject your offer, usually because someone else made a better offer, and yours simply didn't rise to the top of the stack. The seller's agent should contact your agent with the bad news.

You Might Make the B-Team

Instead of rejecting your offer outright, a seller might suggest that you make a backup offer to purchase the house if the chosen deal falls through. Your backup gives the seller a little extra security and saves the hassle of readvertising.

If you submit a backup offer, ask the seller to give you a final yes or no within a few days or to specify that the exact terms of the agreement are to follow. This protects you in case you find another property, lose interest, or want to renegotiate terms with the seller. (You wouldn't want the seller to be able to interpret your offer as binding.)

Even if the seller doesn't offer you a backup position, there's nothing to stop your real estate agent from checking in with the seller's agent during the escrow period. Deals sometimes fall through! If the timing's right, you could make it very convenient for the seller to accept your offer without having to put the house back on the market.

The Seller Counteroffers

Rather than accept your offer as written or reject it outright, the seller might decide that your offer is worth considering but needs improvement (usually a higher price). The seller will then give you a counteroffer, with an expiration time or date for your reply. A counteroffer is a good sign— it means the seller is interested in negotiating with you. But, as retired Massachusetts broker Nancy Atwood warns, "Sometimes the buyer and seller forget that they have the same goal in mind, which is the purchase of the home. I was once involved in a transaction where the buyer and seller were fighting over a couple thousand dollars, on an $800,000 property! Eventually they did relent and split the difference, but it caused some unnecessary stress on both sides of the table."

Mel: *Which reminds me, where's your report card?*

Cher: *It's not ready yet.*

Mel: *What do you mean, "It's not ready yet?"*

Cher: *Well, some teachers are trying to low-ball me, Daddy. And I know how you say, "Never accept a first offer," so I figure these grades are just a jumping-off point to start negotiations.*

From the movie *Clueless*, 1995

The counteroffer might, depending on practices in your state, be structured like a whole stand-alone contract, or it might incorporate your original offer, essentially saying, "I agree to the terms of the offer, except with these changes." If the new terms are satisfactory—for example, you're willing to pay what the seller proposes or give the seller extra time to move out— you can accept the seller's counteroffer.

When a seller receives multiple offers, the seller might return multiple counteroffers, asking people to submit new, better offers. It's kind of like being outbid on eBay: You can then decide whether you want to put in a new offer, but your competitors will be doing the same thing.

If the seller gives you a counteroffer that you don't like, you can reject it and simply walk away, or you can counter the counteroffer. Leshnower counsels, "Don't feel that walking away is failure. It's just another step in the hunting process."

You and the Seller Negotiate

You and the seller can continue to exchange counteroffers until you reach agreement or give up. Each time, you'll include expiration dates for your counteroffers. If an expiration date passes, negotiations are over—no deal. If, however, one of you accepts the other's counteroffer, you'll sign or take other steps to finalize the agreement in a signed contract, as described next.

More Than Words: What's in the Standard Purchase Contract

When you and the seller agree and write a contract, it will probably look like pages and pages of a legal document—which it is! Luckily, you'll probably be spared creating it from scratch. Your state might require you to use certain forms, or a Realtor association might provide a standard preprinted form for your use, called something like "Contract to Purchase" or "Offer to Purchase." These fill-in-the-blanks forms contain state-specific legal language so you won't forget to deal with important issues. But they usually leave space for you to customize, too.

> **CAUTION**
>
> **Customize with caution.** Avoid adding nonstandard language unless it's absolutely necessary. Unless you're an attorney, drafting the language on your own could be dicey. And having your real estate agent attempt to draft anything more than is involved in filling in the blanks could create legal trouble, as the agent could be considered to be practicing law without a license.

If you're using an attorney, he or she might start with some boilerplate and customize it to your purchase. Leshnower adds, "Never believe anyone who tells you that this is a standard contract and you cannot amend, change, or add to it. In fact, with today's technology, a contract that looks boilerplate could actually already contain alterations. The willingness of a seller or purchaser to bend really depends on who is more needy."

CAUTION

Bank sellers can be especially stubborn about changing their contract terms. If you're buying a distressed property, such as a foreclosure or short sale, get ready: Massachusetts attorney Ken Goldstein says, "I've seen situations where the financial institution presents the purchase and sale agreement and says, 'No changes.' They expect buyers to sign onto even the most onerous of terms—such as one saying the seller can terminate the agreement at any time, for no reason. Sometimes it's all just bluster, and I can push for changes in the contract."

To form a legal contract, your final agreement must be in writing and signed by both you and the seller. So if the seller or the seller's agent calls you and says, "We accept your offer," wait for that signed agreement before taking further action.

Whether you use a standard form or a fully customized document, certain key terms and phrases are likely to be in it (though these, too, vary by state). Read it carefully, using the summary of common terms below for both decoding and making sure it contains the protections you want. We'll discuss many of these terms further in this and later chapters:

TIP

Ask questions. If you don't understand the meaning of a term or document, don't hesitate to ask your real estate agent or attorney for a plain-English explanation. As attorney Richard Leshnower notes, "There should be nothing in the contract that you don't understand!"

- **Parties.** The names of the buyer and seller.
- **Property description.** The property address and a physical description (which might be as simple as "a single-family house" or might refer to attachments containing a complete metes and bounds legal description and a survey) and details about what the property includes, such as a garage.
- **Offer or purchase amount.** The price you'll pay, as long as the seller agrees and all the other terms are met.
- **Earnest money amount.** How much you'll deposit when the transaction begins but forfeit to the seller if you back out of the transaction for a reason not allowed in the contract.

- **Down payment amount.** How much you'll pay in cash toward the purchase price (or, put another way, a contingency saying that the deal will close only if you qualify to finance a certain percentage of the purchase price).
- **Contingencies.** Conditions that must be met for the sale to be finalized, such as obtaining loan approval.
- **Loan amount and conditions.** How much you'll borrow, and on what terms and with what restrictions, to finance the purchase.
- **Title.** The seller promises to be in a legal position to sell you the property without any outstanding debts or other liens or encumbrances.
- **Seller representations.** You can require the seller to make certain promises about the property, for example, that to the seller's knowledge, the roof is free of defects or, in a condo or co-op, that the seller knows of no mold or pest problems in the building.
- **Fixtures and personal property.** Fixtures (items permanently attached to the property, like built-in appliances or fences) stay with the house unless you or the seller specify otherwise, while personal property leaves, unless you and the seller agree otherwise.

> **TIP**
>
> **Buying personal property from the seller?** "It's best to make these arrangements outside of the settlement," recommends loan officer Sylvia M. Gutierrez. "Any personal property listed on a purchase contract will have to be independently appraised and the lender will reduce that value from the purchase price used in calculating the allowable loan amount based on loan-to-value." For significant purchases of personal property, consider consulting with an attorney to draw up a purchase contract and to ensure you're complying with applicable sales tax laws.

- **Rights of use.** If you're buying a condo, co-op, or townhouse, you might have the right to use portions of the property that you either don't own yourself or that you own jointly with others, such as a specific parking space.
- **Possession.** The date you can possess (move into) the property.

TIP

Your lender can require you to occupy the home within 30 days after closing. That's to make sure you're using the property as a home, not an investment. (Mortgage interest rates on investment properties are normally higher and have special qualification requirements.)

- **Prorations and assessments.** How you and the seller will split recent and upcoming fees like mortgage interest, property taxes, and community association fees. If, for example, language is used saying "as of the date of possession," and that date falls on a Wednesday, the seller would have to pay expenses through Tuesday and the buyer would pay from Wednesday onward.

- **Closing agent (or escrow holder).** Who will act as intermediary, assisting with preclosing tasks and holding onto any money that you or the seller deposit in advance. This could be a title company, escrow company, or attorney(s).

- **Fees.** A list of the various fees to be paid before and during the closing—including escrow fees, lender's fees, recording fees, title search fees, deed preparation fees, notary fees, and transfer taxes—and who will pay them.

- **Expiration date.** The time limit for the seller to accept your offer.

- **Closing date.** The date the transaction finalizes and the house is legally yours. In some states, instead of an actual date, the contract will give a certain time window or say "on or before" or "on or after" a certain date.

- **Agent payment or commissions.** Who will pay and how much will be paid to the real estate agents representing you and the seller.

- **Damage to property.** How any damage to the property during escrow (such as a fire) will affect the agreement. Also, if local authorities place a notice of violation on the property after the date of contract, who will be responsible for repairing and removing the violation.

- **Resolving disputes.** How you and the seller will resolve any legal disputes, and whether you'll use alternative methods before going to court (such as mediation or arbitration).

- **Entire agreement.** A statement that you and the seller don't have any other agreement and that if you want to alter the one you have, you'll do it in writing and both sign it. This is important language to take to heart. Many buyers are disappointed to later discover that verbal assurances regarding what items of property would stay or go with the house are not enforceable.

- **Time is of the essence.** This confirms that if a date was important enough for you to write into the agreement—for example, the closing date—it's a fundamental part of it, and if either you or the seller don't make the date (or modify the agreement), then you'll have breached the contract.

- **Signatures.** No matter who goes first, you don't have a contract until both of you have signed.

> **CAUTION**
>
> **Put co-op agreements in writing.** When buying stock in a co-op, your state's laws might not require a written agreement. But to prevent any "he said, she said" disputes, get it in writing, anyway. Your co-op contract should look similar to a regular home purchase contract, but also cover such matters as your board application and approval process.

Your agent or attorney can tell you of any state-specific contract require-ments. Your contract might also include other terms—for example, it could address an existing lease if the property is being rented to a tenant or could specify how documents must be transmitted (in person or electronically).

Too Much? Not Enough? How Much to Offer

The most important term in an offer—and the first thing the seller will look at—is the price. If you offer far less than a seller thinks the house is worth, your offer might be rejected outright. But if your offer is very high, the seller might snatch it up quickly—and you might overpay. Find balance by evaluating:

- whether the market is hot or cold
- how long the house has been on the market

- the amounts that comparable properties have sold for
- your agent's opinion
- the seller's position (confident or desperate?), and
- your own state of mind.

Whether the Market Is Hot or Cold

Part of what determines a house's relative worth is how hot or cold the local real estate market is. In very hot markets, some sellers set prices deliberately low, and you'll have to decide on a price that will outdo the competition without going overboard. In a cold market, or where the house has sat unsold for a long time, many sellers accept offers below the asking price.

CAUTION

Stick to your budget. If a house costs more than you can afford, it's not the house for you—even if it's a great deal. You don't want to land in dire financial straits. Be especially careful if your employment is seasonal, you depend on a bonus, or you face other income insecurity.

Unless you're in a really hot market or competing with multiple bidders on a hot property, you might try offering less than you're ultimately willing to pay, with the expectation that the seller will counteroffer. If you can't reach a compromise, you can walk away.

> EXAMPLE: Soledad tours a home and decides to make an offer. The asking price is $385,000, but she thinks it's worth between $365,000 and $375,000. Soledad offers $360,000. The seller counteroffers for $367,000, which Soledad accepts.

What if you're in a hot market? Settling on an appropriate price can be tough, because you want to outdo the competition without breaking your own budget to bits. And although you might hear the term "bidding war" used in reference to real estate, this isn't normally like an auction, where you know what the other bids are and have a chance to outdo them. (Exceptions exist, however. In some markets, sellers are turning to auction apps, where you can continue raising your bid after others come in.) You'll have to wow the seller with your offer price, along with finding other ways to make your offer stand out (discussed later in this chapter).

> **EXAMPLE:** Arif wants to buy a house in San Francisco in 2016, and can't believe the news he's reading of bids going hundreds of thousands of dollars over asking. He sees a two-bedroom place in an okay neighborhood listed for $900,000. His budget is $950,000, but he was hoping not to have to go that high. In fact, he tells his agent that he'd like to offer list price—after all, that's the amount the seller is asking for, right? However, they learn (through the seller's agent) that nine other people intend to submit bids on the home. Arif's own agent says she wouldn't be surprised to see the place go for over $1 million. He decides to bid his full budget of $950,000 and hope for the best.

In multiple-bid situations, adviser Daniel Stea tells his clients, "The price you offer should depend in part on your level of interest in the house: A for hot, B for warm, or C for cool. If your reaction to a house is at Level C— you like the place, but wouldn't be crushed if you didn't get it—then you might put in a bid at a reasonable price, knowing there's a fair chance you'll be outbid. If you REALLY like the house, at level B, it's time to be more aggressive in offering an amount above market value in order to increase your chances of being selected. But if it's an A-level house, and you absolutely must have it because your life depends on it, then get out your checkbook. That's when you'll simply need to overpay, in the sense that you're now partaking in the feeding frenzy. In the end, human emotions rather than objective market value often rule the day."

How Much Comps Have Sold For

To gauge a property's worth, you'll want to know how much houses with similar features have sold for in the area in the last three to six months. Your real estate agent should provide you with a list of comparables. Make sure the comps really are comparable—for example, an older home with an original kitchen isn't worth the same amount as a similar home with a remodeled, state-of-the-art kitchen in the same neighborhood.

If you spend several months searching and your agent gave you a list of comps at the beginning, ask for an updated list.

> **CAUTION**
>
> **Offering far too much could mess up your loan financing.** If you offer more for a house than it's worth, either because you don't know any better or because you desperately love the place, it could cost you the deal. Your lender will eventually require you to have the house appraised and won't lend you more than its appraised value. At that point, your main choices include backing out of the deal or getting the money from another source. To avoid having you back out, the seller might also agree to lower the price.

Your Agent's Opinion

Ask your agent about the value of the home you're interested in and what a reasonable offer price is. Your agent should be experienced enough, and familiar enough with the market, to express a helpful opinion. The agent will also know how to take other variables into account—for instance, the seller's eagerness to get rid of the place.

Of course, this assumes you're working with your own agent. A dual agent has to tread carefully when the buyer asks for pricing advice, and might not be able to do more than provide you with comps. The seller's agent is obligated to get the most money possible for the seller and might encourage you to bid more aggressively than is necessary.

The Seller's Position

When you make an offer, think about what the seller wants from the deal. For example, if you know that the seller has rejected several offers, the seller might be holding out for top dollar—but if the house is overpriced, you can possibly get around this by asking for other concessions, like payment of closing costs. Or if you know the seller has already put in an offer on another home but needs money from the current sale in order to proceed, you might get away with offering less.

Clues That a Seller Might Accept a Lower Price

Here are some signs that a seller might be motivated to unload a house:

- The house has been on the market a long time, with no real interest.

- The house has been put on the market more than once in the past few years without a successful sale.

- The seller has put in an offer on a new home that's contingent on the sale of the current home.

- The MLS or other listing describes the seller as "motivated" or says "seller will consider all offers."

- The seller has already moved out.

- The seller has dropped the price at least once.

- The seller has changed real estate agents at least once.

- A previous offer on the house recently fell through.

- The house is being sold in winter, when buyer interest is generally low.

- The seller plans to move out of the area by a specific date.

- The seller has a major life change on the horizon (getting married, having a child, divorcing, or retiring).

- The seller inherited the house but doesn't live in it.

- The house is an investment property and rents are falling.

If the seller is sitting pretty—the market is superheated and the seller knows the house will go fast—then you'll have to strategize accordingly. Assume that the seller is looking at numerous high-priced offers and that yours will somehow have to stand out. Unfortunately for your finances, this has led sellers in some hot markets to offer absurdly high earnest money deposits—in the $100,000 and up range—and to make them nonrefundable. If you're tempted to go this route, at least talk to a lawyer about including language that protects you from losing the deposit if the seller backs out of the deal for some egregious reason.

TIP

Find out all you can about the seller's motivation. Even if the sellers aren't saying why they're selling, your agent might be able to uncover clues about how motivated they are, such as how long the house has been for sale, whether it's vacant, and whether the seller has tried (unsuccessfully) to sell in the past. Don't be hesitant to play detective yourself, either. Search online for the seller's name and see what comes up. Some examples of what one of the authors of this book has found online include: A seller who revealed on Facebook that he knew the asking price was high but really wanted to move (hello, low offer!), sellers who posted they were putting their house on the market just as a "test" (don't waste your time on that one), and other clues, such as divorces, medical issues, and job transfers.

TIP

If going low on the offer price, it's extra important that your agent presents the offer in person. Realtor Rob Jensen explains, "Sometimes sellers can be a bit delusional about what their house is worth. However, a buyer's agent who just emails in a low-price offer and leaves it at that isn't going to change the seller's outlook. Your agent needs to establish personal rapport and make a persuasive case to the seller's agent—and possibly the actual sellers, if they attend the meeting—for why your offer is actually a strong, fair, and realistic one. By now, you might have actually gotten to know your local market better than the listing agent or seller, because you've been looking hard at the competition! If your agent can highlight what you've learned, you'll have the best shot at the seller conceding."

Your State of Mind

Fatigue ("I'm so tired of looking at houses"), anxiety ("If we don't get this house, real estate prices will go up"), and excitement ("I love this house!") can all affect the terms you're willing to offer. Don't let your emotions control the process. Instead, focus on the externals: the objective value of the house based on market conditions and comparable properties, your agent's opinion, and the seller's position. Remember, if this house doesn't work out, another one will come along.

Best thing we ever did   **Sleep on it.** Ross and Yasmin found an okay house for sale on the fringes of a great neighborhood. Ross says, "We liked the place, but we weren't sure we wanted to make an offer. Then we discovered that another buyer was writing up an offer that night. 'We're going to lose it!' we thought, and drafted our own offer, submitting it that very day. The counteroffer from the seller came back to us with less-than-thrilling terms, including the full asking price. We decided to sleep on it this time. The next morning, both of us realized that we'd worked ourselves into a frenzy over a house we didn't love, just because we were so anxious that someone else was going to get it. We walked away and have since bought a home we like much better."

Keeping Your Exit Routes Open: Contingencies

Let's say you agree to purchase a house with a beautifully remodeled bathroom. But then you learn that underneath the shiny exterior, old pipes are leaking and rusting—an expensive repair job. Suddenly, you feel like you're overpaying.

You can avoid this trap, and others like it, by including a list of contingencies in your offer: conditions that must be met before the deal will be finalized. For example, to protect against the above situation, you'd make your offer contingent on a professional inspection of the property and your satisfaction with the results.

Most offers include a set of standard contingencies that protect either you or the seller. You and the seller will agree on a date by which each contingency must be met. These contingency deadlines are a big part of the reason that most house purchase agreements allow several weeks before the closing.

Financing

Unless you're paying cash, your contract should include a financing contingency, stating that the agreement will be finalized only if you obtain adequate financing. Of course, if you're already preapproved for the loan you want, removing this contingency will hopefully not be a problem. But remember that your preapproval probably came with conditions, such as an appraisal. This contingency lets you make sure you actually get the loan. You can also use the financing contingency period to shop around for a better deal.

Usually, the financing contingency requires you to submit a loan application within a reasonable time period, such as five days. There are two strategies you can take with your financing contingency. One is to be as specific as possible: Protect yourself from having to accept any old loan by specifying not only how much money you must succeed in borrowing (on one or more loans), but at what interest rate and with how many points, or other terms. If you go this route, be realistic. If the going interest rate is around 5%, and you condition your offer on getting a 4% loan, you're not likely to be able to meet that contingency, and you'll look less attractive to the seller.

The other strategy is to make the financing contingency as subjective as possible. For example, you could make the deal contingent on securing a loan that's "acceptable" to you—this gives you a lot of flexibility when your lender gives you its final decision on the loan it's offering you. In fact, some states' standard forms already include similar subjective language. You'll want to discuss which strategy works best in your area with your agent.

Appraisal

The appraisal contingency says that you'll buy the home only if its professionally appraised value is at least as much as the amount you've contracted to pay for it. In some states the appraisal contingency is tied into the financing contingency; in others it's a separate contingency. This both protects your lender and ensures you don't overpay.

This contingency has increased in importance in recent years, says Massachusetts attorney Ken Goldstein: "Due to changes in how banks must choose appraisers, you might end up with one who, perhaps unfamiliar with your local market, appraises the house for less than its purchase price; or for even less than the loan amount. We've seen many transactions fail for insufficient appraisals. While you might be able to go back to the seller and get a lower purchase price, also protect yourself by including an appraisal contingency."

TIP

If you pay all cash, definitely add an appraisal contingency. A lender usually requires a property appraisal, which buyers can avoid by buying with cash. But as Richard Leshnower notes, "You still want to make sure the house is worth the price. Include a contingency allowing you to have the house appraised and back out if the appraised value is less than the negotiated price."

Inspections

Most homebuyers have their potential home examined by at least one, and more likely two or more, inspectors. You'll want a general inspector to find any defects that can affect the property's value; a pest inspector to check for termites, dry rot, and more; and possibly other inspectors to check for things like soil stability or environmental hazards like lead-based paint or radon gas.

If you didn't already take care of this in the precontract phase (as is traditional in some states) your contract should include a contingency allowing you to conduct inspections within a certain time and to back out of the agreement if you don't like the results or you and the seller can't agree on how to deal with needed repairs.

Some contracts will also allow you to ask for approval of a survey of the property boundaries. If you're buying a newly built home, ask that several inspections be done over the course of construction.

TIP

In some states, buyers routinely do a precontract inspection. For example, in New York, after submitting an offer, the buyer has some time before the seller drafts the contract—and may use this time to schedule an inspection, so that by the time the contract is signed, there's no need for this contingency. Richard Leshnower notes, "The advantage is that you know what you're getting into, and the seller knows you won't be pulling out of the deal based on a defect found during an inspection."

Co-op buyers are in a different situation. You're not buying the property itself, you're buying shares in a corporation, and the corporation bears responsibility for the physical property. However, Richard Leshnower advises, "Getting an inspection is the prudent thing to do. If something is found to be wrong that's the responsibility of the cooperative corporation, you want to know that they will make the repair. For example, if the floor sags or creaks, support beams may have to be installed. You want to know before you purchase that this will be done and not have to fight about it later." You will also want to make sure the building is well maintained and in good condition, by checking the co-op records and talking to the property manager, board of directors, and residents.

Attorney Review

If anyone other than your attorney drafts the final contract (particularly if it's not the standard form contract used in your state), you can include a contingency giving your attorney time to review it and requiring that you be satisfied with the results. You'll ordinarily set a time limit of several days after the seller accepts the offer. Being able to call in your legal eagle is especially useful when the deal is complicated or you need help understanding legal terms.

Review of the Preliminary Title Report

When you purchase a property, you normally assume that the seller has good title—meaning full ownership and the right to sell it to you, without any debts (technically called liens or encumbrances) against it. To be certain, your contract should give you the right to hire a title officer or an attorney to review the title history (if a problem turns up, you can back out) and to obtain actual title insurance in case of later surprises.

Review of CC&Rs or Other Community Association Documents

If you're buying in a common interest development, you need the time and opportunity to review documents like the CC&Rs (if you haven't already), master deed, bylaws, rules and regulations, and budget. If you're buying a co-op, you'll want to examine the proprietary lease as well.

These documents will tell you how well funded and well run the association or co-op is, affecting how much you can expect to pay in fees and special assessments. You'll also see what the rules are, whether you can live with them, and how they've been applied. For example, a co-op's proprietary lease might specify who can live in the unit or whether rooms can be subleased, while the minutes from a board meeting might tell you that a former owner tried unsuccessfully to challenge the sublease provision. If you don't like what you see, this contingency allows you to back out.

Co-op Board Approval

If you purchase a co-op, the transaction will have to be approved by the co-op's board of directors, which will want to make sure you can afford to make maintenance payments. If you're unable or unwilling to pay your fair share, the others in the co-op will be financially responsible. This contingency says that the board must accept you, or the deal is off.

Obtaining Homeowners' Insurance

You'll be required by your lender to get hazard insurance—possibly including flood insurance, depending on where you live. Making the sale contingent on actually getting it protects you if the property is uninsurable. You can also require the seller to provide a CLUE ("comprehensive loss underwriting exchange") report. Drawn from an insurance industry database, it details the house's history of claims and damage awards. The more claims, especially serious or water-related ones, the harder it will be for you to get insurance. Even if an insurance company initially agrees to insure you, it can rescind that promise *after the closing* if it investigates a prior claim and discovers a significant risk.

Reviewing the Seller's Disclosure Report

In many states, you don't need this contingency—state law itself will condition the sale on the seller's filling out a form disclosing property conditions, defects, environmental hazards, and more, and on your being satisfied with what you read before closing the sale.

But in some states, no such laws exist, or they make an exception for certain properties, such as condos. One way to protect yourself is by asking the seller to provide written disclosures about the property's condition. (The other way is to get a thorough inspection.)

Final Walk-Through

Also called the buyer inspection, this allows you to take a last look at the house, usually a day or two before the closing. If it's an existing house, the purpose is for you to make sure the seller has made any agreed-upon repairs and actually moved out, cleaned up, and left the place in good condition. If it's a new house, it's your opportunity to make sure the place is finished and meets your specifications. We discuss this in Chapter 14.

What About Home Warranties?

Some offers are contingent on the seller's purchasing a home warranty for the buyer (a service contract mostly covering repairs to major appliances). Don't let this become a sticking point; home warranties are of questionable value, anyway (see Chapter 12).

Other Customized Contingencies

Although we've discussed the typical contingencies, others might be included in preprinted offer forms, or you can draft your own (with the help of your agent or attorney). You might, for example, want to make your offer contingent on verifying that zoning laws allow you to convert the detached garage into a small apartment. We've even heard of cases where buyers made offers after having viewed the house only through an online, virtual tour—then added a contingency giving them a chance to see, and like, the house in person!

Keep in mind that the more contingencies you have and the less reasonable they are, the less attractive your offer becomes. If the seller has multiple offers, particularly at similar prices, the ones with the most contingencies usually lose.

Putting Your Money Where Your Mouth Is: The Earnest Money Deposit

Once you've gone to the trouble of making an offer, you want to show the seller that you're really committed to buying the property. Traditionally, you do this by putting up a cash deposit called "earnest money," a "good-faith" deposit, or a "binder." If all goes well, that money is either returned to you or is applied toward your down payment or closing costs (you'll specify which in advance).

But if you inexplicably back out after you have a contract, you forfeit your earnest money (or you might have to negotiate with the seller, or even go to court, to get it back). The rationale is that the seller might have lost other opportunities to sell to other buyers by relying on your deal.

The amount of the deposit will depend on where you're buying; it's usually from 1% to 10% of the purchase offer amount. In some areas, the property listing specifies how much the seller wants for a deposit; your real estate agent can advise you on how it's handled in your area. For example, if local practice is to draft only a brief offer, you might submit only a small earnest money deposit offer, such as a flat $500, but then submit a larger amount—perhaps even half the down payment—when the contract is signed.

From your perspective, it's best to keep the earnest money amount as small as possible while still showing good faith and remaining competitive for your market—just in case you back out of the deal. (Even if it's for a valid reason laid out in the contract, if the seller contests it, the money could be inaccessible to you until the dispute is resolved.) You'll normally place the earnest money with your escrow agent or attorney, who will hold it in a special account, inaccessible to the seller.

> 💡 **TIP**
>
> **Know your state's laws regarding earnest money.** For example, in California, a maximum of 3% of the purchase price can be kept as a non-refundable deposit unless the seller can demonstrate that a greater amount is reasonable. (Cal. Civil Code § 1675(c).)

Do many buyers end up losing their earnest money deposit? "Not really," says attorney Ken Goldstein. "In the few instances I've seen where a buyer changed his or her mind and didn't have a good reason to walk away, the two parties typically compromised. Say, for instance, the buyer got an unexpected job offer from across the country. He understands that the seller has been banking on the closing for several weeks and lost opportunities to sell to others; but at the same time, giving up the $50,000 deposit would be a huge hit. The buyer might go to the seller, and ask, "Will you consider accepting $20,000? Both parties usually understand the other's position in such a situation, and try to negotiate."

Divvy It Up: Who Pays What Fees

An inspection fee here, an insurance premium there. Your purchase contract should deal with who pays every dollar of every charge involved in buying the house. Common ones include:

- closing agent's or escrow agents' fees for services
- title fees (title search, title insurance for both the buyer and the lender, and attorneys' fees if needed to clarify title)
- transfer taxes (city, county, and state)
- inspections (usually paid by the buyer)
- survey or Improvement Location Certificate (ILC) cost (see "Is That Tree on Your Side or Ours?" in Chapter 11 for more information on ILCs)
- administrative fees (deed preparation, notary, or recording fees), and
- home warranty policy premium (if any).

Who normally pays which fees depends on local custom, which your agent can advise you on. Many preprinted forms have these fees already listed, and you'll check the box to indicate who pays what. You could just ask the seller to pay for everything, but unless you're in a cold market, the seller probably won't agree to this and it could start negotiations off on the wrong foot. Additionally, your offer will likely address real estate agent or broker fees separately from the costs discussed above.

Deal or No Deal: Picking an Expiration Date

Your offer to the seller should include an expiration date—language that says, "After this date, the offer is no longer on the table." Without this, the seller could take his or her sweet time before accepting your offer. (You can also leave the expiration date open, then revoke your offer in writing later, but using an expiration date is easier.) Another good reason to put a little pressure on the seller is if you're preapproved for financing for a maximum of 30 or 60 days or face other time constraints.

Some agents advise giving the seller a very short time—like 24 hours—to respond to your offer. That's to prevent the seller from using your offer to "shop" for others—telling other potential buyers, "You better get in now, and for more than this." In a hot market where a seller might be able to move a property quickly, a short expiration period can be a good idea. But if you're in a relatively balanced market, the seller might interpret this as a pressure tactic.

If you're making an offer on a bank-owned property or a property advertised as a short sale (requiring bank approval), it's possible you won't hear from the seller for several weeks or even months. If this seems likely (the listing will often indicate a long response time), you could leave out an expiration date or choose one in the more distant future, then revoke your offer in writing if you find another house in the meantime.

Think Ahead: Closing Date

Your offer might also include a closing date: the date the transaction will be completed and the house becomes yours. (Some offers don't specify an actual date, and instead indicate that the closing will be "within 30 days of signing," "no later than" a certain date, or "on or before" a certain date, for example.) Richard Leshnower notes that, "Each of these wordings has a special meaning and should be considered carefully so that you know what to expect or how to comply." Assuming you set an exact or near-exact closing date, consider:

- **How much time you'll need.** You'll need time not only to complete all the contingencies, but also to prepare yourself to move. Between four weeks and two months is normal.

> **TIP**
> **Agreeing to close within a "reasonable time" is risky.** Some contracts use vague phrases like this. But what's reasonable to you might be different from what's reasonable to the seller. Far better to set a date at the beginning, then later, if necessary, agree with the seller (in writing) to change it.

- **Impact on your first interest payment.** Loan interest is paid in arrears —meaning that at the beginning of one month, your payment is partly for the interest that accrued the previous month (on October first, you pay the interest that accrued in September—it's the opposite of how you're used to paying rent). However, you'll prepay that cost when you close (so if you close September 15, you'll prepay the interest that accrues between September 15 and 30). (After that, you will shift to a more regular schedule, and your next payment won't be due until the beginning of November—covering not only a share of the principal, but the interest that accrued during October.) If you close at the end of the month, you pay only the few days left before month's end. If you close at the beginning of the month, you pay interest for the entire month. Closing at the end of the month keeps some cash in your pocket—at least for a short while.

- **Moving date.** If you plan to move the day you close (which is ambitious), schedule the closing as early in the day as you can.
- **Year-end tax concerns.** If you're buying toward the end of the year, keep taxes in mind. Any points and interest paid before the new year can become deductions for this year's taxes. On the other hand, if you don't expect to itemize your deductions this year but will the next, it's probably worth waiting. Check with a tax adviser for the timing of any other deductions.
- **Property taxes.** Depending on what state you live in, you might be able to lower your property taxes through a "homestead" or "principal residence" exemption. (Some states limit this to certain groups, like the elderly or disabled, and other states don't have it at all.) If such an exemption is available, you might need to be living in your home by the 1st of January. Check with a tax adviser.
- **Your lender's patience.** Make sure the closing date is set before your lender's commitment—or any interest rate lock—expires. You might be able to extend the commitment, but at a price.

Strategies in a Cold Market: What to Ask For

If you're buying in a cold market, your offer might be the only one the seller sees, which you can use to your advantage. Virtually every aspect of the purchase agreement—price, closing date, who pays various fees, and what the seller leaves behind (such as custom decorations)—becomes negotiable. Your agent can suggest other things to ask for, such as a $5,000 to $10,000 credit at closing, a year of paid property taxes, or a year of paid assessments (for a condo).

If your offer is significantly below the asking price (what's considered "significant" depends on numerous factors and is worth discussing with your agent), one way to soften the blow to the sellers is to write a letter of explanation. You could, for example, highlight recent home price trends, assure the sellers that you love the home, and have no wish to insult them, but explain that for the price that they're asking, you can get more house elsewhere.

Strategies in a Hot Market: Making Your Offer Stand Out

If you're in a particularly hot market, or just know that other buyers will be aching to get their hands on a particular house, you've got to work harder to make your offer the top pick. Here are some steps you can take:

- **Act quickly.** Chances are you're not the only one who likes this house, so you might have to submit an offer immediately.
- **Have your agent personally present your offer.** Unless the seller refuses, this can show the seller why you're better than the rest.
- **Offer more money.** Your offer will stand out if it's the highest, even by a few thousand dollars.
- **Tell your personal story.** When you submit your offer, include a letter explaining why you want to purchase the property and what you like about it. Include information that you think will be important to the seller, based on both the home itself and what you know about the seller personally. For example, if the garden is lovingly cared for, your letter might mention your own green thumb. Although some real estate professionals scoff at this idea, it's not ridiculous if it works—and a seller who is attached to a home will appreciate knowing that it will be cared for by the next owner.

TIP

Will offer videos be the next big thing? Adviser Tara Waggoner, a real estate broker (see Chapter 15), says, "We had a client who'd been outbid on several houses, then got her heart set on one particular house. She created a 60-second video for the sellers explaining how much she loved the house, her financial capability, and her willingness to do anything possible to accommodate the seller, such as arranging a rent-back if they weren't ready to move right away. It worked, and she bought the house! I see a lot of sellers who really appreciate it when prospective buyers like their home. This is an emotional process, not merely a financial one."

- **Limit contingencies.** In some very hot markets, buyers are willing to forgo inspections—but this is a risk we wouldn't advise taking, since the house could have serious, but not immediately obvious, structural or other problems. Another possibility is dropping the finance contingency if you can round up enough cash, even in the short term.

Best thing we ever did

Start with an all-cash offer. Octavio and Gina were trying to buy a house in a hot market and had already been outbid twice. Octavio recalls, "On our third offer, we not only bid more than we ever thought possible, but we made a high down payment (emptying our savings) then got both our parents to lend us the rest on a short-term basis. That let us make an offer with no financing contingency. It worked—we got the house, and then were easily able to get a mortgage and repay our parents."

- **Get preapproved.** This shows that a lender has proclaimed you loan-worthy—and the seller can be confident that you'll likely meet the financing contingency.
- **Offer better nonmonetary terms.** You might find a seller motivated by things other than money, such as the need to close quickly (perhaps to pay the mortgage on a new house) or to rent the property back from you for a while (to look for a new house).

Contracting to Buy a Brand-New Home

If you're buying a newly constructed home from a developer, the process will probably differ from what we've described above. Whether or not you've got an agent representing you, the developer is likely to pressure you to use its standard purchase offer and contract. While these might look like what you'd get from a local real estate agent, they can be very different, and the variations won't be written to benefit you.

The developer's form contract could, for example, allow the developer to substitute comparable products for the products you select (so if the flooring you chose is no longer available, the developer will select "comparable" flooring). It will also likely allow a big cushion for late delivery. If you see these terms, you'll have to argue to change them—and ignore the developer's insistence that the standard form can't be altered (it can).

To add to the challenge, you might not have a real estate agent to help you negotiate, understand, and interpret the contract language. In that case, you should either have the document reviewed by an attorney before signing or include a contingency allowing your attorney to review it before the deal is done.

If you feel the agreement is too one-sided, you can alter or write in additional terms—the developer, like any seller, can decide whether it wants to deal with you on those terms. For example, you might:

- **Limit your earnest money deposit.** If you put down less cash, you'll have less at stake if the developer's performance is lacking.
- **Add a drop-dead date.** Choose a date by which the house must be completed, or you have the option of walking away.
- **Negotiate a holdback.** Add a clause requiring that a portion of the purchase price be set aside if the house isn't complete at closing, which you can then use to have the work completed.
- **Request several inspections and walk-throughs.** If your house will be constructed according to your specifications, negotiate to have professional inspectors *and* you (by yourself) go through it several times—not just right before closing. That's to make sure the installations are happening on time, and that everything is being done right.
- **Get the same quality.** If you're buying a home that looks like the model, add a clause saying that you'll get the same or better quality, not simply that the quality will meet local building codes. How will you know you're getting equivalent products and materials? Adviser Tara Waggoner (who has helped numerous buyers purchase newly built homes, and whom you'll meet in Chapter 15), says, "Before signing the contract, insist that the builder give you a 'specification

sheet,' commonly called a 'spec sheet.' This will contain such details as the type of insulation, plumbing, air conditioning, water heater, paint, kitchen hardware, and other finishings. You can later compare this against what was actually used in your house."

Always Late ... But Worth the Wait?

One of the most frequent complaints from buyers in new communities is that their homes aren't built on time. Even reputable builders might face delays from rain or other problems. Here are some terms you can include in your offer to compensate you for delays:

- pro rata rent, based on your current home
- pro rata hotel rental, based on the market price of an acceptable hotel
- pro rata mortgage payment
- credit toward upgrades based on pro rata mortgage costs, or
- reduced price or free upgrades in exchange for allowing late delivery.

TIP

Don't back down. Realtor Mark Nash advises, "Buyers need to go head to head with pushy developers. If they don't, they're asking to be taken advantage of."

What's Next?

Once you and the seller have signed a contract, it binds you both. Now it's time to arrange your inspections, pull your financing together, get homeowners' and title insurance, remove contingencies, and close the deal. We discuss these topics in Chapters 11 through 14.

Toward the Finish Line: Tasks Before Closing

Meet Your Adviser

Sandy Gadow, a nationally recognized expert on real estate closing and escrow, and author of *The Complete Guide to Your Real Estate Closing*, widely considered the "bible of escrow and closing." Sandy offers closing advice, money-saving insider tips, and coverage of other real estate topics at her website, www.sandygadow.com.

What she does   Sandy travels all over the United States and abroad to research, track, and report on the latest developments in real estate practices and closings. With over 25 years' experience as an escrow officer, Sandy has become a frequent contributor to publications nationwide. She writes for national newspapers such as *The Washington Post* and has appeared as a guest on CNN and a speaker on national radio. Sandy continues to have direct contact with homebuyers as a licensed sales associate with Sotheby's International Realty in Palm Beach, Florida, and a mortgage broker with Palm Beach Mortgage.

First house   "It was a shack, really, on two acres of land that I discovered during a hike in California's Point Reyes National Seashore. I was intrigued by the established trees, including redwood, apple, quince, and cypress; the small vineyard; and the investment potential. With a little research, I found that it was an abandoned estate, left to heirs in the Azores. I tracked down some U.S. relatives and negotiated to buy the property—it all wrapped up within 14 days, with no inspections or disclosures. This was my introduction to the property market, but it went smoothly, and I was so excited that I had no time to be nervous. When we moved in, we found cobwebs everywhere, white lace curtains hanging in shreds, beds still made, dusty dishes and glasses on the table, and jars of preserved fruits from the apple and quince trees—a scene frozen in time. It was a huge fix-up effort but is now worth many times more than what I paid for it."

Likes best about her work	"First I should say that, after my first house purchase, I got the 'real estate bug' and decided the best way to learn about investing in real estate was to become an escrow officer. I started working at a local title company shortly thereafter and have been doing that ever since. I wrote my first book, *All About Escrow*, in 1981 because I saw a need to have a training manual for buyers, sellers, Realtors, and escrow trainees and officers. And I still enjoy the fact that the real estate field is always changing, is always interesting, and involves meeting and dealing with new people every day."
Fantasy house	"It would have to be two houses: one in the countryside, in the South of France preferably, where I would work on the land, relax, and eat very well. The other would be in a city, such as London, where I could work and enjoy all the cultural activities, such as museums, theatres, ballets, and concerts, with the bonus of being able to take short-break trips to neighboring countries."
Top tip for first-time homebuyers	"Once you've chosen a mortgage company, your Realtor may suggest a title and escrow company to handle the closing. The Realtor might, based on past interactions, have a good rapport with the title officer, which could facilitate a faster or at least a smoother closing. Also, don't be afraid to ask questions. Buying real estate is a big decision, and you'll want to stay informed every step of the way. Stay flexible and look for alternate solutions—or compromises—if you come across a stumbling block. There might be several options available for you to consider."

H aving signed a written agreement with the seller, you're in the home stretch—literally. But before you send out invitations to your housewarming party, let's focus on the few (but important) steps that remain before the sale closes:

- **Removing contingencies.** You'll need to make sure all the conditions you placed on the transaction (like getting financing and approving your inspections) are met.
- **Getting title insurance.** This is to verify that the seller has good title to the property and to protect you from claims to the contrary.
- **Deciding how to take title.** Especially if you're buying with someone else, you'll need to choose what legal form your shared ownership will take.
- **Getting ready to move.** Prepare yourself, and anyone going with you, for the big change ahead.

Some of your other responsibilities—like arranging inspections and choosing insurance—will require more discussion, provided in future chapters. Then in Chapter 14, we'll describe what actually happens on closing day.

What Have I Done?!

There are a few moments in the homebuying process where buyer's remorse —that sinking feeling that you've made a *huge* mistake—is common. If you're feeling panicked, try:

- **Calling a homeowner.** Talking to a happy homeowner reminds you that it's worth it and that your fears are completely unoriginal!

- **Driving by the house.** Take another look and imagine living there. Bring a loved one who will be excited for you.

- **Watching a home improvement reality show.** Even if you're buying a brand-new house, or not changing a thing, it's fun to see others get creative.

- **Doing something different.** You've probably spent too much time talking with businesspeople and reading official papers. Take a break: a long hike, a movie, or a massage.

Your purchase contract probably gave you at least a few weeks before the closing, unless you're waiting for a new house to be built. If you haven't already, you and the seller will either hire a closing agent or one or more attorneys to help navigate the deal to, and through, the closing.

CHECK IT OUT

For a detailed chart of who typically handles the closing in your state: Refer to *The Complete Guide to Your Real Estate Closing,* by Sandy Gadow (Escrow Publishing Company).

Wrappin' It Up: Removing Contingencies

One of your main objectives for the period before the closing is removing (checking off as "done") contingencies in your purchase agreement. You're probably not the only one with a lot of to-dos: The seller might be working on performing repairs and finding a new place to live. Each of you will need to advise the other of your progress and, with the help of your real estate agents or attorneys, provide written releases when a contingency is removed. If either of you fails to meet or remove a contingency, the other can either call off the purchase or seek to renegotiate.

TIP

If you need more time, ask. If, for example, a general inspection reveals that another specialized inspection is needed, you can ask the seller (in writing) for additional time to remove this contingency. The seller could say no, perhaps using it as an excuse to back out of the deal. Most sellers, however, are motivated to close and will agree to a reasonable request.

Removing Your Inspection Contingency

Your purchase contract should include an inspection contingency. In Chapter 12 we'll explain what the various types of property inspections include and what problems they might reveal. Here, we're just going to talk about what to do when you get the inspector's report that explains the problems. Don't panic: Every house has hidden flaws or defects that you won't know about until the inspection.

After reviewing the report, you'll have to decide whether the problems can be fixed and whether you can live with them if they can't; who should pay for repairs; and what you'll do if you and the seller can't agree on who pays.

Whether the Problems Can Be Fixed

Discuss with the inspector or outside contractors whether the problems can be fixed and how much repairs are likely to cost. A pervasive mold problem, for example, sometimes can't be fixed, but a pet door that violates a fire code shouldn't require a team of specialists.

If a problem can't be fixed, you must decide whether you still want the property. Sometimes—like if repairs will take several weeks—the answer might be "no." In some states, your standard inspection contingency will say that you must give the seller a chance to fix a problem before backing out of the deal. But if the problem truly can't be fixed, you should be able to walk away.

Who Pays for Repairs

Your first inclination might be to ask the seller to pay for everything ("Hey, it's *her* cat that needed the pet door—I don't even have a pet!"). You can certainly try, but don't be so unreasonable that the seller says, "Forget it!"

TIP

"Don't expect the house to be brought up to 'new' condition," says retired Realtor Nancy Atwood. "All homes (except new construction) have issues that we refer to as 'the price of homeownership': loose faucets, old paint, and so forth. Asking for every little thing to be fixed is simply unreasonable."

If you've got some leverage—for example, you know the seller needs to move fast or that the house sat on the market for months before your offer came along—you can push harder for the seller to take responsibility. But if you know that the seller got a later offer that was higher than yours, keep requests to a minimum.

If the seller agrees to be financially responsible for all or some repairs, the two of you can handle it in one of a few ways, including:

- **Reduce the sale price by the estimated cost of repairs.** The advantage to this is that, with a lower purchase price on record, your annual property taxes will be lowered, as will your transfer tax if you live in a state where they're required (and from the buyer, not the seller). What's more, you can do the repairs whenever you like—though you'll have to come up with the cash on your own.

- **Have the seller pay some of your costs at closing.** Ask the seller to give you a credit for the estimated repair costs at closing. Check with your lender before finalizing any credit agreement with the seller, though, as most lenders don't allow credits exceeding the total of prepaid costs (such as homeowners' insurance and homeowners' association fees) and closing costs. The benefit of having the seller pay these costs is that you'll have cash in hand to make the repairs—rather than putting money toward prepaids and closing costs at closing, you can put it toward needed repairs.

- **Trust the seller to hire someone to make the repairs before the closing.** This tends to be a bad idea. The seller might do the repairs on the cheap or, worse, attempt a do-it-yourself job. If you really want the seller to take care of the repairs before you move in, protect yourself. Let the seller know you won't remove the contingency unless: (1) the seller uses a contractor of your choice for the work, (2) the seller uses a "qualified, licensed, and insured contractor," or (3) your own contractor signs off on the work first.

Your lender may require certain repairs to be done before the deal is finalized. (Lenders need to ensure their collateral—the house—is worth enough to cover the loan.) Discuss how to pay for these repairs with your lender—creative solutions are possible, such as taking out a larger mortgage to cover the repairs or reducing your down payment to free up the cash.

New Construction:
Removing the Final Inspection Contingency

If you're buying a newly built home, you hopefully negotiated a "final inspection" contingency, which allows you to bring in a professional to approve the completed work before closing. Be prepared for unpleasant surprises—legions of homebuyers have discovered unfinished construction or major defects just days before they were supposed to move in.

If this happens, your most obvious choice is to delay the closing. However, that could be impossible if you've arranged to move. Your next-best bet is to go ahead with the closing but insist on a written agreement that says the money needed to complete your house will be taken from the purchase price and put into a trust account that the developer can't touch until the work is done. (Be sure to get your lender's approval before you sign the agreement.) To keep the developer's feet to the fire, also add new deadlines to this agreement and state that if the work isn't done by these deadlines, the money must be withdrawn from the trust account and given directly to you. You can then hire outside contractors to finish the job.

Get an attorney's help drafting an addendum to your agreement. If the developer's contract prohibits this kind of agreement or if the developer won't agree, your final option is to make a list of the remaining tasks, assign each a completion date, and insist that the developer sign it before you agree to close. This is normally called a "punch list," and developers commonly agree to it. Unfortunately, you'll have to chase down the developer to get the work done.

Best thing we ever did **Use the final inspection contingency to get us out of a bad deal.** Sarah and Jeff were excited as they arrived at the final walk-through for their new home. "Everything looked perfect," says Sarah. "The house had high ceilings, a swimming pool, a patio area, three large bedrooms and generous-sized bathrooms, and a modern eat-in kitchen with adjoining family room. The backyard looked lush and inviting. But now that the sounds of hammers, drills, and saws were gone, we noticed something awful. The sound of speeding cars was deafening! Looking into the distance, we realized that I-95, the busiest highway in Florida, was hidden behind a row of trees. Factoring that in with a few other facts we'd been trying to ignore—a high local crime rate, and a longer drive to our son's school than we originally thought—we realized we'd made a horrible mistake. Looking closely at our contract, we discovered that the builder had failed to plant four Queen Anne palm trees along the front walkway. After several calls to the lawyer handling the closing, we were able to cancel the deal and have our full $40,000 deposit refunded."

TIP

The developer will bring in a city inspector to do a separate final inspection—and you'll need a certificate of occupancy by the closing. Realtor Mark Nash says, "The developer normally schedules such an inspection a couple of days before closing—you might not even know it's taking place. If the house fails, your lender won't fund your loan. Failures are usually due to basic safety or habitability issues, such as potable water, sewage, or heating." (In some communities, a closing can go forward with a "temporary certificate" that says the house is habitable, even if lacking some features.) Because the lender requires this certificate to close the deal, check with your closing agent to make sure the developer has forwarded it.

Removing a Financing Contingency

To remove the financing contingency that you placed in your purchase contract, you must obtain financing (a loan) on the terms stated there or otherwise acceptable to you. That means either following up with whichever lender preapproved you or finding alternative financing. (If you aren't preapproved, collect the documents described in Chapter 3 and listed on the "Financial Information for Lender" form in the Homebuyer's Toolkit.) In any case, your mortgage broker or loan officer should help you.

If you were preapproved, your lender will probably add a few requirements for your "final" approval, including verification of your credit, income, and employment; a property appraisal; a lenders' title insurance policy; and, in some cases, a property survey.

What If the Appraisal Comes in Low?

Under the Home Valuation Code of Conduct (HVCC), appraisers have had to adopt greater caution than in decades past when it comes to placing a value on the home that's at least as high as its intended purchase price—with sometimes disastrous results. In superheated markets, it's not surprising if the appraisal report comes in at tens of thousand dollars below the price that the buyer agreed to pay.

Your first step to head off appraisal problems, according to adviser Sandy Gadow, is to "request a copy of the appraisal report as soon as it has been prepared. You have a right to receive the full appraisal, including exhibits and attachments, computer valuations and other data, no later than three days before the closing—but there's no reason to have to wait that long."

If your appraisal comes in a minor amount below the purchase price, but is still higher than the amount you wish to actually borrow, your lender should be willing to go through with the loan—after all, it could still foreclose and sell your house for enough to cover the outstanding balance.

But if the appraiser says the home is worth less than you plan to borrow, you might have a problem getting a loan. Don't give up yet, however.

Remember, appraising homes is an inexact science at best, since no two—even if they're "comparable"—are exactly alike. If a low appraisal threatens to kill your deal, here's what to do:

- **Check for mistakes or oversights.** In particular, look for errors concerning the property's square footage and other key facts that contribute to its value. Also check whether the appraiser failed to notice upgrades, improvements, or special features about the property, such as new granite countertops or fabulous landscaping. And look at what comparables the appraiser chose to list—are they in fact inappropriate, because, for example, the sales happened before recent pending sales, or some houses are in a worse school district, or were foreclosures of uncertain condition?

What If the Appraisal Comes in Low? (continued)

- **Check out the appraiser.** Google the name on the report (which will also tell you where the appraiser's office is located and where the appraiser does most of his or her work).

- **Recheck the comparables.** Ask your agent to prepare an updated comparative market analysis, to make sure that the house isn't actually worth much less than you thought. If the appraiser's analysis turns out to be correct, you might want to either back out of the deal (which you can do without losing your earnest money deposit, based on your financing contingency) or use the appraisal to negotiate a lower purchase price.

- **Contact the appraiser directly about any issues.** For example, you might inquire further about the appraiser's knowledge of the house's geographical area, and point out (politely) any mistakes and over-looked comparable properties. Ask that, after rechecking the facts concerning the mistakes that you're alleging, the appraiser prepare an amended report.

- **Get a second appraisal.** You might be able to convince the lender to pay for this, if you can show the lender that the appraiser was wrong for the job, perhaps lacking local experience—or much experience at all. If that doesn't work, you and the seller might agree to split the cost of a second appraisal. Get a list of approved appraisers from your lender before choosing one. Have your agents prepare a list of comparable properties and key property features to give the new appraiser. Then, assuming the new report is favorable, submit it to your lender.

Both your agent and the seller's agent should get involved in this process, since you've all got the same goal—to convince the lender that lending you money with which to buy this house does not present an unreasonable risk. If all else fails, and you're still convinced the house is worth what you offered, you might want to come up with a higher down payment in order to reduce the amount you're borrowing.

The appraisal assures the lender that you're not borrowing more than the house is worth. While the lender or broker will probably coordinate the appraisal, you'll receive a copy of the report.

Once the various requirements are met, the lender will give you an "approval" or "commitment" letter mentioning the exact dollar amount, which you can show to the seller as you remove the financing contingency. If you're borrowing from a family member or friend, you'll need a letter from that person explaining how much you're borrowing and on what terms (as described in Chapter 7). For safety's sake, don't remove the financing contingency until you have the lender's written approval or commitment in hand. And be sure to verify that the interest rate is identical to the one promised to you by the lender.

TIP

It's not final until closing day. All commitment letters have some conditions attached, allowing the lender to back out if your financial status changes before closing. Homebuyers have been known to stop paying their credit card bills, thinking they already had their loan commitment—thereby destroying their eligibility. Similarly, until you've closed on your home, don't make any major purchases (such as getting a car or buying a bunch of furniture for your new place), quit your job, loan someone money, or shift money between bank accounts—any one of these actions could disqualify you from getting the loan.

Community Interest Developments: Special Contingencies

If you're buying into a community interest development (CID), you probably have additional contingencies to take care of, namely:

- **Approval of documents.** Your contract should require that you be given, and have a chance to approve, documents such as the CC&Rs or master deed, budget, rules and regulations, and meeting minutes. This is your last opportunity to critically examine (with the help of your real estate agent or attorney) whether you're ready to be subject to the rules of the community association and whether it's financially stable.

- **Membership in the community association.** You might, depending on where you're buying, need to submit an application to join the community association and to pay a move-in fee. If so, try to do this as many weeks as possible before the closing. Your application will need to be accepted before the sale can be completed.
- **Co-op board approval.** This is required before you join a co-op and usually involves an application and interview. You'll have to provide detailed personal financial information, plus letters of personal and professional reference, possibly including a recommendation from your landlord. You'll also need to provide details regarding your transaction, like a copy of your contract and a commitment letter from your lender. The co-op can reject you if you lie on the application; if you can't comply with requirements of the proprietary lease (for example, you have a pet, which the lease prohibits); or if you seem difficult, inflexible, or hard to live near— which they'll discover by interviewing you.

Removing Other Contingencies

Other contingencies can be removed in much the same way as described above. For example, your agreement should contain a final walk-through contingency, allowing you to give your property (whether newly built or old) one last look to make sure it's in good shape and the seller has moved out. Because this often happens right before closing, we address it in Chapter 14.

Getting title insurance was probably another contingency in your contract—you'll find a whole section on it below. You might also have made the sale contingent on your successfully obtaining homeowners' insurance, which is fully discussed in Chapter 13.

Review your purchase agreement, particularly any deadlines for completing and removing any other contingencies. If you fail to meet the deadline for a contingency, that contingency may not be enforceable anymore. For example, if you forget to have the property inspected before the inspection contingency deadline, you might not be able to back out of the deal if your (tardy) inspection does reveal an issue. Your real estate agent or attorney should help you understand, keep track of, and meet these deadlines, but they're not perfect; you should stay well informed, too.

Aack! If the Seller Won't—Or Can't—Transfer the Property

Some deals go sour even when you've done everything you're supposed to. Here's what will happen next, if:

- **The seller calls it off.** The seller might have a change of heart about moving or think a better offer is around the corner. If so, try to resolve the dispute according to the terms of your agreement— which could mean an arbitration, mediation, or a lawsuit. You'll probably be able to recover the amount you spent getting into the arrangement, but a court is very unlikely to order the sellers to move forward with the deal.

- **The seller dies.** In theory, the dead seller's estate must honor the purchase contract. Still, the transfer might slow down, especially if the executor or administrator of the estate doesn't understand the law and doesn't want to sell. Get an attorney's help.

- **The seller won't move out.** Despite the change of ownership, some sellers just decide to stay put! You might have to go to court to evict the seller, just as you would a tenant, and to recover some of your costs. Retired Realtor Nancy Atwood recalls, "We had a case where the seller's mother, who lived in the in-law apartment, simply refused to move. The buyers ended up renting to her for a year, by which time they'd all gotten very friendly, and the buyer was sad to see her go!"

- **The house is destroyed.** If fire, flood, or another calamity severely damages or destroys the house, look to your purchase agreement for guidance. If the seller still has legal title or physical possession, you probably won't be responsible, but if you've already received title or physical possession, you will be.

If You Can't Remove a Contingency

If you can't remove a contingency—for example, your loan falls through or you can't find adequate homeowners' insurance—your range of options include waiving the contingency so that the deal will go through, settling for something less than you hoped for (for example, getting a higher-interest loan), or pulling out of the deal. (Of course, you can't waive contingencies that the seller negotiated for in order to protect the seller's own interests.)

To waive a contingency, you'd execute a written release form. This form notifies the seller that even though you agreed to terms that can't be met, you'll still go through with the deal.

If the seller is eager for the deal to go through, you might be able to renegotiate the terms and offer less money for the house.

If you do decide to pull out of the deal because of the unmet contingency, you and the seller should sign a release cancelling the contract (your state might require this). You'll get your earnest money deposit back, provided the seller agrees that the contingency can't be met and the deal is over.

Will It Really Be Yours? Getting Title Insurance

Soon after your purchase agreement is signed, your closing agent will launch the process of getting you title insurance (except for a co-op, where it's not needed). As the buyer, you have the right to choose the title company. Because most buyers don't have a burning preference for a certain title company, usually your closing agent or attorney will give you a strong recommendation.

Title insurance protects you from the possibility that your seller, or previous sellers, didn't really have 100%, free and clear ownership of the house and property and can't rightfully transfer full ownership to you.

How Much Title Insurance Will Cost

On average, premiums are a one-time fee of around $3 per $1,000 of a house's purchase price, with variations depending on what state or county the house is in. A few states' laws set baselines—but not limits—on premiums (thanks to industry lobbying). The policy limit, or maximum payout, is usually set as the purchase price of the property.

In most Western states, the seller pays for title insurance; elsewhere, it's the buyer's responsibility. You probably settled this when you negotiated the purchase contract.

TIP

Buying in Iowa? By law, only state-sponsored title insurance (called a title guarantee) is offered within your state. It costs about half as much as a private policy. Nevertheless, Iowa consumers can buy title insurance from an out-of-state company.

How a House's Title Can Get Clouded

Before we talk about what title insurance covers, let's focus on how a house's title can have problems ("clouds" or "defects") in the first place. At the most extreme, the seller might not really own the place—there have been instances of renters posing as sellers. Typical title issues are less worthy of a crime show, but more complicated. For example, the seller might have copurchased ten years ago with a brother he hasn't talked to since and doesn't realize that he needs his brother's signature to sell. Or a problem might be lurking in the more distant past.

"Bankruptcy is a common source of title issues," says Massachusetts attorney Alicia Champagne. "When our office performs title searches, we have to be really careful about it. For example, we had a sale transaction where the seller had bought the house while single, then married a woman with a bankruptcy in her recent past. We needed to make sure not only that the new spouse had signed off on the deed, but that her bankruptcy case had been discharged. If not, it might have been necessary to petition the court to release the property from the bankruptcy process."

Not all title problems involve the whole house, either. For example, there might be a lien on the house—that is, an individual, a business, or even the government might have, within the public records, legally claimed the right to be paid from the proceeds of the property's sale, in order to settle the owner's debt to them.

The types of debts that sometimes lead to liens often include taxes, spousal and child support, homeowners' association fines, and contractors' fees (mechanics' liens). These liens stick to the house like glue, until the house is sold or foreclosed on.

It's also possible that your new neighbors, the public, or the government have the right to walk across or use parts of the property. This right is called an "easement." Most properties have some easements attached to them, usually by utility companies. These can be a good thing for you as the owner—perhaps your property comes with an easement to access your house using a private road belonging to someone else. Of course, they can also be inconvenient or worse, such as if neighbors have the right to access their property via your driveway or the community's Internet provider has to enter your yard to access a box every time there's an outage.

Uncovering and Removing Clouds on Your House's Title

You probably want the security of knowing the title is clear before the house is yours, right? That's what the title insurance company wants, too, to avoid paying later claims to you. Accordingly, a "title search" will be your title insurance company's first task (or your attorney's, depending on which state you live in—we'll just use the term "title insurer" from now on).

The search involves combing through as many as 50 years' worth of public records concerning the house, including past deeds, wills, trusts, divorce decrees, bankruptcy filings, court judgments, and tax records. Adviser Sandy Gadow has found that, "In almost all real estate transactions, there are title issues that must be cleared up in order to transfer ownership of the home from seller to the buyer." According to the American Land Title Association (ALTA, at www.alta.org), title companies must undertake "extraordinary work" to address title issues in over one third of all real estate transactions. ALTA also reports that spousal fraud—in which one spouse signs on behalf of the other, adding or taking that person out of the title, for example—is a common problem.

The preliminary title report (sometimes called a "title insurance commitment," "commitment of title," or "encumbrance report") gives everyone a chance to eliminate trouble spots before proceeding with the sale—or to call the sale off, if anything too serious is uncovered. It also lets everyone know the conditions under which you'll be offered insurance. For example, some things that can't be known or cleared up will be excluded from coverage.

Your closing agent should send you (and your agent and attorney) the preliminary report. Review it and ask your attorney or closing agent questions until you understand it. If the report refers to recorded documents such as easement agreements or building-and-use restrictions, ask for copies of the actual documents to see what they contain.

Also look at the included plat map (showing the boundaries from when the area was first subdivided). It's easy to read, showing the property's location and size. Look for any inconsistencies—for example, between the map and what you've observed in person ("Wait, there's a fence there!"). Don't take this map as the last word, however, because only a surveyor can tell you exactly where the boundary lines are drawn (see "Is That Tree on Your Side or Ours?" below). If easements are mentioned in the report, ask the title insurer to point out where they are on the plat map (they won't be shown).

TIP

Big reason to read the preliminary title report: Only you know your plans for the property. Says Sandy Gadow, "What if you're fantasizing about building a swimming pool, but never bothered to tell anyone? Finding out there's an easement in the way could prevent you from building the pool. Make your future plans for the property known to your closing agent, attorney, or real estate agent."

Fortunately, you shouldn't be the one who has to act on any title defects. You won't, for example, have to call the seller and say, "Hey, pay off your taxes and child support already." Since you're being promised clear title, it's the seller's problem, not yours. The closing agent will normally call the seller's real estate agent if the report shows a defect. Most sellers agree to remove any liens by paying them off through a deduction from the purchase money at closing.

After All That Prelim Work, Why You Still Need Title Insurance

After the title search process, you can feel pretty comfortable that the house will be yours alone (subject to a few easements and exclusions). So why do you need a title insurance policy? It's protection for you and your lender in case the report missed any clouds on the title.

If you're taking out a mortgage loan, your lender will require, at a minimum, that you buy a "lender's policy" (also called a "mortgagee's policy"). This reimburses the lender for any mortgage payments you can't make because you've lost the house to someone else's claim on it. The lender will likely also require you to buy an "owner's policy," covering your own legal fees and other losses, as yet another step toward protecting its collateral.

Even if you're not taking out a loan from an institutional lender, you should still buy an owner's policy. No title search, no matter how complete, can predict when a long-lost relative will turn up or whether paperwork buried for years under a misspelled name will reveal a claim concerning the property.

Why Buyers of Newly Built Houses Need Title Insurance

If you're the first owner of a newly built house, you still need title insurance. The land your new house will sit on might have had a string of past owners, and what's more, if your own developer fails to pay its subcontractors or suppliers, they can file liens against your property.

You might, however, qualify for a discount if your developer previously bought title insurance on the land. The title insurer might also ask that your developer sign an affidavit stating no knowledge of judgments or liens attached to your property and that all people who supplied labor or materials for the house have been paid in full.

What's Excluded From Your Title Insurance Policy

Any issues revealed by the title search that can't be wiped out will be listed as exclusions in the preliminary report—and ultimately within the title insurance policy itself. If you aren't happy about what's going to be excluded, you can cancel the sale. Some issues won't be worth the fuss, however, such as easements allowing your local power company to come check your meter.

Is That Tree on Your Side or Ours?

One of the biggest sources of homeowner angst is figuring out where your property ends and the neighbors' property begins. Bad news here: Your title insurance policy won't help forestall such boundary line disputes. Most policies include a basic plat map, but it's nothing you can draw a precise line by (although if it's clearly wrong, your title insurance will cover you).). If you want certainty, call in a professional surveyor, who can put in markers denoting the exact boundaries. Many lenders insist on having either a survey or an Improvement Location Certificate (ILC) done.

The cost of a survey can run into the thousands of dollars. Before hiring a surveyor, do some research to see if a boundary issue is likely. Start by asking the seller whether past disagreements have arisen with the neighbors over property lines, fences, trees, driveways, and the like. Look around the property for anything that looks out of place (like a neighbor's shed that is too close to your house), and take a look at aerial photos of the property online (Google Maps, Zillow, and sometimes the local tax assessor's website are all good sources of aerial property views that might even include rough boundary lines). If you spot any possible problems, ask your surveyor about doing an ILC. An ILC is created by a surveyor, and it shows the locations of improvements in relation to the property line. ILCs are usually far less expensive than surveys, and they will either put any concerns to rest or indicate that a more comprehensive survey is necessary.

If you feel you need a survey, ask the seller to pitch in. You can save money by asking the seller whether a previous survey was done and getting it updated.

For more information, see *Neighbor Law: Fences, Trees, Boundaries & Noise*, by Attorneys Emily Doskow and Lina Guillen (Nolo).

One of the most important limitations on coverage concerns future events. Once the policy's effective date is established, anything you do to cloud your property's title—for example, failing to pay your mortgage or a contractor who then files a lien—is considered your own problem. Your title insurance policy covers you only for events that arose before you bought the house.

You'll also find some standard, boilerplate exclusions in your title insurance policy, such as for boundary line disputes, unrecorded easements, taxes, special assessments and mechanic's liens, and mineral and water rights. You'll need to decide (probably with input from your lender) whether to buy extra coverage (endorsements) for these items if it's available. Lenders often require you to buy endorsements against unrecorded easements and liens, defects that might be found only by an inspection or survey of the property (which your title insurance company won't do), mining claims and water rights, and rights of people currently living on the property (for example, if you're buying a duplex with rental tenants).

> **TIP**
>
> **Get some additional coverage for free.** Some title companies might be willing to issue an owner's policy "without the standard exceptions," giving you coverage against boundary encroachments and construction liens. In return, the seller must sign an affidavit stating that there's been no construction recently that wasn't paid for, and you must provide a report from a surveyor—which your lender may order, anyway.

Yours, Mine, or Ours? What to Say on the Deed

The final step in the transaction occurs when your escrow agent or attorney prepares a new deed and files it in the public land records office. We're not there yet—but you'll need to decide in advance what the deed should say about how you've decided to legally own the place. Depending on where you live, your and any cobuyers' choices as to how to take ownership might include:

- sole property
- joint tenants with right of survivorship
- community property
- community property with right of survivorship
- tenants by the entirety, or
- tenants in common.

Your closing agent or attorney should be able to tell you which options are available in your state.

TIP

Your choice isn't permanent. Be careful about how you take title—it can affect important things like tax liability and division of the property if you die. But you can change your deed later (though you might need all the other owners' consent first).

Sole Property

If you're buying a place on your own, you'll hold it as your sole property, and your deed will reflect that. The property belongs to you alone.

If you're married but nevertheless purchasing the house on your own, you can still own it as sole property. In that case, talk to an attorney, to discuss not only what to put on the deed, but how to make sure it remains your sole property. For instance, this might require you to make all the payments on any mortgage or other house-related expenses like property taxes, repairs, and upgrades. Your spouse might also need to sign a quitclaim deed giving up any interest in the house. However, that won't necessarily preclude your spouse from claiming an interest based on later contributions—for instance, if you use community property (like your salaries) to make mortgage payments.

Joint Tenants With Right of Survivorship

If you buy the property with at least one other person, you can take title in joint tenancy with right of survivorship. In most states, joint tenants must own equal interests in the property (50/50 if there are two of you). The most important feature of such ownership is that if one of you dies, the co-owner automatically gets the other share of the property, without the need for probate.

It's common for married couples, domestic partners, and those in committed relationships to take title this way. It's not so popular among other cobuyers, who might not want to leave their half-interest to their co-owner. Some states restrict joint tenancy—for example, in Texas it can be created only by a separate written agreement.

Community Property

This one's for married couples (and in some places, registered domestic partners) only, and then in only a handful of states (listed below). But it's usually the most beneficial option where available. Couples that own their homes as community property each own half of the property, which they can pass on to whomever they please through their wills. They can't sell or give away their share while living unless the other spouse consents.

Community property ownership often comes with significant federal tax advantages. (As of 2013, when the Supreme Court issued its *Windsor* decision, these advantages also apply to married same-sex couples.)

When one spouse dies, the *entire* property is revalued, for capital gains tax purposes, to its current market value. This new value is sometimes referred to as a "stepped-up basis." When the house is eventually sold, the stepped-up basis is treated as if it were the original purchase price to determine the amount of profit on the sale. The higher your stepped-up basis, the lower your profit, and the lower your capital gains tax obligations. This beats the tax benefits available to buyers in joint tenancy—they also get a stepped-up basis, but for only half the property when one owner dies. For more information, see IRS Publication 555, *Community Property*, available at www.irs.gov.

Community Property States

The states that currently have community property laws include Alaska (a somewhat unusual law, in which community property is never automatic but can be chosen), Arizona, California, Idaho, Louisiana, Nevada, New Mexico, Texas, Washington, and Wisconsin.

Community Property With Right of Survivorship

In a few states, another way to hold title is "survivorship community property" (currently available in Alaska, Arizona, California, Idaho, Nevada, Texas, and Wisconsin). Property held this way doesn't have to pass through probate when one spouse dies, but instead goes straight to the other spouse. It's similar to joint tenancy but limited to married couples (or registered domestic partners). It still carries the other benefits of community property, as well.

Tenants by the Entirety

Another option usually reserved for married folk—and in some states, those in registered civil unions or similar "official" relationships—is tenancy by the entirety (available in about half of the United States). Its main advantage is protecting the property from creditors. You and your spouse each own the *entire* property and can sell it only with the other's consent. In most states, if one spouse is in debt, creditors can't come against that person's share of the property—a major difference from joint tenancy. However, it's similar to joint tenancy in that if one spouse dies, the other gets the place without probate hassles.

Tenants in Common

If you're unmarried and buying with another unmarried person, you might choose to own the property as tenants in common (TIC). This allows you to hold property together in unequal shares. For example, if you're buying with a friend and have agreed on a 60/40 ownership split, your deed can reflect that. If you don't specify your shares in the deed, the split will be assumed to be equal.

With a TIC, you really have to trust your buying partner. The law will allow either of you to sell your share of the property without the other's consent, unless you make a separate arrangement. That means you could find yourself with a new housemate, perhaps one you don't like. Also, each of you owns an undivided portion of the entire property—you own 60% of the entire house, not just the large upstairs unit you and your co-owner have agreed you'll live in. You'll have to separately agree on who lives where.

If one of you dies, the other doesn't have any right to the deceased's share of the property. Instead, that person's share will pass according to the will or living trust or, if there is no such document, according to state law (which would normally give the property to a close family member). Discuss all these issues before purchasing, and create a separate written agreement—preferably with an attorney's help—covering the use and possible sale of the property. For a refresher on the legal and practical issues of joint ownership, see Chapter 9.

Get Ready, 'Cause Here I Come: Preparing to Move

Even as you're busy with these preclosing tasks, you have another logistical issue to take care of: moving. Don't wait until the last minute to plan for how you'll transition from your old home to your new one.

Renters: Give Notice

If you're renting, you'll need to give your landlord proper notice that you're moving out. How much notice varies by state, but if you're a month-to-month tenant, one month is normal. If you have a fixed-term lease, you are legally responsible, with some exceptions, for paying the rent through the end of the lease term. If you can afford to pay both rent and a mortgage for a little while, plan some overlap. This will lower your stress in case the sale is delayed or final construction or repairs take longer than expected. It will also allow you to focus on the sale instead of on the move—more time reading agreements and handling contingencies, less time searching for boxes and bubble wrap.

If you have a roommate who won't be coming along, be sure to work out details such as finding a replacement and getting the security deposit back.

CHECK IT OUT

The Tenants section of Nolo.com includes information on notice requirements and rules to end a month-to-month tenancy, legal issues involved with breaking a lease, and relevant roommate issues.

Make Sure the Lights and Water Will Be On

You'll want to contact local providers of electricity, water, gas, and garbage/recycling about two weeks before you're due to move into the home, to set up your new account. (If the seller hasn't already given you the relevant contact information, a simple Web search should pull this up.) If you're in a condo or co-op, trash pickup may be part of your monthly fees—check with the association.

How do you prove you'll soon own the home? Some utilities might ask you for a copy of the purchase contract.

> **CAUTION**
>
> **It's typically easier to transfer services than to restart them.** In other words, you don't want to wait until the seller has already canceled the service to put in your request. To make sure the transfer goes seamlessly, some agents recommend that buyers negotiate with sellers to pay for the original service to continue for 48 hours after the closing.

Arrange Your Move

Even if you've always used three friends and a pickup truck, your first home might be the time to consider hiring a mover. It's much easier (especially if you're moving into or out of a space with a lot of stairs), usually faster, and not always more expensive.

Within the "move your stuff for money" arena, you have several options. The most expensive is the full-service mover, who packs everything for you and whisks it away. Another option is to pack everything up yourself, then have the mover pick it up—this tends to be cheaper. Finally, there are companies that deliver storage units to you, then pick them up and ship them to your new pad. These are typically the cheapest, but of course you do most of the heavy lifting.

> **TIP**
>
> **Need to access a condo unit using an elevator?** If so, Realtor Mark Nash cautions, "You'll probably need to plan ahead for moving day by reserving use of the elevator. And you can do this only after you've paid your move-in fee."

If you decide to use a mover, get recommendations from family, friends, and colleagues, and check online reviews. Then get in-person, written quotes from at least three different companies. If you're being quoted extremely low rates over the phone, be suspicious—reputable moving companies are usually in line with each other, and looking at the goods allows them to make reasonable estimates based on the amount of stuff you actually have.

If you're moving a long distance or interstate, choose an interstate mover licensed by the Department of Transportation (DOT). Ask for a license number, and look up basic information at www.protectyourmove.gov (by the Federal Motor Carrier Safety Administration). Your state might also have licensing requirements for in-state movers, and it's a good idea to check up on those.

Long-distance moves are charged by weight. Plan for the truck to be weighed twice—once when it's full of your stuff and again when it's empty. And know this: Movers regulated by the DOT can't charge you more than 110% of a given nonbinding estimate, so don't let the mover pull a fast one.

 TIP

Can you live without your stuff for a few days? Some movers offer a discount if you'll allow a pickup or dropoff that coincides with another customer's. For example, if you can wait three days for someone moving to the same area, the company can move you together.

 CHECK IT OUT

For more moving help and quotes, see:

- www.moving.com, where you can compare prescreened movers' rates
- www.homebulletin.net, a directory unaffiliated with any moving companies
- www.movingease.com, which gives quotes from up to seven "top movers," and
- various moving mobile phone apps, for example, Sortly (to help categorize items by room) and Wunderlist (keeping track of tasks and errands).

Children's Books on Moving

Here's some comforting material for kids of various ages:

- *Because of Winn-Dixie*, by Kate DiCamillo (Candlewick; Ages 9–12). A stray dog helps Opal make new friends among the unusual residents of her new hometown.
- *The Monster in the Third Dresser Drawer & Other Stories About Adam Joshua*, by Janice Lee Smith (HarperTrophy; Ages 4–8). A spunky boy copes with moving, the strange boy next door, and a new school.
- *Before I Leave*, by Jessixa Bagley (Roaring Brook). Zelda, a hedgehog, sadly tells her anteater friend Aaron that he can't come along to her family's new home. But before the move, they spend a lovely afternoon playing and eating ice cream.
- *Ben Says Goodbye*, by Sarah Ellis (Pajama Press). When his friend Peter moves away, Ben decides to move, too—under the dining room table, to become a cave boy who talks only in grunts.
- *Moving Molly*, by Shirley Hughes (William Morrow & Co; Baby–Preschool). Molly's new neighbors help her adjust to her new country home.

If you decide to move yourself, you might want to rent a truck big enough to accommodate your worldly goods, especially if you're going a significant distance. You might also want to call friends and family now, to ask for help.

Get the Kids Ready

A move can be traumatic for little people. According to child and family therapist Debbie Ostrow, "One of the reasons moving is tough on children is that they've usually had very little input into the process—they just feel like their lives are being disrupted. You can help counter that by letting them play some small role in decision making, for example, choosing a new color to paint their bedroom or where to place their bed or the posters on their wall." Here are some other ways to help make the transition easier:

- **Share it.** If you live far away but you've got pictures of the new place, show them. If you can drive by, do it. For the younger ones, remind them frequently about the new move. Reading children's books about moving can also help.

- **Keep the comforts close by.** Pack comforting items—toys, games, pictures, whatever—in easily accessible places. Though you might be tempted to get rid of a ratty blanket, don't do so now if it's something your child treasures.
- **Get schools squared away.** Particularly if it's the middle of the school year, do what you can to make your child's transition comfortable. Order school records. Find out whether your child is likely to be ahead of, or behind, the current curriculum and whether adjustments should be made. Take the little one to see the new school.
- **Make sure there's time to say goodbye.** You might wish to plan a going-away party, or just go out to your favorite local restaurant.
- **Get medical and dental records.** If you're going to be changing providers, make sure you have records to hand over.
- **Research activities in the new home.** Especially if you're moving during the summer, research opportunities for the kids to get involved in activities that will help them make friends.
- **Prepare to childproof.** If you have young children, make a list of hazards in the new house and purchase safety devices ahead of time. Have either a playpen or child gates ready to corral a curious little one on moving day. Have a few "emergency" safety latches, locks, and outlet covers on hand until you're sure of what you need in your new place. You can also hire professionals to childproof your new place—some businesses can perform same-day service. Search online for "professional baby proofer" in your area.

Get the Pets Ready

For those of you with furry, scaly, and many-legged friends, here are a few important tips for making the transition:

- **Arrange transport.** Moving companies don't take pets, so plan ahead. If you're moving a long distance, some animals can be shipped on airplanes, though often as cargo, in a pressurized (though dark) cabin. You might have to be the one to transfer your pet between planes, if you have a stopover. If your dog or cat is small enough, you might be able to take it with you in the plane for an additional fee. If driving, make sure your car is equipped to handle your pet comfortably. Get a nervous cat a pet-carrier or make sure the pets in your aquarium will get sufficient fresh water or oxygen during the transport.

- **Get vet records.** If you'll be seeing a new animal care provider, obtain a copy (digital or otherwise) of your pet's medical records.
- **Get a new license or tags.** Get your pet a new identification tag— some pet stores have engraving machines, or you can order these online. Also get a current animal license (if applicable), or update the current license to reflect your new address. If your pet is found wandering, authorities will be able to contact you in your new location. Finally, if your pet has an identifying microchip, update your contact information with the microchip company.
- **Set up space.** Keep your pet's immediate physical needs in mind as you pack, keeping food, a litter box, or other tools accessible.
- **Make sure enclosures are safe.** If your new house has an enclosed area like a fenced yard where the pet will stay, make sure there are no escape routes or hazards. You can check this out when touring the property with your home inspector.
- **Don't leave animals alone.** They don't understand why you packed up and shipped out. Leaving pets alone in a new environment can cause them anxiety. Plan to be home as much as possible in the first few days.
- **If you're moving to a new state, check its government website for laws on bringing in pets.** Some states require you to obtain entry permits, or to undergo inspection at the border, at which time you may be asked to present a health certificate from a veterinarian. Pets traveling to Hawaii must spend time in quarantine.
- **Make sure the new house has been cleaned of old pet odors.** Otherwise, your dog's or cat's territorial instincts may be aroused— and it might start marking the space.

What's Next?

You're almost ready for the closing itself—but not quite. First, we need to explore the ins and outs of property inspections (Chapter 12) and homeowners' insurance (Chapter 13).

Send in the Big Guns:
Professional Property Inspectors

Meet Your Adviser

Frank Lesh, founder of Home Sweet Home Inspection Company and spokesman-ambassador for the American Association of Home Inspectors (ASHI).

What he does

Frank is a home inspector who founded Home Sweet Home Inspection Company in 1989. He has been a member of ASHI since 1991, served as ASHI's president in 2007, and has recently retired as ASHI's executive director. Frank's new roles are as ASHI spokesperson as well as ambassador, which involves establishing, developing, and maintaining good relations with public and private organizations. Frank is still involved in the Great Lakes Chapter of ASHI. He is committed to maintaining quality among home inspectors and believes the key to being successful is his ability to communicate effectively with people. After over 25 years of inspecting, Frank can't help but look at potential problem areas whenever he goes to a house as a guest. His wife rolls her eyes and threatens him if he doesn't stop inspecting the house! By the way, she can usually find him in the basement, explaining what's wrong with the plumbing or the electrical system to anyone who will listen.

First house

"My first house was actually a three-flat apartment building that I bought in 1973. It was about 60 years old. My future mother-in-law wanted to buy it for an investment, but was discouraged because of some maintenance issues I found. What I learned from the experience was not just a lot of do-it-yourself repairs, but also how to deal with tenants' concerns."

Likes best about his work	"I like turning problems into opportunities. The challenge of having a finite amount of money with which to achieve a desired goal encourages me to be creative. Adding people to the mix turns everything into an extremely interesting experience."
Fantasy house	"My favorite type of home is Prairie style. The overhanging roof helps to shield the summer sun yet allows the winter sunshine to come in. The simple, uncluttered look is also appealing to me. Because I like to tinker, I'd need a workshop or garage for all my toys and tools."
Top tip for first-time homebuyers	"Get a professional inspection! And no matter where you're buying, watch out for water—whether it's in the basement, the roof, the siding, or whatever. Water is the most destructive element affecting homes, and water damage is difficult or expensive to fix."

Your purchase contract should have included a contingency saying you could back out if you weren't satisfied with the results of one or more professional inspections. While many sets of eyes—the seller's, your real estate agent's, and yours—have all examined the property, it's entirely possible that no one had the expertise to identify certain problems. As adviser Frank Lesh likes to say, "A house does not have a 'check-engine' light."

This close to the finish line, you might be tempted to close your ears to your prospective home's dirty little secrets—but you'd regret it later. Horror stories abound: people who moved in only to discover that the basement floods when it rains or the attic becomes a dance club for squirrels at night. Avoid nightmares by picking up the phone, scheduling an inspection or two, and paying attention to the results.

This chapter will explain:

- what inspections your home needs, and how to arrange and budget for them
- what's involved in a general house inspection
- how to interpret and follow up on your general inspection report
- what's involved in a termite or pest inspection
- when you should hire additional, specialized inspectors, and
- why inspections of newly built homes—before and after they're done—are a must.

Home Inspection Overview: What, When, and at What Cost?

Most buyers arrange at least one general inspection of their house's physical and structural components. In many situations, buyers also commission specialized inspections to investigate things such as pests, structural stability, roofing, septic systems, wells, and chimneys. Often, the need for these additional inspections becomes apparent when the general inspector spots a potential problem. Or, you or your agent might be concerned about an area of the property that the inspector's report specifically excluded. If the house has features requiring special attention (like a pool) or is located in an area where particular hazards (like radon) are common, your general inspector might inspect or test for these for an additional fee.

No state's laws require buyers to have a home inspection, so how many inspectors you bring in and how much you ask them to inspect is mostly up to you. (The exception would be if you're getting an FHA loan and the FHA's appraiser spots potential repairs needed for health and safety or to preserve the property's continued marketability. In that case, the FHA might require an inspection.)

On the other hand, relying on the seller's disclosures or an inspection report the sellers paid for can be dangerous. Sellers need to disclose only things they are aware of. And no matter how authoritiative the report they gave you looks, it's possible they didn't hire the best inspector out there, or that something's gone kerplunk in the house since the inspection. Investing a bit of money now can save you thousands of dollars later.

Some problems are easier to overlook than you might think. Adviser Frank Lesh provides the following example: "Few homeowners clean their gutters and downspouts more than once a year—though they should, particularly in areas with harsh winter weather. Stuff piles up there: balls thrown by children, bird nests, and so on. That can create ice damming, in which snow melts and refreezes, then expands and migrates under the roof shingles, causing a leak. Even an honest homeowner who's reasonably attuned to home maintenance could be unaware that this is happening. And until the problem is truly severe, it's hard to spot. The leaks are often in the attic, in that thin area where the roofline meets the wall. It's dark and full of insulation. A good home inspector will get up there and check for rusty nails and other signs of moisture. Not even a roofer will spot this problem—they usually inspect the *top* of the roof."

TIP

You'll be in good company. Over three-quarters of all homebuyers obtain a home inspection before buying their homes. (*Source:* American Society of Home Inspectors, www.ashi.org.)

SEE AN EXPERT

The tighter your budget, the more important the inspection. If you have gobs of money and something wrong turns up after you move in, you can simply fix it. But if a $1,000 repair is going to break the bank, then you need to not only have the inspection, but to choose your inspector carefully.

General inspections can be a relative bargain—usually between $200 and $2,000, depending on the house's square footage, selling price, age, and number of rooms, as well as local market conditions. Specialized inspections also vary in price, anywhere from around $100 for a radon test to $2,000 for an engineering inspection.

TIP

Don't rely on a home warranty to cover undisclosed defects. Most cover only appliances and other mechanical systems (such as heating) and leave out expensive structures or problem areas (such as the foundation, walls, or roof). See Chapter 13 for details on home warranties.

House Calls: Your General Home Inspection

The general home inspection will likely be your most important one. Its findings could make a difference to both your negotiations with the seller and your future home maintenance budget.

What a General Home Inspection Includes

Assuming you use a professional inspector (a licensed one, if you're in a state where that's offered), the investigation and resulting report will probably cover all the items listed in "Standard Inspection List," below. The report will describe the items' condition and any defects or damage. As adviser Frank Lesh explains, "Inspectors look at a house as a system. While roofers would be able to tell you about the condition of the roof, and plumbers could advise on the state of the plumbing, a good inspector will understand and observe how all these various components fit together and interact. Sometimes what looks like an isolated defect actually has a hidden cause. For example, moisture in the attic could actually be a result of previous attempts to increase ventilation there. (A "stack effect" occurs, in which warm, moist air, perhaps from a kitchen or bathroom, is drawn upward.) We're the only discipline that looks at the whole system in this way."

But not all home inspections are created equal. In fact, many states don't offer an inspector's license, so people with varying specialties—or lack thereof—can decide what services to charge you for in the name of a "home inspection." Most good general inspectors started out as either contractors, builders, or engineers. (We're assuming you've already evaluated the inspector's basic qualifications, as covered in Chapter 5.)

Before hiring the inspector, confirm exactly what will be inspected, what won't be (perhaps because the inspector isn't licensed to do so), and what inspections (such as radon, or simply the inspector crawling into the subspace or attic) are optional for an extra fee.

ONLINE TOOLKIT

Check out actual inspection reports: You'll find one (with personal information removed) in the Homebuyer's Toolkit on the Nolo website. (See the appendix for the link.) An excerpt is shown below.

Standard Inspection List

Most inspections that meet industry standards will evaluate the house and garage, from top to bottom, including the foundation; electrical and plumbing systems; roof; heating, ventilation, and air-conditioning systems; water heater; waste disposal; doors, windows, floors, and ceilings; walls; exterior, including grading, drainage, retaining walls, porches, driveways, walkways, and any plants or vegetation affecting the house's condition; insulation; smoke detectors; smoke and carbon monoxide detectors; floor surfaces and paint; and fireplaces and chimneys. If you're buying a townhouse or condo, some of the exterior items, such as drainage, might not be included, because they're not part of your property.

Sample From Home Inspection Report, by Frank Lesh

Home Sweet Home Inspection Company		
_____ Street, Downers Grove, Il		

Report Summary

Crawl Space		
Page 6 Item: 1	Crawl Space Conditon	• The crawlspace floor is wet. I recommend installing visqueen plastic sheeting. Also, see Roof, gutters and down spouts. • Both crawlspace sump pumps have extension cords. This is a shock hazard. • The sump pump is on the floor.
Heating		
Page 7 Item: 4	Heat Distribution Condition	• The ductwork is rusting in the crawlspace. Water is dripping out. This is a health hazard. I recommend replacing it.
Cooling		
Page 8 Item: 1	Cooling Condition	• The a/c unit fins were bent. This will affect the efficiency of the system.
Plumbing		
Page 9 Item: 3	Drain/Waste/Vent Condition	• There is a plumbing leak at the master bathroom. • There is a plumbing leak at the hall bathroom shower.
Bathroom		
Page 11 Item: 1	Master Bathroom	• The master bathroom tub diverter sprays. • There is a slow sink and tub drain in the master bathroom.
Electrical		
Page 12 Item: 1	Service Entrance Condition	• The overhead power lines are touching foliage.
Page 12 Item: 3	Circuits & Conductors Condition	• There is exposed wiring and an open junction box in the attic. This is a fire hazard. • There is exposed non-metalic sheathed wiring (Romex) in the basement. This is not allowed in some jurisdictions.
Page 13 Item: 4	Outlets Condition	• There is an ungrounded outlet strip in the basement. This is a shock hazard. • The master bathroom gfci did not operate. • Correct the electrical deficiencies listed above.
Kitchen		
Page 14 Item: 3	Dishwasher condition	• The drain hose from the dishwasher should be raised to prevent it from leaking back toward the dishwasher.
Page 14 Item: 10	Dryer condition	• The dryer exhaust is flexible plastic. This is a fire hazard. Replace with metallic pipe.
Interior		
Page 16 Item: 4	Stairs condition	• The steps to the basement are uneven. This is a trip hazard.
Page 16 Item: 5	Fireplace condition	• The fireplace flue has a build up of creosote. • The firebox brick has gaps in the mortar. • This is a fire hazard.
Page 16 Item: 7	Windows condition	• There is a broken window crank in the breezeway. • There are 4 broken window seals in the breezeway.
Attic		
Page 18 Item: 5	Insulation condition	• There is some misplaced insulation.
Roofing		

Page 1 of 24

Sample Report. ©20xx

What a General Home Inspection Doesn't Include

Even a comprehensive home inspection doesn't cover every possible problem area of a home. When you get the inspection report, you'll see that it lists items or areas the inspector couldn't or wouldn't investigate.

Don't worry—it's not because the inspector is slacking. Instead, many of these disclaimers arise because the inspector can't see through walls, pull up carpeting, or dig underground. And no one expects the inspector to take a dip in the pool or hot tub. Also, because the average home is estimated to contain 60,000 bits and pieces, inspectors might look at only representative samplings of things like electrical outlets and windows.

Safety is another important limitation. The inspector isn't required to risk injury. Exactly where an inspector draws the line varies: One house's crawl space, for example, might be accessible, but another's too narrow or wet. "You never know what you'll find," says adviser Frank Lesh. "I once inspected a home built in the 1800s, and got curious about a brick wall in the cellar that didn't match the other walls. I found an entry hole, ventured in, and discovered that it was an old tunnel to the river. It had been part of the underground railroad, for people escaping slavery."

Further limitations can arise if unscrupulous or lazy sellers create barricades, for example by piling up boxes in front of the door to a room or leaning bicycles near the back of a garage. If this happens, contact the seller and ask that the blockage be removed immediately. If that doesn't work, follow up with a request that the seller clear the area and allow it to be inspected again, at the seller's expense.

Lesson learned the hard way **Should've had them move the potted plant earlier.** Attorney Ken Goldstein remembers, "I had a client who'd bought a house with an enormous potted plant in the living room; so big it would have taken a couple of people to move. The buyers allowed the sellers to leave a few items in the house until the closing, including the plant. When the buyers moved in, they discovered that the pot had been covering up a hole in the floor. They could see right through to the basement."

If your property has unusual features, such as a swimming pool, hot tub or sauna, solar or geothermal energy system, security system, seawall, breakwater, or dock, the inspector will probably not evaluate them. The exception would be if the inspector happens to have specialized expertise and is willing to put it to use. If you know these will be issues for you, seek out inspectors with those specialties.

Finally, every property has a unique array of appliances, furnaces, water heaters, and other manufactured items—some of which might have been recalled due to safety concerns. Most experienced inspectors know about major recalls and will mention them in their reports. But to be thorough, do your own search: Note the brand name, manufacturer, model, and serial number, then search the site of the U.S. Consumer Product Safety Commission, www.cpsc.gov/en/Recalls.

CAUTION

Make sure the water, gas, and electricity are on before holding inspections, especially if the home is vacant. The inspector will charge a fee to reinspect the home if utilities are turned off. And if they're off, make sure the seller arranges for them to be professionally reconnected—never attempt to turn on gas, water, or anything else yourself.

Tagging Along at Your General Home Inspection

You and your real estate agent normally can—and should—show up while your house is being inspected. There's nothing like seeing problems for yourself and being able to ask questions (though, to give the inspector some space and make sure the inspection doesn't drag on so long that you get charged extra, you should probably save most questions until the end).

TIP

"If an inspector asks you not to show up until he or she is finished, hang up the phone," advises retired Austin, Texas inspector Paul MacLean. You should wonder why someone you hired doesn't want you—the paycheck—to watch how he or she works.

As a bonus, the best inspectors will give you practical tips above and beyond the report, such as home maintenance advice and remodeling options. Plan on spending two or more hours at the general inspection, and definitely not less than one hour. Many unhappy consumers tell stories of inspectors who took only an hour to complete a general inspection and missed something important.

Here's how to make the most of the inspection:

- **What to bring.** Have something on hand to take notes, photos, and or video with. (Ask the inspector for permission with regard to photography, though—some aren't comfortable with being photographed or recorded.) Make a list of any potential trouble spots you saw on prior visits—such as cracks in the walls or signs of basement leakage. Also bring copies of any past inspection reports provided by the seller, as well as any disclosure form that the seller filled out. That way the inspector can follow up on the issues mentioned. You can also use the inspection as a chance to take your own second look. You might bring a measuring tape to verify that furniture and appliances will fit as planned, or download a measurement app onto your smartphone and use it to create a floor plan.

- **What to wear.** Wear comfortable clothing that you don't mind getting scuffed, and bring a dust mask in case you venture into the crawl space or attic or onto the roof. You aren't obligated to follow along everywhere, and the inspector might not encourage it (you'll be doing so at your own risk—no fair suing the inspector if you're injured).

- **What not to do.** Don't crowd the inspector or interrupt with questions about your remodeling plans. Be attentive, but give the inspector space to do his or her job. Try not to be one of the buyers who blurts out nervous questions like, "Is everything okay?" before the inspector has even had a chance to look. Save unanswered questions for the end of the inspection, or ask the inspector to orally summarize the findings.
- **But don't be shy about checking things the inspector might skip.** Most inspectors examine only samples of multiple features like windows and light fixtures. You, however, can check each one for yourself. If you find defects, ask the inspector to include them in the report.

TIP

Don't make it a family affair. We asked retired California inspector Paul A. Rude what he wishes people would do differently during the inspection. His reply: "Bring fewer people along. Often the whole family wants a chance to see the house, and they're feeling festive, planning for new curtains, and maybe taking care of a crying baby. All of this is distracting if I'm trying to explain why the house might need $100,000 in repairs."

Say What? Understanding Your General Home Inspection Report

Within two to three days of the general home inspection, the inspector should send you a written report. Make sure the inspector sends it directly to you as well as to your real estate agent. We know of at least one horror story where an agent went on vacation and forgot to forward an inspection report containing information about sewage issues—the buyers had to spend thousands of dollars on repairs after moving in.

Some inspectors give you a descriptive narrative report. Some include digital photos (nice, except that some inspectors use them to replace actual explanations of the problem). At the other end of the spectrum, some cookie-cutter franchise operations give you a computer-generated, check-the-box report, where each item is be simply marked "serviceable," "not serviceable," "repair or replace," or something equally vague.

No matter what your report looks like, read the entire thing, even if your agent summarizes it for you. Realize, however, that some of the report is just boilerplate—for example, disclaimers regarding areas that the inspector takes no responsibility for. The purpose is usually to head off lawsuits.

Lesson learned the hard way **Shoulda read the report.** After the inspection, Julian's real estate agent told him that the report showed "no major defects." Julian's exact words were, "Awesome." He closed the sale and moved in. That winter, Julian watched water leak into the house through its aged roof. He says, "I finally read the report, ready to yell at the inspector for incompetence. But no, the leaky roof was right there! There went hundreds of dollars that I could have asked the seller to spend if I'd been paying attention."

How Bad Is It, Really?

Every house has problems, and most can be fixed or lived with. The seller has no obligation to provide you with a flawless house, and the inspection isn't a repair list—it just gives you an opportunity to negotiate. Plus, the inspector wouldn't be doing the job right without describing everything from a missing cover plate on an electrical outlet to a crack in the foundation. And the inspector has to worry that if the report leaves something out, you—or a subsequent buyer—might one day respond with a lawsuit.

The inspector should be able to prioritize the necessary repairs and explain whether they need immediate work. But don't expect the inspector to tell you that your house has "passed" or "failed." While buyers and agents frequently ask whether a problem is serious or is a "defect," some inspectors rightfully shy away from making such judgments. One buyer's defect is another buyer's "no big deal." The inspectors don't want to scare you unduly—nor do they want you to later complain that they didn't ring sufficiently loud alarm bells.

Don't ask the inspector to give you an exact estimate of repair costs, either. That's partly because you shouldn't be hiring the inspector to do the repairs (which creates a conflict of interest), so any cost estimates are hypothetical. It's also because some repairs might need a closer look or can be approached in more than one way—for example, crumbling mortar between chimney bricks might be fixed with either a quick patch or a complete teardown and rebuild. You and a separately hired contractor would decide on the solution.

It's okay to contact the inspector after reading the report and ask for clarification or more information. Like every professional, inspectors have their own jargon, and you might need a translation of some of the report's more arcane language. Other common questions include, "How important is this really?" or "How soon do I need to fix this?" And if you notice something missing from the report, ask for a written addition.

Getting Estimates for Repair Needs

If not to the inspector, to whom do you talk about the cost and other details concerning repair needs that turned up in the report? You'll need to make some educated but quick decisions about whether the problems justify backing out of the sale or at least asking the seller to provide compensation for the repairs (as discussed in Chapter 11). Your inspector might be able to recommend follow-up professionals.

Your real estate agent can also help here, but be careful. This is a time when agents face the specter of their commission evaporating if the sale falls through. Agents have been known to bring in less-than-scrupulous contractors upon whom they can rely to provide unrealistically low estimates.

Termite or Pest Inspections

Years ago, most everyone got a pest inspection, to check for fungus, dry rot, and "wood-boring organisms"—creepy crawlies that dine on homes, such as termites, carpenter ants, powder-post beetles, and carpenter bees. Almost no one got a general home inspection. Today, the pattern has reversed. The standard home inspection is the broader in scope, focusing on many aspects of the home's structure and features, while pest inspections remain a separate specialty.

In regions with pest problems, it's common and wise to get both types of inspections. Most parts of the United States do have some sort of pest trouble, whether it's termites in the West, old-house borer beetles in the East, or carpenter ants in the Midwest and South. In fact, if the house is in a pest-prone area, your bank or lender will probably insist on a pest report, and that any problems be corrected before you move in.

Your seller might have had a pest inspection done before putting the house on the market—and if you're lucky, has already had the repairs done. But, as with every inspection, you might still want to hire your own, independent pest inspector.

Ask your real estate agent about the reputation of the seller's pest inspector. Your bank or lender, in fact, might demand a second inspection after the first one is more than 30 days old (structural pests can be quick eaters).

In a few states, a combination pest/home inspection is common or even standard. But it's worth trying to find separate specialists if you can, since finding one who is truly expert in both house structure and the various pests is difficult. Adding to the confusion, a regular home inspector might alert you to obvious signs of pests (They might, however, have to be careful how they word this: In some states, it's illegal for anyone but a licensed pest inspector to make any determinations about pests in your home.) The general inspector will then likely suggest a follow-up pest inspection.

How Gross Are They? Termite Facts

- Termites actually eat wood (well, technically, protozoa in their gut do the digesting). All that wood gives the termites gas—enough, some believe, to boost global warming.

- Termites move slowly but will keep on trekking for up to one-half an acre in search of a tasty wood source.

- A termite colony may contain between 100 and 1-million-plus termites.

- Subterranean termites can, in a major infestation, destroy a house in two years.

- At least you're not househunting in Africa— one species there builds cement-like mounds that are the largest non-man-made structures in the world. If the termites were as big as people, their towers would be 180 stories high.

Budget around $150 to $300 for the pest inspection. Plan to tag along—it won't take as long as the general inspection, usually no more than one or two hours.

When to Get Other, Specialized Inspections

Your general inspection and pest inspection may be enough. But, your general inspector is like a family physician, who gives you the big picture and may need to refer you to a specialist for potentially serious conditions or complications. Consider hiring more inspectors if:

- Your inspector recommends them, such as for electrical or plumbing issues; structural engineering issues like a damaged foundation; a house on a steep hillside; unusual construction types like a house built on a pier; a defect in a retaining wall; drainage or soil problems; and toxic substances like asbestos, lead, or radon.
- You know you're allergic or sensitive to, or are worried about, particular substances, such as toxic mold.
- You notice a potential problem in an area your inspector's report doesn't cover, such as unpleasant aromas around the septic tank.
- The property has special features such as a swimming pool, septic tank, or boathouse.
- The seller's disclosure report revealed potential problems, such as the presence of lead or asbestos, that your general inspector didn't test for.
- You're interested in finding out more about the home's energy usage and efficiency (as described in, "What's Involved in a Home Energy Assessment," below).

TIP

"What's the 800-pound gorilla in your area?" Every geographic area has some potential natural disaster. How your home stands up to this gorilla's pounding should be among your first priorities in a home inspection. On the West Coast, it's earthquakes, floods, or mudslides; in the southeastern United States, it's hurricanes; in the northern states, it's extreme cold weather and snow.

What's Involved in a Home Energy Assessment

Retired California inspector Paul A. Rude explains, "Assessing a home's energy efficiency is becoming more common—and more critical—as energy costs rise and as state and local governments adopt regulations to combat climate change. A technical evaluation is beyond the scope of a typical home inspection, as it's time-consuming and requires specialized expertise and equipment that most inspectors don't have. But many inspectors will point out obvious issues, such as inadequate attic insulation, drafty windows, or an older furnace that's far less efficient than a modern one would be.

"Whether to get a separate energy assessment depends mainly on the home's age and location. Some states, including California, now require specific energy evaluations for new homes. These may include blower-door tests to check the home's resistance to air leaks, pressure tests of heating and cooling ducts, and calculations of expected energy usage. These tests are usually conducted before a home is put on the market, but you can ask the builder for proof that they were performed and that the home met the standards.

"Tests may also be required of older homes in certain areas. Realtors are usually aware of such requirements, but you may want to consult your local building department or housing agency for details.

"An energy assessment tends to be most useful in areas with hot summers or cold winters. The monthly cost of heating or cooling a poorly insulated home with inefficient appliances can be hundreds of dollars higher than for a more efficient home. It doesn't take too many years of high utility bills to eliminate the advantage of a lower purchase price.

"Specialized energy assessments can also be useful for planning improvements in older homes—though, if the home is 50 years old or more, you can be pretty sure that it is nowhere near meeting current standards, unless previous owners have installed major upgrades."

Trouble in Paradise: Inspecting Newly Built Homes

If you're buying a newly constructed house, you have every right to expect it to be in mint condition—like a shiny new raincoat. But if you're like many homebuyers, you might soon discover missing buttons and leaking seams. It's been called an "epidemic" of bad workmanship.

It's not hard to understand the source of the problem: Builders are under tremendous time and financial pressure; profit margins can be slim; and anything that takes extra time or resources cuts into the bottom line. Meanwhile, experienced contractors or subcontractors are in short supply. So, some developers cut corners; hire unqualified, inexperienced workers; or just plain make mistakes.

Worse still, once developers finish a project, they usually move on —and try to avoid phone calls. Some even set up shell corporations and intentionally go bankrupt. And some states' laws (lobbied for by developers' associations) allow the developer a chance to fix the property before you sue, without necessarily specifying a timeline. That gives the developer every incentive to delay fix-ups.

The upshot is that you need to monitor the process well before the house is built. Get not only a general inspection of the completed house, but interim inspections during its construction. Yes, this will cost hundreds more than an average general inspection, but it's worth it. And don't count on a city inspector or the developer's so-called "third-party" inspector to do the job—they're not necessarily on your side, nor focused on quality control issues. City inspectors look primarily for code compliance, and the quality and scope of their inspections varies considerably among jurisdictions.

TIP

"I was inspecting a couple of new homes every week, and I always found problems," says retired Texas inspector Paul MacLean. "The worst was in a two-story house, where the master bedroom upstairs had a whirlpool. I filled up the tub and turned on the jets. Next thing I know, a subcontractor who happens to be downstairs is yelling, 'Hey, do you know you've got water coming through the ceiling?' The plumber hadn't hooked things up correctly."

Problems With Newly Built Homes

Here are some all-too-common defects:

- **improper weather detailing** around windows, doors, chimneys, and decks, and improperly installed siding (causing leaks)

- **poorly graded land or faulty sewer and water main connections** (causing flooding, sewer, and drain backups)

- **roof problems,** such as improperly installed shingles and poor design

- **ventilation problems,** most often in the attic, roof, kitchen, and bathrooms, such as blocked or improperly installed vents (leading to mold and moisture problems), and

- **building code violations,** such as improper rail heights on stairs, ungrounded electrical outlets, loose wiring, flues too close to wood, and pipes that don't extend to the drain.

Hopefully, your purchase contract included the right to make all these inspections. Now you just need to follow through and schedule them. Remember, no one has lived in this house before, and you don't want to be the first to find out that the chimney top was cemented over, the drains flow under the house without connection to further piping, or the hot water or power turns off without warning (all real stories).

Unfortunately, even if your purchase contract allows inspections—and even if state law backs up your right to an independent inspection—you might encounter extreme resistance from your developer. When demand for their properties is high, developers have been known to refuse outright, figuring someone will be in line behind you, ready to buy with no inspection. In a slow market, however, you have more leverage. Do what you can to claim your rights.

Also prepare for the possibility of later trouble. Many common defects appear only with time, or are already hidden by finished surfaces by the time an inspector gets a look at the place. It's a good practice to obtain the names of contractors who participated in the construction in case you need eventual repairs or modifications. Key contractors include those installing the foundation, framing, roofing, windows and doors, siding, electrical system, plumbing, and heating system. Also obtain as much information as possible on brand names, model numbers, and warranties on components such as roofing, windows, and appliances.

 CHECK IT OUT

Still not convinced of the need for new-home inspections? Find out about real complaints or class-action lawsuits against specific builders at www.hobb.org, by HomeOwners for Better Building.

What's Next?

Completing the inspection, and negotiating over repairs and removing the inspection contingency, is a major step toward buying your first house. Now take steps to protect its future physical condition by learning how to select the best homeowners' insurance policy.

Who's Got Your Back?
Homeowners' Insurance and Home Warranties

Meet Your Adviser

Amy Bach, J.D., consumer advocate and expert on insurance matters, and the executive director and cofounder of a national nonprofit called United Policyholders (www.uphelp.org; follow her on Twitter at @UPHELP). United Policyholders (UP) is a trusted information resource and a respected voice for consumers of all types of insurance in all 50 states. For over 22 years, UP has been helping people make good insurance-buying decisions and navigate full, fair, and timely claim settlements.

What she does   The core of Amy's work is promoting insurance consumer rights, for both purchasers of insurance (home, rental, and more) and victims of fires, hurricanes, floods, and earthquakes. In recognition of her work, *Money Magazine* honored her as a "Money Hero" in 2012.

The organization Amy heads, UP, serves consumers by maintaining an extensive free online self-help library and distributing tools, information, and resources through three programs: Roadmap to Preparedness, Roadmap to Recovery, and Advocacy and Action.

Amy frequently provides information to the media on insurance matters, and has been quoted in *The New York Times*, *The Wall Street Journal*, CNN, Fox News, *The Philadelphia Inquirer*, *Real Simple*, and *USA TODAY*. She has written numerous publications, including *Wise UP: The Savvy Consumer's Guide to Buying Insurance*, *The Disaster Recovery Handbook*, and consumer tips and guides available at www.uphelp.org. Amy is a member of the U.S. Treasury Department's Federal Advisory Committee on Insurance and an official consumer representative at the National Association of Insurance Commissioners where she is a member of the Consumer Participation Board of Trustees.

First house	"My first (and only) house is a wood-frame Arts and Crafts home built in 1912 in San Francisco. Because I've worked with thousands of people who've lost everything in natural disasters and came up short on their insurance, I have plenty of coverage and a very diligent, consumer-oriented agent. And because we live in an earthquake-prone region and ours is a 'soft-story' home (meaning it sits on top of a garage), we carry insurance for that risk in addition to our basic coverage, even though the cost and high deductible are painful. "
Fantasy house	"A solidly built, multilevel tree house with lots of decks and windows, radiant floor heating, recessed lighting and sconces designed by a lighting professional, comfortable chairs, and functional simple furniture. A large soaking tub in the master bath under a self-cleaning, watertight skylight. A game room with vintage pinball machines and a shuffleboard game. And of course the house can't be in an area prone to tornadoes or severe hurricanes."
Likes best about her work	"Being genuinely useful. Not a day goes by that someone doesn't thank me or United Policyholders for helping them solve a problem."
Top tip for first-time homebuyers	"When insuring your new home, be proactive about putting adequate protection in place. Don't just buy the cheapest policy you can find. Aim to buy enough insurance to cover what it would cost to rebuild your home—not what you paid for it. Keep good notes about your conversations with your insurer in a safe place for future reference."

Once you own a home, you'll want to protect it from the bad stuff, such as fire, break-ins, flooding, or lawsuits.

While you can't control Mother Nature or prevent every accident, you can protect yourself and your assets by buying and maintaining an insurance safety net.

A standard homeowners' insurance policy includes four essential types of coverage, which we'll explain in this chapter. They include:

- coverage for the structure of your home
- coverage for your personal belongings, the "contents" of your home
- additional or temporary living expenses due to your "loss of use" in the event you are unable to live in your home because a fire or another event has damaged or destroyed it, and
- liability coverage to protect you in case someone seeks compensation for an injury on your property or caused by a member of your household (including your pets).

CHECK IT OUT

The United Policyholders' website (www.uphelp.org) offers tips, videos, and tools for properly insuring your home at a price you can afford, avoiding being underinsured, and being a savvy insurance consumer. See "Shop Smart" and other publications at www.uphelp.org.

When buying a home, you might also be solicited to buy a home warranty (or the seller might buy it for you as part of the deal). This is a service contract, not a form of insurance—but since it's related to protecting you financially from stuff that goes wrong in your home, we'll also discuss it in this chapter.

Coverage for Your House

Properly insuring your dwelling requires buying a high enough limit to cover reconstruction costs and coverage of local risks. If you're in a high fire, hurricane, or flood risk area, try to buy a policy that doesn't exclude those risks.

Our changing climate makes it harder than in the past to fully insure a home. Insurance companies have reacted by adding new exclusions and limitations, so be a savvy consumer and shop proactively.

The "dwelling" part of your policy should pay to repair or rebuild your home if it is damaged or destroyed by fire, hurricane, hail, lightning, or another peril covered in your policy. For example, homeowners' insurance should pay to repair a roof after a tree falls during a windstorm, replace a kitchen after a cooking fire, or fix ceiling damage from a leaking tub upstairs.

The biggest things to worry about are:

- A "total loss" is where your home is so damaged that it needs a rebuild. The amount of coverage for this scenario will depend on what type and how much coverage you buy, as explained in, "Is Your Homeowners' Coverage Enough to Rebuild Your House?" below.
- Will your policy cover the local and specific risks that could damage or destroy your particular home given where it's located (earthquake or flood zone) and how it's built (slab on grade foundation or elevated)?

Types of Coverage

There are two main types of coverage within homeowners' insurance policies, and the difference between them is financially significant. Replacement cost (RC) coverage is superior because it pays to rebuild your home as it was before the damage, up to policy limits. Actual cash value (ACV) coverage is inferior but cheaper, because it pays only replacement cost minus depreciation. Consider adding riders to cover increased repair/rebuilding costs due to changes in building codes and increases in materials and labor prices.

Most standard policies (other than flood insurance policies) cover other structures that are detached from your home, such as a garage, tool shed, or gazebo. Typically, these structures are covered for about 10% of the amount of insurance you have on the structure of your home. If your property has unique features that require extra coverage, talk to an insurance representative about purchasing it.

Coverage to Replace Personal Possessions/"Contents"

You'll want to be able to replace the stuff inside your house if it's stolen, damaged, or destroyed on or off your premises. Most home insurance policies also cover items you've temporarily taken outside your home—for example, items stolen from a car, hotel, or even your child's dorm room.

You can buy RC coverage or ACV on the contents of your home. Tailor your coverage to your specific needs, and keep an eye on the list of special caps found in most policies for jewelry, furs, valuable papers, money/coins, electronics, firearms, fine art, and collectibles. A typical cap is around $2,000 per category.

Remember, actual cash value covers "as-is" values versus replacement cost coverage, which replaces old with new.

> EXAMPLE: The RC of a couch you bought in 2013 will be the thousands of dollars it would cost today to replace one of like kind and quality. The ACV of that couch will be the few hundred dollars a willing buyer would have paid you the day before the loss if you'd listed it on Craigslist or sold it at a garage sale. Aim to insure for RC wherever possible.

Most insurers will set the limit (maximum payout) of your contents coverage as a percentage of the limit on your structure. You can increase it through add-ons (riders or endorsements) or stick with the basic coverage. Contents coverage is usually 50%–70% of your structure coverage limit. So if you've got $375,000 in insurance on your house, you'd get $187,500 worth of coverage for its contents. If this sounds like more than enough, and it is for most people, great.

The ideal way to protect your stuff is to use a video camera or cell phone to record the inside and outside of your home. Ideally, pair the video with a detailed inventory of your home and its contents and work with a good agent or broker to customize your coverage. You can use one of United Policyholders' online home inventory tools to draw up a list of your worldly goods—furniture, clothes, jewelry, toys, sports and camping equipment, art, light fixtures, appliances, electronics, DVDs, and garden equipment. Present it to the insurance company and store a copy securely offsite.

An ideal time to create an inventory is when you're unpacking and moving into a new home. You can easily do it any time, however, with a cell phone camera, notebook, or computer. Your inventory will be super useful if you ever have a loss and need to make a claim.

Got Expensive Items Needing Separate Coverage?

If you own big-ticket items, such as valuable jewelry, furs, or antiques, that would be capped at $2,000 in the typical policy, you can buy a floater or rider to increase the coverage and you can "schedule" (a fancy insurance word for "list") individual items.

Scheduling valuables will protect you if, for example, you leave your wedding ring or expensive watch in a hotel room, or your home is burglarized.

Before you purchase a floater, the items to be covered should be professionally appraised. The cost of this service will depend on where you live.

Is Your Homeowners' Coverage Enough to Rebuild Your House?

Approximately two thirds of homes destroyed in disasters are underinsured. Don't blindly trust that the policies offered to you will be adequate.

Your homeowners' insurance should cover the cost of rebuilding your home from the ground up, without reference to sale price or market value. Aim to buy enough coverage to completely rebuild the structure (and replace your belongings) in the event of a total loss. (Insuring your home for only the amount of your mortgage protects your lender, not you.)

The Current Standard: Replacement Cost Coverage With Limits

The label replacement cost is now standard on most home insurance, but buyer beware: An insurance policy is a contract full of legalese ifs, buts, and limits—regardless of that comforting label.

The bottom line is this: Your Coverage "A" limit for the structure is the *most* money you'd be able to collect from your insurer if your home were destroyed. So if you truly want replacement cost coverage, your Structure (Coverage A) limit should be reasonably close to the likely price of rebuilding *your individual home* from the ground up. And, you should be covered for debris removal, other structures, and building code compliance. This latter coverage is essential, particularly for any home older than ten years.

When you're buying a policy, the insurance company's representative will likely ask you about the house's size, location, number and type of rooms, building materials, amenities, and more. Then the rep will estimate your house's replacement value and give you a quote that includes an amount for the structure and contents.

Insure Your Home to Value

Before you accept an insurance company rep's numbers and close the deal, consider this: Factoring in unique features and the quality of materials in order to accurately calculate a home's true replacement cost can't be done in just a few minutes. So if a sales rep spits out a recommended Coverage A limit in less than a half hour, chances are good the calculation is inaccurate.

Find a more conscientious sales rep, or ask the insurer to send out an expert to appraise your home's replacement cost, or get a second opinion from a local builder or use an online home replacement calculator to do your own math. If you're like most people, your home is your biggest asset, so you don't want to underinsure it.

Consider Extended Replacement Cost Coverage

By spending a little more, you can buy a set amount of extended replacement cost (ERC) coverage, which will kick in if you suffer a large or total loss and find your basic coverage insufficient.

You can typically pick the amount of extended/extra coverage. Most insurers offer between 20% to 100% of your basic A limit, and the cost of the "E" in the ERC is often well worth it. If you live in California, the law requires your policy to contain an extended coverage amount that kicks in when needed.

Will Your Living Costs Be Covered While the House Is Being Rebuilt?

If your house needs major repairs or rebuilding, you probably don't want to pitch a tent outside. Standard policies include a loss of use provision to cover the extra costs of living elsewhere, like temporary rent and restaurant meals. This is usually referred to as additional living expense (ALE) coverage.

If you can afford a policy with 24 months of ALE, that's a safer bet than the standard 12 months. California law, for example, now requires every policy to contain 36 months of this coverage. It's almost impossible to rebuild and move back in within a year after a serious or total loss.

Some policies limit ALE coverage to a set dollar amount or a percentage of the total insurance on your house. You want enough ALE coverage to rent comparable digs in your area for at least 24 months.

Damage Your Homeowners' Insurance Won't Cover

Standard home insurance typically covers losses due to fire, lightning, explosion, riot or civil commotion, damage caused by aircraft or vehicles, smoke, vandalism or malicious mischief, theft, volcanic eruption, falling objects, weight of ice, snow, or sleet.

Standard home insurance typically will not cover losses due to earthquakes, flood, war, nuclear accident, landslide, mudslide, or sinkholes. In recent years, many insurers have capped and limited coverage for water and mold damage and added exclusions related to sewer backup/sump pump failure.

Before you buy or renew homeowners' insurance, ask lots of questions about what's excluded. It's very hard to access and read—let alone understand—the actual policy wording and all its exclusions and limitations, so asking questions and keeping good notes on the answers is very important.

If you understand what's excluded, you have the option of checking out another insurance company or buying extra or separate coverage. The key is to buy added coverage for hazards that can cause huge damage or are big risks in the area where you live—like earthquakes in parts of California, hurricanes and flooding in coastal areas, or local concerns such as sinkholes.

Who Should Buy Flood Insurance

You should buy flood insurance if you have to or need it and can afford it. Standard homeowners' policies don't cover damage from flooding, yet flooding is the United States' most common natural disaster. Torrential rains, melting snow, overflowing creeks or ponds, a weak levee, or heavy rain running down a steep hill can all cause flooding. If you live in a designated flood zone and have a mortgage, your bank will require you to buy it. If you're not in a flood zone but want to be safe, buy it if you can. The federal flood maps are often outdated, and thousands of people whose homes were damaged by Superstorm Sandy and Hurricanes Katrina and Rita had no flood insurance because they weren't in designated flood zones.

Basic flood insurance is available through the National Flood Insurance Program (www.floodsmart.gov) and some private insurers. The maximum amount of coverage you can buy through the NFIP for a one-to-four-family structure is $250,000, and $100,000 for personal property. Private insurers sell higher limits but are selective about the homes they'll insure.

NFIP policies don't cover finished basements or outbuildings and pay only actual cash value on your contents/personal possessions. There is a 30-day waiting period before flood insurance coverage takes effect, so don't wait until the middle of a storm to buy it. The cost of flood insurance varies according to the location and history of your property.

You can plug some of the holes in an NFIP policy by buying a DIC (difference in conditions) policy or excess flood insurance on top of a basic policy. Coverage options include structure, contents, and loss of use and can be customized to the needs of the homeowner. DIC and excess flood are available through independent agents or from regular homeowners' insurance companies that have arrangements with a specialized insurer.

CHECK IT OUT

Could your house flood? Could your house flood? After checking
the seller's disclosures, get more information from FloodSmart.gov (under
"Understand your risk," click "Flood Map Service Center"). Also check with your
local flood control board or city building department. Note, however, that due to
climate change, the fact that an area hasn't flooded in the past is not a guarantee
it won't in the future, so get a quote for adding flood insurance before you decide
to "go bare" for this common peril. A nearby wildfire that denudes hillsides can
cause unusual flooding.

Who Should Buy Earthquake Insurance

Standard homeowners' policies don't cover damage from an earthquake
—and you don't need to live in California to experience one. The U.S.
Geological Survey estimates that earthquakes pose a hazard to 143 million
Americans nationwide. The top five earthquake-prone states include
California, Oregon, Tennessee, Utah, and Washington.

CHECK IT OUT

Watch out for fracking. It's been linked to earthquakes and land
subsidence in Oklahoma and elsewhere. If your home is near fracking sites, avoid
buying a policy that excludes losses due to fracking. Ask these questions *before* you
buy or renew insurance. If you wait until after a loss, it's too late to add coverage.

You can protect your home from earthquake damage by adding an
endorsement to your home policy or by buying a separate policy. In California,
earthquake insurance is available either through private insurers or through
the California Earthquake Authority (www.earthquakeauthority.com).
The CEA has improved its products in recent years by offering options that
let you pick and choose your deductible and whether you want to insure
only your structure and not your stuff. (Outside California, earthquake
insurance is very affordable.) Consider your home and its location and do
the math: Could you finance a major repair or rebuild out of pocket after
an earthquake? If not, bite the bullet and buy the coverage.

CHECK IT OUT

Is your house in earthquake territory? After checking any disclosures from your seller, go to the U.S. Geological Survey website at earthquake.usgs.gov for more information.

Protection for Others' Injuries: Liability Insurance

Liability insurance protects you and your assets from claims and lawsuits for bodily injury or property damage that you or family members cause to other people. The classic example is if someone slips and falls on your front steps and sues you. In that case, the liability portion of your home insurance should cover legal fees and damages a court orders you to pay.

Liability insurance also pays for damage caused by your pets. So, if your dog bites someone or accidentally ruins your neighbor's expensive landscaping, you are most likely covered. However, many policies now exclude coverage for certain specified dog breeds.

Your liability coverage extends beyond your home, to anywhere you go in the world. If the Italian waiter trips over your pocketbook, breaks an arm, and sues you, you'll be covered.

Liability coverage does have its limits, however, and buying higher than the minimum is a prudent move. You'll need either additional coverage or a separate policy to protect against losses from injuries related to your car, home-based business, nanny or other domestic worker (in some states), tenants (if any, including Airbnb-type renters), and some pets (depending on their breed, behavior, or other circumstances).

Get Enough Liability Coverage to Cover Someone's Injuries

Liability limits—that is, the maximum amount your insurer would pay out on a claim—typically start at about $100,000. However, experts recommend that you purchase at least $300,000 worth of protection.

Medical care costs, lost earnings, and lawsuits can get expensive fast. The purpose of liability insurance is to protect your home and savings from being tapped to compensate an injury victim.

Some people feel more comfortable with even more coverage, which an umbrella or excess liability policy will provide. It will cover you for libel and slander claims, as well as offer higher liability limits. Generally, umbrella policies cost between $200 to $350 for $1 million of additional liability protection.

TIP

Agreed to rent your house back to its former owners after the closing? This is an increasingly common arrangement, but be sure your investment will be properly insured. Your insurance company will most likely allow a 30-day rent-back period, but for anything longer, you will likely need a landlord or rental dwelling policy. Landlord policies provide property insurance coverage for any physical damage to the structure of the home caused by fire, lightning, wind, hail, ice, snow, or other covered perils. It also offers coverage for any personal property you might leave on-site for maintenance or tenant use, like appliances, lawnmowers, and snow blowers. The policy also includes liability coverage; if tenants or their guests get hurt on the property, it would cover legal fees due to injury claims, and medical expenses. Your tenant's personal possessions are not covered under your policy. Tenants are often unaware of that fact and mistakenly assume they don't need to carry renters' insurance. So, in a post-sale lease-back (or standard rental transaction), a best practice is to alert tenants in writing that if they want protection, they'll need to buy it.

Pet Liability Issues

Around one third of all homeowner liability claims are caused by dog bites. Although these and other pet-related injuries are ordinarily covered, the costs have been going up, and the insurance industry is getting stricter about this. If you've got a rottweiler, Doberman, German shepherd, chow chow, pit bull, husky, or other breed with a bad reputation or that state or local law forbids ownership of, your insurance company might refuse liability coverage altogether or raise your premium. A few states, such as Michigan and Pennsylvania, prohibit insurers from singling out entire dog breeds. But the insurer can still exclude a "bad" dog, that is, one with a bite complaint filed against it.

Do your best to find liability coverage for your dog, whether as part of your homeowners' insurance or separately. With the average cost of a dog bite claim at nearly $30,000, it's a good idea to up your liability limits, too.

Your Out-of-Pocket: Homeowners' Insurance Costs

Homeowners' insurance can cost as little as $800 per year or as much as $8,000 or more per year, depending on many factors, including:

- where you live (Texas, Louisiana, Mississippi, Florida, and Oklahoma tend to be the most expensive, and Washington, Oregon, Idaho, Utah, and Wisconsin the least)
- risk factors—both the house's and yours
- discounts offered by your insurance company
- how high a deductible you agree to
- your track record on insurance claims, and
- how much you shop around.

Risk Factors That Affect Your Insurance Rates

Topping the list of factors that an insurance company will look at before quoting you a price are:

- the house's age (newer homes are considered less risky, having been built according to modern codes)
- the house's size, condition, and number of rooms
- other physical aspects of the house and property (brick versus wood frame construction, custom cabinets versus stock, granite counters versus laminate)
- the geographical location of the property (near water, set on a steep slope, or in hurricane territory)

- proximity of a fire hydrant or other water supply and a fire station
- claims filed on the property by the current or past owners (usually up to five years ago)
- your credit-based insurance score, and
- your history of filing insurance claims.

TIP

In many areas of the U.S., insurers are getting pickier about the homes they'll insure. It's becoming fairly common for insurers to use drones or send out an inspector and require the homeowner to fix or replace items before it will issue a policy on the home. Older roofs and brush around homes are red flags for many insurers. If your home has an older roof, your insurer might sell you only ACV coverage for that item, unless you agree to replace it. Homeowners with swimming pools, trampolines, and/or other high-risk conditions can expect to pay higher insurance rates.

Discounts for Lowered Risk

Most insurance companies will knock a little off your premium if your house:

- has smoke alarms and fire extinguishers
- has deadbolt locks
- has burglar and fire alarms that report to a central service
- has weather-resistant features, such as hurricane shutters and roof ties
- has sump pumps with battery backup systems, and lightning protection systems
- was built within the last ten years
- has a gas shutoff/seismic safety valve
- has a bolted foundation and shear panels, or
- was built using fire-resistant construction, such as block or masonry. (If you live in an area vulnerable to earthquakes, however, masonry homes are more costly, because of the shifting that takes place in an earthquake.)

Your own personal characteristics can sometimes also get you discounts or reduced rates, for example, if you're a nonsmoker, over 50, or have a good credit rating. (The theory is that you're less likely to start fires or to be generally irresponsible.)

Insurance Deductibles

Choosing a deductible is part of buying home insurance. Deductibles affect what you pay for your insurance (the premium) and what you can recover in benefits after a loss.

Although you won't have to actually pay out the amount of your deductible in order to collect benefits, the deductible creates a shortfall in your repair/rebuild budget that you'll have to make up for by paying out of pocket or by cutting corners on the project. If you suffer a loss that's below your deductible, you won't recover any policy benefits.

Types of Deductibles

Your home policy can have one of three types of deductibles:
- a flat/set deductible, such as $500 or $2,500
- a percentage deductible of 1%–15%, or
- a combo of a flat deductible that applies to fire and theft losses plus a percentage deductible that applies to a hurricane or an earthquake.

TIP

You might not have much choice when it comes to percentage deductibles. Insurers have been increasingly adding percentage deductibles to home insurance policies. Claiming they need this protection to stay solvent, these high deductibles allow them to avoid paying claims where the loss doesn't exceed the deductible, and reduce their payouts across the board. On Long Island, N.Y., it's now standard for homeowners to have a 5%–7% deductible for windstorm/hurricane losses. In California, it's common for homeowners to have a 15% deductible for earthquake losses. In wildfire-prone areas of Colorado, homeowners insured with one leading company are now carrying 1% or 2% deductibles for all claims.

How to Choose a Deductible

For your basic home insurance deductible for fire, theft, and so forth, consumer advocates including UP's Amy Bach and former Texas Insurance Commissioner Bob Hunter recommend that you choose $2,500 or even $5,000, if your lender allows it. (Some require borrowers to carry a deductible no higher than $1,000.)

The recommendation that you carry a higher basic deductible is based on three facts:

- You can save as much as 20% on the overall cost of your insurance.
- Paying smaller claims ($5,000 and under) out of pocket protects you from having a "record" and being charged more for your insurance due to being classified as having a high-risk history.
- It's statistically unlikely you'll suffer a large loss, but if you do, you should have plenty of protection above the deductible.

"Named Storm" and Percentage Deductibles for Earthquakes, Hurricanes, and Hail

If you want coverage for earthquakes or hurricanes, you can expect a separate, percentage deductible to apply to those losses, as follows:

- **Earthquakes:** Deductibles for earthquake coverage range from 2% to 20% of the replacement value of the structure. If you buy $400,000 of insurance on your home, for example, a 15% deductible means you'll have a $60,000 shortfall in your repair/rebuild payout. But while you might be thinking, "Why would I pay for that?" remember that if you go without earthquake insurance, your deductible (and payout shortfall) will be 100%!
- **Hurricanes/windstorms:** There are two kinds of wind damage deductibles: hurricane deductibles, which apply to damage solely from hurricanes; and windstorm or wind/hail deductibles, which apply to any kind of wind damage. Whether a hurricane deductible applies to a claim depends on the specific "trigger" selected by the insurance company. These triggers vary by state and insurer and usually apply when the National Weather Service (NWS) officially names a tropical storm, declares a hurricane watch or warning, or defines a hurricane's intensity by wind speed.

When buying or renewing your home insurance, discuss your deductible options with the company or companies you're considering, and find out how they will be applied in the event of a loss. This is a biggie. In some states, policyholders have the option of paying a higher premium in return for a traditional dollar deductible. But in coastal areas you might have no option other than choosing the amount of the percentage deductible.

Consider Insurance Costs When Choosing a Home

When looking for a home, it has become important to consider the cost of insuring it. Coastal and flood zone properties and homes in the urban wildland interface and high wildfire risk areas cost significantly more to insure. Remember, you will be paying for insurance the entire time you live in your home. If you feel you won't be able to afford the coming years' insurance premiums and deductible payments, then you might want to consider a different home.

TIP

Got a home-based business, or working from home? A typical homeowners' policy provides only $2,500 in coverage for business equipment. To properly insure your home-based business, there are three ways you can go:

- **Home-based business policy endorsement.** Adding this to your homeowners' policy doubles your insurance for business equipment. You can also add a homeowner's liability endorsement to protect you in case delivery people or others fall on your property and sue you.

- **In-house business policy/program.** This provides more comprehensive coverage. Usually it covers up to three employees.

- **Business Owners Policy (BOP).** This is created specifically for small businesses. A BOP covers business property and equipment, loss of income, extra expense, and liability. A BOP offers much broader coverage than the other two policies, but does not include coverage for professional liability, automobiles, workers' compensation, health, or disability benefits for your employees. These coverages must be purchased separately.

Shopping Around for Homeowners' Insurance

Home buyers often just go with the insurance company their real estate agent recommends. But doing some price and coverage comparisons—preferably between three or four companies—could save you hundreds of dollars *and* make a big difference in the quality of your protection if you suffer a loss and need that insurance safety net.

Price should not be your only concern. Coverage is really important, so ask questions before you pick the company you're trusting to protect your biggest asset. While all policies have lots of exclusions, some exclusions are broader than others—especially for water damage.

Look for a company that is financially healthy. Check financial ratings through organizations such as Demotech, Standard & Poor's, or A.M. Best. An A– rating or better indicates a solid company that will be able to pay your claims.

Websites that rank or grade insurers on reputation for reliability, fairness, and customer service can be helpful. Find an agent who will take the time to discuss your insurance needs and explain options to you clearly and accurately, and not just give you the "company line."

You can buy insurance in one of three ways:

- an insurance company that sells insurance directly to customers without a middleman (via a toll-free phone number or the Internet)
- "captive agents," who represent only one insurance company, or
- agents or brokers who represent more than one insurance company.

Each option has its own advantages. Ask friends and real estate agents for recommendations. Also, if you're happy with your car insurer, contact that company's representative to ask whether it offers a multipolicy discount (often 5% to 15%). Check with your state insurance department as well, which might track local insurance rates and complaints. You'll find the link to that department in the "State-by-State" section of the United Policyholders online resources.

Types of Insurance Companies

Depending on whether you live in a coastal area or an area considered high risk due to past disasters, you might not be able to buy insurance through a brand name you recognize. If that's the case, aim for a licensed company that is admitted to do business in your state and that has an A or A+ financial rating from A.M. Best.

Here are the basic types of insurance companies:

- admitted, licensed, shareholder-owned, or mutual, such as State Farm or Nationwide
- nonadmitted/surplus/excess, such as Lloyds of London and its many affiliated companies
- government-run or quasi-government-run insurers of last resort (examples include Citizens Insurance of Louisiana, the Texas Windstorm Association, the California Earthquake Authority, the California Fair Plan, and the National Flood Insurance Program), and
- "take out" companies that took incentives offered by the state (such as Florida or Louisiana) to take customers out of a state-run insurer of last resort.

Jointly Owned, Jointly Insured: What Your Community Association Pays For

If you're buying a condo, a co-op, or another property in a common interest development, the community association should have a "master policy" that includes hazard and liability coverage. It will cover common areas such as the roof, walkways, and structure of the building in which your unit is located, but not the contents of your unit or your personal liability. You must buy your own unit owner's policy and make sure it includes coverage for loss assessments the HOA might impose to cover repairs to common areas.

It's well worth examining the master policy for completeness. Many condo owners have learned only after a flood or an earthquake that their associations hadn't bought insurance for these hazards, or not enough. Worse yet, a clause in your association's covenants, conditions, and restrictions (CC&Rs) might allow it to collect from you personally if its master policy doesn't cover the full extent of a loss.

The master policy's coverage generally stops at your unit's bare walls, ceilings, and floors, or it might also include your cabinets, plumbing, appliances, carpeting, wallpaper, wiring, light fixtures, and more. Check with your association for details, then buy insurance to fill gaps. Special condo and co-op policies are available.

If the association has decided not to buy flood or earthquake insurance for the common areas and the overall structure but you feel it should, request in writing that it reconsider the decision. You can buy coverage for the interior of your own unit and your personal assets, and you might want more liability coverage than the association has bought for itself if you entertain often or conduct business out of your home.

Home Warranties for Preowned Houses

Another form of home protection is what's called a preowned home warranty. This is not an insurance policy; it neither overlaps with nor replaces your homeowners' insurance. Instead, it is a service agreement offered to the sellers and/or buyers during the sale of a home, which provides repair and replacement for certain home systems and appliances if they break down due to normal wear and tear. (If you're buying a newly built home, however, this type of warranty isn't available; skip to the next section for information.)

Here's an example of the difference between a homeowners' insurance policy and a home warranty: Let's say your hot water heater were to burst and destroy a wall in your home. The warranty would pay only to repair the water heater itself. Your homeowners' insurance would pay to fix any damage done by the water heater.

The home warranty applies only to certain mechanical systems and appliances in your house, such as the furnace, plumbing, and electricity, and for an added fee, the air conditioner, spa, pool, and roof. If one of these breaks due to normal wear, you call your warranty company. If the company believes you're covered, it sends a repairperson. You pay a set fee for parts and labor, usually $50 to $100.

If you purchase a policy, make sure to look into several different companies' warranties, and read the exclusions. Common policy exclusions include inaccessible areas, your failure to have the item serviced as often as recommended (will you remember to change your A/C filter once a year?), and improper installation. The policy might also require you to pay to upgrade a system to current building code standards before it pays for repairs. And if your toddler flushes a teddy bear down the toilet, that's an accident, not "normal wear and tear," and the warranty provider will probably pass the buck to your insurer.

Home warranties cost around $300 to $800 per year, depending on your house. Many sellers will offer to pay for the first year, as a way of inspiring confidence. Or, your own real estate agent might offer to pay, in the name of customer satisfaction.

If the seller or your agent isn't paying for the home warranty, however, do some homework before deciding whether to buy one on your own. Angie Hicks, founder of Angie's List (a national consumer rating service) says that users of home warranty or home service companies are often their least satisfied group of reviewers. You might find a company with great consumer ratings and go for the peace of mind that comes with easy access to repair pros—or you might prefer to save your money and put it toward an annual repair fund. Setting aside $5,000 per year for home repairs is recommended.

In any case, if you're debating whether to get a home warranty, decide now, because they become unavailable after the closing.

For the protection of consumers, home warranty companies are often regulated and licensed by the state department of insurance. Check with the appropriate department or the Better Business Bureau in your state to see whether any complaints have been logged against the companies you're considering (or being offered). Pick a company with a long history in your state.

Home Warranties for Newly Built Houses

If you're buying a newly built house, don't consider one that isn't backed with a builder's warranty. Reputable builders won't balk at this. What this means in many cases is that the builder promises to assess any problem and arrange for repairs. (Get this in writing.) In other cases, it means the builder buys you a warranty.

No matter where the warranty comes from, read it carefully to find out who the actual provider is and what it covers. You might even want to have an attorney review the warranty. If, for example, it's coming straight from the builder, the attorney could look into matters like whether the builder formed a single-purpose entity to construct the home and issued the warranty in that name. This all-too-common strategy means that by the time you might a warranty claim, the single-purpose entity might no longer exist or might be judgment proof.

For the first year, the warranty should cover workmanship and materials on everything from the roof to the structure to the mechanical systems. The builder is off the hook for appliances or fixtures whose manufacturers provided separate warranties. The best builders will also plan to schedule one or two inspections during the first year, in order to find and repair any nonemergency problems.

After that year, most builder warranties cover mechanical systems (plumbing, electric, heating, and A/C) for two years and the basic structure for ten years.

As with any warranty, damage due to normal wear and tear isn't covered. It will also be your responsibility to take care of normal upkeep, such as annual servicing on the heating and air conditioning system, and simple maintenance like caulking the seams around windows and tubs.

CHECK IT OUT

Most states also regulate builder warranties. Check your state government website for consumer information, for example, via www.usa.gov. Some states' laws mandate warranties on new construction (often for up to one year) even if the builder put nothing in writing.

What's Next?

You're almost there—proceed to the next chapter, on closing the sale!

Seal the Deal:
Finalizing Your Homebuying Dreams

Meet Your Adviser

Sylvia M. Gutiérrez, loan officer in the South Florida market (NMLS # 372427; sylviagutierrez.com), and author of *Mortgage Matters: Demystifying the Loan Approval Maze* (Real Works Press), which won both the 2016 Bruss Silver Award and the Best First-Time Author Award from the National Association of Real Estate Editors (NAREE).

What she does

"Much of my typical day involves interacting with real estate agents, CPAs, and financial advisers, stepping in when their customers need a checkup of their current mortgage or are buying a home. For home-buyers, I'll take a look at their financial situation and identify what loan products will help meet their short- and long-term goals. I also help educate consumers, by giving homebuying seminars. Sometimes, I'll attend brokers' open houses or Sunday open houses, speaking to potential buyers and real estate agents about market trends or new loan programs. As a volunteer, I am a director on the board of the Mortgage Bankers Association (MBA) South Florida chapter, and formerly served as co-chair of the Diversity and Inclusion committee of the National Association of Mortgage Professionals."

First house

"It was the first in a string of houses! I wasn't in the mortgage business at the time, and like most people, my husband and I relied on the advice of family and friends. To satisfy my husband's risk aversion, we took out a 15-year mortgage and saved up enough to make a 10% down payment on an affordable, newer home, far from most of our life activities. The high monthly payments were affordable, because—at that time—housing ratios were maxed out at 28/36. So less than 28% of our total monthly income went to housing (in the mortgage heyday, lenders increased this amount to 50%). We stayed there only four years, needing room for our growing family. (In hindsight, we should have considered a 30-year adjustable rate mortgage with initial interest fixed for at least five years.)"

Fantasy house	"My vision of a fantasy home has changed many times over the years! Now, I just want something that's small, easy to clean, near a part of town where all the fun is, and has ocean access."
Likes best about her work	"Being a perennial student. The mortgage industry is constantly changing, and I've seen it through many cycles. Also, hearing the unique story of every family I work with makes each transaction an interesting challenge. Every family has its own set of hopes and hurdles to clear. It's rewarding to help my customers identify short- and long-term financial goals, realize their dreams of homeownership, or find ways to sustain homeownership, and it's satisfying to see them come back to me, time and again, for their second home, investment, or construction loan financing."
Top tip for first-time homebuyers	"Get your finances in order, to a point where you're paying off your credit cards completely every month. Understand what it means to be ready to buy a home. If you've been living with Mom and Dad, and they've been paying your house-related bills (not to mention food), the change to your current spending habits might be a shock. (And you might need to have a conversation with Mom and Dad about how much it really costs to support you there.) You might try doing a mock trial for six months, practicing setting aside the money you'll need in order to make not only your mortgage payments, but to pay for electricity, Internet, cable access, telephone, groceries, car and student loans, insurance, lawn care, and so on. Also consider your other financial needs and goals. Maybe you're helping support parents or adult children, or want to send your kids to private school. Only you can decide where your money should go and thus plan around these things. I see too many people overextend themselves, forgetting that they'll need some assets in reserve for lean times—or for something special."

At last, you're approaching closing day, when the house officially becomes yours. You should have the easiest job of anyone involved: familiarizing yourself with documents that other people prepare and signing your name. That doesn't mean you can sit back and put your feet up, though. You'll need to stay in close contact with your team as they take care of the myriad tasks in the last hours before the closing. And be aware that some little surprise or bump in the road might (and often does) come along on closing day. Fortunately, most real estate closings work out fine in the end, usually because the professionals involved have the experience to save the day.

This chapter will tell you what to expect during the last hours leading up to the closing, and on the closing day itself, including:

- what a closing is—the who, what, and where of it
- how to conduct a thorough final walk-through
- tasks that you're personally responsible for in the last days and hours before the closing
- what to expect when attending your closing, including what identification documents you'll need to bring and documents you'll have to sign, and
- when you can move in.

TIP

The world won't end if your closing gets delayed. According to retired Realtor Carol Neil: "In my 30-plus years of experience, I've never had an escrow where something new didn't come up at the last minute, leading to scrambles or even a delayed closing date. I worked on one sale where the lender, at the 11th hour, asked for the buyer's divorce papers—even though he'd already been divorced for about 15 years! Homebuying is like childbirth: You think you might not survive the process while it's happening but later forget the pain and love the results."

Speaking of delays, however, you will still want to do your best to ensure that the closing does happen on schedule. As adviser Sylvia M. Gutiérrez explains, "Your lender might have to push the closing back another three days if it doesn't take place as scheduled. This is due to regulatory rules that require a lender to give you three business days to review your closing disclosure. If you're thinking of canceling the closing, be sure to ask your lender how this will affect your interest rate, closing fees, and available closing dates."

Preview of Coming Attractions: What Your Closing Will Involve

A closing (also sometimes called a "settlement" or "time for performance") is a meeting or a nearly simultaneous series of events during which you pay the seller and the seller transfers ownership rights to you. All of this will be orchestrated by your closing agent or, in some states, your respective attorneys.

The closing can't happen until both you and the seller have either complied with or renegotiated all the terms of your purchase agreement. The two sides have, no doubt, been working hard to bring this about for weeks, by having inspections and possibly repairs done, arranging for financing, and removing other contingencies. But during that time, you were still hanging onto your purchase money, and the seller still owned the house. The closing was created so that each of you could feel safe handing over what you own to the other.

Of course, if you're not paying in cash, your lender actually holds much of the money for this transaction. The lender will be doing some last-minute investigating behind the scenes—expect your employer to receive a call to reverify your employment within the ten days leading up to the closing. And you yourself might have to fulfill some last-minute lender requests for additional documents or statements. When the lender decides that all is "clear to close," you'll be able (as part of the closing "ceremony") to sign off on your loan and transfer your down payment to the seller. Your lender will then (using the closing agent as intermediary) pay the seller the remainder of the purchase price.

But enough generalities: What about *your* closing? The biggest logistical questions in the days leading up to it are:
- When will it be?
- Where will it be?
- Who will attend?

When. The exact date of your closing, or an approximate date, should have been specified in your purchase agreement. If the date wasn't made absolutely clear, your closing agent will help you and the seller decide when you'll all be ready and coordinate dates with your lender.

Contact your lender at least ten days before closing to confirm that all documentation is in and has been reviewed by the underwriting team. Then once you've gotten the all-clear from your lender, your closing agent will coordinate with everyone involved to set the date, time, and place for closing. Your closing appointment could still change, though: Attorney Ken Goldstein says, "It's not unusual, in the final days, for the time and even the date of the closing to be revised by mutual agreement, in order to meet changing schedules."

*L*esson learned the hard way   **Don't schedule your closing on a weekend.** Marge and her husband Theo lived a long way from their closing agent's office, so, as Marge explains, "We thought we were lucky when she volunteered to come in on a Saturday. But then she got really annoyed when we wanted to read everything (our real estate agent hadn't given us drafts) and when a complication arose with our loan. Our mortgage broker wasn't available by phone, and it took three hours to sort everything out. By the end, we were all exhausted. Theo and I had to force ourselves to go out and celebrate afterwards, but I'm glad we did."

Where. The meeting will most likely take place at the office of either your escrow officer or attorney, the registry of deeds, your real estate broker or your builder's sales office, or (in rare cases) your lender's office. The choice of location depends on local custom, convenience, and ultimately the terms of your purchase and sale agreement.

Who. Of course you'll be there, preferably well rested and fresh, along with any cobuyers. Don't bring children! A closing is a serious, sometimes intense experience demanding your full attention. Hire a babysitter (for double the time you think it will take), and give yourself plenty of time for the meeting (and maybe a grownups-only celebratory meal afterwards).

TIP

What if an emergency comes up and you or a cobuyer can't be at the closing? One possibility is to arrange to sign everything a few days beforehand, for example, if you'll be traveling. Another (which not all lenders allow) is to prepare a document called a "specific power of attorney" giving signing power to a trusted friend, relative, or lawyer for the limited purpose of bringing about the purchase (or sale) of the property. (If the document doesn't list the specific intent, a lender will most likely reject it.) The power of attorney should include an expiration date—perhaps a few days after the closing. Check with your attorney or closing agent for details of how the power of attorney needs to be formatted and possibly recorded with a government office.

Your real estate agent should definitely be at the closing, offering support and carrying a packet of documents in case anyone forgot anything. You might also be accompanied by your mortgage broker and your attorney, if you have one. If you haven't used an attorney up to now, but are worried about last-minute issues or complications—for example, if a recently completed survey reveals that the house's garage is over the neighbor's property line—you can hire one before the closing.

Best thing we ever did **Have our lawyer at the closing to deal with the sleazy seller.** Mackenzie and her husband Don had agreed to buy a fixer-upper within walking distance of their jobs on the University of Michigan campus. "But," says Mackenzie, "We had a feeling our seller wasn't the most scrupulous character. He'd been renting out even the damp, gross basement spaces to students, and the place was a total wreck. Our suspicions were confirmed on closing day, when our lawyer discovered an outstanding water bill of some $800. The seller tried first to pretend that he'd paid it (he hadn't), then to argue that it wasn't up to him to pay it! It was quite a scene. But our lawyer eventually helped make him understand that he had to pay it in order to transfer the deed."

TIP

Save on attorneys' fees. Bringing an attorney to the actual closing can get expensive if the attorney's time is mostly spent watching people sign papers. Often, a good middle course is for the attorney to receive the key documents for review the day before the closing—which is probably the earliest they'll be ready— and to report any findings to the buyer by phone. The attorney could also agree to be reachable by phone if a problem comes up at the closing table.

Unless you're meeting at the lender's office, the lender won't normally send a representative, but will send the documents straight to the closing agent. If questions come up, your mortgage broker will normally contact the lender. The lender won't authorize disbursement of the funds until the settlement agent has confirmed that it has complied with all the lender's instructions. Sometimes, meeting those final contingencies can take place a few hours after you've signed, and the disbursement of funds would take place later—making yours what's called a "dry" closing. You'll get your keys only after the seller has received all the funds.

TIP

Who will answer last questions about your loan? Many buyers develop new questions on closing day when all the loan documents are in front of them. Closing agents can't always answer these. Be sure to study the most recent Loan Estimate and the Closing Disclosure well ahead of time so that all will be familiar to you. Then make sure that your mortgage broker or, if you have none, your direct lender, will either be represented at the closing or give you a direct-line phone number and a promise to be available on closing day.

Another person who might be in the room is a notary public (unless the settlement agent plays this role). The notary is charged with the brief but all-important task of making sure that you and anyone else signing documents are, in fact, who you say you are (by checking your photo ID) and stamping the documents to confirm this.

Whether the seller and/or the seller's agent or attorney will attend the closing depends on local custom. They might handle their end of things separately—the seller has far fewer documents to sign, and might have already signed and sent them via overnight delivery, or might give an attorney signing authority (a power of attorney). And, signing documents—anywhere between ten and 75 of them—will, in fact, be your main task at the closing.

TIP

Differences with co-op closings. Co-op buyers normally meet at the co-op attorney's office, and a representative of the seller's bank or lender will be there (to bring the stock certificate proving the seller's ownership of the co-op, which they've been holding as security for their loan—and must destroy before you get a new certificate). Other folks in attendance will include an attorney or other representative of the co-op, the attorneys and real estate agents for both sides, a representative of your bank or lender, probably a paralegal who brings the checks, and the seller. Instead of recording a deed, your lender's attorney might record a UCC-1 financing statement to publicly show its lien on your co-op shares.

Is It Really Empty?
Final Walk-Through of an Existing House

Taking a last look at the house before the closing is both fun and vitally important. Never skip this step! The walk-through is your chance to make sure that the seller has (in accordance with your agreement) moved out of the house, made any agreed-upon repairs, left behind all fixtures or other agreed-upon property, and left the place clean and trash free. Once the house has closed, it's a lot harder to run after the seller saying, "Wait, I thought you were leaving the stove?!" (You might be able to sue, but you'll have more interesting things on your mind by then.) Be careful on your walk-through—but also don't let last-minute jitters make you see major problems when you're really looking at minor cracks or dust balls.

Final Walk-Through Checklist (Existing Home)

Use this checklist to walk through the house and make sure everything is in good order or repair. You'll want to make sure that the seller has made any agreed-upon repairs, left behind all fixtures or other agreed-upon property, and left the place clean and trash free. Add any other relevant items (inside and outside) or questions you might have (such as the name of the architect who did a recent kitchen remodel) to the list. Note any problems and try to work them out with the seller before the closing. If the seller agrees to do additional work or repairs, be sure to get the details in writing, including how the costs will be paid.

☐ The keys fit in the locks, keys have been provided for every door, and you know how to use them.

☐ The lights and fans work when you turn switches on and off.

☐ The fixtures (such as light fixtures, towel racks, toilets, sinks, and cabinet knobs) are present and are the same ones you expected.

☐ The doorbell rings.

☐ The alarm or security system works, and the seller has left the company's contact information and any entry codes and remotes.

☐ The faucets turn on, no leaks are evident under or around the sinks, and all toilets flush.

☐ The stove, oven, refrigerator, garbage disposal, dishwasher, microwave, and other appliances are empty and work.

☐ The garage door opener works, and the seller has left the remote.

☐ The ceilings, walls, and floors are in the condition you expected.

☐ The heating and air conditioning work.

☐ The windows are in the condition you expected.

☐ The sump pump, if there is one, works (to turn it on, you'll normally need to fill the pit with water).

☐ None of the seller's trash or personal items remain in the house, garage, attic, basement, yard, or sheds.

☐ The seller has left you any brochures or warranties regarding the furnace, appliances, and other fixtures.

☐ Other.

NOTES:

You'll normally want to schedule the final walk-through within the five days before the closing—preferably the day before, if not on the closing day itself. The closer to the closing day, the more time the seller has to move out completely—but the less time remains to fix any problems. There's no perfect balance!

"We typically do the final walk-through on the closing day itself here in Massachusetts," says attorney Ken Goldstein. "The first thing I ask at closing is, 'How was your walk-through? Anything we need to talk about?' When I wake up on the morning of a closing and it's raining outside, I start to worry. There's a fair chance that the buyer's answer to my question will involve water in the basement or some other leakage."

Arrive at your final walk-through with your real estate agent. The seller's agent might also be there as well as, in rare cases, the seller.

ONLINE TOOLKIT

Bring the "Final Walk-Through Checklist (Existing Home)" provided in the Homebuyer's Toolkit on the Nolo website. (See the appendix for the link.) A sample is shown above. It lists all the things you should check out, like the windows, faucets, and appliances.

Also bring along a copy of your purchase agreement and any follow-up writings explaining what the seller has agreed to repair or leave behind.

Then take a good, hard look around. "I tell people to remember the steps their home inspector took earlier and roughly follow these," says attorney Ken Goldstein. "Turn on faucets and appliances, flush the toilets, and so on." Next, make a list of what remains to be done, and negotiate accordingly. If it's just a matter of removing the old magazines from the garage, the seller should be able to handle that before closing. If you find a more serious problem—one that appears to be new or previously hidden, such as a mysterious puddle in the crawl space or a foundation crack revealed after the boxes were moved—quickly get a contractor's estimate or "cost to cure." Then try to negotiate to withhold enough money from the seller's proceeds to cover repairs after the closing.

Depending on the timing of your walk-through, the sellers might not have actually moved out yet. In that case, focus on whether repairs have been completed, and check that nothing has been removed that should have stayed behind. If, for example, there are holes in the wall where a mirror fixture used to hang, or the light fixtures have been downgraded, bring this up with the seller's agent. If most of the seller's possessions are in boxes, ask about trashy-looking items that no one seems to have taken an interest in packing.

And if the seller has only a few hours in which to pick up and move, your real estate agent might need to get assurances about what will happen (preferably in writing) or, at worst, delay the closing or negotiate to have the seller rent the place back from you for awhile.

What if you've just noticed a problem that was probably there before and your inspector could have seen, such as cracks in the ceiling? You might just have to live with it. This isn't a new inspection, it's your chance to confirm that the house is in the same condition in which you agreed to buy it. These can be tough calls, so confer with your real estate agent before rushing to judgment.

Even if the seller moved out ages ago, you shouldn't be held responsible for any damage that occurred while the place sat empty, so long as the seller still owned the home. The seller is normally responsible, under the contract, for fixing any damage due to vandalism, dumping, spontaneous leaks, or even the seller's moving company. After all, the seller's homeowners' insurance should still be in effect.

TIP

If the seller is at the walk-through, get friendly. Establishing a relationship you can draw on later, after your agents and the others are gone, can be invaluable. If negotiations were tough, try to put the business side of the transaction behind you, and ask practical questions like, "How do the burners on this vintage gas stove light?" and "Is that a fruit tree?" Also ask the seller for contact information, including a forwarding address. (You'll no doubt get some of the seller's mail, and can your conscience handle throwing away a letter from a long-lost relative?) Years from now, you might also need to call with questions like, "Where can we buy replacement tiles for the ones you installed?" or "What's this urn full of ashes in the attic?" If the seller isn't at the walk-through, you might want to get in touch or meet soon after the closing, for the same purpose.

Final Walk-Through Checklist (New Home)

Use this checklist to walk through your new house and make sure everything inside and out (from flooring to landscaping) has been finished and is in good shape. Then, create a "punch list" of what remains to be done. Work out with the developer how and when needed changes will be made and how this will affect your closing date.

☐ Construction and finishing work is complete, with no missing trim, hardware, or paint, no exposed wires, and all water gutters pointed away from the house.

☐ The landscaping is complete, with grading sloped away from the foundation (no trenches right next to the house). All agreed-upon trees have been planted (often the last thing to be done).

☐ No damage, scrapes, or gouges are visible on counters, walls, floors, appliances, or other surfaces.

☐ All fixtures, carpets, and appliances are the ones you specified.

☐ The keys fit in the locks, keys have been provided for every door, and you know how to use them.

☐ The lights and fans work when you turn switches on and off.

☐ The faucets turn on, no leaks are evident under or around the sinks, and all toilets flush.

☐ The stove, oven, refrigerator, garbage disposal, dishwasher, microwave, and all other appliances work.

☐ The garage door opener works.

☐ The ceilings, walls, and floors are in the condition you expected, with finishes on the flooring and woodwork even and complete.

☐ The heating and air conditioning work.

☐ The sump pump, if there is one, works (to turn it on, you'll normally need to fill the pit with water).

☐ All windows open and close, and all doors and cabinet doors are hung correctly and open and close smoothly.

☐ Electric, phone, and cable connections are functioning.

☐ Other.

NOTES:

Is It Really Finished?
Final Walk-Through of a New House

By now, you've hopefully seen your new house at various stages of construction—perhaps as recently as a week ago, if you negotiated for a series of walk-throughs in your purchase contract. But now you're at the very last walk-through, your first opportunity to see the house in its final form. Bring your original contract or addendum specifying products, extras, and upgrades.

The developer might accompany you, which is helpful for learning where things like the circuit breaker and the water shutoff valve are; how the heat, appliances, and other systems actually work; how you'll need to maintain them; and whether they're covered by any warranties. (Some builders call this the "orientation.") Expect also to be handed a pile of instruction pamphlets (or make sure to get these even if the developer isn't personally there).

This is also a common time to bring in a professional inspector for the final new-home inspection, as discussed in Chapter 12.

TIP

Gather all your new home's plans, documents, and more. Developers can be difficult to contact after the home is yours. Insist on copies of architectural plans, names of all the contractors and subcontractors, and any written warranties that came with building materials and appliances. These will come in handy for later repairs, matching new materials to old, and so forth.

ONLINE TOOLKIT

Use the "Final Walk-Through Checklist (New Home)" in the Homebuyer's Toolkit on the Nolo website. (See the appendix for the link.) A sample is shown above. This will help you assess whether everything (such as flooring, landscaping, and sinks) has been finished and is in good shape.

Don't let the developer rush you! Then create a so-called "punch list" of what remains to be done. Your developer might have a standard form for this.

At the end of your walk-through, the developer will review the list and should agree to make the needed changes by the closing. If that looks impossible, your best bets are either to delay the closing (taking into consideration your mortgage interest rate lock-in period) or to get a written agreement saying that the developer will put enough money to complete your house into an account that the developer can collect on when the work is done. And you can add new deadlines within this agreement, saying that if the work isn't done by these deadlines, the money will be returned to you. Consult an attorney if you're not satisfied with the developer's assurances.

TIP

Now is when you have the most leverage. Right before the closing, the developer is looking forward to cashing out and moving on. Be pleasant, meticulous, and assertive as you press for everything to get done—and delay the closing if you have to. As soon as the developer has your money, you're history—the developer is mentally already moving on to the next project.

Lesson learned the hard way

Don't arrange your life around closing day. When Flora bought a newly built condo in Portland, Oregon, the last inspection was scheduled on a Friday, with closing the following Monday. Flora says, "I arrived Friday to find workers running in all directions. I went around with my punch list of things that should have been done and kept checking off 'not done,' 'not done.' But we couldn't put off the Monday closing—I was living in someone's basement, and my husband was flying up from California. The developer never finished all the items on the punch list; we later sued."

Your Last Tasks Before the Closing

Below are the most important things for you to do in the approximately 24 hours leading up to the closing.

Check and Double-Check Final Closing Cost Amount

Your closing costs include everything that you (and the seller) will have to pay to anyone connected with the sale, including your loan fees and points; title and homeowners' insurance premiums; transfer and property taxes; recording fees; attorneys' fees; adjustments between buyer and seller for prepaid or unpaid taxes, utilities, and condo fees; and down payment. You will also receive, in the closing package, a mortgage payment coupon, in case you don't receive your first bill in time for its due date. Many people are surprised by how high their closing costs go—several thousand dollars is not uncommon—but they must be in line with the fees the lender disclosed to you in the Loan Estimate.

Co-op buyers might pay a little less, because title insurance isn't available to them (as owner of shares in a corporation rather than land), and the taxes are normally lower because it's not considered a real estate transfer. On the other hand, co-op owners might be required to pay a move-in deposit, a stock transfer fee, and a fee for any credit checks run by the owners' association board.

Condo owners should also be prepared for a few closing costs not owed by ordinary homeowners, such as a move-in fee or move-out deposit and fees for credit checks run by the community association. Buyers of brand-new condos often pay two months' extra common area fees (capital contributions), to establish working capital for the association. This is not a prepayment.

 TIP

Remember next April: Some closing costs are tax deductible. These include the discount points and any prepaid interest you pay for your mortgage, and any reimbursement you pay the seller for already-paid local property taxes. Many other closing costs, while not tax deductible, can be figured into your house's adjusted cost basis, helping to reduce your capital gains when you eventually sell.

Sample Closing Disclosure

Closing Disclosure

This form is a statement of final loan terms and closing costs. Compare this document with your Loan Estimate.

Closing Information

Date Issued	4/15/2013
Closing Date	4/15/2013
Disbursement Date	4/15/2013
Settlement Agent	Epsilon Title Co.
File #	12-3456
Property	456 Somewhere Ave
	Anytown, ST 12345
Sale Price	$180,000

Transaction Information

Borrower	Michael Jones and Mary Stone
	123 Anywhere Street
	Anytown, ST 12345
Seller	Steve Cole and Amy Doe
	321 Somewhere Drive
	Anytown, ST 12345
Lender	Ficus Bank

Loan Information

Loan Term	30 years
Purpose	Purchase
Product	Fixed Rate
Loan Type	☒ Conventional ☐ FHA
	☐ VA ☐ _____
Loan ID #	123456789
MIC #	000654321

Loan Terms

		Can this amount increase after closing?
Loan Amount	$162,000	**NO**
Interest Rate	3.875%	**NO**
Monthly Principal & Interest *See Projected Payments below for your Estimated Total Monthly Payment*	$761.78	**NO**
		Does the loan have these features?
Prepayment Penalty		**YES** • As high as **$3,240** if you pay off the loan during the first 2 years
Balloon Payment		**NO**

Projected Payments

Payment Calculation	Years 1-7	Years 8-30
Principal & Interest	$761.78	$761.78
Mortgage Insurance	+ 82.35	+ —
Estimated Escrow *Amount can increase over time*	+ 206.13	+ 206.13
Estimated Total Monthly Payment	**$1,050.26**	**$967.91**

		This estimate includes	In escrow?
Estimated Taxes, Insurance & Assessments *Amount can increase over time* *See page 4 for details*	**$356.13** a month	☒ Property Taxes ☒ Homeowner's Insurance ☒ Other: Homeowner's Association Dues	YES YES NO
		See Escrow Account on page 4 for details. You must pay for other property costs separately.	

Costs at Closing

Closing Costs	$9,712.10	Includes $4,694.05 in Loan Costs + $5,018.05 in Other Costs – $0 in Lender Credits. *See page 2 for details.*
Cash to Close	$14,147.26	Includes Closing Costs. *See Calculating Cash to Close on page 3 for details.*

Sample Closing Disclosure (continued)

Closing Cost Details

Loan Costs		Borrower-Paid At Closing	Borrower-Paid Before Closing	Seller-Paid At Closing	Seller-Paid Before Closing	Paid by Others
A. Origination Charges		**$1,802.00**				
01 0.25 % of Loan Amount (Points)		$405.00				
02 Application Fee		$300.00				
03 Underwriting Fee		$1,097.00				
04						
05						
06						
07						
08						
B. Services Borrower Did Not Shop For		**$236.55**				$405.00
01 Appraisal Fee	to John Smith Appraisers Inc.					$405.00
02 Credit Report Fee	to Information Inc.		$29.80			
03 Flood Determination Fee	to Info Co.	$20.00				
04 Flood Monitoring Fee	to Info Co.	$31.75				
05 Tax Monitoring Fee	to Info Co.	$75.00				
06 Tax Status Research Fee	to Info Co.	$80.00				
07						
08						
09						
10						
C. Services Borrower Did Shop For		**$2,655.50**				
01 Pest Inspection Fee	to Pests Co.	$120.50				
02 Survey Fee	to Surveys Co.	$85.00				
03 Title – Insurance Binder	to Epsilon Title Co.	$650.00				
04 Title – Lender's Title Insurance	to Epsilon Title Co.	$500.00				
05 Title – Settlement Agent Fee	to Epsilon Title Co.	$500.00				
06 Title – Title Search	to Epsilon Title Co.	$800.00				
07						
08						
D. TOTAL LOAN COSTS (Borrower-Paid)		**$4,694.05**				
Loan Costs Subtotals (A + B + C)		$4,664.25	$29.80			

Other Costs

		Borrower-Paid At Closing	Borrower-Paid Before Closing	Seller-Paid At Closing	Seller-Paid Before Closing	Paid by Others
E. Taxes and Other Government Fees		**$85.00**				
01 Recording Fees	Deed: $40.00 Mortgage: $45.00	$85.00				
02 Transfer Tax	to Any State			$950.00		
F. Prepaids		**$2,120.80**				
01 Homeowner's Insurance Premium (12 mo.) to Insurance Co.		$1,209.96				
02 Mortgage Insurance Premium (mo.)						
03 Prepaid Interest ($17.44 per day from 4/15/13 to 5/1/13)		$279.04				
04 Property Taxes (6 mo.) to Any County USA		$631.80				
05						
G. Initial Escrow Payment at Closing		**$412.25**				
01 Homeowner's Insurance $100.83 per month for 2 mo.		$201.66				
02 Mortgage Insurance per month for mo.						
03 Property Taxes $105.30 per month for 2 mo.		$210.60				
04						
05						
06						
07						
08 Aggregate Adjustment		– 0.01				
H. Other		**$2,400.00**				
01 HOA Capital Contribution	to HOA Acre Inc.	$500.00				
02 HOA Processing Fee	to HOA Acre Inc.	$150.00				
03 Home Inspection Fee	to Engineers Inc.	$750.00			$750.00	
04 Home Warranty Fee	to XYZ Warranty Inc.			$450.00		
05 Real Estate Commission	to Alpha Real Estate Broker			$5,700.00		
06 Real Estate Commission	to Omega Real Estate Broker			$5,700.00		
07 Title – Owner's Title Insurance (optional) to Epsilon Title Co.		$1,000.00				
08						
I. TOTAL OTHER COSTS (Borrower-Paid)		**$5,018.05**				
Other Costs Subtotals (E + F + G + H)		$5,018.05				
J. TOTAL CLOSING COSTS (Borrower-Paid)		**$9,712.10**				
Closing Costs Subtotals (D + I)		$9,682.30	$29.80	$12,800.00	$750.00	$405.00
Lender Credits						

Sample Closing Disclosure (continued)

Calculating Cash to Close

Use this table to see what has changed from your Loan Estimate.

	Loan Estimate	Final	Did this change?
Total Closing Costs (J)	$8,054.00	$9,712.10	YES • See **Total Loan Costs (D)** and **Total Other Costs (I)**
Closing Costs Paid Before Closing	$0	– $29.80	YES • You paid these Closing Costs **before closing**
Closing Costs Financed (Paid from your Loan Amount)	$0	$0	NO
Down Payment/Funds from Borrower	$18,000.00	$18,000.00	NO
Deposit	– $10,000.00	– $10,000.00	NO
Funds for Borrower	$0	$0	NO
Seller Credits	$0	– $2,500.00	YES • See Seller Credits in **Section L**
Adjustments and Other Credits	$0	– $1,035.04	YES • See details in **Sections K and L**
Cash to Close	$16,054.00	$14,147.26	

Summaries of Transactions

Use this table to see a summary of your transaction.

BORROWER'S TRANSACTION		SELLER'S TRANSACTION	
K. Due from Borrower at Closing	**$189,762.30**	**M. Due to Seller at Closing**	**$180,080.00**
01 Sale Price of Property	$180,000.00	01 Sale Price of Property	$180,000.00
02 Sale Price of Any Personal Property Included in Sale		02 Sale Price of Any Personal Property Included in Sale	
03 Closing Costs Paid at Closing (J)	$9,682.30	03	
04		04	
Adjustments		05	
05		06	
06		07	
07		08	
Adjustments for Items Paid by Seller in Advance		**Adjustments for Items Paid by Seller in Advance**	
08 City/Town Taxes to		09 City/Town Taxes to	
09 County Taxes to		10 County Taxes to	
10 Assessments to		11 Assessments to	
11 HOA Dues 4/15/13 to 4/30/13	$80.00	12 HOA Dues 4/15/13 to 4/30/13	$80.00
12		13	
13		14	
14		15	
15		16	
L. Paid Already by or on Behalf of Borrower at Closing	**$175,615.04**	**N. Due from Seller at Closing**	**$115,665.04**
01 Deposit	$10,000.00	01 Excess Deposit	
02 Loan Amount	$162,000.00	02 Closing Costs Paid at Closing (J)	$12,800.00
03 Existing Loan(s) Assumed or Taken Subject to		03 Existing Loan(s) Assumed or Taken Subject to	
04		04 Payoff of First Mortgage Loan	$100,000.00
05 Seller Credit	$2,500.00	05 Payoff of Second Mortgage Loan	
Other Credits		06	
06 Rebate from Epsilon Title Co.	$750.00	07	
07		08 Seller Credit	$2,500.00
Adjustments		09	
08		10	
09		11	
10		12	
11		13	
Adjustments for Items Unpaid by Seller		**Adjustments for Items Unpaid by Seller**	
12 City/Town Taxes 1/1/13 to 4/14/13	$365.04	14 City/Town Taxes 1/1/13 to 4/14/13	$365.04
13 County Taxes to		15 County Taxes to	
14 Assessments to		16 Assessments to	
15		17	
16		18	
17		19 ·	
CALCULATION		**CALCULATION**	
Total Due from Borrower at Closing (K)	$189,762.30	Total Due to Seller at Closing (M)	$180,080.00
Total Paid Already by or on Behalf of Borrower at Closing (L)	– $175,615.04	Total Due from Seller at Closing (N)	– $115,665.04
Cash to Close ☒ From ☐ To Borrower	**$14,147.26**	**Cash** ☐ From ☒ To Seller	**$64,414.96**

Sample Closing Disclosure (continued)

Additional Information About This Loan

Loan Disclosures

Assumption
If you sell or transfer this property to another person, your lender
☐ will allow, under certain conditions, this person to assume this loan on the original terms.
☒ will not allow assumption of this loan on the original terms.

Demand Feature
Your loan
☐ has a demand feature, which permits your lender to require early repayment of the loan. You should review your note for details.
☒ does not have a demand feature.

Late Payment
If your payment is more than *15* days late, your lender will charge a late fee of *5% of the monthly principal and interest payment.*

Negative Amortization (Increase in Loan Amount)
Under your loan terms, you
☐ are scheduled to make monthly payments that do not pay all of the interest due that month. As a result, your loan amount will increase (negatively amortize), and your loan amount will likely become larger than your original loan amount. Increases in your loan amount lower the equity you have in this property.
☐ may have monthly payments that do not pay all of the interest due that month. If you do, your loan amount will increase (negatively amortize), and, as a result, your loan amount may become larger than your original loan amount. Increases in your loan amount lower the equity you have in this property.
☒ do not have a negative amortization feature.

Partial Payments
Your lender
☒ may accept payments that are less than the full amount due (partial payments) and apply them to your loan.
☐ may hold them in a separate account until you pay the rest of the payment, and then apply the full payment to your loan.
☐ does not accept any partial payments.
If this loan is sold, your new lender may have a different policy.

Security Interest
You are granting a security interest in
456 Somewhere Ave., Anytown, ST 12345

You may lose this property if you do not make your payments or satisfy other obligations for this loan.

Escrow Account
For now, your loan
☒ will have an escrow account (also called an "impound" or "trust" account) to pay the property costs listed below. Without an escrow account, you would pay them directly, possibly in one or two large payments a year. Your lender may be liable for penalties and interest for failing to make a payment.

Escrow		
Escrowed Property Costs over Year 1	$2,473.56	Estimated total amount over year 1 for your escrowed property costs: *Homeowner's Insurance Property Taxes*
Non-Escrowed Property Costs over Year 1	$1,800.00	Estimated total amount over year 1 for your non-escrowed property costs: *Homeowner's Association Dues* You may have other property costs.
Initial Escrow Payment	$412.25	A cushion for the escrow account you pay at closing. See Section G on page 2.
Monthly Escrow Payment	$206.13	The amount included in your total monthly payment.

☐ will not have an escrow account because ☐ you declined it ☐ your lender does not offer one. You must directly pay your property costs, such as taxes and homeowner's insurance. Contact your lender to ask if your loan can have an escrow account.

No Escrow		
Estimated Property Costs over Year 1		Estimated total amount over year 1. You must pay these costs directly, possibly in one or two large payments a year.
Escrow Waiver Fee		

In the future,
Your property costs may change and, as a result, your escrow payment may change. You may be able to cancel your escrow account, but if you do, you must pay your property costs directly. If you fail to pay your property taxes, your state or local government may (1) impose fines and penalties or (2) place a tax lien on this property. If you fail to pay any of your property costs, your lender may (1) add the amounts to your loan balance, (2) add an escrow account to your loan, or (3) require you to pay for property insurance that the lender buys on your behalf, which likely would cost more and provide fewer benefits than what you could buy on your own.

Sample Closing Disclosure (continued)

Loan Calculations

Total of Payments. Total you will have paid after you make all payments of principal, interest, mortgage insurance, and loan costs, as scheduled.	$285,803.36
Finance Charge. The dollar amount the loan will cost you.	$118,830.27
Amount Financed. The loan amount available after paying your upfront finance charge.	$162,000.00
Annual Percentage Rate (APR). Your costs over the loan term expressed as a rate. This is not your interest rate.	4.174%
Total Interest Percentage (TIP). The total amount of interest that you will pay over the loan term as a percentage of your loan amount.	69.46%

Questions? If you have questions about the loan terms or costs on this form, use the contact information below. To get more information or make a complaint, contact the Consumer Financial Protection Bureau at **www.consumerfinance.gov/mortgage-closing**

Other Disclosures

Appraisal
If the property was appraised for your loan, your lender is required to give you a copy at no additional cost at least 3 days before closing. If you have not yet received it, please contact your lender at the information listed below.

Contract Details
See your note and security instrument for information about
• what happens if you fail to make your payments,
• what is a default on the loan,
• situations in which your lender can require early repayment of the loan, and
• the rules for making payments before they are due.

Liability after Foreclosure
If your lender forecloses on this property and the foreclosure does not cover the amount of unpaid balance on this loan,

☒ state law may protect you from liability for the unpaid balance. If you refinance or take on any additional debt on this property, you may lose this protection and have to pay any debt remaining even after foreclosure. You may want to consult a lawyer for more information.

☐ state law does not protect you from liability for the unpaid balance.

Refinance
Refinancing this loan will depend on your future financial situation, the property value, and market conditions. You may not be able to refinance this loan.

Tax Deductions
If you borrow more than this property is worth, the interest on the loan amount above this property's fair market value is not deductible from your federal income taxes. You should consult a tax advisor for more information.

Contact Information

	Lender	Mortgage Broker	Real Estate Broker (B)	Real Estate Broker (S)	Settlement Agent
Name	Ficus Bank		Omega Real Estate Broker Inc.	Alpha Real Estate Broker Co.	Epsilon Title Co.
Address	4321 Random Blvd. Somecity, ST 12340		789 Local Lane Sometown, ST 12345	987 Suburb Ct. Someplace, ST 12340	123 Commerce Pl. Somecity, ST 12344
NMLS ID					
ST License ID			Z765416	Z61456	Z61616
Contact	Joe Smith		Samuel Green	Joseph Cain	Sarah Arnold
Contact NMLS ID	12345				
Contact ST License ID			P16415	P51461	PT1234
Email	joesmith@ficusbank.com		sam@omegare.biz	joe@alphare.biz	sarah@epsilontitle.com
Phone	123-456-7890		123-555-1717	321-555-7171	987-555-4321

Confirm Receipt

By signing, you are only confirming that you have received this form. You do not have to accept this loan because you have signed or received this form.

_____   _____   _____   _____
Applicant Signature   Date   Co-Applicant Signature   Date

Your task, on the day before the closing, is to find out whether your total closing costs are adding up as you expected and get ready to pay that amount. By law, your lender is required to give you the Closing Disclosure at least three business days before closing. The Closing Disclosure will look very similar to your original Loan Estimate. The fees and other figures shown there should be in line with those on the estimate, with no more than a 10% upward fee adjustment. If later changes were made to your loan application that affected your loan terms, for example, the fees or rate, you should have received an updated Loan Estimate. (Ask your lender for a copy of the most recently issued Loan Estimate, just in case.)

ONLINE TOOLKIT

The Homebuyer's Toolkit on the Nolo website contains a blank Closing Disclosure form. (See the appendix for the link.) Open it to see the full list of possible closing costs. A sample is shown above.

Here are some things to pay particular attention to on the Closing Disclosure: Check the spelling of your name, property address, interest rate (fixed or adjustable), loan amount, number of months' term, monthly payment, prepayment penalties (if any), balloon payment (if any), mortgage insurance (if any), lender credits (if any), and seller credits (if any). Take a look at the figures used for estimates for property taxes and homeowners' insurance and the estimated cash required for closing. Discuss with your settlement agent its preference for receiving funds for closing. Typically, no personal checks are allowed. Usually a wire transfer coming from a previously disclosed bank account or a cashier's check identifying the remitter is acceptable.

CAUTION

Be wary of wire fraud. As adviser Sylvia M. Gutiérrez warns: "You should accept wiring instructions only from the closing agent in person or while you're talking with them directly on the phone. We've seen an increase in legit-looking wire instruction phishing emails attempting to scam buyers and lenders."

At the closing itself, you'll receive a final version of the Closing Disclosure form. But now's a great chance to check for oddities, errors, or failures to credit you for fees you've already paid. For example, your earnest money deposit should show up as a credit, as should any prepaid items, such as the appraisal, credit report, or application fee, reducing what you'll owe at closing. If you're buying a newly constructed house, your advance payments to cover customizations or upgrades should also be credited against your closing costs. Bring up any errors or questions with the closing agent *before* you get to the closing. All monies changing hands should be shown on the Closing Disclosure form.

Thankfully, the problem of buyers being hit with last-minute "junk fees"—or additional, padded amounts designed to increase the lender or settlement agent's profits—has diminished since the passage of current lending rules. But if you nevertheless see unexpected or questionable fees, ask about them.

CAUTION

Don't pay junk fees that exceed legal limits. Certain costs can't exceed the estimates given on the Loan Estimate, and other costs have tolerances that can only be increased by a maximum of 10% and for very specific reasons. For a full list of which costs can't be changed, review the sample Loan Estimate that appears in The Homebuyer's Toolkit on the Nolo website.

Assuming you find no problems, the "Cash to Close" figure found on Page 3 of the Closing Disclosure is the amount that you'll need to show up with at closing. Have your real estate agent, closing agent, or attorney confirm that the amount is, in fact, final.

Make Payment Arrangements

For convenience, many buyers pay their entire closing costs in one lump sum. (The closing agent saves you from having to write separate checks to everyone.) We're assuming you haven't already deposited money with the closing agent, which some buyers do several days in advance—usually more than they think they'll need, with the idea of getting a refund after closing. This allows buyers to use a personal check, which you can't do at the closing itself.

Of course, if you've got money coming from different sources (a bank account here, a family member there), compiling it into a lump sum before giving it to the escrow agent might not actually be so convenient. (You should also realize, adviser Sylvia M. Gutiérrez notes, that "Your lender will need to know from where you're getting the money, as required by the Patriot Act and Anti-Money Laundering Rules.") The important thing is to make sure you'll be transferring the money—every last cent of it—in an acceptable form (sometimes called "good funds"). That usually means either a certified or cashier's check or having funds wired directly from your bank or investment company showing your name as the remitter or, if gift funds have been previously approved by your lender, the donor information. "I've run into problems where people think they can get good funds out of a stock brokerage account at the last minute," warns Attorney Ken Goldstein. "These usually require some advance time." A briefcase full of five-hundred-dollar bills would probably work, too, depending on how many bodyguards you normally travel with.

If wiring some or all of the funds is your plan, double-check how much advance notice your bank needs. Wiring can be a same-day deal, but one of this book's authors nearly had her California house closing delayed because the wired funds mysteriously got stalled in an office in Texas. Adviser Sylvia M. Gutiérrez recommends "wiring funds to the settlement agent 24 to 48 hours in advance of closing. And if you're liquidating funds from a stock account, initiate the liquidation at least five days prior to settlement. If you're having funds disbursed or loaned from a retirement account, initiate the withdrawal three to four weeks prior to settlement."

Although personal checks aren't usually accepted at the closing, because of the uncertainty over whether they'll clear, it's a good idea to bring your personal checkbook along and make sure a few hundred dollars will be in your account. This is in case any last-minute incidentals crop up

Read Your Documents and Raise Any Last Issues

By the time you walk in the door to your closing, all possible negotiations and issues should have been settled. Closing day is not the time to tell the seller, "You never removed the pet door!"

Start by reviewing the escrow instructions, and any letters or instructions from your lender, to make sure you've done everything requested. Also ask your mortgage broker and real estate agent to give you complete sets of any draft documents that have been prepared to date and to explain to you (if they haven't already) what the documents mean.

Finally, call your real estate agent, closing agent, and mortgage broker or loan officer to double-check that they're not waiting for anything else from you. (And, just in case, that they still have tomorrow's closing on their calendar!)

Prepare What You'll Bring to the Closing

Other than money, the buyer might be expected to bring only a few documents, depending on practices in your state. For example, you could be asked for proof of homeowners' and flood insurance and an original copy of any inspection reports, if your real estate agent hasn't already forwarded these to the closing agent. But if you're in doubt, or think you might be the only one holding any possibly relevant document, bring it. Also bring receipts or other proof of things you've already paid (such as inspection fees, credit report, loan application or appraisal fees, or homeowners' insurance) in case any last questions arise about whether these can be deducted from your closing costs.

Finally, bring two forms of proof of your identity, at least one with a photo. Many people forget a driver's license, passport, or other photo identification. You'll need to show these to the notary, who stamps the documents after you sign them.

The Drum Roll, Please: Attending the Closing

No matter what time your closing is scheduled for, plan to take the day off work and to get there in plenty of time. Although a normal closing lasts no more than an hour or two, surprises can happen. Also, your closing agent might have more than one closing scheduled that day, and an earlier one might run over.

Whether or not you're meeting in one room, who signs the documents *first* isn't really an issue. The seller could, for example, sign the deed transferring ownership to you before you've signed anything—but would have the protection of knowing that the closing agent won't record the deed until you've signed your documents and the loan has been funded.

We'd love to tell you to read every document one last time before signing, but that's probably not realistic—it would take hours. By now, you should have seen many of the documents in draft form and read them when you weren't under time pressure. As mortgage expert Russell Straub says, "It's important to get your questions answered, but if you wait until the closing to read everything, you're really throwing sand in the gears."

Just listen carefully as your team of professionals explains what each document is; compare the filled-in portions and numbers (not the boilerplate) with your own notes; and raise questions about things that don't appear as you'd expected. If you have an attorney representing you (and not simultaneously representing the seller), you can rely on the attorney to tell you what a document generally means and whether it's safe to sign.

Closing Documents Related to Your Mortgage Loan

One major set of documents you'll deal with at the closing are those concerning your loan. Before you sign, look at every number to make sure it's what you were expecting and that no one mistakenly added any zeros.

TIP

Expect a little sticker shock. Annemarie Kurpinsky, a California real estate agent, says, "Buyers tend to think in terms of the house's purchase price—as in, 'I'm buying it for $800,000.' But the closing can be daunting, because you're now confronted with loan documents showing how much you'll REALLY be paying, after the interest and other costs are added up. To relax, try focusing on all the reasons you chose this house in the first place, on how it will be a good investment over time, and on the fact that you don't need to pay this all at once!"

Below is a summary of the main documents you'll be given. However, there will probably be more. For instance, your lender might have you sign an affidavit promising that you'll live in, not rent out, the house (if the loan you applied for is conditioned on your using the property as a primary residence). You can expect a:

- **Promissory note, or "Note."** You're stating that you're borrowing X amount of money and personally guaranteeing to repay it.
- **Mortgage or Deed of Trust.** Here's where you agree to have a lien put on your house as security for the loan. It turns your house into collateral, which the lender can claim in foreclosure if you fail to repay or to otherwise follow the terms of the note (if you "default"). The lender will record your mortgage with the appropriate local government office.
- **UCC-1 Financing Statement (co-ops only).** Since co-op financing involves no mortgage, your lender might instead fill out and record this document, to show its claim on your property interest.
- **Closing Disclosure.** You should have seen an earlier draft of this, within at least three days prior to your scheduled closing. Here, the lender confirms your interest rate, the annual percentage rate (APR), and the total cost of the loan over its life. The disclosure itemizes each payment to be made by you and the seller, not only for the house, but for all other costs, such as services performed in connection with the sale, insurance premiums, paying off liens, and more. (The seller will need to sign it, too.) Before stuffing this into your files, check whether your closing agent included a refund check with it (for any extra money that you deposited ahead of time).
- **Monthly payment letter.** This tells you how much money you'll pay in monthly loan principal and interest. It might also include amounts that your lender requires you to put into escrow each month for payment to third parties such as the tax collector or insurance companies (homeowners' or PMI). Your closing agent will take care of setting up this account on closing day. Adviser Sylvia M. Gutiérrez warns, "Be sure to set aside the payment coupon containing instructions on sending your first payment to the lender. Don't assume you'll get a bill right away, or that the autopayment you set up from your checking account has been initiated. Sometimes the lender experiences a slight delay in setting up your account, and if you don't track this yourself, you could wind up late on your first payment!"

Closing Documents Related to Transferring the Property

Another important set of closing documents serves to transfer the property to you. At a minimum, these include the items below, though others might be added depending on where you live, for example, to account for local transfer taxes. Some documents you won't even have to sign—you'll just receive them from the seller: perhaps a certificate saying that the house has smoke detectors, or a certificate of occupancy showing that the house has passed a municipal or local inspection for basic habitability and legal compliance. Expect to see:

- **Deed (or "warranty deed").** The seller signs this to tell the world that title of the property has been transferred to you, the new owner. (The deed also states the purchase price, or enough information that the price can be figured out—which is how services like Zillow obtain this information.) Make sure your name is spelled correctly and that it accurately shows the manner in which you and any cobuyers have opted to take title (for example, as joint tenants). Your closing agent will, as the last step in closing on the property, file a copy with the appropriate public records office.

- **Co-op buyers only: Stock certificate and proprietary lease.** Instead of a deed, co-op buyers receive a stock certificate indicating how many shares they own in the corporation and a proprietary lease outlining their rights to live in a certain unit. Your lender will probably keep these in its files.

- **Bill of sale.** This document attests to the transfer of any personal property from the seller to you. In other words, if the sale includes any nonfixtures such as a children's swing set, curtains, or a floor rug, the bill of sale creates a record of this agreement.

- **Affidavit of title and ALTA statement.** Here, the seller swears to the title insurance company to have done nothing to cloud the house's title and to know of no unrecorded contracts, easements, or leases regarding the property. The seller signs the affidavit, but both you and the seller sign the ALTA statement to finalize your request for title insurance.

Once all the documents are signed, you'll be given a complete set for your records. Some closing agents will put them onto a CD or flash drive for you. Keep everything in a safe place, such as a safe deposit box. Don't assume that your closing company will keep a copy for you—they're allowed to toss most of your records after five to seven years.

The final task, after the meeting is over, is for your closing agent or attorney to record the property deed that shows you as the new owner, in the appropriate public records office. In some areas, this is done electronically. In others, someone (the closing agent or a messenger) must go to the appropriate office in person. The sale hasn't truly "closed" until the deed is recorded, even if you're already sipping a glass of wine at a nice restaurant.

Can I Move In? Taking Possession

After waiting so long, it's hard to believe you've actually got the right to move in or, in legal terms, take possession. That right normally kicks in at the end of closing—receiving the keys is a pretty good clue. In fact, from the standpoint of your lender, you have not only the right, but an obligation to move in. Some lenders mandate you do so within 60 days of the closing, to demonstrate that you're not an investor. But before you tell the movers when to arrive, check two more things:

Tunes to Celebrate By

Here are some house-inspired songs to play as you dance with joy:

- "Home," by Phillip Phillips ("Just know you're not alone; Cause I'm going to make this place your home...")

- "Our House," by Madness ("Our house, in the middle of our street ... Our house, was our castle and our keep ...")

- "This Is Not the House That Pain Built," by Dar Williams ("My house is hard to find, but I'll give you directions, You can visit sometime ...")

- "Our House," by CSNY ("I'll light the fire, you put the flowers in the vase that you bought today ...")

- "More Than One Way Home," by Keb' Mo' ("Well there's more than one way home, Ain't no right way, Ain't no wrong ...")

- "Come-On-A My House," by Rosemary Clooney ("Come on-a my house my house, I'm gonna give you candy ...")

- "Home," by Bonnie Raitt ("And all through my brain, Came the refrain, Of home and its warming fire.")

- **Your purchase contract.** Your contract will probably contain a clause titled or mentioning "possession." That clause will most likely say that the seller must deliver possession at closing (in other words, you can move in). However, in a few states, different arrangements are common—for example, that buyers won't take possession for one or two days after the closing (as in Georgia), or that the seller can stay for up to seven days after paying a deposit (as in New York). Also, you might have agreed to give the seller extra time, perhaps to move out or close on another property.

- **Your state's practices around waiting for the deed to be recorded.** Although the house is yours once the title has been transferred from the seller to you, the deal isn't technically closed until the deed has been recorded with the appropriate government office. And customs regarding whether you'll need to actually wait for the recording to receive the keys and take possession are stricter in some states than in others. In Massachusetts, for example, recording is taken very seriously, and retired Realtor Nancy Atwood found that, "You might have to wait for 45 minutes at the closing attorney's office until the messenger has recorded the deed." By contrast, in Michigan, where most closings take place at a title insurance office, once all the papers have been signed, the seller receives the payment check and simultaneously gives the buyer the keys. The seller, buyer, and lender all rely on the title company to take care of recording the deed.

TIP
Now that you've got the keys, should you change the locks? Not a bad idea, as we'll discuss in Chapter 15.

What's Next?

You've done it! Time to move in, settle down, sing at the top of your lungs, and enjoy knowing that no landlord will be knocking on your door to protest. For tips on settling in, see Chapter 15.

Settling Into Your New Home

Meet Your Adviser

Tara Waggoner, MBA, a real estate broker with eXp Realty (www.exprealty.com) and coach with The Tara Waggoner Group, offering mentoring, coaching, and training to real estate professionals and people looking to enter the industry (www.linkedin.com/in/whynotwaggoner).

What she does   "I coach and train real estate agents (beginner and seasoned) wanting to take their business to the next level, as well as investors who want to create another stream of income. I see myself as a true client advocate, strong negotiator, customer service rep, contract review person (making sure all the i's are dotted and t's crossed), and calming influence (both with agents and clients). Every transaction has its twists and turns, and every buyer wants to tear his or her hair out at some point in the process. Every day is a new and exciting day with client concerns. I've pretty much seen it all by now and can keep a level head and propose solutions."

First house   "It certainly wasn't my dream house. I was tired of seeing money thrown out the window renting and was wondering why I was still doing so while already working as a real estate agent. I was overly critical, letting my experience as an agent get in the way of actually choosing a place, always hoping I'd find the best deal around. Then I swung to the other extreme—I practically woke up one day and picked a home. It was a model townhome in a gated community. I didn't heed the very advice I would have given my clients—didn't ask for the discounts I could have gotten, didn't thoroughly check out the builder, and focused too much on minor issues like decorating. Of course, the homebuilder went bankrupt. I sold after a little over four years, and barely broke even on the place. Now I make sure my clients don't make the same types of mistakes!"

Fantasy house	"The style would be 1920s to 1950s bungalow, one story, with subway tiles, Restoration Hardware features, and a large pool for the kids, located right smack dab near the city."
Likes best about her work	"At the end of the day, I like to see the client's smile at the closing table. And leading up to that moment, I also enjoy receiving not only encouragement, but actual incentive to make sure my customers are truly satisfied. As a broker associate with eXp Realty, this lets me take the time to do that—and ensures that I receive regular customer feedback—because of its nontraditional, technology-based business model. So I never feel I need to hurry someone into a sale. Say, for example, I'm working with a home-buying couple who start out thinking that they want to spend up to the limits of their budget for a $500,000 downtown condo with city views. But I notice that the wife is pregnant and they've got a dog. I can gently say, 'Hey, maybe moving to the suburbs and paying $400,000 for a place with a yard would be better all around,' and then take a step back while they do some realistic thinking about their home-buying wants and needs."
Top tip for first-time homebuyers	"First off, don't rush. The right place isn't likely to come along the first week. Also, when you work out your budget to see how much you can afford, don't forget that you want to enjoy life after moving in. (Always get a lender approval letter before you go out touring homes with your Realtor.) Take into account family trips, date night, summer camp, and those other miscellaneous items. You don't want to be house poor—that's not fun."

There's nothing like waking up the first morning in your new home—ready for the fun parts of homeownership, like settling in and making the space your own. We'll give you some creative ways to make your mark (without going broke), including how to:

- tell the world where you are
- get comfortable socially
- make sure your new home is as safe as it can be
- decorate, design, and remodel on a budget
- organize your records and finances, and
- get back on your feet financially.

Just don't try to do it all in one day!

Tell the World You've Moved

Most everyone in your daily life, or even in your social media networks, probably knows you've moved. Nevertheless, you might have forgotten to keep some key service providers and people in the loop. Here are ways to remedy that.

Set Up Services

You'll want to get in touch with:

- **Electricity, water, gas, and garbage/recycling companies.** Contact your local providers and arrange for your new account. The seller has probably given you the relevant information. If not, a simple Web search should pull it up. If you're in a condo or co-op, trash pickup may be part of your monthly fees—check with the association.
- **Other financial service providers.** Your bank, insurance carriers (such as auto), pension and investment plan providers, and others need to know where to find you.
- **Medical providers.** Notify your doctor, dentist, and any specialists, along with your health insurance provider, pharmacy, and any online medical services you use (such as prescription or medical supply delivery).

- **Telephone, Internet, and TV provider (cable/satellite).** It might be economical to get a "bundled" subscription through one provider. If you change phone numbers from a landline, contact your provider to find out if forwarding calls to your new number is possible.
- **Postal Service.** Fill out a change of address form online at USPS.gov, or do it at a post office. This is supposed to forward your mail for 12 months, except periodicals, which are forwarded for only 60 days. (But plan for slipups, in which your mail is occasionally delivered to your old address.)
- **Subscriptions.** You can often update your address at a periodical's website. Don't forget to contact alumni magazines or newsletters you get from nonprofits, too. And what about your favorite retail catalogs?
- **Credit card companies.** Make sure creditors know where you are— you'd hate to get behind on a payment when you've just proven how responsible you are.
- **Department of Motor Vehicles.** Go to your state's DMV website or www.dmv.org to get information on updating your car registration and driver's license.
- **Parking permit provider.** If you need a residential parking permit, you'll need to let the appropriate permit-issuing entity know. Try your new city's website.
- **Registrar of voters.** Go to USVoteFoundation.org and click "State Voting Information" for links to information on each state's elections offices, which have change of address forms online.

Notify Friends and Family

To make sure you keep getting Great Aunt Margaret's holiday fruitcake or your college friends' wedding invitations, send out new-address announcements. You can send traditional emails or make your own cards, but online vendors will also send customized emails or custom-print announcements on a design of your choosing. Check out:

- TheStationeryStudio.com for paper announcements (under "Announcements"), and
- PaperlessPost.com for online and printed announcements.

Thanks a Million! (Or $200,000)

Your real estate agent probably spent a lot of time and energy helping you find the perfect abode—and maybe even gave you a nice gift. For a good agent, consider a similar gesture, such as a bottle of champagne. And remember, the best gift of all is referring other potential homebuyers or sellers to your agent.

A fun and cheap method of announcing your move is to share photos of your house online. Try the following free image-hosting websites, some of which will even create custom slideshows for you to share on your Web page or social networking profiles (like Facebook):

- photos.google.com
- Flickr.com
- Imgur.com, and
- Instagram.com.

Home, Hearth, and Hors d'Oeuvres: Settle in Socially

Once you're sure your old friends know where you are, it's time to have them over—and maybe meet some new friends, too. Below are a few tips.

Housewarming on a Budget

Nothing says "Welcome Home" quite like a party. A housewarming is a great way to thank the people who helped you find, purchase, and move into your home; show off your new digs, and get to know the neighbors. Some homebuyers invite the professionals who helped out: the real estate agent, mortgage broker, attorney, or closing agent.

You're probably not looking to break the bank on the first fete. Sympathetic partygoers will likely be happy to contribute a dish, but if "potluck" feels like a dirty word, try sticking toothpicks into a few of your favorite finger foods and picking up some bottles of decent wine. And while some people go so far as to register for gifts, Miss Manners has opined, "Hoping to furnish one's quarters on other people's budgets is not a proper reason for giving a housewarming party."

Get to Know the Neighbors

Whether or not you invite the neighbors to your housewarming party, you'll probably want more intimate opportunities to get to know them. Here are some possibilities:

- **Have a neighbors-only party.** An after-work cocktail hour, weekend high tea or barbecue, or dessert evening works well. The neighbors will probably be more relaxed among each other than with your regular crowd.

- **Knock on doors.** Don't wait for the neighbors to come to you! Bring cookies or another small gift, like a bar of handmade soap or a coupon for "one emergency cup of sugar or equivalent."

- **Look for community activities.** You might have just moved in, but you'll also want to get out sometimes. Whatever your interests (knitting, tennis, reading, cooking, running, or gardening), there's probably a local group that fits. Ask your neighbors, check locally focused groups on social media, search online, or visit community gathering places (such as libraries and recreation centers).

> ### The Fastest Way to a Neighbor's Heart
>
> Be the neighborhood's favorite new baker with Mom's Crunchy Granola Cookies:
>
> 1. Combine and beat with rotating mixer until creamy: 1 cup shortening; ¾ cup brown sugar, firmly packed; ⅜ cup granulated sugar; 2 eggs; 1 T hot water; 1 tsp. vanilla.
>
> 2. Add and mix with a wooden spoon: 1½ cups flour, 1 tsp. baking soda, 2 cups crunchy granola. Optional: Stir in ½ cup walnuts and ½ cup raisins OR a 6 oz. package butterscotch chips OR all three.
>
> 3. Drop by teaspoonfuls on ungreased cookie sheets and bake at 375° for ten minutes, or until golden brown around the edges.

CHECK IT OUT

When good neighbors turn bad. Being a neighbor isn't always about cookies: To prevent or deal with neighbor-related disputes over things like fences, noise, easements, or joint-use agreements, check out *Neighbor Law: Fences, Trees, Boundaries & Noise*, by Attorneys Emily Doskow and Lina Guillen (Nolo).

Find Activities for the Kids

Your children might feel as out of the social loop as you do. Here are some fun ways you can help them adjust and to maybe make some new friends yourself:

- **Volunteer at school.** You can participate by becoming a room parent, going on field trips, and generally helping out in the classroom (unless your kids are teens—then your presence might not be appreciated).
- **Start a carpool, playgroup, or babysitting co-op.** If your kids' school isn't within walking distance, start or join a carpool with nearby parents. Playgroups and babysitting co-ops are also great ways to meet and get to know other families. Check out BabyCenter.com, www.redtri.com, and www.mother.ly for ideas.
- **Have a kids' party.** Just because no one's having a birthday doesn't mean that you can't have a party. Decorate the house, serve up some kiddie treats, and play a few games.

The Safest Home in Town: Yours

Given that every unfamiliar noise in a new house can sound treacherous, you're already probably thinking about home security. Take these easy follow-up steps:

- **Change the locks.** If you don't, you won't know who has keys to your front door (the seller's wacky houseguest from two years ago and several neighbors, perhaps). Call a locksmith or visit a hardware store.
- **Install a "smart" doorbell.** Ring and Nest are just two of the companies selling Internet-connected doorbells with built-in motion detectors and cameras. When someone comes to your door, the doorbell notifies you via your smartphone. You can watch and talk with the visitor through the phone app if you don't want to open the door.
- **Reset the alarm code.** Choose a number you'll remember, share it on a "need to know" basis, and keep the owners' manual on hand in case you're in a jam. If there's no alarm system, now might be the time to consider getting one (prices are more reasonable than you might think, and your homeowners' insurance company might discount your rate if you have a security system).

- **Check smoke detectors and sprinkler systems.** Though the inspector told you whether these were up to code, make sure they're still in good working order. For your family's safety, consider installing them in every bedroom or hallways that lead to bedrooms. And if you're in a building with a sprinkler system, make sure you know how it works and where your unit's sprinkler heads are.

- **Plan an escape route.** In a panicked situation, your halls might feel like a labyrinth. Make sure every family member knows all entrances and exits, how to get out from the second floor, and where to meet up if separated.

> *One Way to Test Your Locks ...*
>
> **Luke:** *It's the kind of lock burglars look for.*
> **Lorelai:** *Why do burglars look for that lock?*
> **Luke:** *Because it's easy to break into. I proved that.*
> **Lorelai:** *You proved that by ...?*
> **Luke:** *Breaking in through the back door.*
> —Gilmore Girls

- **Childproof everything.** If you're a parent, you've probably done this before. Put chemicals and cleaning supplies out of reach, and add child safety locks to all cabinets. Also put important phone numbers (your cell phone, police, fire department, health care providers, and more) as well as your address on a bulletin board or refrigerator for babysitters.

- **Remind the kids how to get home.** Have your kids memorize their new address and telephone number and your full name. Make sure their school has the correct contact information for you.

Cozy Up ... Without Breaking the Bank

Decorating and remodeling—or maybe just choosing your own paint color for the first time—are probably high on your priority list. We'll give you some starter ideas and resources for:

- decorating without maxing out your credit card
- planning a remodel on your own, or finding professionals to help you, and
- beautifying any outdoor space.

Decorating on Your Budget

Though it might be tempting to buy out your nearest home furnishings store or warehouse, your budget is probably telling you to hold back. But hey, creativity thrives within constraints, right? And there's no rush—you'll need time to figure out your needs as you adapt to the space. There are hundreds (actually, thousands) of low-cost resources on decorating (TV shows, magazines, books, websites) to help you plan (or at least fantasize about) all the great things you'd like to do with your new home. (Popular websites include Houzz.com, Remodelista.com, and thespruce.com.)

"It helps to keep an open mind," says adviser Tara Waggoner. "For example, take a look at the special rack in the paint or lumber section of your local Lowe's or Home Depot where they put materials cut or created for customers who never came back to buy them. The deep discount you'll get may make up for the fact that the paint color perhaps wasn't exactly what you originally had in mind."

Other ways to be kind to your pocketbook include:

- **Inventorying.** Make a list of what you already have, and find the holes. For example, a rug you haven't used in years might fit perfectly in your new hallway.
- **Prioritizing.** Distinguish what you need (a bedside lamp) from what you want (sleeker cabinet knobs). Rank your priorities from highest to lowest, and space purchases out to fit your budget.

> **TIP**
>
> **Small price, big impact.** You don't need to replace all your furniture to get a fresh look. Consider sprucing up your rooms with candles, pictures, or thrift store vases or adding color with paint, pillows, or a tablecloth. Check out TheBudgetDecorator.com.

- **Researching.** Shop around for the best deals. Consider buying used (from Internet vendors or at discount shops), consignment stores, flea markets, or end-of-the-season clearances. Or even get stuff for free from people in your area, on sites like Freecycle.org or the "Free" section of craigslist.

CHECK IT OUT

Crafty community. Even if you've never picked up a glue gun, you'll find easy decorating tips at www.craftster.org, from how to stencil a patio umbrella to how to make fabric area rugs.

Remodeling on the Cheap

If you bought a fixer-upper, you might be spending time and money just making the place habitable. Our book can't cover all the bases—plenty of others do—but here are some cost-cutting tips to use from the get-go. And don't forget to check out the resources in Chapter 8 on doing home repairs.

Remodeling on Your Own

If you're planning to remodel on your own, you'll need tools to do it. Some are easy to afford—you can just go to the hardware store for a hammer—but others are a larger investment. Consider renting tools, or borrowing them from your neighbors (responsibly) or buying used (check for local listings at www.craigslist.org). Finally, find out if your community has a tool-lending library. No matter what, you'll probably have questions once you get started. Reap the benefit of others' knowledge by checking out sites like:

- DIYNetwork.com
- DoItYourself.com, and
- HomeDoctor.net.

Be sure that a project is doable before you begin. The websites listed above all have sections dedicated to user comments to help you gauge how much elbow grease and expertise you'll need for your project. Many offer detailed blogs that take you through a real remodel.

CAUTION

Whether it's a DIY or professional job, check the zoning and get the right permits. That includes getting permission from your homeowners' association (HOA), if you have one. "Failure to take these steps," according to adviser Tara Waggoner, "can create huge and expensive problems when it's time to resell. I know of one family who enclosed a patio, turning it into livable space, without so much as notifying their HOA. It turns out they didn't use proper roofing materials. Later, the HOA made them replace the roof before it would authorize them to sell."

Finding and Hiring Professionals

Professionals exist for a reason, and you shouldn't be embarrassed to use one, no matter how handy you are. Bringing in a general contractor (who oversees a team of subcontracting professionals) is a smart move if you're attempting a complex or extremely large project. For more limited projects, you can hire your own carpenters, plumbers, electricians, and so forth.

Get Greener Now, Get More Green Later

As long as you're remodeling, consider the short- *and* long-term benefits of making your home more energy efficient. Sustainable construction and architecture will lower both your energy consumption and the amount you spend on utilities. And when you sell, you'll be able to play up the house's upgraded insulation, sealed crawlspace, energy-efficient window glazes, or tankless water heater. Ask your contractor which features might be feasibly incorporated in the remodel, or see www.smarterhouse.org for more information.

To look for a general contractor, get recommendations from friends and check out neighborhood groups on social media and Yelp.com. As with any professional, conduct a thorough interview before hiring, making sure this one is bonded and insured and has experience with the type of work you need; then sign a contract laying out what work is included and the price.

Though it might be tempting to get the whole project done in one fell swoop, this isn't always a good strategy for the cash-strapped first-time owner. One project will be a big enough learning experience—simultaneous ones can make you crazy. And if you have a young child (whose immune system will be sensitive to the raw materials in the air), or don't have time to work around the chaos, you'll want to keep the house livable during construction.

Gardening and Landscaping

If you've just moved into a home that's beautifully landscaped, you might not realize how much time, effort, and money was put into making it just so. If you don't have a green thumb (and aren't in a CID where the community association takes care of such things), think about hiring a professional to take over.

Ask the seller or neighbors whom they use (it's not uncommon for a whole neighborhood to have the same gardener). Local nurseries provide good recommendations, too. Realize that gardeners come with all levels of expertise and prices, from the expensive landscape architect to the college kid who likes wielding a hedge clipper. You're probably looking for someone in the middle: a gardener who specializes in maintenance rather than design but has enough experience to know a weed from a seedling and can help recognize plant diseases and suggest solutions.

> *If I wanted to have a happy garden, I must ally myself with my soil; study and help it to the utmost, untiringly .... Always, the soil must come first.*
>
> —Marion Cran, gardening expert and author

Large trees, however, definitely need a professional, preferably a certified arborist. Bad pruning can kill the tree or make it look bad or grow faster. And tree pruning is dangerous work—don't risk a lawsuit by employing an inexperienced worker. Look for membership in either the International Society of Arboriculture (ISA, at www.isa-arbor.com), the Tree Care Industry Association (TCIA, at www.tcia.org), or the American Society of Consulting Arborists (ASCA, at www.asca-consultants.org).

If you didn't inherit a landscaped garden, you're probably going to want to use your own green thumb. Check your local nurseries for the types of plants that suit your space and ask questions about whether they're native, the type of care they'll need, whether they're susceptible to munching by deer or other natives, and their cycle (annual, perennial). And don't forget that not all plants need to be purchased—trading plant cuttings with friends is satisfying and free; see the articles at YouGrowGirl.com.

In fact, there are plants that thrive on neglect, perfect if you've got a huge pile of dirt for a backyard and don't want to take care of a needy garden. For more ideas than you can shake a hoe at, check out the community at DavesGarden.com.

Making It Green

Want to assuage your enviro-guilt for all the gas the moving van used? Here are some ways you can save energy and protect the environment from within your own home—and many of them cost little or nothing:

- **Hang laundry.** A $5 clothesline will cut down your gas or electricity bill, since you won't be running the dryer. And it will leave your clothes smelling fresh. (Check to see if your community allows outdoor clotheslines—some don't.)

- **Wash your clothes in cold water.** Modern detergents don't need hot water to work, and heating the water uses lots of energy. Biodegradable and earth-friendly detergents are available. If you can't skip fabric softener, choose one that's soy based, or throw vinegar into the rinse cycle to soften your clothes.

- **Lower the thermostat.** Two degrees lower in the winter and two degrees higher in the summer could save up to 2,000 pounds of carbon dioxide per year.

- **Clean or replace furnace and air conditioning filters.** Keeping your furnace and air conditioning filters clean will help them function efficiently. An electrostatic filter will cost more up front than a paper or fiberglass one, but can be cleaned and reused.

- **Turn down the water heater.** Most people find 120 degrees to be warm enough, and the addition of an insulating water heater blanket (around $10–$20) can reduce heat loss by 25%–40%.

- **Use the dishwasher.** Modern dishwashers tend to be more efficient than handwashing, since they use less than ten gallons of water per load. And they're effective enough that you can feel justified in not prerinsing your dishes, which wastes water. Wait to run the dishwasher until it's completely full, and let dishes air dry if you can.

- **Reduce water use.** A low-flow showerhead will still have good water pressure, but will release (and waste) a lot less water. And if you can't yet afford a low-flow toilet, put a gallon milk jug filled with rocks into the tank to displace the water.

- **Get rid of the junk mail.** While you're switching over your address, cancel catalogs you don't need at CatalogChoice.org. Pay your bills—and get your statements—online.

- **Make your own cleaning products.** You can use some common household supplies—like vinegar, baking soda, and lemons—to make environmentally friendly products. For formulas, go to CrunchyBetty.com and search for "cleaning products."
- **Replace lawn with native plants.** This will decrease water use, as will watering early in the morning (to prevent evaporation) and keeping the grass three to four inches long. Getting rid of the gas mower will also have a positive environmental impact.

> *Ready to Discover Your Inner Martha Stewart?*
>
> *Martha Stewart's Homekeeping Handbook: The Essential Guide to Caring for Everything in Your Home,* by Martha Stewart (Clarkson Potter), covers just what it says (in over 750 pages).

- **Plant trees.** A $10 annual membership to the Arbor Day Foundation (www.arborday.org) gets you ten free trees. Trees shade your home, reducing the temperature in warm spring and summer months; and deciduous trees will drop their leaves in the fall, too—letting sunlight in and potentially lowering the heating bill.

There's a Place for It: Organize Your Records

Boring, boring, but money saving! Knowing where your home-related records are is part of the responsibility of owning a home and will help you collect on your insurance, claim tax deductions, and more. In this section, we'll run through the various categories of documents, including which ones to keep and why.

But first, a basic word on where and how to keep these documents. The basic rule is "in more than one place." More than one homeowner has carefully stored all their key documents in a large box only to lose the box.

Fortunately, your title or closing company is likely to make this easy for you by giving you both a paper copy of all the documents relevant to your closing as well as a CD and/or flash drive with scanned versions of the same. And in case those get lost, it's a good idea to upload the documents to the "cloud"—Google Drive and DropBox are just two examples of the many programs you can use.

For hard copies (or items that don't go through your closing agent, such as your home inspection report), it's a good idea to buy a locking file cabinet and keep the key somewhere secure. Then create folders with relevant titles such as "Closing Documents," "Repair and Improvement Receipts," "Product Manuals," "Homeowners' Insurance," "Tax Deductions [*year*]," and more. You'll get more ideas from the topics below and might want to put copies of some documents in more than one file.

It's also wise to find a location outside your house in which to keep copies of critical records, such as your house deed, loan, and insurance papers. If a fire or another disaster makes your house temporarily uninhabitable, easy access to these will make your life much easier. A safe deposit box is good, as is a secure place at a trusted friend's house (for weekend access).

Your Purchase and Ownership Records

Below are the basics: documents that prove you own the house, and those concerning your house's ongoing financing and insurance:

- **Closing documents.** These serve to prove your ownership of your property, a top priority.
- **Loan documents.** Keep all documents associated with your mortgage accessible, as well as documentation of other financial arrangements like promissory notes to family members. The Closing Disclosure signed by your lender can be particularly important to have around—especially if you live in a CID, where the homeowners' association might require you to come up with a copy in order to claim such things as your mailbox and fitness room keys.
- **Inspection reports.** These set a baseline for future comparison. If problems pop up later, they allow you to look back at whether the inspectors predicted them or overlooked something they should have caught.
- **Insurance policy.** In a minor or major emergency, you'll want to know how to contact your insurance company and what you're covered for. Having the contract handy will make dealing with company representatives much easier at a potentially troubled time.
- **Association records.** If your home is governed by a community association, keep all the relevant documents, like the CC&Rs.

You'll want to be able to check on things like whether you can put up a basketball hoop or are really liable for a new fee.

Your Tax Records

Even if you've always stuffed your tax-related documents in a shoebox, homeownership gives you a good time to start over—with the possibility of some tax deductions, if you itemize, as well as tax credits. (Also, you never know when you'll be audited.) Here are some of the most important ones to keep track of:

- **Interest and points.** The interest you pay on your mortgage or home equity loan might be tax deductible, as might be points you paid up front. (For more on these, turn back to Chapter 1.) Your lender will normally send you a post-year-end statement totaling your interest payments, so add these to your files.
- **Property tax.** You might be able to deduct state and local property taxes from your federal taxes. Keep a copy of the tax statement you receive, with notes on how you paid it (for example, a personal check number).
- **Home business.** If you work at home, your tax prep will be more complicated than the average Joe's, but that could also translate into more deductions.
- **Energy-efficient improvements.** If you make any energy-efficient improvements that qualify for tax credits, be sure to keep copies of your receipts (and make sure those receipts clearly identify what you purchased).
- **Moving expenses if you're a military member moving in accord with military orders.** Qualifying members of the U.S. armed forces can take an "above-the-line" deduction (meaning it doesn't depend on itemizing) for moving and storage expenses. (See IRS Publication 521, *Moving Expenses*.)

CHECK IT OUT

Keep what you've earned. If you're running a business from your home, learn which deductions you qualify for and which ones you don't using *Home Business Tax Deductions*, by Stephen Fishman (Nolo).

- **Any other deductible expenses.** To find out more about home-related deductions go to www.irs.gov; download IRS Publication 530, *Tax Information for Homeowners*.

Your Home Maintenance Records

All homes require upkeep, and keeping track of your maintenance and improvement efforts will help you figure out how old the roof and other things are, provide information to later potential buyers, and in some cases, show the IRS why your capital gains tax should be reduced when you sell. Here are some documents to save:

- **Utility bills.** When you sell your home, many buyers will want to see about two years' worth of utility bills to see what their average expenses would be. (You can discard the older bills.)
- **Professional services.** Careful records of what's been done, who did it, when, and how much you paid will be helpful in two ways. First, you'll be able to check whom you used if you want to bring them back (or avoid them). Second, you'll be able to hand these documents over when you sell your home, so prospective buyers can see what's been done and hire professionals familiar with the property, if they choose.
- **Manuals and warranty information.** Keep all the info you'll need in order to replace, return, or otherwise deal with your house's appliances. Hopefully the seller left you relevant manuals and warranties; most warranties carry over to subsequent homeowners.

The Art of Organizing

Bookstores and websites are full of great resources for those who love to organize. (You know who you are—one clue is if the Container Store is your home away from home.) *Real Simple* magazine and organizing guru Julie Morgenstern both have useful books to keep your place decluttered. And if you want to hire a pro, check out the National Association of Productivity & Organizing Professionals, www.napo.net, for leads.

- **Repair and improvement receipts.** Keep records of and receipts for your repairs and improvements to the house. The distinction between them can be complicated, so for now, you might just want to save everything. When you sell, you can figure out which projects qualify as improvements that lower your capital gains tax liability. IRS Publication 530 (cited above) tells you more and includes a suggested chart for tracking home improvements.

Your Personal Records

Keeping track of essential forms was helpful in securing your home and will continue to be important while you own your home. Keep separate files for:

- **W-2s and other IRS-related papers.** Keeping track of your income from all sources, whether it's a salary, royalties, or eBay business, is the first step in preparing to file your taxes. Also track incoming money that might look to the IRS like income, but really wasn't, like a gift or reimbursement.
- **Health insurance records.** In case of emergency, every member of your household should know your and their health insurance information. Also consider creating documents showing who's authorized to make health care decisions for you if you aren't able to; see "Living Wills and Powers of Attorney for Health Care: An Overview" and related articles in the Wills, Trusts & Probate section of Nolo's website, Nolo.com.
- **Auto insurance.** Though you should keep a copy of your car registration and current insurance information inside the car itself, you should also keep them on file, in case of loss or theft. Make sure you can easily find the vehicle identification number.

Back to the Future: Get Your Finances on Track

You've already made a budget (in Chapter 3). It might be time to revisit it to realistically account for the expenses of homeownership, which can be different from and higher than renting. (Of course, some of these expenses will be deductible, and if you alter your exemption status, this can also change your monthly cash flow.) The point is to make sure your budget is realistic and to stick to it, especially since you'll probably be tempted to do a lot at once—like buy furniture, restock your pantry, and remodel the outdated bathroom.

Here are some other ways to make the most of what you've got:

- **Hire a tax professional.** A pro can help you take maximum advantage of your brand-new investment and avoid incomplete filings with the IRS.

- **Check out additional resources.** In fact, you might want to literally check these out, at the library. See favorite books like *The Complete Tightwad Gazette*, by Amy Dacyczyn (Villard), and *Pinch a Penny Till It Screams*, by Madeline Clive (Lucerna Publishing).

- **Eat in more.** You've got a new kitchen, so experiment! There are hundreds of great websites (*Epicurious* magazine's site, www.epicurious. com, is one of our favorites). And if you're really pinching pennies, check out *Dining on a Dime Cook Book: 1000 Money Saving Recipes and Tips*, by Tawra Jean Kellam and Jill Cooper (T and L Group), and *The Frugal Family's Kitchen Book*, by Mary Weber (Cranberry Knoll Publishers LLC). An Internet search for "frugal recipes" will turn up plenty, too.

- **Restart your savings.** With all the financial rigmarole you've just been through, saving might sound like a pleasant dream. However, careful goal setting can help you rebuild funds—plenty of millionaires can tell you the benefits of saving just a little at a time.

Congratulations!

It might be hard to believe, but you've reached your goal. You prioritized your needs, figured out what you could afford, researched where to find it and whom to get to help you, negotiated and closed your deal, and actually moved in. You're at the end of the road, so settle in and enjoy—this is home!

Using the Downloadable Forms

This book comes with interactive files that you can access online at **www.nolo.com/back-of-book/HTBH.html**

To use the files, your computer must have specific software programs installed. Here is a list of types of files provided by this book, as well as the software programs you will need to access them:

- **RTF.** You can open, edit, print, and save these form files with most word processing programs, such as Microsoft *Word*, Windows *WordPad*, and recent versions of *WordPerfect*.
- **PDF.** You can view these files with Adobe *Reader*, free software from www.adobe.com. Government PDFs are sometimes fillable using your computer, but most PDFs are designed to be printed out and completed by hand.

Editing RTFs

Here are some general instructions about editing RTF forms in your word processing program. Refer to the book's instructions and sample agreements for help about what should go in each blank.

Underlines. Underlines indicate where to enter information. After filling in the needed text, delete the underline. In most word processing programs you can do this by highlighting the underlined portion and typing CTRL-U.

Bracketed and italicized text. Bracketed and italicized text indicates instructions. Be sure to remove all instructional text before you finalize your document.

Optional text. Optional text gives you the choice to include or exclude text. Delete any optional text you don't want to use. Renumber items, if necessary.

Alternative text. Alternative text gives you the choice between two or more text options. Delete those options you don't want to use. Renumber items, if necessary.

Every word processing program uses different commands to open, format, save, and print documents, so refer to your software's help documents for help using your program. Nolo cannot provide technical support for questions about how to use your computer or your software.

CAUTION

In accordance with U.S. copyright laws, the forms provided by this book are for your personal use only.

List of Forms

The following files are in portable document format (PDF):	
File Name	**Form Name**
Financial Information for Lenders	LenderInfo.pdf
Real Estate Agent Interview Questionnaire	AgentInterview.pdf
Real Estate Agent References Questionnaire	AgentReferences.pdf
Mortgage Broker Interview Questionnaire	BrokerInterview.pdf
Mortgage Broker References Questionnaire	BrokerReferences.pdf
Attorney Interview Questionnaire	AttorneyInterview.pdf
Attorney References Questionnaire	AttorneyReferences.pdf
Home Inspector Interview Questionnaire	InspectorInterview.pdf
Home Inspector References Questionnaire	InspectorReferences.pdf
House Visit Checklist	HouseChecklist.pdf
First-Look Home Inspection	HomeInspection.pdf
Cobuyer Discussion Checklist	CobuyerChecklist.pdf
Sample Home Inspection Report	InspectionReport.pdf
Loan Estimate	LoanEstimate.pdf
Closing Disclosure	ClosingDisclosure.pdf
Final Walk-Through (Existing Home)	ExistingWalkthru.pdf
Final Walk-Through (New Home)	NewWalkthru.pdf

The following files are in rich text format (RTF):	
File Name	**Form Name**
Dream List	DreamList.rtf
Gift Letter	GiftLetter.rtf
Private Loan Terms Worksheet	LoanTerms.rtf
Questions for Seller Worksheet	QuestionsForSellers.rtf
Condo/Co-op Questions	CondoQuestions.rtf

Index

 **NOLO** *More from Nolo*

Nolo.com offers a large library of legal solutions and forms, created by Nolo's in-house legal editors. These reliable documents can be prepared in minutes.

Create a Document Online

Incorporation. Incorporate your business in any state.

LLC Formation. Gain asset protection and pass-through tax status in any state.

Will. Nolo has helped people make over 2 million wills. Is it time to make or revise yours?

Living Trust (avoid probate). Plan now to save your family the cost, delays, and hassle of probate.

Provisional Patent. Preserve your right to obtain a patent by claiming "patent pending" status.

Download Useful Legal Forms

Nolo.com has hundreds of top quality legal forms available for download:

- bill of sale
- promissory note
- nondisclosure agreement
- LLC operating agreement
- corporate minutes
- commercial lease and sublease
- motor vehicle bill of sale
- consignment agreement
- and many more.